Dynamic Federalism

This book offers a new theory of federalism.

The work critically discusses traditional federal theories and builds on theories that focus on the dynamics of federalism. It offers a definition of federalism and federal organizations that encompasses both new and old types of multi-tiered system. Unlike traditional federal theory, it is well-suited to research both multinational and mononational systems. It also takes into account the complexity of these systems, with bodies of governance at the local, regional, national, and supranational level.

The book is divided into three parts: the first part outlines the contours of dynamic federalism, based on a critical overview of traditional federal theory; the second part develops comprehensive indexes to measure the autonomy and cohesion of multi-tiered systems; and the third part concentrates on the dynamics of federal organizations, with a special focus on institutional hubs for change.

Dynamic Federalism will be an essential resource for legal, social, economic, and political scholars interested in federalism, regionalism, and de/centralization.

Patricia Popelier is full professor at the law faculty of the University of Antwerp, director of the research group of government and law, and copromoter of the interdisciplinary Centre of Excellence GOVTRUST. She is also senior research fellow at the University of Kent, Centre for Federal Studies. She is the vice president of the International Association of Legislation (IAL) and president of the Flemish Interuniversity Center of Legislation (ICW), convenor of the standing research group on subnational constitutions in federal and quasi-federal systems of the International Association of Constitutional Law, and member of the scientific committee of EURAC – Institute for Comparative Federalism (Bolzano); of the scientific committee of the Sofia Legal Science Network (SLSN); and of the scientific committee of the Ossevatorio AIR (Rome).

Comparative Constitutional Change

Comparative Constitutional Change has developed into a distinct field of constitutional law. It encompasses the study of constitutions through the way they change and covers a wide scope of topics and methodologies. Books in this series include work on developments in the functions of the constitution, the organization of powers, and the protection of rights, as well as research that focuses on formal amendment rules and the relation between constituent and constituted power. The series includes comparative approaches along with books that focus on single jurisdictions, and brings together research monographs and edited collections which allow the expression of different schools of thought. While the focus is primarily on law, where relevant the series may also include political science, historical, philosophical, and empirical approaches that explore constitutional change.

Series Editors: Xenophon Contiades is Professor of Public Law, Panteion University, Athens, Greece and Managing Director, Centre for European Constitutional Law, Athens, Greece.

Thomas Fleiner is Emeritus Professor of Law at the University of Fribourg, Switzerland. He teaches and researches in the areas of Federalism, Rule of Law, Multicultural State; Comparative Administrative and Constitutional Law; Political Theory and Philosophy; Swiss Constitutional and Administrative Law; and Legislative Drafting. He has published widely in these and related areas.

Alkmene Fotiadou is Research Associate at the Centre for European Constitutional Law, Athens.

Richard Albert is Professor of Law at the University of Texas at Austin.

Also in the series:

Icelandic Constitutional Reform
People, Processes, Politics
Edited by Ágúst Þór Árnason and Catherine Dupré

Dynamic Federalism
A new theory for cohesion and regional autonomy
Patricia Popelier

For more information about this series, please visit:
www.routledge.com/Comparative-Constitutional-Change/book-series/COMPCONST

Dynamic Federalism

A New Theory for Cohesion and Regional Autonomy

Patricia Popelier

Routledge
Taylor & Francis Group
LONDON AND NEW YORK

First published 2021
by Routledge
2 Park Square, Milton Park, Abingdon, Oxon OX14 4RN

and by Routledge
52 Vanderbilt Avenue, New York, NY 10017

Routledge is an imprint of the Taylor & Francis Group, an informa business

British Library Cataloguing-in-Publication Data
A catalogue record for this book is available from the British Library

Library of Congress Cataloging-in-Publication Data
Names: Popelier, P., author.
Title: Dynamic federalism: a new theory for cohesion and regional autonomy/Patricia Popelier.
Description: Milton Park, Abingdon, Oxon; New York, NY: Routledge, 2021. | Series: Comparative constitutional change | Includes bibliographical references and index.
Identifiers: LCCN 2020043719 (print) | LCCN 2020043720 (ebook) | ISBN 9780367652821 (hardback) | ISBN 9781003128762 (ebook)
Subjects: LCSH: Federal government. | Decentralization in government—Law and legislation. | Central-local government relations.
Classification: LCC K3185 .P67 2021 (print) | LCC K3185 (ebook) | DDC 321.02—dc23
LC record available at https://lccn.loc.gov/2020043719
LC ebook record available at https://lccn.loc.gov/2020043720

ISBN: 978-0-367-65282-1 (hbk)
ISBN: 978-0-367-65292-0 (pbk)
ISBN: 978-1-003-12876-2 (ebk)

Typeset in Galliard
by KnowledgeWorks Global Ltd.

Contents

Illustrations

Figure

Box

Indexes

Preface

This is a corona-book. It does not deal with the topic of pandemics or crisis management, but it was written during the corona crisis. The first few chapters were discussed at Eurac, February–March 2020, at the outbreak of the coronavirus crisis. I would like to warmly thank Francesco Palermo, Karl Kössler, Elisabeth Alber, Jonathan Fessha, and many others for their hospitality and for their invaluable input. Because of lockdown and other protective measures, all other research visits that were planned during my extremely badly timed sabbatical were cancelled. I would nevertheless like to thank Nico Steytler and Jaap De Visser, Neophytos Loizides, Alain Gagnon, Johanne Poirier, Ben Gussen, and Nick Aroney for their invitations. Undoubtedly, this book would have benefitted from their input and rich environment. I'm looking forward to their – and others' – comments and criticism for follow-up research. Meanwhile, special gratitude goes to Anne Van De Vijver, professor of tax law and one of the finest and most promising colleagues in my faculty, for checking and giving feedback on Chapter 6 and the fiscal arrangement index in the appendix.

Acknowledgement

This book was written with the support of the FWO funding agency and the University of Antwerp, which sponsored my sabbatical. It is output of the Government and Law research group and the BOF funded GOVTRUST Centre of Excellence.

Introduction

A mushrooming amount of literature on federalism and federations makes it increasingly difficult to stay abreast of the latest developments. To explain this phenomenon, scholars refer to the rise of federal and 'federalish' systems that increases the political importance of federalism.[1] Riker's famous opening sentence – "This is an Age of Federalism"[2] – can now be rewritten as "This is an Age of Federalisms". Still, the question remains: why another book on federalism to add to the pile of federalism literature? In other words: what is still missing from federalism literature that this book aims to fill?

Gaps in federalism theory

First, despite generations of study, federalism theory remains underdeveloped. Hueglin has argued that "our conceptual knowledge of federalism has remained more confused than refined".[3] According to him, theoretical accounts are either too wide, making "sweeping assumptions" that do not enable meaningful comparison, or too narrow, offering an institutional checklist that fits only a handful of states and does not lead "beyond narrow institutional analyses".[4] Scholars regularly point out that there is no scholarly agreement on what federalism exactly means and how it functions.[5] The dynamics of federalism have only recently been rediscovered, and the mechanisms of federal change are

1 Jan Erk and Wilfried Swenden, 'The new wave of federalism studies', in Jan Erk and Wilfried Swenden (eds), *New Directions in Federalism Studies* (Routledge 2010) 2.
2 William H. Riker, *Federalism. Origin, Operation, Significance* (Little, Brown and Company 1964) 1.
3 Thomas O. Hueglin, 'Comparing Federalisms: Variations or Distinct Models?' in Arthur Benz and Jörg Broschek (eds), *Federal Dynamics* (Oxford University Press 2013) 27.
4 Thomas O. Hueglin, *A Political Economy of Federalism: In Search of a New Comparative Perspective With Critical Intent Throughout* (Queen's University Institute of Intergovernmental relations 1990) 4.
5 Erk and Swenden (n 1) 1; Anna Gamper, 'A "Global Theory of Federalism"? The Nature and Challenges of a Federal State', (2005) 6 *German Law Journal* 1297.

still underexposed.[6] Further, federalism is usually viewed from the center. It is rarely approached from below, with subnational entities as the unit of analysis.[7] Especially in comparative studies, the study of federalism is said to have "not yet been at the core of the theoretical debates".[8] At most, catalogues of institutional variations have been produced, but explanatory theories, predictions or general classifications of types of federalism are still missing.[9]

Second, old theories have proven to be inadequate to understand new systems of dispersed political authority, whereas recent literature lacks the theoretical foundation for a comprehensive analysis of these developments. According to Riker, federalism became popular as a way of solving the problem of enlarging governments – which was once identified as "one of the most pressing political concerns in the modern world".[10] Meanwhile, multinational systems have discovered that federalism is a way to accommodate autonomy demands by territorially based identitarian groups, while still maintaining the territorial integrity of the state. However, these systems display features that do not agree with older theories.[11] Old theories are mainly concerned with western federations, whereas federalism in Africa and Asia has become attractive precisely as a form of multinational conflict management. These areas recently received some attention in separate studies,[12] but have largely remained exotic outliers in too many comparative works.[13] Likewise, new forms of state, not unitary but not quite federal 'as we know it', have become an unsolvable puzzle for old theories – Spain, the United Kingdom, or the European Union are just a few examples.[14] Instead, a new branch of 'ethnofederalism' is emerging. Gagnon, for instance, distinguishes "two types of federalism": one is called territorial federalism, the other multinational federalism.[15] There is a risk that the ever-growing distance of these branches may prevent us from seeing the bigger picture. Moreover, the fixation on traditional models of federalism has led many scholars to ignore the rise of local entities as new partners in compound

6 César Colino, 'Introduction: the study of change in federations', in Erk and Swenden (n 1) 18. See also Arthur Benz, 'Dimensions and dynamics of federal regimes', in Benz and Broschek (n 2) 70.

7 Michael Burgess and G. Alan Tarr, 'Introduction: Sub-national Constitutionalism and Constitutional Development', in Michael Burgess and G. Alan Tarr, *Constitutional Dynamics in Federal Systems: Sub-national Perspectives* (McGill-Queen's University Press 2012) 6:

8 Jan Erk, *Explaining Federalism* (Routledge 2010) 1.

9 Lori Thorlakson, 'Comparing Federal Institutions: Power and Representation in Six Federations', (2003) 26 *West European Politics* 7.

10 Riker (n 2) 2.

11 See further, Chapter 1.

12 Yonatan T. Fessha and Karl Kössler (eds), *Federalism and the Courts in Africa* (Routledge 2020) and Harihar Bhattacharyya, *Federalism in Asia* (Routledge 2010) to name but a few.

13 See also Bhattacharyya (n 12) 3.

14 See further, Chapter 1.

15 Alain-G. Gagnon, *The Case for Multinational Federalism* (Routledge 2010) 5.

political systems. It has been noticed that efforts to adapt old models of federalism to contemporary forms of state have raised more questions than they have provided answers, and "mostly reflect the difficulty to organize a general federal conceptual framework from systematic studies of federalist theories and practices".[16]

Third, where federalism was once regarded as the monopoly of legal scholarship,[17] other disciplines have taken the lead in what has been called "the new wave of federalism studies".[18] Legal scholars lag behind, especially in the field of comparative federalism.[19] It is regrettable that many legal scholars seem to have retired to the certainties of old theories.[20] One of the consequences is a wide neglect in 'new wave federalism' of the role of courts in federal systems.[21] Empirical scholars that do focus on the role of courts tend to undervalue legal merit to explain court outcomes.[22] Also, 'new wave federalism scholars' take pride in their descriptive analysis, away from "the underlying normative attachment to the subject".[23] However, courts make federalism operational through constitutional narratives, derived precisely from normative accounts of federalism. Federalism, then, is a complex phenomenon that can only be understood by taking an interdisciplinary approach. This means that federalism studies also need the input of legal scholars. Watts already stressed that it is necessary to examine both constitutional law and political practices and processes to understand how federal systems operate.[24] What legal scholarship adds is an emphasis on courts, legal procedures, and legal reasoning, elements that are often undervalued by empirical scholars. At the same time, legal scholars should incorporate insights from other disciplines into their work, and in turn, make their own analyses useful for empirical scientists.

16 Frédéric Lépine, 'Federalism: Essence, Values and Ideologies', in Alain-G. Gagnon, Soeren Keill and Sean Mueller (eds), *Understanding Federalism and Federation* (Routledge 2015) 31–32.
17 Erk and Swenden (n 1) 5–6. See also Lori Thorlakson, 'Comparing Federal Institutions: Power and Representation in Six Federations', (2003) 26 *West European Politics* 2.
18 Erk and Swenden (n 1) 1.
19 Which is exactly the reason why Palermo and Kössler published their reference book on comparative federal law: Francesco Palermo and Karl Kössler, *Comparative Federalism: Constitutional Arrangements and Case Law* (Oxford, Hart, 2017) 1.
20 See also Thorlakson (n 9) 8.
21 Erin F. Delaney, 'Judicial Federalism in Comparative Perspective', in Yonatan T. Fessha and Karl Kössler (eds), *Federalism and the Courts in Africa* (Routledge 2020) 15; Francesco Palermo and Karl Kössler, *Comparative Federalism: Constitutional Arrangements and Case Law* (Oxford, Hart, 2017) 1.
22 See further, Chapter 8.
23 Erk and Swenden (n 1) 3.
24 Ronald L. Watts, 'The Federal Idea and its Contemporary Relevance', in Thomas J Courchene *et al.* (eds), *The Federal Idea. Essays in Honour of Ronald L. Watts* (McGill-Queen's University Press 2011) 16.

What this book offers

This book does not aim to fill all these gaps and give a final answer to all outstanding questions about federalism. Instead, its purpose is to contribute to the development of a theory of federalism that overcomes the weaknesses identified above.

Firstly, the book aims to lay the foundations for a new theory, by offering a concept and a toolbox that is useful for comparative research and for the development of a theory of change. To this end, it does away with institutional checklists and redefines federalism in terms of autonomy and cohesion, instead of the traditional self-rule and shared rule. Indexes are developed to measure federalism. These indexes allow the identification of multi-tiered systems as one of nine forms of state that can be compared with similar and other compound systems. Further, change can be assessed, and constitutional asymmetry can be measured.

Secondly, the toolboxes in this book are developed in a way that can be applied to all forms of multi-tiered systems. This is regardless of whether the systems are federal, confederal, regional, or decentralized, in any part of the world. For this reason, they do not fixate on specific institutions that are deemed essential for federal organizations, but on instruments that have the potential to create cohesion or protect autonomy. This makes it possible to examine similarities and differences between decentralized local entities, autonomous regions, and federal sub-states. References are made to systems in all continents, as well as supranational organizations. Power-sharing arrangements that are typical for multinational systems are not treated separately, but are included in the general framework.

Finally, this book is written with the benefit of my expertize as a legal scholar. This means that it takes an institutional approach and gives due consideration to the role of courts, constitutions, and constitutional reasoning. The inspiration for this book, and the common thread throughout the chapters, is one specific research question: how do constitutions facilitate or curb the dynamics of multi-tiered systems and how can constitutional engineering impact on this? Nonetheless, it builds on literature from other disciplines, theoretical and empirical, including political as well as economic sciences. This book's purpose is also to offer a tool for the empirical study of how multi-tiered systems function, and how they can change.

Structure of the book

The book is divided into three parts that follow after this introduction.

The first part constructs the foundations of a theory of dynamic federalism. Chapter 1 points out the weaknesses of traditional federalism theories. At the same time, it takes building blocks from these theories to develop a new theory of federalism. Chapter 2 revisits another old theory – Friedrich's concept of federalism as a process – as the starting point for a new theory of dynamic federalism. It also introduces this new theory and its basic concepts: the meaning of federalism, the definition of federations and other forms of state, and the notion of change as an inherent part of multi-tiered systems. At the core of the theory is the search for a (perpetually contested) optimal balance between autonomy and cohesion. This requires the building of indexes to measure both dimensions.

The second part offers models for such indexes. They are built around three categories that form the skeleton of multi-tiered systems: status (Chapter 4), powers (Chapter 5), and fiscal arrangements (Chapter 6). First, Chapter 3 provides some guidelines for the interpretation of the indexes and illustrates the use of these toolboxes with reference to results from the Belgian example. The case study itself is set out in the Appendix, so as not to distract from the general theory.

The third part provides some basic observations for the development of a theory of change. Chapter 7 summarizes the insights from federalism scholars with regard to the dynamics of federal systems. Chapter 8 focuses on institutions as hubs for change. These institutions already appeared in the indexes to measure autonomy and cohesion. However, in this chapter, they are now examined as instruments for change, in a search for institutional as well as noninstitutional drivers. This part also features a first attempt to answer the research question underpinning this book.

The book concludes with a summary of the main insights that were developed in the different parts. It also offers a research agenda for follow-up research. Dialogue and case studies are needed to validate and improve the indexes. Skills and methodologies from different disciplines are also required to gain comprehensive insights into the operation and dynamics of multi-tiered systems. Riker considered even writing a mono-disciplinary comparative study of federalism "far too pretentious a project for one man".[25] The same sentiment applies to one woman. As will be repeated further in this book: it takes an entire research community to develop a theory.

25 Riker (n 2) xii.

Part I

Theoretical framework

1 What is federalism? In search of building blocks for a new federal theory

Federalism is a perennially popular research topic amongst constitutional legal scholars and political scientists. Throughout the world, universities and research institutions have established their own centers of federalism studies, many of which are members of the International Association of Centers for Federal Studies (IACFS). Yet, there is no general understanding of what they are actually studying: what are federalism and federal systems, exactly?[1] Even Palermo and Kössler, in their seminal book on comparative federalism, leave the definition open. Not only do they find "no universal agreement on what federalism means" or any consensus "on how to classify federal countries"; they even claim that no such agreement can ever be reached,[2] and any attempt to define federalism is both impossible and futile.[3] Kincaid is also of the opinion that the multiplicity of forms in which the federal concept is applied makes it "impossible for one definition to fit all cases exactly and for generalizations to be set forth without exceptions".[4]

The question is: why should we care? If federalism studies can prosper even without a common agreement on what federalism or federations mean, why would we agonize over a proper definition? Why not simply set aside these discussions and take a pragmatic approach? In this chapter, I will argue that a pragmatic approach is insufficient, and explain why a proper definition matters (section 1.1). I will then turn to traditional definitions of federalism and point out their weaknesses, in order to better establish what a renewed theory needs to offer (section 1.2). These definitions then lead us to the distinction between federalism and federations. The notion of 'federalism' as a principle, pointing to the value of 'federalism' is further explored (section 1.3), because it gives us insights into the core or the essence of federal systems. By analyzing old federal

1 Anna Gamper, 'A "Global Theory of Federalism"? The Nature and Challenges of a Federal State', (2005) 6 *German Law Journal* 1297.

2 Francesco Palermo and Karl Kössler, *Comparative Federalism: Constitutional Arrangements and Case Law* (Hart, 2017) 2–3.

3 *Ibid* 38.

4 John Kincaid, 'Editor's Introduction: Federalism as a Mode of Governance', in J. Kincaid (ed), *Federalism* (Sage 2011, Volume 1) xxi.

theories, this chapter provides us with the building blocks for a renewed theory of 'dynamic' federalism that is set out in Chapter 2. These building blocks are summarized in section 1.4.

1.1 The importance of defining federations

1.1.1 Why a pragmatic approach to the definition of federal systems is insufficient

Palermo and Kössler argue for a pragmatic approach as a coping strategy to avoid difficult definitions. They distinguish two forms of pragmatism, which we can describe as an intuitive method and a generalizing method. A third can be added: the method of self-definition.

Palermo and Kössler compare the most minimal form of pragmatism with Justice Potter Stewart's approach to the definition of obscenity: "I know it when I see it".[5] So, do we know it when we see a federal system? Apparently not. Different eyes see different things. Some argue that Spain is a federal system,[6] others insist that it is not.[7] In the end, the intuitive method conceals an implicit definition that may differ depending on who's talking.

Under the method of self-definition, it is left to the constitutional system itself to decide whether it is federal or not. For Elazar, this is the first test to qualify states as federal: "the desire or will to be federal on the part of the polity involved".[8] Several constitutions include a structure clause, which lists the basic elements that define the state. Constitutions that pronounce the federal structure as a basic trait of the system can be found, amongst others, in Austria, Belgium, Brazil, Ethiopia, Germany, Iraq, Mexico, Nigeria, Pakistan, and Russia. In other cases, the 'basic structure' is not made explicit in the constitution itself, but is recognized by the supreme or constitutional court. For example, federalism is read into the Canadian Constitution as a basic principle,[9] to guide the interpretation of constitutional provisions and to fill in gaps.[10] The Indian Supreme Court reads the constitutional term 'Union of States'[11] as a

5 Palermo and Kössler (n 2) 3.

6 Gemma Sala, 'Federalism without Adjectives in Spain', (2013) 44 *Publius: The Journal of Federalism* 109–134.

7 Ferran Requejo, *Multinational Federalism and Value Pluralism* (Routledge 2005) 82.

8 Daniel J. Elazar, *Exploring Federalism* (University of Alabama Press, 1987 – ed. 1991) 42.

9 Tsvi Kahana, 'Canada', in Dawn Oliver and Carlo Fusaro (eds), *How Constitutions Change. A Comparative Study* (Oxford, Hart 2011) 12–13, 37.

10 Eugénie Brouillet, 'The Supreme Court of Canada: The Concept of Cooperative Federalism and its Effect on the Balance of Power', in Nicholas Aroney and John Kincaid (eds), *Courts in Federal Countries: Federalists or Regionalists?* (University of Toronto Press 2017)151. The Canadian Constitutional Act 1867 itself does not explicitly define its structure, although the Preamble underlines the desire of the Provinces to be 'federally united'.

11 Section 1(1) Indian Constitution.

synonym of a federation and includes 'federalism' as an unamendable component of the system's basic structure.[12]

Self-definition, then, seems to be an easy solution, but ultimately comes up against the same difficulties it tries to avoid. Switzerland is not even the most complex example. The Constitution refers to the Swiss 'confederation',[13] but there is a general agreement that the historical title was kept for pragmatic reasons[14] and that Switzerland is in fact a federal system. The US Constitution also does not use the word 'federal', but nonetheless, the United States is commonly regarded as a federal system, if not the prototype of modern federalism.[15] In other cases, it is more difficult to decide how a state defines itself. For example, the Constitution of Bosnia and Herzegovina only mentions that it "shall consist of the two Entities, the Federation of Bosnia and Herzegovina and the Republika Srpska",[16] but it is not clear whether this is intended as a federal or a confederal set-up. To determine this, there may be discussions about whether a federation can actually consist of another federation. On one hand, can a constitution that leaves so few powers to the central level still be considered a federation? On the other hand, can a system that does not consist of independent states be considered a confederation? Even when a constitution defines a state as a federation, disputes may arise about the real nature of the state's structure. In some cases, federalism is a part of constitutional self-definition, but considered in practice to be a 'paper principle'.[17] Without actually having in mind some idea of what a federation means, how do we distinguish between 'real' federations and those that are only federal on paper? Further, if we do not make any distinction, what can we learn from research on a topic that treats both highly centralized and highly decentralized systems in the same way? How comparable are 'unitary federations' – for example systems that call themselves federal but at the same time emphasize their unity and indivisibility[18] – to federations such as Belgium, which is said to have 'confederal traits'? If these systems are comparable, why include highly centralized systems such as Mexico and Malaysia but not highly decentralized systems such as Spain; simply because the one calls itself a federation and the other does not? And another argument: in Belgium, a highly topical debate has arisen on the definition of a federal and a confederal system, with the leading Flemish party Nieuw-Vlaamse Alliantie (N-VA) striving for a confederation but maintaining that this does not by definition imply separatism.

12 Mahendra Pal Singh, 'India', in Oliver and Fusaro (n 9) 183. See also Palermo and Kössler (n 2) 41.
13 Art. 1, 3 and 5a Swiss Constitution.
14 Thomas Fleiner, 'Constitutional Revision: The Case of Switzerland', in Xenophon Contiades (ed), *Engineering Constitutional Change*, (London, Routledge 2013) 337. See also Giovanni Biaggini, 'Switzerland', in Oliver and Fusaro (n 9) 305.
15 Kenneth C. Wheare, *Federal Government* (Oxford University Press 1953) 1.
16 Art. 3 Constitution of Bosnia and Herzegovina.
17 Palermo and Kössler (n 2) 6.
18 See for example Art. 2 Mexican Constitution, Art. 2 (1) Nigerian Constitution, Art. 1 Iraqi Constitution.

How useful is a theory if, by clinging to the systems' own self-definition, the theory is not able to guide political discussions on the system's future?

Similar questions arise from what Palermo and Kössler call the more "sophisticated form" of pragmatism,[19] which encapsulates a very broad working definition – a method often also used by many other scholars to avoid the thorny exercise of defining federalism.[20] For this, Kössler and Palermo rely on Elazar's definition of federalism as 'self-rule plus shared rule'. They find this to be a convenient definition for "being sufficiently generic that no one can disagree, while at the same time providing a rough idea of what it is all about".[21] The fact that "no one can disagree", however, makes it methodologically unsound: science thrives on falsification. The advantages and disadvantages of this approach are discussed more in-depth further in this chapter, under 'the Elazarian approach'.

1.1.2 Why definitions matter

So, why do definitions matter? Why do we care whether Spain is called a federation or not, if we can simply examine how it works? Why put effort into the matter of definition, classification, and concept-building, if only for their own sakes?[22]

The previous section already hinted at some answers to this question. Basically, defining federalism and federal systems are crucial for the sake of theory, method, and impact.

Firstly, theory depends on conceptual clarity. Insight into the essence of federalism and federal systems is crucial to understanding how states are formed and evolve, and how federalism relates to principles such as democracy and the rule of law. For legal theory, in particular, insight into this essence is vital for deriving normative requirements from the state structure. This is not a merely academic exercise: it has consequences in litigation. For example, in some constitutions, such as Brazil and Germany, the federal structure is shielded from revision by an explicit eternity clause.[23] In India, the Supreme Court developed the basic structure doctrine to invalidate amendments that change the basic structure of the Constitution.[24] However, without a definition, we cannot assess whether a change affects the federal structure. In Germany, courts have defined this in terms of institutional features such as the classification of subnational entities with state quality, minimum material and institutional autonomies, and financial

19 Palermo and Kössler (n 2) 3.

20 For references to scholars that use broad or minimalist definitions for this reason: John Law, 'How Can We Define Federalism?', (2013) 5 *Perspectives on Federalism* 115.

21 Palermo and Kössler (n 2) 3–4.

22 Peter Leslie, 'European Futures: The Unbearable Heaviness of Thinking Federally', in Thomas J. Courchene *et al.*(eds), *The Federal Idea. Essays in Honour of Ronald L. Watts* (McGill-Queen's University Press 2011) 324.

23 Art. 60 para 4 Brazil Constitution; Art. 20 para 3 German Constitution.

24 *Kesavananda Bharati v. State of Kerala* (1973) 4 SCC 225.

independence.[25] This classification action can only have normative qualities if it is based on a theoretical understanding of what federalism means. Otherwise, it is merely a random qualification of features as constitutive of the federal structure. In turn, a jurisprudential definition cannot be upgraded to a general theory, because the court crystallizes federalism in view of the particular constitutional and political context of the system in which it operates.

Next, in terms of method, definitions enable us to select cases for comparative purposes. This is useful, irrespective of whether a mostly similar or a mostly different approach is taken. Under the 'sophisticated form of pragmatism', specific institutions or mechanisms are compared rather than systems.[26] This is a valuable method, but it remains debatable whether we can draw general conclusions without understanding the context of the surrounding federalist system. Imagine that Catalonia wants to better protect its autonomy, and has its eye on the exclusivity principle as a method for the allocation of powers.[27] A comparison with Belgium may lead to the impression that this would indeed be a successful strategy. However, the exclusivity principle in Belgium is linked with axioms of equality and autonomy, and combined with several other mechanisms that put sub-states in a more prominent position. By contrast, exclusivity in Austria functions within a highly centralized system, which mostly means that powers remain exclusively concentrated at the central level. Without these contexts, what can we learn from exclusivity as a principle to allocate powers, other than that it may have varying effects in different countries? These contexts show that the exclusivity principle will not afford more autonomy to the Autonomous Communities in Spain, because their wider context is a system that is more centralized. One may argue that we do not need to define federations if we eventually take context into account. Classifying states as '(highly) centralized' or '(highly) decentralized' does not release us from the task of identifying its constitutive features. If, for example, a high or low centralization grade is constitutive for how a multi-tiered system works, then we need criteria to measure the centralization grade and distinguish systems on that basis. It does not matter whether we use specific labels like unitary, regional, federal, or confederal systems.

Finally, we need to clarify concepts in order to have an impact in debates on the organization of a particular political system. To illustrate this third function, I give two examples.

For the first example, I refer back to Belgium. According to the Belgian constitution, Belgium is a federal state.[28] It is fragmenting and dyadic. It was once a unitary state, but gradually decentralized into a system of subnational entities

25 Markus Kotzur, 'Constitutional Amendments and Constitutional Changes in Germany', in Contiades (n 14) 132; Jens Woelk, 'Germany' in Oliver and Faruso (n 9) 149.

26 Palermo and Kössler (n 2) 6.

27 For this exercise, see my contribution, Patricia Popelier, 'Exclusive Powers and Self-Governed Entities: A Tool for Defensive Federalism?', in Ferran Requejo and M. Sanjaume (eds), *Defensive Federalism*, forthcoming.

28 Art. 1 Belgian Constitution.

that have broad legislative powers.[29] According to the constitution, Belgium consists of six subnational entities – three Communities and three Regions. In reality, Belgium's federal structure really revolves around the antagonistic relationship of the Francophone and Flemish language groups. In Flanders, two Flemish-nationalist political parties desire an independent Flanders. One of them, the leading Flemish party N-VA, now promotes confederalism. A heated dispute has emerged as to what 'confederalism' means. This dispute erupts on a daily basis in newspapers and social media, as well as in academic forums. The N-VA presents a model that delegates practically all powers to the subnational entities, but maintains the Belgian structure as a shell. Another Flemish party, the Christian-democratic CD&V, also advocates confederalism, but only as a way to give subnational entities more autonomy without emptying the central level of practical meaning. Constitutionalists and political scientists have entered the debate, pointing out that confederal systems consist of independent states that cooperate on the basis of a treaty. This means that anyone who promotes confederalism is, in fact, promoting separatism.[30] This definition is discussed further below. This gives a common language to relevant stakeholders and shows what is actually at stake: the integrity of the Belgian state. If federalism and confederalism were not properly defined, people would talk past each other and the entire debate would remain blurred. The definitions should, however, be capable of grasping political reality. This is not the case in Belgium, because emphasizing that confederalism requires a constitutional moment of secession, disregards how the Belgian system (without formal secession) has gradually slid into a very loose association.

The second example is the European Union (EU). Scholars often go to great lengths to qualify the EU as a federal system. At the same time, the term is politically controversial because, as Leslie notes, federalism "means very different things to different people".[31] For Germans, a federal EU means a centralized system, counterbalanced by guarantees to secure the Member States' autonomy. However, in Britain (and arguably also in new, unitary Member States) a federal EU evokes the threat of an overriding dominance of EU institutions.[32] For this reason, Leslie chooses to avoid the term and steer clear of 'semantic disputes'.[33] However, antagonists will refer to federalism anyway, in order to protest deeper European integration. In the absence of a clear definition, these antagonists will be free to deform the meaning of federalism in this way. Therefore trying to avoid "the unbearable heaviness of thinking federally" because of political rhetoric will probably not work. It is more useful to explain how the envisaged model of integration differs from federalism, and then a definition helps to clarify this. Alternatively, the EU is in fact designed as a federalist system, and there is no use

29 For an overview: Patricia Popelier and Koen Lemmens, *The Constitution of Belgium. A Contextual Analysis* (Hart 2015) 15–32.

30 Jan Velaers, *Federalisme/Confederalisme… en de weg er naar toe* (KVAB Press 2013) 22–23.

31 Leslie (n 22) 325.

32 *Ibid* 325.

33 *Ibid* 325.

in disguising this. It is important for the functioning of the European system that all partners be on the same page. Also, we need to recognize the relevant definition before we can derive the necessary legal principles to guide the Court of Justice in resolving disputes between the EU and national governments.

Definitions, then, do matter. According to Law, "the lack of a complete appreciation of the meaning and definition of federalism [...] represents a serious weakness that now requires urgent attention".[34] Another question is how precise we need definitions to be. For any research exercise, a definition that articulates the key inclusion and exclusion criteria for the target population is crucial. In clinical studies, inclusion criteria are key features of the population in the study, while exclusion criteria are features of objects that meet the inclusion criteria but are disqualified because they have additional features that could skew the outcome.[35] Likewise, in federalism studies, a definition that articulates inclusion criteria is needed so that states can be examined within the operational framework of the (in our case) federal system. Broad definitions identify only a few defining features, which expands the range of political systems that fall under this category. Precise definitions add more defining features ('intension'), thereby narrowing the number of eligible states ('extension'). Exclusion criteria can be added as the next step for specific research questions. For example, we might be interested in whether or not federal structures make multinational systems more stable or not. This means that we start with the population of federal systems, and then exclude those systems that are not considered to be multinational. If the definition is too strict and includes too many properties, we might end up with no target population at all. If it is too broad, we end up with a range of arrangements that are so varied that we risk finding no clear answer to whether or not federal structures actually provide stability. In the next section, current definitions are examined to determine whether they are too narrow or too broad.

1.2 Defining federations: the problems of traditional approaches

1.2.1 Hamilton, or a narrow approach to defining federations

1.2.1.1 The Hamiltonian tradition

In what Pinder calls the 'Hamiltonian tradition', forms of state are classified as unitary, federal, or confederal, according to defining institutional features.[36] It is an approach that scholars have adopted with enthusiasm, but with very different lists of defining features.

34 Law (n 20) 92.
35 Cecilia M. Patino and Juliana Carvalho Ferreira, 'Inclusion and exclusion criteria in research studies; definitions and why they matter', (2018) 44 *J. Bras. Pneumol* N° 2.
36 John Pinder, 'Multinational federations: introduction', in Michael Burgess and John Pinder (eds), *Multinational Federations* (London-New York, Routledge, 2007) 2.

It should be kept in mind, though, that the 'Federalist Papers' were written to convince the people of New York to give their support to the new Constitution, which was drafted as a compromise between confederalists and unionists. Hamilton, for one, preferred the abolition of the States,[37] and in presenting the new model his basic concern was not so much the organization of a 'federal' state but, rather, the organization of a 'free' state.[38] What arises from the Federalist Papers, then, is an explanation and a defense of what was called a compound form of government – now called 'federal', but with confusing terms in the Papers because there was insufficient terminology for this new form of state.[39] It was an authoritative commentary on the text of the new, federal US Constitution:[40] not a theory of federalism, but the construction of a very particular form of state. Hence the institutional approach. These features, presented for a new American state, were not intended and cannot be considered as qualifying properties for any federal system.

Yet, the system presented by the Federalist Papers was unprecedented, and therefore, as "the founding instance of this phenomenon",[41] became a model for subsequent federalist systems. Gamper dissected the method for defining federal systems as the identification of those institutional features that are shared by a "small number of historic prototypes that serve as model federal systems".[42] Equally, King suggested the analysis of the institutional features of those systems "which most observers agree to be federations".[43] Still, prominent federal scholars come up with different lists, resulting in a larger or narrower population of federations depending on how small or large the number of features are. What follows are just a few examples from authoritative authors. The overview will show that even if authors want to steer clear from the Hamilton tradition, they easily fall into its trap.

Wheare defines the United States, as a model of a federal government, as an association of states so organized that powers are "divided substantially according to the principle that there is a single independent authority for the whole area in respect of some matters and that there are independent regional authorities for other matters, each set of authorities being coordinate with and not subordinate

37 Harry N. Scheiber, 'Federalism and the Constitution: The Original Understanding', in Lawrence M Friedman and Harry N Scheiber (eds), *American Law and the Constitutional Order: Historical Perspectives* (Harvard University Press 1988) 87.

38 Gottfried Dietze, 'Hamilton's Federalist – Treatise for Free Government', (1957) 42 *Cornell LawReview* 307.

39 Scheiber, (n 37) 88. See also Daniel Halberstam, 'Federalism: History, Policy, Law' in Michel Rosenfeld and András Sajo (eds), *The Oxford Handbook of Comparative Constitutional Law* (Oxford University Press 2012) 578–579.

40 Jean Yarbrough, 'Rethinking "The Federalist's View of Federalism"', (1985) 28 *Publius: The Journal of Federalism* 31.

41 Law (n 20) 100.

42 Gamper (n 1) 1298.

43 Preston King, *Federalism and Federation* (Croom Helm 1982) 73.

to the others within its own prescribed sphere".[44] While this appears to be a very general definition at first sight, the term 'independent' conceals a more rigid system of properties that a system should have in order to qualify as federal system. The definition makes two features explicit: (1) a distribution of powers; (2) in accordance with the principle of exclusivity, at least for a minimum set of central and sub-state powers. In addition, Wheare regards the following features as essential to federal government:[45] (3) a supreme written constitution to make the distribution of powers binding upon central and sub-state authorities; (4) a process of constitutional amendment that involves both levels of authority; (5) an independent body to resolve disputes over the distribution of powers;[46] (6) if not a dual set of jurisdictions, then at least some safeguards against a concentration of jurisdictional power over sub-state/central laws in the hands of federal/sub-state courts; and (7) financial resources for each level of authority sufficient to perform their exclusive functions. More features pop up when Wheare undertakes a comparative analysis. For example, a federal system implies that central and sub-state governments each have their own legislative and executive powers through which they can act directly on the citizen. It also implies that sub-state legislatures have no dominant say in central legislation, for example, through a second chamber representative of sub-state legislatures, and that the central government has no control over sub-state legislation. Wheare warned, however, that these individual institutional features are not of themselves determinative. A system may display features that reveal some interdependency between the States and the federal government, so long as the independence criterion, identified as 'the federal principle', remains dominant in the overall system.[47]

For Ronald Watts, a federal system has: (1) two orders of government acting directly on their citizens; (2) a formal constitutional distribution of legislative and executive authority and the allocation of revenue sources ensuring some areas of genuine autonomy for each order; (3) representation of distinct regional views within the federal policy-making institutions, usually via a particular mechanism in the federal second chamber; (4) a supreme written constitution that is not unilaterally amendable and requires the consent of a significant proportion of the constituent units through the assent of their legislatures or by referendum majorities; (5) an umpire in the form of courts or provision for referendums to rule on disputes between governments; (6) processes and institutions to facilitate intergovernmental collaboration for those areas where governmental responsibilities are shared or inevitably overlap.[48]

44 Wheare (n 15) 2, 35.
45 *Ibid* 55, 57, 60, 71, 97.
46 This is most logically, but not necessarily, a court: *ibid* 66.
47 *Ibid* 16.
48 Ronald Watts, *Comparing Federal Systems* (Queen's University 2008, 3rd ed.) 9; Ronald L. Watts, 'The Federal Idea and its Contemporary Relevance', in Courchene *et al.* (n 22) 15–16.

Building on this, Swenden qualifies the first criterion as a distinction of 'territorial' orders of government and adds two other requirements: (7) federal states are by definition democratic; and (8) do not allow unilateral secession.[49]

Gamper detects a common institutional standard, requiring: (1) the distribution of powers between the central and the constituent entities; (2) the participation of the constituent units in the central level of legislation; (3) the constitutional autonomy of the constituent entities; (4) fiscal equalization (further concretized as autonomous taxation rights); and (5) intergovernmental instruments.[50] As part of these intergovernmental instruments for cooperation and coordination, she also refers to instruments needed for the prevention and resolution of competence conflicts. In the end, Gamper reduces this to two 'most essential' elements - the distribution of powers and participation of the constituent entities. This is only because she considers the other criteria as inherent to these two elements.[51] Still, other inclusion criteria seem to be implied in her list. This becomes apparent when Gamper holds that states are to be called regional instead of federal if they lack a representative chamber or if the constituent entities hold no legislative powers.[52]

Palermo and Kössler abstain from a definition and take a pragmatic approach, but in the end, they nevertheless partly turn to the Hamiltonian approach. They enumerate three – in fact four – characteristics that they deem "necessary but not sufficient".[53] In other words, while these features alone are not sufficient to qualify a state as 'federal', they are nevertheless presented as inclusion criteria. To define a concept, we need to identify "necessary and sufficient conditions".[54] "Necessary" albeit insufficient conditions go partly down that road: they are not helpful to identify a federal system, but they do disqualify systems that fail to meet any of the criteria. These criteria are: (1) the division of state functions between at least two different orders of government that both enjoy political autonomy; (2) the supremacy of the federal constitution; (3) a system of cooperation among the levels, including (to be considered as criterion 4) the judicial adjudication of disputes between and among the entities over the respective constitutional powers.[55]

Gaudreault-DesBiens harshly criticizes the Hamiltonian approach.[56] With Basta Fleiner, he nevertheless enumerates three "defining characteristics" of a federation: (1) the division of powers in; (2) a supreme constitution that; (3) is

49 Wilfried Swenden, *Federalism and Regionalism in Western Europe. A Comparative and Thematic Analysis* (Palgrave MacMillan 2006) 10.
50 Gamper (n 1) 1305.
51 *Ibid* 1306.
52 *Ibid* 1306.
53 Palermo and Kössler (n 2) 39.
54 Law (n 20) 97.
55 Palermo and Kössler (n 2) 39.
56 Lidija R. Basta Fleiner and Jean-François Gaudreault-DesBiens, 'Federalism and autonomy', in Mark Tushnet, Thomas Fleiner and Cheryl Saunders (eds), *Routledge Handbook of Constitutional Law* (London, Routledge 2015) 5. See further in this chapter.

non-modifiable at the will of a single party.[57] In addition, 'key mechanisms' for shared rule in federal systems[58] are presented that cannot be seen as defining properties. They instead point out what should be dealt with in federal states rather than how, such as the allocation of residual powers, or the resolution of conflicts between orders of government. Nevertheless, the authors seem inclined to shift to a more specific property-based list: where they indicate representation of constitutional units not just in any federal body but 'most importantly the second chamber', declare the 'supremacy of federal laws', and call for an 'independent judiciary' to umpire the division of powers.[59] This sounds as if second chambers, federal supremacy, and courts to resolve federalism disputes are institutional features of federal systems.

Apart from these general theories of federalism, scholars studying a specific phenomenon regularly declare this specific element to be a defining property of federal systems. Some consider second chambers to be 'identity bracelets', a necessary condition to qualify a system as federal.[60] Others point out that subnational constitutional autonomy is "of course" one of the defining attributes of federalism.[61] Or they maintain that a federation, by definition, has a subnational judicial branch.[62]

Ultimately, federal systems are contrasted with other forms of government that, in turn, also have to be defined. As a result, confederations are also defined in terms of their institutional features. In doctrine, there is a surprising consensus on the definition of confederations. Confederations bring together: (1) sovereign states; (2) on the basis of a treaty; (3) but do not act directly upon the people; and (4) take decisions on the basis of unanimity.[63] Often, it is also specified that (5) states can withdraw from the confederation at will.[64] What is surprising, is that it is generally accepted that this defines a confederation, although a political system that meets these conditions turns out to simply be an international intergovernmental organization. The sole difference, added by some scholars, is that a confederation cannot be confined to only one goal.[65] Also, older literature enumerates the types of competences that can be transferred to the confederal entity.[66]

57 Basta Fleiner and Gaudreault-DesBiens (n 56) 153.
58 *Ibid* 149
59 *Ibid* 149.
60 Michael Burgess, *Comparative federalism. Theory and Practice* (London, Routledge, 2006) 204.
61 James Gardner, 'In Search of Sub-National Constitutionalism', (2008) 4 *Eu. Const. L. Rev.* 325. See also Werner Heun, *The Constitution of Germany. A Contextual Analysis* (Hart 2011) 50, 80; Christina Fasone, 'What Role for Regional Assemblies in Regional States? Italy, Spain and the United Kingdom in Comparative Perspective', (2012) 4 *Perspectives on Federalism* 176.
62 Maxwell A Cameron and Tulia G Falleti, 'Federalism and the Subnational Separation of Powers', (2005) *Publius: The Journal of Federalism* 246.
63 Palermo and Kössler (n 2) 35. See also Kincaid (n 4) xxii – but see, by contrast, p. xxiii.
64 Jean-François Aubert, 'Essai sur le fédéralisme' (1963) 80 *Revue de droit public* 404.
65 Palermo and Kössler (n 2) 35.
66 For an overview: Aubert (n 64) 404.

1.2.1.2 *What is wrong with the Hamiltonian approach?*

The Hamiltonian approach is useful from a normative perspective. It helps courts to select minimum requirements that the (constitutional or organic) lawmaker must respect to uphold the federal principle as articulated by the constitution. Courts, however, do not appear to have found a recipe with universal validity. Instead, they shape a specific type of federal state that is consistent with the constitution, in the particular political context, and the national sentiments of the state in which they function. In contrast, as a universal doctrine, the Hamiltonian approach is unsatisfactory for at least ten reasons.

i The cherry-picking problem
The lack of consensus about the precise set of properties is problematic because it allows cherry-picking. One can pick any of these lists of characteristics to randomly include or exclude a specific political system in comparative studies. This was already signaled by Livingston. He stated that federal government can be defined in many different ways, depending on which institutional criteria are selected, and thus "definitions can be devised to fit almost any circumstances" – an exercise which he found "interesting but of little worth".[67]
Likewise, in political debate, one can pick any feature in the list to support a political preference for institutional reform (e.g. a demand for subnational constitutional autonomy) or status quo (e.g. to maintain a bicameral Parliament) and give it the pretense of normativity.

ii The circular reasoning fallacy
More fundamentally, the variety of lists reveals that the Hamiltonian approach falls short as a defining mechanism. Consensus about institutional features is only possible if a list relies on a preexisting definition of what federalism means. In other words: we need to define federations before we can infer essential institutional features from them. Federalism points to the core value of federal arrangements that apply irrespective of the specific shape they take in different countries or at different times. I will discuss this in the next sections of this chapter, under the 'value of federalism'. For now, it suffices to stress that at its core, federalism has to do with the distribution of power between the central authority and territorial subunits. A catalogue of characteristics, then, should always connect with this core idea. Thus, Basta Fleiner and Gaudreault-DesBiens present key mechanisms of federal systems that all have the aim of guaranteeing "the representation of the federation's diversity within federal institutions, in view of achieving a proper balance between unity and diversity".[68] A closer look at the proposed characteristics, however, reveals that this is not always the case.

67 William S. Livingston, *Federalism and Constitutional Change* (Oxford University Press 1956) 300.
68 Basta Fleiner and Gaudreault-DesBiens (n 56) 149.

One example is the requirement that a federal state should be a democratic form of government. Riker has already warned about this 'ideological fallacy'.[69] Friedrich held that although democracy facilitates the federalizing process, the two concepts are not necessarily linked. Friedrich also noted that federalism even conflicts with a specific type of democracy, conceived as the absolute and unrestrained rule of the majority.[70] Yet, Swenden adds a requirement for federal and regional legislators to be directly elected in a free and open election process, as a corollary of 'self-rule'.[71] However, in a broad definition of federalism, the notion of 'self-rule' (contrasted to the notion of 'shared rule') relates to the status of territorial entities, and not to the people themselves. For methodological reasons, different constitutional principles should not be mixed. If authoritative states are excluded by definition, we risk missing out discovering how, and understanding why, this specific characteristic may compromise the functioning of federal institutions. Of course, authoritative states can also get excluded from the target population in the next phase, if the research question for a specific study presupposes democratic government. This means that '(non) democracy' is an exclusion criterion, not an inclusion criterion. Also, the distinction should be kept in order to analyze the more complex relationship between federalism and democracy.[72] In promoting self-rule by political units that are closer to citizens, federalism provides citizens with more opportunities for political involvement. This may also be considered a threat to democracy where it frustrates majority rule.[73] In fact, empirical research has disproven the correlation between federalism and democracy.[74] I come back to this relationship further in this chapter when federalism as a value concept is discussed.

Another example is the referendum requirement. Watts adds this as an alternative to the judicial resolution of federal disputes, i.e., disputes about whether the federal or sub-state government remains within the scope of its powers.[75] Thorlakson holds that in the absence of judicial interference, new federal competencies in Switzerland are the result of a process of formal

69 William H. Riker, *Federalism: Origin, Operation, Significance* (Little, Brown and Company 1964) 13–15; 139–145. Also critical: King (n 43) 88–89.

70 Carl J. Friedrich, 'New Tendencies in Federal Theory and Practice', (1965) 14 *Jahrbuch des Öffentliches Rechts* 8–9; Carl J Friedrich, *Constitutional Government and Democracy: Theory and Practice in Europe and America* (Blaisdell Publishing Company 1968) 196.

71 Swenden (n 49) 10.

72 For the interference of patterns of democracy with patterns of federalism, see Arthur Benz, 'Dimensions and Dynamics of Federal Regimes', in Arthur Benz and Jorg Broschek (eds), *Federal Dynamics. Continuity, Change, & the Varieties of Federalism* (Oxford University Press 2013) 72–74.

73 Basta Fleiner and Gaudreault-DesBiens (n 56) 145.

74 Jan-Erik Lane and Svante Ersson, 'The riddle of federalism: does federalism impact on democracy?,' (2005) 12 *Democratisation* 163–182.

75 Watts (n 48) 7.

constitutional amendment which includes a popular referendum.[76] Yet, if the federal authority simply usurps powers by legislating in a particular policy field, there is no court to challenge this overreach. The reply to this critique is that the federal legislation in question can be stopped by the popular vote process. Wheare, for example, accepts the Swiss referendum as an alternative for judicial oversight of federal laws, because it allows citizens to decide whether or not to validate the law.[77] However, disputes can be resolved through different mechanisms, judicial or extra-judicial, but not through referendums. In a referendum, people do not decide whether a proposal is in accordance with the constitutional distribution of powers; they vote on the content of the proposal, based on their political preference. If they downvote a proposal, this is not because they find it beyond the competency of the federal or sub-state authority; it is because they do not favor the proposal, whether it is adopted by the federal or the sub-state legislature. If in doctrine referendums are presented as an alternative to constitutional review – a continuing discussion in Switzerland – then this has to do with mechanisms to protect fundamental rights, rather than at which level the government should act. The threat of a referendum, so the argument goes, is more effective to secure the recognition of the people's interest than the retrospective review by the Federal Supreme Court.[78] Irrespective of one's position in the debate, referendums are discussed as an alternative to constitutional review only as a way to make the government responsive and to protect people against government abuse, and not as an alternative to the resolution of federalism disputes. They can be an alternative for a federal arrangement as a kind of market for political competition: people can force governments to take their preferences into account by direct vote (in a referendum) or by voting with their feet (in a federation), and they can combine both in a federation with sub-state referendums.[79] But referendums do not resolve federalism disputes.

iii The lack of universal validity

The third problem with the Hamiltonian approach is that the preferred list gives us insight into the characteristics of specific federations, but not into the essence of any federal state. As a result, federalism studies too often remain country-specific and lack sufficient theoretical basis.[80] Yet, in the 1950s already Livingston warned against sets of institutional criteria to qualify a

76 Lori Thorlakson, 'Comparing Federal Institutions: Power and Representation in Six Federations' (2003) 26 *West European Politics* 11.

77 Wheare (n 15) 61, 68.

78 Christine Rothmayr, 'Towards the Judicialisation of Swiss politics?', (2001) 24 *West European Politics* 80.

79 Bruno S. Frey and Iris Bohnet, 'Democracy by Competition: Referenda and Federalism in Switzerland', (1993) 23 *Publius: The Journal of Federalism* 80.

80 Jan Erk, *Explaining Federalism. State, society and congruence in Austria, Belgium, Canada, Germany and Switzerland* (Routledge 2008) 1; Thorlakson (n 76) 1.

constitution as federal or not, because "no societies are the same and each will require different instruments" in accordance with their specific features.[81]

Duchacek illustrated this when testing a set of ten 'yardsticks' drawn from the US model: (1) exclusive control over foreign relations; (2) immunity against secession; (3) an independent sphere of central authority; (4) participation of territorial units in constitutional amendments; (5) indestructible identity and autonomy of the territorial components; (6) their residual and significant power; (7) equal or favorably weighed representation of unequal units; (8) two independent sets of courts; (9) judicial review; (10) a clear division of power. Having tested them on a wide set of multi-tiered systems, Duchacek's conclusion was that they do not give "an acceptable answer to the question [of] what constitutes real federalism".[82] The author confirmed his conclusion fifteen years later.[83]

Lists of characteristics are of limited value because they are too closely related to the specific shape that a federation takes at a given moment. Even when, following Gamper's method, different jurisdictions are compared to identify their shared characteristics, the Hamiltonian approach always relies on a prior selection of what are considered to be – randomly, intuitively, or traditionally – model federations. As a consequence, systems that are commonly regarded as federal but have not been included in the set of model federations do not necessarily meet all the institutional requirements.[84]

The characteristics, then, do not show us how to design a federal state. Instead, they show us how to copy a 'particular' federal state – how to become the United States as it were – or how to design the mean of a set of particular states. Even more, they show us how to design a particular federal state or the mean of a set of particular states 'at a particular moment'. Duchacek, revisiting his ten yardsticks, contrasted the last one, exclusive national control over foreign relations, with developments in the last decades. Subnational entities have "dramatically increased their activities across international borders in either a regional or global framework".[85] Clearly, Hamiltonian lists risk becoming outdated before you know it. Another illustration of this is identified by Wheare. His definition reflected the US system of dual federalism, thereby disqualifying Germany as a federal state, along with other models of so-called executive federalism. The definition was highly influential, but came under attack with the rise of cooperative federalism, which Wheare's theory was unable to capture.[86] Even when the focus

81 Livingston (n 67) 6, see also p. 9 and 302.

82 Ivo Duchacek, *Comparative Federalism* (University Press of America 1987) 274.

83 Ivo Duchacek, 'Consociational Cradle of Federalism', (1985) 15 *Publius: The Journal of Federalism* 46.

84 Sala (n 6) 111. See also Thorlakson (n 76) 3 to note that the approach is "unsatisfactory because it is too narrow and rigid, and applies formal constitutional criteria that few systems match".

85 Duchacek (n 83) 45.

86 See Law (n 20) 93.

remained on the United States alone, the model had to be reshaped. This resulted in a shift from a dual state model based on exclusive competences to the concurrent power paradigm based on the doctrine of preemption.[87]

iv A biased selection of model federations

If institutional features of 'any' federation are drawn from the institutional design of existing systems, it is relevant which systems are selected as model federations. According to Gamper, "all theories of federalism are more or less based on a small number of historic prototypes that serve as model federal systems".[88] As the first model of modern federalism, the United States has left a dominant mark on how contemporary scholars envisage the design of federations – which Diamond criticized as "a parochial tendency of contemporary observers who take American federalism as the very model of federalism as such".[89] Other model federations are usually Germany and Switzerland.

These old-school models usually present similar features. First, if not necessarily created by aggregation, they at least all have a history of the unification of formerly independent states or former colonies.[90] This explains why residual powers with the sub-states and subnational constitutional autonomy are frequently identified as properties of 'real' federations. Next, while some are multicultural, none are multinational. This is defined as systems in which significant groups voice important political autonomy claims for territorial entities based on linguistic, religious, cultural, or ethnic identities[91] – i.e. systems where linguistic, religious, cultural, or ethnic differences are persistent markers of political identity and bases for fragmentation.[92] As a result, they are organized in a symmetrical way.[93] Basically, the model federations share basic assumptions which Choudry and Hume have summarized as follows: "once pre-existing political units have come together in a federal state, they shall remain members of a single political community bound in a common constitutional order; this new political community is

87 Robert Schütze, *From Dual to Cooperative Federalism: The Changing Structure of European Law* (Oxford, Oxford University Press 2009) 94.

88 Gamper (n 1) 1298.

89 Martin Diamond, 'The Ends of Federalism', (1973) 3 Publius: The Journal of Federalism, 131. See also Thomas O. Hueglin, 'Comparing Federalisms: Variations or Distinct Models?', in Benz and Broschek (n 72) 28 and Douglas V. Verney, 'Federalism, Federative Systems, and Federations: The United States, Canada, and India', (1995) 25 *Publius* 84 on the American terms in which federalism writers define federations.

90 See also Stepan's criticism of Riker's definition of federalism, which comes down to the US model of a coming-together federation: Alfred Stepan, 'Federalism and Democracy: Beyond the U.S. Model', (1999) 10 *Journal of Democracy* 20–21.

91 Alfred Stepan, 'Towards a New Comparative Politics of Federalism, Multinationalism, and Democracy: Beyond Rikerian Federalism', in Edward L. Gibson (ed), *Federalism and Democracy in Latin America* (John Hopkins University Press 2004) 39.

92 Sujit Choudry and Nathan Hume, 'Federalism, Devolution and Secession: From Classical to Post-conflict Federalism', in Tom Ginsburg and Rosalind Dixon, *Comparative Constitutional Law* (Cheltenham, Edward Elgar 2011) 363.

93 Critical of the inability of traditional federal theory to capture constitutional asymmetry: Maja Sahadžić, *Asymmetry, Multinationalism and Constitutional Law. Making Legitimacy and Stability in Multinational States* (Routledge 2020) 3, 12, 14.

a nation that inhabits the entire history of the state and possesses the right to self-government; and debates over the design of the federal system are debates about how this nation should organize itself internally and thus do not raise the prior question of whether the nation should continue to exist".[94] Consequently, traditional federal theory is called "a misfit"[95] for multinational systems, because it does not deal with the burning questions of national pluralism:[96] can different political nationalities coexist within one federal state, and does this reduce or fuel the instability that comes with minority nationalism? Yet, these kinds of divided, multinational states present the most salient issues of contemporary federalism.[97] As a result, a new 'branch' of federal theory emerged under the names of 'ethno-federalism', 'post-conflict', 'pluralist', or 'multinational federalism', as opposed to the established 'monistic federalism'.[98] General federal theory, however, should be able to cover all types of federalism.

v A barely hidden sense of superiority

Systems that do not meet the inclusion criteria that define a federal state are classified as 'regional' or 'quasi-federal'. This is contrasted with model federations – those systems that are generally agreed upon as federal, such as the United States and Germany. A normative flavor is added to this. Robust models of federations are 'fully-fledged', 'true', or 'mature' federations, quasi-federations are not – or not yet. The idea is that quasi-federations are incomplete.[99] They aspire to become a federation just like the United States or Germany, but they have not quite got there. A little effort is needed before they reach their goal: the development of their true federal self. But do they really aspire to become the next United States or Germany? Is Spain a quasi-federation aspiring to become a federal system, even if its constitution stresses the "indissoluble unity of the Spanish Nation",[100] without any mention of federalism? Sometimes multi-tiered states such as Indonesia[101] deliberately avoid self-defining themselves as 'federal' precisely because they do not aspire to become a 'true' federation, for fear that this carries the seed

94 Choudry and Hume (n 92) 363.
95 Alain-G. Gagnon and Arjun Tremblay; 'Federalism and diversity: a new research agenda', in John Kincaid (ed), *A Research Agenda for Federalism Studies* (Edward Elgar 2019) 131.
96 Ferran Requejo, 'Plurinational federalism and political theory', in John Loughlin, John Kincaid and Wilfried Swenden (eds), *Routledge Handbook of Regionalism and Federalism* (Routledge, 2013) 34, 38. See also André Lecours, 'Federalism and nationalism', in Kincaid (n 95) 142.
97 Michael Burgess, 'The penumbra of federalism', in Loughlin, Kincaid and Swenden (n 96) 45–46. See for this question Jan Erk and Lawrence M. Anderson (eds), *The Paradox of Federalism* (Routledge 2010).
98 Basta Fleiner and Gaudreault-DesBiens (n 56) 144. See, for example, Requejo (n 7) 152 p.
99 Sala (n 6) 109 quotes the various adjectives that have been used to describe Spain as "something other, or even less, than a federation": imperfect federalism, noninstitutional federalism, incomplete federalism, unfulfilled federalism, and quasi-federation.
100 Section 2 of the Spanish Constitution.
101 Simon Butt, 'Provincial Asymmetry in Indonesia: What is so 'Special' about it?', in Patricia Popelier and Maja Sahadžić, *Constitutional Asymmetry in Multinational Federations*, 229.

of separatism. Likewise, the United Kingdom, despite devolution, shudders at the idea of federalism.[102]

vi The epistemological obstacle and the embarrassment of intermediate constructs The Hamiltonian approach ranks states according to the unitary-federal-confederal trichotomy.[103] However, the properties of these concepts are not mutually exclusive. As a result, political systems sometimes present features that exclude them from either category. For intermediate forms between unitary and federal systems, the categories 'regionalist state', 'hybrids', or 'quasi-federation' were created, as general waste containers without specific properties. For intermediate forms between federal and confederal systems, such as the EU, what remains is – as Law puts it – "a conceptual void, an unidentified and unnamed 'black hole'.[104] For the EU in particular, all the efforts that are made to describe the EU in terms of a federation thereby mixing description with intention, create confusion instead of conceptual clarity.[105]

In the 21st century, however, these intermediate forms are the real challenge. Complex systems, mostly disaggregating, with prominent positions for regional as well as local sub-entities, have replaced the (either unitary or federal) nation-state as the dominant form of political organization.[106] According to Requejo, federations need confederal traits and asymmetry to accommodate multinationalism.[107] If federal theory remains focused on traditional, past-century models of nation-states, it is not capable of dealing with the most pressing issues faced by contemporary multi-tiered systems.[108] This is why the Hamiltonian approach has been considered an "epistemological obstacle" in constitutional discourse, which obstructs our insights into what is really at stake.[109] According to Watts, 'hybrids' are on the rise "because statesmen are often more interested in pragmatic solutions than in theoretical purity".[110] But if theoretical purity does not grasp political reality, then there's something wrong with the theory, rather than with the

102 Michael Keating, 'Why no Federalism in the United Kingdom?', in Alain-G Gagnon, Soeren Keil and Sean Mueller (eds), *Understanding Federalism and Federation* (Routledge 2015) 177.

103 Aubert (n 64) 403.

104 Law (n 20).

105 Leslie (n 22) 324.

106 John Loughlin, 'Reconfiguring the nation-state. hybridity vs. uniformity', in Loughlin, Kincaid and Swenden (n 96) 3–4; Cheryl Saunders, 'Federalism and Constitutionalism: challenges presented by dominant conceptions of the unitary state', in Kincaid (n 95) 41.

107 Requejo (n 7) 63, 69–78.

108 See in this respect Requejo (n 7) 62–63 in his critique on the state-centred approach of classic federalism.

109 Jean-François Gaudreault-Desbiens and Fabien Gélinas, 'Prolégomènes à une étude renouvelée du fédéralisme', in Jean-François Gaudreault-Desbiens and Fabien Gélinas (eds), *Le fédéralisme dans tous ses états* (Brussels, Bruylant 2005) 5.

110 Watts, 'The Federal Idea' (n 48) 16; Ronald L. Watts, 'Comparing Federal Political Systems', in Gagnon, Keil and Mueller (n 102) 13.

statesmen. This explains Elazar's call for a rethinking of federal theory to respond to what he calls a crisis in (American) thinking about federalism.[111]

John Law presents an effort to solve the problem without losing the idea of catching federal systems in terms of defining institutional features. He defines federal systems as forms of government in which there is a division of powers between two levels of government of equal status. 'Equal status' in turn is analyzed in terms of three properties: (1) constitutional protection of the regional governments, seen as "the absence of a right for the general government unilaterally either to abolish them or to reduce their powers"; (2) the direct effect of the law of the general government; and (3) majority-voting in the decision-making process of the general government.[112] At first sight, this definition of 'equal status' is quite surprising. This is because the properties do not guarantee equal weight, for example, in shared decision-making or equal status of federal and sub-state laws with a neutral priority principle in case of conflict. Further reading clarifies that the properties are intended to emancipate the EU level in order to qualify the EU system as federal, i.e., a 'federal union of nation states':[113] Majority voting, Law states, put an end to the blocking power of individual Member States. He claims it enabled the EU level to evolve into an equal relationship with the Member States instead of acting as their agent, with Member State autonomy having been sacrificed for efficiency gains.[114] Law's equality criterion, then, reminds us of Wheare's independence criterion. This was also there to secure that the federal government, instead of being the subordinate agent of the States as it was considered to be under the Confederation, was their "equal and co-ordinate partner".[115] This criterion is affected by the same deficiencies, the latter being molded too much to the US model, while the first to the EU model. Equal status is not secured if the central government by mere majority voting is able to use its powers in ways that encroach upon the sub-states' domain, especially in fragmenting federal systems.

vii Denial of political reality: the federal construct as a package deal

The specific institutional design of multi-tiered systems is the result of a package deal.[116] This is why in reality states rarely conform to all the institutional features that are considered to be properties of federations.[117] The

111 Daniel J. Elazar, 'Federalism vs Decentralization: The Drift from Authenticity', (1976) 6 *Publius: The Journal of Federalism* 9.
112 Watts, 'The Federal Idea' (n 48) 105–106.
113 *Ibid*, 107 and 109–111.
114 *Ibid* 107.
115 Wheare (n 15) 3, 5.
116 Vicki C. Jackson, 'Comparative constitutional federalism: its strengths and limits', in Gaudréault-Desbiens and Gélinas (n 109) 148–151. See also Riker (n 69) 12–13 on 'the federal bargain', albeit confined to military threat and expansionist motives.
117 Ronald L Watts, 'Typologies of federalism', in Loughlin, Kincaid and Swenden (n 96) 19.

traditional theory is therefore praised for being precise, but criticized for the "serious default" of being estranged from reality.[118]

The design reflects the power relations that existed during the bargain. For example, during the foundation of the United States, the original confederate States were dominant and had to be convinced to accept a new power balance. This is why the original US federation was designed as an 'Enumerated Powers Federalism', where the States' powers are protected by constraining the federal authority to a limited list of enumerated powers.[119] By contrast, in fragmenting states, new constituent entities are created that have to negotiate for powers that were taken as given in coming-together federations, such as the power to adopt their own constitutions or residual powers. Hence, so-called properties of federal systems are simply part of a package deal, rather than being an essential part of federations.

As a result, constitutionalists, while teaching federalism *in abstracto*, are inclined to describe their own multi-tiered system as '*sui generis*'. This means that it results from the specific societal, political, economic, and historical features that explain why the package deal turned out this way in that particular country. If the theoretical model and political reality are not sufficiently connected, the *sui generis* narrative prevails. This obstructs the development of theory, for, as Schütze reminds: "the *sui generis* idea is not a theory. It is an *anti*-theory as it refuses to search for commonalities; yet, theory 'must' search for what is generic".[120] For example, it has been pointed out that federal systems in Africa have been considered *sui generis* cases, ill-suited to comparison. Therefore federal scholars remained blind to the challenges African federalism poses to traditional federal theories and the assumptions that underpin these theories.[121]

viii The risk of missing out: the problem of rigid definitions

Fear of Missing Out – FOMO – is a trendy word to pinpoint the social anxiety of persons with a compulsive concern that they might miss an opportunity.[122] The Hamiltonian approach suffers from a related but reverse deficiency: the risk of missing out. By concentrating on a specific institution or procedure that is considered an attribute of federal systems, one misses out on alternatives that serve the same function. As Wheare rightfully noticed, before providing a rigid definition of his own (and revealing a male-dominated nature of the academic world): "Where common usage differs so much, the academic man must be careful not to adopt too rigid a definition".[123]

118 Aubert (n 64) 403, 408.
119 Randy E. Barnett, 'Three Federalisms', (2008) 39 *Loy. U. Chi. L.J.* 286–287.
120 Schütze (n 87) 3.
121 J. Tyler Dickovick, 'Federalism in Africa: Origins, Operation and (In) Significance', (2014) 24 Regional & Federal Studies 554–566.
122 On the origins of the term, see Joseph Reagle, 'Following the Joneses: FOMO and conspicuous reality', (2015) 20 *FirstMonday*. Available at: https://firstmonday.org/ojs/index.php/fm/article/view/6064/4996. Last accessed: July, 27, 2020.
123 Wheare (n 15) 1.

The risk of such rigid definitions is that theory creates blinders that saddle systems with obsolete institutions, instead of creatively looking for more effective mechanisms. For example, federal scholars have long been fixated on second houses, whereas it is clear by now that executive-based institutions are far more effective for securing subnational interests in federal decision-making.[124] The risk increases where properties are described in detail. For example, 'a mechanism to rule on disputes between governments' offers more leeway as a standard than 'a court to rule on disputes between governments'.

To catch the variations within federal systems, then, it seems wiser to list functions or, in Thorlakson's terms, 'key dimensions',[125] rather than precise institutions or procedures. But even then, hard cases remain. For example, what should be done with asymmetric federations, where some subnational entities meet most but not all criteria? This might be because they are not sufficiently represented at the central level and are not involved in the procedure to revise the 'political contract' that distributes competences. This is, for example, the position of the German Community in the Belgian federal system. In the end, Thorlakson also ends up with a comparison of the 'usual suspects' in comparative federalism: the United States, Australia, Canada, Switzerland, Germany, and Austria.

ix The absence of a global/local perspective

By extracting general theory from specific federal systems, the focus remains on relations between one central and one subnational level of authority within a system. Only rarely does traditional federal theory look outside the state borders. Duchacek formulated 'exclusive national control over foreign relations' as a yardstick, albeit as a controversial one, only to discover later that real-life federations had greatly surpassed this criterion.[126]

States today are increasingly being embedded in a more global legal environment.[127] Scholars have tried to either construct yet another category for the resulting supranational systems – 'postmodern confederations' in Elazar's words[128] or tried to rank them under the redefined category of federations. More global legal systems, however, may also change the power relations of central and subnational authorities within the national federal system.[129] This is true, especially for the EU Member States. If the EU is

124 Francesco Palermo, 'Beyond Second Chambers: Alternative Representation of Territorial Interests and their Reasons', (2018) 10 *Perspectives on Federalism* 49–70. See already Aubert (n 64) 412 for a rejection of the idea that second chambers protect the interests of the sub-states.

125 Thorlakson (n 76) 6.

126 Duchacek (n 83) 45.

127 Loughlin (n 106) 13, 16.

128 Daniel J. Elazar, *Constitutionalizing Globalization: The Postmodern Revival of Confederal Arrangements* (Rowman & Littlefield Publishers 1998), in particular at p. 40–41; Daniel J. Elazar, 'The New Europe: a Federal State or a Confederation of States?', (1998) 4 *Swiss Pol. Sc. Rev.* 124.

129 See Watts, 'The Federal Idea' (n 48) 24 for the trends toward multi-level federal organization.

considered to be a federal system, then federal theory needs to accommodate the exponential increase in the different levels of authority, the relationships between these levels, and the dynamics of these relations. This is where Law's theory, aimed at including the EU as a federal system,[130] fails.

At the same time, by concentrating on only two levels of authority, the definition does not account for the dynamics between multiple levels within the national system. Within a strict definition, local entities are not recognized as sub-state levels within a federalist system. Yet, scholarship increasingly draws attention to the local level as a 'third order of government'.[131] The constitution in some federalist systems, such as South Africa, Brazil, Mexico, Nigeria, and India, expressly recognize these levels in this way.[132] This creates dynamics that also impact on the regional level. It has been pointed out in the literature how local decentralization can be used to weaken regional levels of government.[133]

In reality, more levels can sometimes be discerned even without counting the global level. For example, Bosnia Herzegovina comprises a federation with its own subunits, apart from local entities.

x Missing out on the topical issues: the sovereignty debate

In the Hamiltonian approach, the notion of sovereignty often looms around the corner to confuse the debate. 'Sovereignty' was a paradigm in constitutional law that could not simply be dismissed when confronted with new compound forms of political organization, e.g., with the Swiss Confederacy or the United Provinces of the Netherlands. Therefore, unitary, federal, and confederal systems are often distinguished based on the location of sovereignty. This would be in the central government in unitary systems, in the member states in confederal systems, or spread over various levels of political authority in federations.[134] In reality, this model is not always put in practice. The Ethiopian constitution, for example, defines Ethiopia as a federal system, but lays all sovereign power in the Nations, Nationalities, and People of Ethiopia.[135]

Within federalism theory, this has generated competitive models of federalism. The first is a dual-type of federalism where sovereignty is divided into separate blocks, one residing with the central authority, while the other with the subnational entities; the second is a cooperative type of federalism where sovereignty is shared by both levels of authority.[136] In its original definition,

130 Law (n 20) 109–111.

131 See Palermo and Kössler (n 2) 281–320 for this development.

132 Kincaid (n 4) xxvi; Nico Steytler, 'Non-centralism in Africa: in search of the federal idea', in Kincaid (n 95) 181. For example Art. 40.1 South African Constitution; Art. 1 Brazilian Constitution.

133 J. Tyler Dickovick, 'Municipalization as Central Government Strategy: Central-Regional-Local Politics in Peru, Brazil, and South Africa', (2006) 37 *Publius; The Journal of Federalism* 1–25.

134 Watts (n 117) 20, 22.

135 Art. 8(1) Ethiopian Constitution.

136 Palermo and Kössler (n 2) 46; 87–88; Schütze (n 87)5.

however, sovereignty means absolute and indivisible power, as rooted in European constitutional theory.[137] The notion of divided sovereignty is conceptually unthinkable from that perspective.

The sovereignty concept traditionally preoccupied in particular Germanic federalism scholarship, but has gradually faded.[138] Still, the notion of sovereignty as a defining element of federal forms is wide-spread. For example, King defined a federation as "an institutional arrangement, taking the form of a sovereign state, and distinguished from other such states solely by the fact that its central government incorporates regional units in its decision procedure on some constitutionally entrenched basis".[139] Watts, in turn, stresses that in a federation, each unit "has sovereign powers derived from the constitution rather than from another level of government".[140]

The notion is, in particular, used to include subnational constitutional autonomy as a – or even 'the' – defining institutional feature to distinguish federal systems from regional states.[141] As a result, courts in Germany and Australia have identified full-fledged subnational constitutional autonomy as essential features of a federal system, whereas the Russian Constitutional Court stated the opposite because sovereignty resides in the federation.[142]

For non-European scholars, sovereignty usually does not have this connotation of absolute and indivisible power.[143] Instead, sovereignty is vested in the people, and all (central, subnational, or local) government powers are delegated this power.[144] Still, federalism blurs the notion of sovereignty as the will of the people. Whitaker observed that a federation "denies by its very processes that the national majority is the efficient expression of the sovereignty of the people: a federation replaces this majority with a more diffuse definition of sovereignty".[145] Hence, the sovereign *demos* is represented by both the people as a single entity, and by a plurality of territorial entities, connecting population and territory.[146] But if sovereignty connects people and territory, and if all powers are delegated, the sovereignty concept makes it difficult to distinguish between decentralized unitary systems with elected local governments, and federations.

Either way, the sovereignty concept does not grasp the complex arrangements and developments that occur in practice. For example, the Federation

137 See Palermo and Kössler (n 2) 87; Schütze (n 87) 30.

138 In more detail: Gamper (n 1) 1301–1305.

139 King (n 43) 77.

140 Watts, 'The Federal Idea' (n 48) 15.

141 Heun (n 61) 50.

142 See Heun (n 61) 50, Elena A Kremyanskaya, Tamara O Kuznetsova, Inna A Rakitskaya, *Russion Constitutional Law* (Cambridge Scholars Publishing 2014) 71 and Palermo and Kössler (n 2) 127–128 for this case law.

143 Palermo and Kössler (n 2) 88. To Friedrich, *Constitutional Government* (n 70) 195 this constitutes a "perversion of the classical meaning of sovereignty".

144 Elazar (n 8) 41.

145 Reginald Whitaker, *A Sovereign Idea* (McGill-Queen's University Press 1992) 167.

146 Brunetta Baldi, *Federalism by degree* (Working Paper Institute of Governmental Studies, University of California, 1999) 7.

of Bosnia and Herzegovina is a federation in itself but at the same time a federated unit of Bosnia and Herzegovina, and therefore, not a sovereign state. In turn, the definition of confederations as associations of independent, and thus sovereign states, makes the theory unfit to explain supranational models of compound government, such as the European Union.[147] It also makes it unfit to grasp political developments that gradually turn the federal system into a confederal one without a separatist moment as the breaking point – i.e., unfit to make a sensible contribution to the confederalism debate in Belgium that was referred to above.

For all these reasons, there is growing recognition that sovereignty, if not irreconcilable with federalism,[148] is at least unable to provide a full insight in the phenomenon of federalism and is too often the subject of controversial debate.[149] It is therefore recommendable, as Aroney holds, to avoid the notion of sovereignty altogether as a conceptual device for federalism.[150]

1.2.2 Elazar, or a broad approach to defining federalism

1.2.2.1 The Elazarian approach

Elazar contributed to federalism in the same way that Lincoln contributed to democracy: by capturing the principle in a device that is both vague and attractive enough for everyone to understand what it is roughly about. Democracy is the government by the people, for the people, with the people. Federalism is the combination of self-rule and shared rule.[151]

Elazar distinguished between federalism as a political principle and federations as a form of federalism. As a political principle, federalism is about "the constitutional diffusion of power so that the constituting elements in a federal arrangement share in the processes of common policy making and administration by right, while the activities of the common government are conducted in such a way as to maintain their respective integrities." Federal political organizations, then, distribute powers among general and constituent governing bodies in such a way that the existence and authority of all are protected. It is a combination of autonomy (self-rule) and joint decision-making (shared rule).[152] Two elements are crucial: federalism is about power relations, and it is also about the territorial division of power. This territorial aspect is what distinguishes

147 See also Erik Fossum and Markus Jachtenfuchs, 'Federal challenges and challenges to federalism', (2017) 24 *Journal of European Public Policy* 477 on how the sovereignty debate has 'plagued' the European literature on federalism.

148 Friedrich, *Constitutional Government* (n 70) 195; Carl J. Friedrich, *Trends of Federalism in Theory and Practice* (Frederick A. Praeger 1968) 8.

149 Palermo and Kössler (n 2) 41–42.

150 Nicholas Aroney, 'Formation, Representation and Amendment in Federal Constitutions', (2006) 54 *Am. J. Comp. L.* 314–315.

151 Elazar (n 8) 5, 12.

152 *Ibid* 5–6.

federalism from consociationalism.[153] While both principles are related,[154] they have separate meanings, with consociationalism referring to the joint exercise of power by non-territorial subgroups.

This broad definition is valuable for three reasons: it is uncontested, it brings us to the core of what federalism is about, and it does not pin systems down to a particular set of institutions. All scholars accept – even if only for pragmatic reasons[155] – that this constitutes the core of federalism. This is the basic idea that people have in mind when talking about federalism,[156] even if they disagree on the exact definition. This is also, in fact, what makes federalism so appealing in the contemporary world. As Watt points out, it provides "the closest institutional approximation to the complex multicultural and multidimensional economic, social and political reality of the contemporary world".[157] This common agreement is based on the fact that the definition touches the core, but at the same time encompasses a variety of forms of state. Elazar emphasized that the essence of federalism is not to be found in a particular set of institutions, but revolves around the relationships between the political partners.[158] Moreover, the broad definition does not confuse the debate with the notion of sovereignty: Elazar pointed out that federalism "cuts around the issue of sovereignty".[159]

The first and last arguments should be nuanced somewhat. While other scholars have used a similarly broad definition that concentrates on power relations between central and territorial decentral governments as the core of federalism, they sometimes stress self-rule and ignore shared rule. For example, according to Riker, a federal system is "a political organization in which the activities of government are divided between regional governments and a central government in such a way that each kind of government has some activities on which it makes final decisions".[160] In this system: "(1) two levels of government rule the same land of people, (2) each level has at least one area in which it is autonomous, (3) there is some guarantee (even though merely a statement in the constitution)

153 *Ibid* 7–8.

154 On the relationship between both: Arend Lijphart, 'Non-Majoritarian Democracy: A Comparison of Federal and Consociational Theories', (1985) 15 *Publius: The Journal of Federalism* 3–15; Duchacek (n 83) 35–48; Daniel J. Elazar, 'Federalism and Consociational Regimes', (1985) 15 *Publius: The Journal of Federaliusm* 17–34; Soeren Keil, 'Federalism as a tool of conflict resolution', in Kincaid (n 95) 151–161.

155 Palermo and Kössler (n 2) 3. See above, section 1.1.

156 At least, in contemporary debate and referring to political organizations. The origins of federalism are theological, and refer to partnership circles of families and communities, to define the relationship between man and God. See Elazar (n 8) 5 and Daniel J. Elazar, 'The Political Theory of Covenant: Biblical Origins and Modern Developments', (1980) 10 *Publius: The Joirnal of Federalism* 3–30.

157 Watts (n 48) 14.

158 Elazar (n 8) 12.

159 Elazar (n 8) 12.

160 William R. Riker, 'Federalism' in F.I. Greenstein and N.W. Polsby (eds.), *Handbook of Political Science. Vol. 5. Governmental Institutions and Processes* (AddisonWesley 1975) 101. See also Riker (n 69) 5–6.

of the autonomy of each government in its own sphere".[161] Likewise, Wheare stressed the self-rule part: "To be sure, most of those who use [the term 'federal government] agree in this, that they have in mind an association of states, which has been formed for certain common purposes, but in which member states retain a large measure of their original independence".[162] Or Dahl: federalism implies that "competences of subunits are constitutionally beyond the scope of the authority of the national government, and other matters are constitutionally outside the scope of the authority of the smaller units".[163] And the last example, Halberstam, where he defines federalism as "the coexistence within a compound polity of multiple levels of government each with constitutionally grounded claims to some degree of organizational autonomy and jurisdictional authority".[164]The latter definitions are clearly based upon the aggregative form of US dual federalism, even if they do not rule out some degree of shared rule. Apparently, then, even broad definitions cannot hide the defining person's origins. Even for Elazar's definition, one might debate whether both aspects are as important. As Palermo and Kössler noticed, in coming-together federations shared rule is a compensation for the sub-states' loss of independence. By contrast, in decentralizing systems, subnational representation in central institutions is usually "non-existent or extremely weak".[165] There, subnational entities gain autonomy, which gives them little to bargain for involvement in central decision-making. This gives some perspective to the assumption that the 'self-rule, shared rule' notion adequately covers all federalist systems.

There are also some problems attached to this broad definition on a more fundamental basis. This was already highlighted in section 1.1, where the so-called 'sophisticated' pragmatic approach was discussed. This is further elaborated in the next section.

1.2.2.2 What is wrong with the Elazarian approach?

i Missing out on the fundamentals: the problem of broad definitions

With an all-encompassing definition, federalism risks becoming what Duchacek called "one of those echo words that evoke a positive response but that may mean all things to all men".[166] In this way, the "descriptive lowest common denominator" of multi-tiered systems is used to define federalism.[167] This is most helpful for those eager to qualify an otherwise "hybrid" form of state as federal. But this definition also applies to all kinds of administrative decentralization in countries that are not federal, nor wish

161 Riker (n 69) 11.
162 Wheare (n 15) 1.
163 Robert Dahl, *Democracy, Liberty, and Equality* (Norwegian University Press, 1986), 114
164 Halberstam (n 39) 580.
165 Palermo and Kössler (n 2) 42.
166 Duchacek (n 82) 191.
167 Erk (n 80) 3.

to be called federal. Prominent scholars have at some length illustrated the fundamental difference between unitary states, federal systems, and confederations.[168] For instance, it is held that, with each different 'federal agreement' behind each form of state, there will be a different response to the question of whether federalism can accommodate multinationalism.[169] It is therefore doubtful whether it is helpful to gain deeper theoretical insight into the phenomenon by bringing such a wide variety of state forms on the same level.[170] Instead, to be useful, a definition of federalism must be inclusive enough to accommodate variations, but sufficiently exclusive to distinguish federations from other types of state arrangements.[171]

To the first argument, one can reply that Elazar's term constitutes an overall term for federalism as a political principle, but not for federations as a particular form of state. In fact, Elazar identifies a range of 'federalist' arrangements, of which 'federations' are just one type, along with unions, constitutionally decentralized unions, confederations, federacies, associated statehoods, condominiums, leagues, and joint functional authorities.[172] Watts adds federal-unitary and federal-confederal hybrids to this list.[173]

According to Hueglin, this leads to a form of 'typological escapism' that brings little theoretical insight into what federalism really is.[174] There is, however, the advantage that 'federalism' as a principle can be used to analyze power division in different forms of state. At the same time, conceptual clarity is preserved by reserving the term 'federation' for a particular type form of state.[175] This distinction between federalism and federation goes back to King[176] and is broadly accepted in scholarship. King defined federalism as a political philosophy or ideology.[177] Burgess emphasizes their relationship by defining federalism as "a normative principle that recommends a particular set of values and principles which, when translated in practice, create a level of institutionalization that produces federation as one among other federal forms".[178] This broadens the notion from a principle of political organization to a value-laden concept. I come back to this point later in this chapter.

168 See e.g. Wheare (n 15) 13.
169 Requejo (n 7) 47–48.
170 Erk (n 80) 3. See also Edward L. Rubin, 'Federalism as a Mode of Governance: Autonomy, Identity, Power, and Rights', in Amnon Lev (ed), *The Federal Idea* (Hart 2017) 125.
171 Thorlakson (n 76) 4–5.
172 Elazar (n 8) 38–64.
173 Watts (n 117) 21, 24–25.
174 Hueglin, (n 89) 28.
175 Thorlakson (n 76) 4.
176 King (n 43) 20, 74.
177 *Ibid* 75.
178 Burgess (n 97) 46.

ii Missing out on the topical issues: the shift to a debate on categorization

At the same time, the federalism-federation distinction creates new difficulties. First, as Choudry and Hume point out, the focus on a typology of institutional manifestations of the federal principle "may draw political actors into debates over categorization [...] that divert attention from the concrete political problems to which federalism is a response.[179] Again, the current Belgian political debate over a future confederal model that was referred to above illustrates this point. Bickering politicians and lecturing scholars are so preoccupied with the question of whether in theory a confederal model implies separatism or not, that the more fundamental question of whether and how the Belgian form of state can be organized to accommodate identitarian differences in a more satisfying way, is ignored. Secondly, there remains a need for a sharper definition of federations.

To distinguish federations from other federal forms, the whole discussion that appeared in section 1.2.1 begins anew. For example, King and Burgess consider the 'constitutionally entrenched involvement of the constituent units in the central decision making process' as the critical feature of federations.[180] This time the set of defining characteristics is reduced to two: involvement of the constituent units in the central decision-making process; and a constitutional basis for this entrenchment. This explains why Burgess considers second chambers as the 'identity bracelet' of federations. "Put simply", Burgess states, "every federation must have a second chamber in the legislature for it to be an authentic federal state".[181] Burgess adds that federations incorporate the values that define federalism.[182] Arguably, this could mean that we exclude systems that have a second chamber to represent constituent units, but do not involve this second chamber in a meaningful way. This, however, would leave us with only a few examples, with Germany as the most prominent form of federalism. Also, it would turn a blind eye to those systems that have no or only a weak second chamber, but involve territorial units in an informal, and therefore, nonconstitutionally entrenched way. For example, in Austria[183] – or as in Belgium – through partly but not entirely overlapping national groups

Others concentrate on the coordinate vs subordinate relationship of central and subnational entities.[184] According to Duchacek what distinguishes federations from other forms, is primarily the fact that the territorial units have their own source of power. In contrast, in states with territorial segments (decentralized local units, or overseas departments) this power is

179 Choudry and Hume (n 92) 359.
180 King (n 43) 77, 142, 146; Burgess (n 97) 47.
181 Burgess (n 60) 204.
182 Burgess (n 97) 47.
183 Ferdinand Karlhofer and Günther Pallaver, 'Strength through Weakness: State Executive Power and Federal Reform in Austria', (2013) 19 *Swiss Political Science Review* 41–59.
184 Verney (n 89) 85.

derived from the central power, based on delegation, and is revocable.[185] Again, the definition is problematic and appears to be based on the model of coming-together-federalism, composed of previously independent states with preexisting constitutions. In these federations, the sub-states' power to adopt and amend their own constitutions is self-evident, and subnational powers are plenary unless limited by the federal constitution. In falling-apart federations, however, powers are transferred to the newly established constituent units and, therefore, derived from the central power. In the end, it seems that the distinction between administrative decentralized states and federations is more a matter of degree rather than a clear-cut categorization.

iii Complications resulting from a value-laden definition of federalism

We can conclude that a broad definition does not solve the problem. The idea of 'federalism' as a principle that underpins different forms of 'federal' arrangements and refers to values is more interesting. This is because it leads us to the essence of the research topic. According to Burgess, federalism refers to 'a particular set of values and principles'. In Elazar's definition, a 'value concept' is a "term that carries with it an essence, which is interpreted in a variety of ways under different circumstances as long as they adhere to the essentials of the concept, so that they serve to allow people to 'hone in' on a particular set of deep structural meanings".[186] Finding the essence of federalism, then, is crucial for the development of a federal theory. It allows for variety according to time and context, and helps us to identify 'true' federations in the multitude of federal-like arrangements. It is therefore further explored in the next section. This section is limited to explaining how the federalism-federation dichotomy complicates the definition exercise in two ways.

First, it complicates the identification of 'federations'. The truism that there can be federalism without federations, but no federations without federalism,[187] raises some doubts when it no longer refers to organizational arrangements, but to a set of values. How can we be sure that a federal arrangement, i.e., one that meets the criteria that are proposed as defining features (whatever they are), really breathes the spirit of federalism? The institutional arrangement, and the dynamics that bring it to life, are influenced by extra-legal factors such as political systems and actors. If they do not live up to the values that define federalism, we might very well end up with a federal arrangement on paper, i.e., a federation without federalism. For example, Burgess qualifies Ethiopia and Malaysia as federal systems in form, but not in practice.[188] This is also why the Soviet Union was so often renounced as 'a sham federation'. Yet, Raffass shows up as a myth the idea

185 Duchacek (n 83) 42.
186 Elazar (n 8) 15–16.
187 King (n 43) 76.
188 Burgess (n 97) 55.

that the United States, unlike the Soviet Union, was established as a form of 'voluntary integration'.[189]

This means that not only are we still stuck with the problem of defining 'a federation', but the exercise is still not finished once we have identified the systems that meet this definition. Instead, within this set of systems, we need to distinguish between those systems that are 'true' federations because they live up to the values and principles that define federalism and those that do not.

Secondly, all this shifts the debate to the identification of these 'values and principles' that bring an institutional arrangement to life. Some insight into the value of federalism is needed to answer a number of questions. Is the essence of federalism also the essence of federations? In other words, is federalism an exclusion criterion in the sense that out of all the state forms that meet the institutional definition of federations (broad or narrow), we must exclude those that do not live up to this core? If so, why does the essence of federalism not suffice in of itself to define what a federation is? The following section is devoted to these questions.

1.3 The value of federalism

In brief: traditional federal theory has offered us the distinction between 'federalism' and 'federation'. Federalism can be seen as a principle of political organization – further referred to as a 'federalist organization' – but it can also be seen as a value concept. This leads us to the trichotomy of federalism, federal political organization, and federation.[190] As a value concept, federalism points to the essence of federalism, irrespective of context or concrete form. In this section, we are interested in federalism as a value concept in order to find the essence of federalism that persists over time and across countries and allows for a variety of forms. For this reason, we need to search through the literature to find what is considered to be the value of federalism. We need to test the suggestions against two conditions: a condition of specificity and a condition of universality.

The specificity condition requires that the proposed value has some relationship with federalism as a principle of political organization – i.e., the broad definition following the Elazarian approach. Only then can we use the essence of federalism as a driver for the organization of the state and as a reference point for courts to assess federalism conflicts. The universality condition implies that the proposed value covers very different forms of state and does not select one specific model as superior. This avoids an ethnocentric view and ensures that the value remains concentrated on the essence of federalism, instead of being mixed with other value concepts.

These conditions are not met when the essence of federalism gets confused with the value of liberal democracy. Burgess regards 'liberty' as the expression of the liberal democratic state, procedural justice, and the rule of law. To him, this is a

189 Tania Raffass, *The Soviet Union: Federation or Empire?* (Routledge 2012).
190 Watts (n 48) 8.

federal value underlying the principle of self-determination.[191] From this angle, he distinguishes six models: mature, flawed, incomplete, emergent, transitional, and aspiring federal democracies.[192] This does not meet the specificity condition, because the values of liberty and liberal democracy, and the ensuing categorization, do not refer to the power relations between levels of authority within one system. Instead, liberal democracy has a value of its own, irrespective of the centralist or decentralist form of state. As a result, the value concept of liberal democracy does not give us any indication as to which systems, in the wide range between unitary states and confederations, can be recognized as federalist. Federalism and democracy may therefore be considered values that reinforce each other,[193] but should not be confused with one another. In fact, the relation between democracy and federalism seems much more nuanced and complex than any normative account may suggest.[194] Likewise, liberty does not constitute the essence of federalism in the way that it defines democracy and the rule of law: individuals cannot be free in political systems without democracy or the rule of law, but they can be free in nonfederalist political systems. Instead, as Hueglin advocates, federalism should be taken more seriously "as a normative proposition of political legitimacy in its own right".[195] Nor is the universality condition observed. One category is selected as superior: the federations that are labeled 'mature' because they are full liberal democracies. This turns federalism into an ideological concept[196] and easily leads to a western bias.

Yet, the notion of democracy resurfaces regularly in federalism scholarship, but this time linked with the notion of a federalist political organization. Even the Canadian Supreme Court defined federalism in terms of its ability to enable citizens to participate in governance at several levels of authority.[197] It is, however, not the only value that is mentioned. Besides 'liberty',[198] and 'enhancing democracy',[199] values such as 'peace and prosperity',[200] 'preventing national

191 Michael Burgess, *In Search of the Federal Spirit* (Oxford University Press) 2012, 22–23.

192 Burgess (n 97) 55–58. Comp. also Watts (n 110) 26–27.

193 Inman, despite admitting that he has no evidence on this point, sees federalism's greatest contribution from its ability to enhance the transition to democracy itself. See Robert P. Inman, 'Federalism's Values and the Value of Federalism', (2007) 53 *CESifo Economic Studies* 522–560, reprinted in Kincaid (n 4) Vol. 1, 283.

194 Jan Erk and Wilfried Swenden, 'The new wave of federalism studies', in Jan Erk and Wilfried Swenden (eds), *New Directions in Federalism Studies* (Routledge 2010) 8.

195 Thomas O. Hueglin, 'Federalism and political theory: a case of mutual neglect', in Kincaid (n 95) 24.

196 King (n 43) 21. See also Frédéric Lépine, 'Federalism: Essence, Values and Ideologies', in Gagnon, Keil and Mueller (n 102) 45.

197 *Reference Re Secession of Québec* [1998] 2 SCR 217, para 66.

198 See also, amongst others, Elazar (n 8) 33, Erwin Chemerinsky, 'The Values of Federalism', (1995) 47 *Florida L. Rev.* 538, John Kincaid, 'Values and Value Tradeoffs in Federalism', (1995) 25 *Publius: The Journal of Federalism* 35–41. This is also at stake in Proudhon's theory on federalism, see R. Vernon, 'The Principle of Federation: an introduction', reprinted in Kincaid (n 4) 149.

199 Kincaid (n 198) 35–41. For a nuanced discussion: Chemerinsky (n 197) 527–528.

200 Kincaid (n 198) 32–35.

tyranny',[201] 'providing laboratories for experimentation'[202], 'community',[203] 'utility or efficiency',[204] and 'national pluralism'[205] are also mentioned. Often, these values meet the specificity condition, meaning that they give guidance as to how to allocate competences to one or the other level of authority. For example, the idea that powers must be allocated to this level of authority that is best placed to enhance democracy can be translated into the legal principle of subsidiarity. The principle's starting point is that powers should in principle be allocated to the subnational units because they are closer to the people, but the central government may interfere for reasons of efficiency or democracy.[206] For example, in cross-border matters where decisions in one unit impact upon the living conditions of people in another unit, it may especially be more democratic to make a decision at the central plane, where all affected persons can have a voice. The values are, however, more problematic under the universality condition. Often, the values are country-specific, selected for the purpose of a specific type of political system or society. For example, Requejo introduces national pluralism as a value to accommodate multinational systems.[207] Elazar's emphasis on 'liberty', for which he found inspiration in the original, biblical notion of 'federalism' as a covenant,[208] is driven by the US context that is based on the idea of individual liberty.[209] At the heart of this are "humans [that] are able to make constitutional choices".[210] This may explain why the United States currently has a preference for designing the Senate as a chamber representing the 'people' of the states rather than the states themselves, even though the absence of an institutional link weakens the entities' voice in central decision-making.

These values cannot simply be dismissed, even though they do not meet the universality condition. This is because they do serve as guiding principles for the allocation of powers and in federalism disputes, and because they are linked to the specific context of a state. As Watts observed, the motivations and interests within a society, as well as the legal constitutional structure, are important considerations for understanding the operation of federations.[211] In fact, the constitutional structure reflects the 'motivations and interests within a society', and therefore, gives it legal meaning. Rather than pointing to the essence of federalism, however, they reveal the 'purpose' of a federalist form in a given political system. These purposes are manifold and depend upon the origins of the

201 Nuanced: Chemerinsky (n 198) 524–527.
202 Kincaid (n 198) 41–43. Nuanced: Chemerinsky (n 198) 528–530.
203 Chemerinsky (n 198) 536–538.
204 *Ibid* 536–538; Kincaid (n 198) 41–43.
205 Requejo (n 7) 47.
206 W. Vandenbruwaene, 'What Scope for Subnational Autonomy: the Issue of the Legal Enforcement of the Principle of Subsidiarity', (2014) 6 *Perspectives on Federalism* 51–52.
207 Requejo (n 7) 47.
208 Elazar (n 156) 19–21.
209 Verney (n 89) 88–92; Lépine (n 196) 45.
210 Elazar (n 8) 33.
211 Watts, 'The Idea of Federalism' (n 48) 17.

country, its history, its demography, or simply its size. Federalism can be a tool for peace-making, for effective defense, for economic prosperity, for multinational conflict management, for the separation of powers, for enhancing democracy, or for efficient management of large states.[212] These varieties of purposes explain the variety of federalist systems.[213] The value concept that points to the essence of federalism should have a more universal scope, but should also give room for this variety of purposes.

Livingston adds that purposes may shift, which in turn may change the functioning of institutions even without formal amendment.[214] For this reason, Livingston sees the 'essence of federalism' in the society itself rather than in the institutional structure.[215] Livingston is right to stress that it is not a set of institutional criteria that can determine whether a system is federal, because different societies may require different instrumentalities.[216] However, identifying the structure of society as the essence of federalism would make this essence too context-bound. Every society has its own features that determine the purpose and organization of the state structure in a given country. Instead, society is what drives a system to choose for a federalist structure. It is the beating heart, rather than the essence.

Livingston's argument is that while historical, cultural, economic, political, and other determinants may differ, in the end, the different mixtures of these elements create different groups with varying demands for self-expression. If these groups are located within specific territories, the system can take a federalist form; if they are scattered throughout the country, it cannot.[217] In reality, however, a federalist system is not necessarily constructed along the lines of subgroups. An example is Switzerland. Livingston's response is that "federal organization is not perfect in every case", but maintains that "federalism is nothing if it is held to embrace diversities that are not territorially grouped".[218] Yet, in some countries, like Nigeria, a federalist structure is used precisely to break up ethnic groups in order to create stability.[219] In turn, federalist systems are also created in homogeneous societies. According to Livingston, there will always be some distinction between the territorial areas that leads to different interests, because otherwise, there would be no need for federalism.[220] Such functional differences, however, are also present in large nonfederalist countries.

212 For a discussion of purposes, see Kincaid (n 4) xxiii-xxv and Kincaid (n 198) 29–44. Inman (n 193) 261, discerns three categories of values: economic efficiency, democratic participation, and the protection of personal rights and liberties.
213 Diamond (n 89) 130.
214 Livingston (n 67) 1–2; William S. Livingston, 'A Note on the Nature of Federalism', (1952) 67 *Political Science Quarterly* 84.
215 Livingston (n 67) 2; Livingston (n 214) 84.
216 Livingston (n 214) 91.
217 Livingston (n 67) 2; Livingston (n 214) 85.
218 Livingston (n 67) 3; Livingston (n 214) 85–86.
219 Rotimi Suberu, 'Federalism in Africa: The Nigerian Experience in Comparative Perspective', (2009) 8 *Ethnopolitics* 72.
220 Livingston (n 214) 87.

In these cases, the federalist option may be inspired merely by administrative efficiency.[221] Moreover, the territorial division may create or deepen differences in society.[222] In fact, Livingston seems to reduce the essential purpose of federalist systems to the need to manage groups in a multinational state. While it is true that, "the more diverse a society is, the more it demands means of self-expression",[223] at the same time alternative, nonfederal solutions can deal with multinationalism, and federalism can serve other purposes. Society, then, can be seen as a factor that determines how a system is organized and how it operates in fact, but society as such does not reveal the essence of a state structure.

More promising is the frequently recurrent idea of 'balance' in federal theory. For example, Stein defines federalist political organizations as systems where "the institutions, values, attitudes, and patterns of political action operate to give autonomous expression both to the national political system and political culture and to regional political subsystems and subcultures". He adds: "The autonomy of each of these systems and subsystems is counterbalanced by a mutual interdependence. This balance maintains the overall system".[224] Basta Fleiner and Gaudreault-DesBiens, as mentioned above, are in search of key mechanisms that guarantee "a proper balance" between unity and diversity.[225]

This idea of 'balance' can potentially serve as a value concept for federalism, as it meets both conditions. First, it fulfils the specificity requirement, as it is very clearly related to the organization of a multi-tiered state and the demarcation of power relations. It can guide the allocation of powers and the resolution of federalism disputes. This is because it requires political actors to allocate powers in a way that establishes a proper balance of powers, and requires courts to invalidate an exercise of powers that distorts this balance. Second, the universality condition is met, because the concept remains neutral as to what this balance entails exactly. It may point to equal-power relationships, give dominance to the central level of authority, or let the subnational entities prevail. I will come back to this in Chapter 2 for a discussion and a categorization of states along these lines. Here, it is sufficient to stress that this gives room for the articulation of specific, context-bound purposes in any given federalist system. At the same time, no category is identified as superior to others, or as the ideal model to which other federalist forms aspire. Whatever the 'proper' balance is, it simply depends on the characteristics of a specific political system.

221 Verney (n 89) 82 even refers to multinational Canada and India as states that adopted federalism as a means of making governance more manageable in large states.

222 See also Hueglin (n 195) 16–17 on how the sociological approach underestimates the dynamics of an institutional and procedural trajectory over time.

223 Livingstone (n 214) 89.

224 Michael B. Stein, 'Federal Political Systems and Federal Societies', (1968) 20 World Pol 731.

225 Basta Fleiner and Gaudreault-DesBiens (n 56) 149. See also Watts (n 48) 23.

1.4 Conclusion: building blocks for a renewed federal theory

The discussion of broad and narrow definitions of federations, and of the federalism/federalist political organization/federation has given us the contours for a renewed federal theory. The trichotomy has proven useful to encompass all systems that are organized around the essence of federalism, while still making distinctions between the various forms of state. It avoids the 'circular reasoning fallacy'[226] and makes sure that characteristics to distinguish forms of state are not taken randomly, but follow from a predefined notion.

'Federalism' refers to the essence of federalism, i.e., the core that remains present throughout the various forms a federalist organization may serve. It is a value concept for which the previous chapter phrased conditions of specificity and universality. Maintaining a proper 'balance' between different levels of authority was identified as a value that meets these conditions. This is not a mere academic notion: legal principles can be derived from it, which guide courts in the resolution of federalism disputes. Therefore, the subsidiarity principle relates to federalism in the same way that the legality principle relates to democracy, and the legal certainty principle relates to the rule of law.

In the following chapter, a theory of federalism is developed that revolves around the proper balance as a value concept that reveals the essence of federalism. It will identify federalist political organizations, and categorize forms of state derived from the idea of federalism. The chapter will also test the validity of the theory. This is done on the basis of the building blocks that this chapter has derived from an analysis of the weaknesses of traditional theory. These building blocks can be formulated as a set of conditions. A condition of flexibility is added to the conditions of specificity and universality.

The 'condition of specificity' was already defined to identify the value of federalism. Applied to federal theory, the condition means that not only the value, but also the definition of a federalist political organization and the categorization of forms of state must derive from the idea of shared rule and self-rule between territorial levels of authority. Also, the characteristics that distinguish federalist forms of state must all derive from that idea. In traditional theory, this condition was not always met, either in the search for the value of federalism or in the enumeration of defining characteristics following the Hamilton approach. The specificity test also means that definitions must be sufficiently sharp to distinguish and compare forms of state in a meaningful way.

The 'universality condition' was defined as the requirement that the value of federalism covers very different forms of state and that not one specific model is selected as superior. For a general theory, this means, amongst others, that a federation cannot be defined in such a way that it coincides with a specific model state. In this way, universality allows for theory-building, because it avoids

226 See above, section 1.2.1(ii).

having to take the refuge of the notion of *sui generis* federations.[227] Instead, there is room for variety within categories, and 'intermediate constructs' occupy a place of their own. This condition also protects against cherry-picking.[228] It cannot be used to support political demands for a particular mechanism by presenting them as defining features of any federation – for example obtaining full-fledged subnational constitutional autonomy, allocating residual powers with the subnational entities, or bicameralism. Universality also has a time dimension. The theory must not only grasp a variety of federalist forms of state, but also variations over time in one particular model. Finally, other forms of state have to be considered as valuable in themselves, not as models that are in transition or aspire to become the superior form of state. This was identified as a weakness of traditional theory: that it is based upon specific model federations which are considered superior, with 'intermediate' categories being viewed as 'immature' federations.[229]

The 'flexibility condition' means that theory and definitions are not too rigid. This is linked with the universality condition, but concentrates in three ways on the adaptive power of the theory. First, the theory must be construed in such a way that we do not miss out on alternatives. This means that functions are more important than particular institutions or procedures, and that forms of states are better delineated through key dimensions that serve as indicators, rather than through particular defining features.[230] Next, it must be able to adapt to structural changes in state structures, such as state fragmentation, and the embedment of federalist entities into more global systems.[231] This requires that the theory is not fixated on old, state-centered notions such as sovereignty.[232] Instead, it must be able to accommodate the "paradox of global integration and regional fragmentation occurring simultaneously as the old-style nation-state struggles to maintain a place for itself in a world where the historic attributes of national sovereignty are being eroded by transnational and subnational political forces and economic imperatives" – "a job for federalism", according to Kincaid.[233] Finally, it must incorporate adaptations of a particular system over time, and also take into account the contextual factors that influence both the shaping and the functioning of federalist political organizations. It must also take into account possible changes in contextual factors and the resulting changes in the purpose of federalism in a given country.[234] This means that the form of state must be seen as a package deal[235] that can be renegotiated, and that the theory must take

227 See above, section 1.2.1(iii) and (vii).
228 See above, section 1.2 (i).
229 See above, section 1.2.1 (iv), (v) and (vi).
230 See above, section 1.2.1 (viii).
231 See above, section 1.2.1 (ix).
232 See above, section 1.2.2 (iii).
233 Kincaid (n 197) 30. Likewise: Watts, 'The Federal Idea' (n 48) 22.
234 See above, section 1.3.
235 See above, section 1.2.1 (vii).

account of the various political, social, economic, and institutional factors that determine the purpose,[236] the package deal, and its adaptations.

A federal theory that meets these three conditions should, ultimately, be able to serve the three functions identified above: (1) it must give more insight in what federalism really means and how it functions, allow for structuring and categorizing, and propose normative principles that guide the resolution of federalism conflicts; (2) it must propose a research agenda and allow for systemic and methodical research from any discipline – legal, political, sociologic, or economic – interested in federalism. Ideally, these disciplines are combined, to allow for a holistic approach to federalism. This means, among other issues, that the theory must give adequate indicators to allow for a useful comparative study; (3) it must be helpful to grasp federalist developments in any singular political system and contribute to political debate. The confederalist debate in Belgium and the qualification of the EU were given as examples throughout this chapter.

With these building blocks, we can now commence with the construction of a renewed theory, under the name of 'dynamic federalism'.

236 See above, section 1.2.3 for the variety of purposes.

2 Dynamic federalism: 'federalism as a process' revisited

The previous chapter distinguished between federalism as a value, federalist systems as political organizations, and federations as a form of state. Federalism as a value concept refers to maintaining the proper balance between different levels of territorial authority. In this chapter, the contours of a dynamic federalism theory are outlined. This theory builds on Friedrich's idea of federalism as a process and develops this concept further. I will, therefore, first highlight very briefly the main ideas of Friedrich's theory of federalism as a process, and point out its weaknesses that need to be remedied (section 2.1). I will then lay down the contours of a theory of dynamic federalism (section 2.2). Next, this enhanced theory is assessed against the criteria developed in Chapter 1 (section 2.3). Finally, I will draw some relevant conclusions about this enhanced theory of federalism as a process (section 2.4).

2.1 Friedrich on federalism as a process

Under Friedrich's approach, forms of state can be "represented as differences of degree in the relation of government to the territory affected by it, between two extremes, complete unity and complete separateness".[1] Friedrich sees federalism primarily as a federalizing process, rather than as a fixed design.[2] This process may develop in two directions. At some times it is a process by which either a number of separate political communities enter into joint arrangements. At other times it is a process by which one particular political community differentiates itself to the point where distinct political communities make separate decisions.[3]

This means that federalism is essentially dynamic, and that it allows for institutional diversity – Friedrich himself stressed the need for an all-inclusive

1 Carl J. Friedrich, *Constitutional Government and Democracy: Theory and Practice in Europe and America* (Blaisdell Publishing Company 1968) 4th ed., 189.
2 Friedrich (n 1) 1989–1990; Carl J Friedrich, 'New Tendencies in Federal Theory and Practice', (1965) 14 *Jahrbuch des Öffentliches Rechts* 1; Carl J. Friedrich, *Trends of Federalism in Theory and Practice* (Frederick A. Praeger 1968) 7, 173.
3 Friedrich 1965 (n 2) 2; Friedrich 1968 (n 2) 7, 177.

understanding of federalism.[4] It is also able to accommodate new political trends and structures,[5] and the process is more important than the institutional arrangement in itself.[6] Federalism itself is conceived as a balance in the pursuit of specific objectives, interests, and traditions of the territorial units, and common objectives, interests, and traditions. It is this balance that determines the distinction between forms of state. In turn, the particular conditions of time and place determine this balance. This means that no form of state is inherently superior over another,[7] and one form cannot be considered more or less 'natural' than the other.[8] A consequence is that federalist organizations must provide themselves with the instruments that enable institutional change in accordance with their changed preferences.[9] This defines a 'federal spirit' that can be conceived as "a firm determination to maintain both diversity and unity by way of a continuous process of mutual adaptation".[10]

However, Friedrich's theory is still problematic in several ways.[11]

First, this theory has been criticized for its vagueness about how to identify federal systems at any particular time,[12] and for the ambiguous portrayal of the relationship between process and structure.[13] The distinction between 'federalism' (conceived as a process) and 'federations' (as a form of state) reminds us of the problem of definitions that was discussed in the previous chapter. For Friedrich, describing forms of state as a matter of design is still meaningful – for example, Friedrich resorts to the classic assumption that "a federal regime presupposes a bicameral representation"[14] – but no sharp line can be drawn.[15] The distinction between forms of state lies in the balance of interests: "a federation is a union of groups, united by one or more common objectives, but retaining their distinctive group character for other purposes",[16] with a constitutionally entrenched distribution of powers as an essential feature.[17]

Moreover, Friedrich attached a very particular function to federalism. This function is the restraint of power and the protection of the political community against the excesses of governing power.[18] In Chapter 1, however, it was

4 Michael Burgess, *In Search of the Federal Spirit* (Oxford University Press 2012) 140.
5 *Ibid* 172.
6 Friedrich 1968 (n 2) 173.
7 Friedrich (n 1) 226.
8 Friedrich 1965 (n 2) 13.
9 Friedrich 1968 (n 2) 7.
10 *Ibid* 175.
11 For a very detailed discussion of the theory and its critics, see Burgess (n 4) 131–173.
12 Anthony H Birch, 'Approaches to the Study of Federalism', (1966) XIV *Political studies* 15–33, reprinted John Kincain (ed), *Federalism*, Vol.1, 322; Burgess (n 4) 139.
13 Burgess (n 4).
14 Friedrich (n 1) 210.
15 Friedrich (n 1) 189; Friedrich 1965 (n 2) 1.
16 Friedrich 1965 (n 2) 2. See also Friedrich 1968 (n 2) 8, 177 and Friedrich (n 1) 189.
17 Friedrich (n 1) 194; Friedrich 1965 (n 2) 4–5.
18 Friedrich (n 1) 195; Friedrich 1965 (n 2) 5. See also Burgess (n 4) 143.

emphasized that political systems can have very different reasons for organizing themselves in a compound way. By portraying the operation of federalism as 'a pattern of opposition', Friedrich sets high expectations for federalism: for example, the capability of federalism to multiply the opportunities for citizens to participate in political life, or to enhance confidence in and loyalty to a constitutional polity.[19] While in some cases federalism has this potential, this is not necessarily the case. For example, federalism may lead to such complexity in the distribution of powers that it is difficult for the citizen to hold the responsible actors to account or to have access to the relevant center of power. Further, in multinational multi-tiered systems, federalism can easily enhance distrust rather than trust.[20]

Third, there is the impression given that federal organizations are the endpoint of the process. Von Krosigk notices that when Friedrich applies his theory to European integration, it is still dynamic where it designs federalism as a process, but becomes static where the federal state is conceived as the normative goal.[21] This is unfair to Friedrich's general theory, considering his insistence that the distinction between forms of state is not a matter of maturity, but rather a question of which balance is preferred.[22] Still, the formulation of federalization as a process toward a compound community is a precursor to the reintroduction of the idea of superiority. For example, Baldi admits that not all federalizing systems end up as a federation, but argues that this leaves them incomplete.[23] This definitely calls for a clear definition of what a federation is, to take away the impression that federal organizations are the ideal arrangement which every entity in the federalizing process aspires to achieve. Holding on to federations as the endpoint of the process would ignore the reality that the development process continues once the system has become federalized. It would also, therefore, underestimate the risk that the federalizing process may lead to the dissolution of a political system.

Until recently, the idea of federalism as a process has usually been identified in the literature on decentralization. Friedrich's position was that there was "much to be said" for viewing federalism as a particular form of decentralization. His only objections were that decentralization gives the center primacy, from which powers are delegated to the subunits. In his view, this does not correspond to reality, and decentralization (unlike federalism) is sometimes unrelated to distinctive community formation.[24] These, however, are very fundamental

19 Friedrich (n 1) 208.

20 See Ferran Requejo, *Multinational Federalism and Value Pluralism* (Routledge 2005) 74 and Nico Steytler, 'Non-centralism in Africa: in search of the federal idea', in John Kincaid (ed), *A Research Agenda for Federalism Studies* (Edward Elgar 2019) 176–177.

21 Friedrich von Krosigk, 'A Reconsideration of Federalism in the Scope of the Present Discussion on European Integration', (1970) 9 *Journal of Common Market Studies* 206.

22 Friedrich 1965 (n 2) 13.

23 Brunetta Baldi, *Federalism by degree* (Working Paper Institute of Governmental Studies, University of California, 1999) 5.

24 Friedrich 1968 (n 2) 4–5.

differences. They explain why, for example, decentralization alone is not able to accommodate multinationalism.[25] Scholars have debated how federalism and decentralization are related. Do federations differ from unitary states merely by their degree of decentralization? This would mean that de/centralization is a process and federalism and decentralization largely overlap. Alternatively is it a difference in character? This would mean that de/centralization is a dichotomy and federalism is not just another word for decentralization.[26] In dynamic federalism theory, de/centralization is an important aspect of federalism, but federalism comprises more than the process by which policy and fiscal powers move to decentralized units or to the center. Instead, it contains the entire institutional arrangement of a system, including representation in parliamentary, executive, and judiciary institutions. Empirical data show that several types of multi-tiered systems can achieve a high score for self-rule factors. Generally, however, those systems that are regarded as 'federal' also have a high score for shared rule, which often translates itself as regional influence over nation-wide decisions.[27]

In this chapter, I will therefore give particular attention to definitions. I will also develop the idea of balance, irrespective of the system's purpose and not as an endpoint, but as an essentially contested notion. And I will develop this idea of balance not only with regard to powers but also with regard to status.

More recently, more emphasis has been put on the dynamics of federal systems as a way to adapt to new circumstances and respond to societal problems.[28] According to Colino, "an adequate empirical theory of federalism should be able to explain why and how federations and federal institutions change and adapt to domestic or external changes as part of their capacity to survive and respond to societal or policy problems. Also, such a theory should indicate how stable a federation is and what factors make it persist or adjust".[29] Chapter 7 will further discuss this topic. To grasp the drivers and mechanisms of change, however, we first need a picture of the institutional set-up. Change can then be defined as either the difference in institutional balance between cohesion and autonomy at two different moments in time; or as the difference in institutional balance on the one hand and factual balance on the other. The next chapters will provide the tools to establish the institutional set-up, before considering the matter of change in federalist systems.

25 Requejo (n 20) 65.
26 For this discussion, see Paolo Dardanelli, 'Decentralization', in Kincaid (n 20) 107.
27 Sean Mueller, 'Federalism and the politics of shared rule', in Kincaid (n 20) 170.
28 César Colino, 'Introduction: the study of change in federations', in Jan Erk and Wilfried Swenden (eds) *New Directions in Federalism Studies* (2010) 16. See in particular Arthur Benz and Jörg Broschek, *Federal Dynamics. Continuity, Change, & the Varieties of Federalism* (Oxford University Press 2013) and Jan Erk, *Explaining Federalism. State, society and congruence in Austria, Belgium, Canada, Germany and Switzerland* (Routledge 2008).
29 Colino (n 28) 16.

2.2 Contours of a theory of dynamic federalism

There is a common understanding that federalism is about the relationship between territorial levels of authority.[30] Practically all states can be described as 'permanent fields of tensions between integration and differentiation'.[31] As discussed in the previous chapter, Livingston argued that there will always be some distinction between territorial areas that leads to different interests.[32] These differences, however, are not necessarily based on different group characteristics. Federalism is also present in very homogeneous societies. But the mere subdivision of a country into districts with political governors easily leads to distinction and some sense of 'local identity', even if only for the sake of administrative efficiency. Federalism as a value concept seeks a response to these tensions in the search for a proper balance between integration and differentiation. In other words, this means the balance between 'optimal plurality' and 'indefeasible homogeneity',[33] or between demands for regional autonomy, and the need for cohesion or efficiency of the overall system.[34]

2.2.1 Multi-tiered systems in search of a proper balance

Federalism presupposes a subdivision of the political system in territorial entities with some political power. This points to the so-called 'federalist organization', which, described by Diamond, is the institutional expression of tension between units that want to remain small and relatively autonomous, and the system as a whole that wants to remain large and relatively consolidated.[35] A synonym for this is a 'multi-tiered system'. Multi-tiered systems are all systems with multiple

30 Jean-François Aubert, 'Essai sur le fédéralisme' (1963) *Revue de droit public* 402; Ivo D Duchacek, *Comparative Federalism: The Territorial Dimension of Politics* (New York, Holt, Rinehart and Winston 1970 – reissue University Press of America 1987) 191; Daniel Halberstam, 'Federalism: History, Policy, Law' in Michel Rosenfeld and András Sajó (eds) *The Oxford Handbook of Comparative Constitutional Law* (Oxford University Press 2012) 580–581; Sean Mueller, *Theorising decentralisation* (ECPR Press 2015) 4; Preston King, *Federalism and Federation* (Croom Helm 1982) 19; William S Livingston, *Federalism and Constitutional Change* (Oxford University Press 1956) 2–3; Edward L Rubin, 'Federalism as a Mode of Governance: Autonomy, Identity, Power, and Rights', in Amnon Lev (ed) *The Federal Idea* (Hart 2017) 125, 132. Contrary: Frédéric Lépine, 'Federalism: Essence, Values and Ideologies', in Alain-G. Gagnon, Soeren Keil and Sean Mueller (eds), *Understanding Federalism and Federation* (Routledge 2015) 37.

31 S Wim Couwenberg, 'Staatsvorming, soevereiniteit en subsidiariteit', in Jan Velaers (ed) *Publiek recht, ruim bekeken* (Maklu 1994) 102–104.

32 Livingston (n 30) 4.

33 Peter Häberle, 'Legal Comparison for Constitutional Development – The relevance of Federalism and Regionalism', in Luther Jörg., Passaglia Paolo and Tarchi Rolando (eds), *A World of Second Chambers* (Giuffrè Editore, 2006) 54.

34 Friedrich 1968 (n 2) 7; Friedrich (n 1) 193.

35 Martin Diamond, 'The Ends of Federalism', (1973) 3 *Publius: the Journal of Federalism* 130.

tiers of government, characterized by a central level of government as well as subnational entities with public policy powers.[36] Throughout the rest of the text, I will use the term 'MTSs' for multi-tiered systems, and 'SNEs' for subnational entities. The term MTS avoids confusion between federations and other types of MTS, and is more appropriate for systems that explicitly wish to distance themselves from federations.

The starting point is that MTSs seek a balance between cohesion and subnational autonomy. King – and Burgess behind him – was critical of the notion of federalism as a balance, perceived as an immobile equilibrium, centralist nor decentralist, and closer to constitutionality than territoriality.[37] Mueller counters this by stating that balance is to be understood as an aggregate, with a more centralist position in some domains and less centralist in others.[38] To him, the end result of equal balance is a normative principle and the key to success for federalist organizations.[39] In a theory of dynamic federalism, however, the notion of 'balance' differs in two ways. First, it is not a balance – the middle point – on a continuum between centralization and decentralization, as it is usually conceived.[40] Instead, it points to the proportion of centralization on the one hand, and of cohesiveness on the other. Balance does not mean 'equal proportions' altogether, but 'correct' proportions to keep the system in a steady position. Each component can be given a different value, as long as, following the definition of a federalist political organization, some core of autonomy and interdependence is secured. Consequently, balance does not imply immobility: what is considered as the optimal balance, can change over time. Hence, the question is not where the key to success lies for all federalist organizations, but what proportion of institutional cohesion and autonomy is optimal for a given society.

Considering this balance between cohesion and autonomy, the constitution will employ instruments to secure autonomy, and instruments to create and maintain cohesion. While definitions of federalism usually concentrate on autonomy, they tend to ignore the need for cohesion. Lev maintains that the theorization of federalism – especially in public law – is constrained by the

36 Robert Agranoff, 'Power Shifts, Diversity and Asymmetry', in Robert Agranoff (eds) *Accomodating Diversity: Asymmetry in Federal States* (Nomos 1999) 12–13; Patricia Popelier and Maja Sahadžić, 'Linking Constitutional Asymmetry with Multinationalism. An Attempt to Crack the Code in Five Hypotheses', in Patricia Popelier and Maja Sahadžić (eds), *Constitutional Asymmetry in Multinational Federalism* (Palgrave MacMillan 2019) 4.

37 King (n 30) 56–68; Michael Burgess, *Comparative Federalism. Theory and Practice* (London, Routledge, 2006) 45–46.

38 Sean Mueller, 'Switzerland: Federalism as an Ideology of Balance', in Gagnon, Keil and Mueller (n 30) 108.

39 Mueller (n 27) 162. The author describes Swiss federalism in particular as 'an ideology of balance', Mueller (n 38) 105.

40 E.g. Mueller (n 30) 7 where he sees centralized/decentralized states as the desired empirical outcome of federalism as an ideology.

conception of the political community.[41] This concept is easily translated into theories of sovereignty but is a difficult match with federalism. This may explain why cohesion, which links with the idea of a political community, is not included in the definition of federalism.[42]

'Autonomy' means the ability of SNEs to organize themselves and make their own decisions, and to secure their interests in central decision-making. It contains not only elements of a SNE's ability to rule itself ('self-rule'),[43] but also aspects of 'shared rule' which allows SNEs to control central decisions.

'Cohesion' aims to secure the integrity of the entire system by linking all tiers through mutual respect, common interest, and solidarity.[44] For example, this might be achieved by voicing a general interest that transcends the separate territorial interests through joint decision-making, by establishing instruments that further the creation of a common public sphere and inter-regional solidarity, or by encouraging commitment of territorial representatives to the general interest. Federalism scholars have been reproached for having concentrated on 'self-rule', but having neglected the importance of 'shared rule'.[45] More than that, centralist processes are often criticized for encroaching on subnational autonomy, but the perspective of cohesion is rarely considered. Yet, the 'federal spirit', i.e. the commitment to living together peacefully, in mutual recognition and respect, is regarded as a fundamental value and a condition for success.[46]

This 'balance' between autonomy and cohesion is context-bound. It depends upon the purpose of the form of state and societal, economic, political, and geographical factors. For example, we might expect that in large, homogeneous states with a highly integrated economy that divide power for reasons of effective governance, the 'proper balance' is more centralistic.[47] In divided, multinational states in search of peaceful survival, the 'proper balance' may point to either central or subnational dominance.[48] This might depend on the extent to which

41 Amnon Lev, 'Introduction: Federalism and Public Law Theory', in Amnon Lev (ed) *The Federal Idea. Public Law Between Governance and Political Life* (Hart 2017) 3.

42 At most its potentially cohesive effects are discussed, see Alain-G. Gagnon and Arjun Tremblay; 'Federalism and diversity: a new research agenda', in Kincaid (n 20) 131–132 for the urgent question of whether federalism can help to maintain the cohesiveness of a (multinational) democracy.

43 Mueller (n 27) 163.

44 Maja Sahadžić, *Asymmetry, Multinationalism and Constitutional Law* (Routledge 2020) 216.

45 Mueller (n 27) 162.

46 Burgess (n 4) 2012, 322. See also Friedrich 1968 (n 2) 175–176, Livingston (n 30) 316 and Sahadžić (n 42) 216.

47 But see Milton J Esman, 'Federalism and Modernization: Canada and the United States', (1984) 14 *Publius* 21–38 for a more nuanced discussion.

48 Wilfried Swenden, 'Territorial strategies for managing plurinational states', in John Loughlin, John Kincaid and Wilfried Swenden (eds), *Routledge Handbook of Regionalism and Federalism* (Routledge 2013) 62–65 outlines several strategies for multinational entities, which largely come down to combinations of autonomy and participation.

the recognition of diversity is considered a condition or a threat to the integrity of the system as a whole. For multinational MTSs, finding the proper balance is especially challenging because they endeavor to manage conflicts that are generated by distrust in the central government, which is itself perceived as serving exclusive rather than inclusive interests.[49] We can hypothesize what the proper balance is under which circumstances. For instance, Mueller maintains that secession is more likely to be triggered by the combination of high degrees of both self-rule and shared-rule as well as the combination of high degrees of self-rule and little or no shared rule. 'Shared rule' is envisioned as 'regional influence over nationwide decisions', which means that Mueller balances two aspects that determine subnational autonomy. Arguably this conclusion is even more accurate if the system scores lowly on cohesion. Ultimately, however, the 'proper balance' cannot be predefined. This does not make it too vague to serve as a concept for federal theory, if we construct the 'proper balance' as a 'constitutionally defined and contested concept'.

2.2.1.1 A constitutionally defined concept

This means, firstly, that constitutional arrangements will define what is meant by proper balance. The constitution is based on consent, which means that constitutional arrangements of the state's form are the expression of what the constituent regards as the proper balance. For this, we need to take into account structural clauses with self-definitions, as well as those provisions that determine how the system actually operates.

Structural clauses may emphasize the autonomy of the SNEs[50] or stress the unity of the system. For example, fragmenting MTS, despite giving important powers to SNEs, tend to declare that they are 'one and indivisible', or declare the 'indissoluble unity' of the nation.[51] In post-colonial systems such as Indonesia or Myanmar, an emphasis on the unitary character[52] is part of the nation-building project.[53] In the case of Indonesia, it is also a reaction against imposed ideas of federalism, which are suspected of intentions to divide the country.[54]

49 See Nico Steytler, 'Non-centralism in Africa: in search of the federal idea', in Kincaid (n 20) 176–177.

50 For example, Art. 1, 3 and 5a of the Swiss Constitution emphasize the sovereignty of the Cantons and the subsidiarity principle.

51 Art. 5 Italian Constitution resp. Art. 2 Spanish Constitution.

52 Art. 1(1) Indonesian Constitution; Art. 2 and 6(b) Myanmar Constitution.

53 Harihar Bhattacharyya, 'Federalism in Asia: beyond the diversity problematic', in Kincaid (n 20) 187. See for Myanmar in particular: Michael G Breen, 'Asymmetry or Equality? Ethnic Nationalities in a Bamar-Dominated State', in Popelier and Sahadžić (n 36), 345.

54 Simon Butt, 'Provincial Asymmetry in Indonesia: What is so 'Special' about it?', in Popelier and Sahadžić (n 36) 229.

Unity is also stressed in other forms of nation-building, e.g., in South Africa, where centralism was deemed vital for the transformation of the society under a post-apartheid regime.[55] Yet, even when constitutions call the system federal, they may emphasize the unity and indivisibility of the system, e.g., in Mexico, Nigeria, or Iraq.[56]

Self-definition is an important factor because it instructs courts and other safeguarding agencies where the boundaries lie. It is, however, not sufficient in and of itself. As mentioned in the previous chapter, not all constitutions self-define the form of state, or the structural clause that contains the self-definition may be misleading. Switzerland, for example, considers itself to be a federation although the constitution, for pragmatic reasons, still refers to the Confederation.[57] Another matter is how the system is organized: by the constitution, or through organic laws or other legal acts. Three categories determine how the system divides the power relations between central and SNEs: status, powers, and fiscal arrangements.[58] Within these categories, mechanisms are introduced to safeguard autonomy, cohesion, or both. 'Status' concerns the identification of the SNEs, including territorial boundaries, their involvement in the central and intergovernmental decision-making bodies and procedures, and their powers of self-organization. It also concerns representation of the central government in governing institutions and the procedures for voicing the public interest. 'Powers' refers to the allocation of legislative, executive, administrative, and judicial powers to the central government and SNEs, in combination with the location of residual powers. It covers policy instruments (constituent, legislative, executive, judicial, taxation, and treaty-making powers), allocation techniques, and the policy fields in which the central and subnational entities can use their powers. 'Fiscal arrangements' points to the financial relations between the

55 Art. 1 South African Constitution defines South Africa as 'one, sovereign' state although Art. 40 distinguishes three interrelated spheres of government. On the underlying reasons, see Nico Steytler, 'The Constitutional Court of South Africa: Reinforcing an Hourglass System of Multi-Level Government', in Nicholas Aroney and John Kincaid (eds), *Courts in Federal Countries: Federalists or Regionalists?* (University of Toronto Press 2017) 330. Lidija R. Basta Fleiner and Jean-François Gaudreault-DesBiens, 'Federalism and autonomy', in Mark Tushnet, Thomas Fleiner and Cheryl Saunders (eds), *Routledge Handbook of Constitutional Law* (London, Routledge 2015) 148 point out that the term federalism was shunned because it was associated with apartheid politics.

56 Art. 2 Mexican Constitution, Art. 2 (1) Nigerian Constitution, Art. 1 Iraqi Constitution.

57 See Thomas Fleiner, 'Constitutional Revision. The Case of Switzerland', in Xenophon Contiades (ed), *Engineering Constitutional Change* (Routledge 2013) 337. See also Giovanni Biaggini, 'Switzerland', in Dawn Oliver and Carlo Fusaro (eds) *How Constitutions Change. A Comparative Study* (Hart 2011) 305.

58 See for this trichotomy Francesco Palermo, Carolin Zwilling and Karl Kössler (eds), *Asymmetries in Constitutional Law* (Bozen/Bolzano, Eurac 2009) and Sahadžić (n 43) 32.

central and the subnational levels of authority: revenue powers, expenditures, and financial equalization.[59]

2.2.1.2 *An essentially contested concept*

Federal theorists often stress the importance of safeguards: once the federal arrangement is made, it must be protected. This is because the elements that Bednar calls the 'authority boundaries' are continuously contested.[60] This puts an emphasis on obstacles to constitutional changes, and safeguards for the status quo. As discussed in the previous chapter, this is why constitutional entrenchment and judicial review regularly pop up in the list of institutional requirements. Safeguards, however, can take various forms: judicial review is one, intergovernmental conciliation procedures is another. Preferably, they are combined, as each instrument has its own timeline and flaws. For example, courts are slow and can only behave in a reactive way.

At the same time, many forces push for changes to the power relations that are defined in the constitution. These forces can be both political and judicial, which means that the safeguards of the status quo can also act as drivers for change.[61] Gardner concludes that constitutions cannot, "through careful engineering, be made to stabilize themselves at their initial design specifications".[62] Bednar takes this to be an essential feature of federalism: "All of the pushing and pulling, and the variety of interpreters, mean that the boundaries are always being questioned" – which is precisely what leads us to a theory of federal dynamics.[63]

This observation casts the value of proper balance as an essentially contested concept. In a dynamic concept of federalism, constitutions are not meant to 'stabilize themselves at their initial specifications'. Instead, the concept of stability in itself is a dynamic notion that requires a constant rethinking of power balances and needs room for flexibility and adaptation.[64] Constitutions are therefore conceived as providers of instruments that can recalibrate power relations when new developments put important values at risk. These values might include efficient government, the survival of the state, or group identity. This means that contesting constitutional power relations is inherent to federal arrangements. Such instruments are necessary to address the instability that results when the

59 See Francesco Palermo and Karl Kössler, *Comparative Federalism: Constitutional Arrangements and Case Law* (Hart 2017) 201. For the emphasis on intergovernmental financial relations in the definition, see A. Valdesalici, 'Defining Fiscal Federalism', in Alice Valdesalici and Francesco Palermo (eds) *Comparing Fiscal Federalism* (Leiden, Brill, 2018) 19–21

60 Jenna Bednar, 'Federalism theory: the boundary problem, robustness and dynamics', in Kincaid (n 20) 27.

61 *Ibid* 33.

62 James Gardner, 'The Theory and Practice of Contestatory Federalism', (2018) 60 *William & Mary L. Rev.* 588.

63 Bednar (n 60) 33.

64 Sahadžić (n 43) 148–149, 163.

division of powers and resources in an MTS is no longer accepted as legitimate by political actors at the different levels.[65] The capacity to respond to change, then, is regarded as an important factor for the survival of MTSs.[66] Flexibility is essential to respond to the exigencies of the moment,[67] particularly in multinational states where the organization of diversity through federal arrangements is simultaneously the device for stability and the seed for instability.[68] This is also the case when subgroups are not territorially defined: scholars argue that forms of dynamic or 'living' consociationalism are more successful, with their power-sharing arrangements that guarantee adaptability and cooperation.[69] Contestation creates dynamics, which means that MTSs continuously move in opposite directions. As a consequence, a theory of dynamic federalism does not distinguish, as in traditional federalism theory, between 'mature' and 'emergent' federations. It does not regard federations as systems where a stable balance has been established, and other MTSs as systems that "are still in the process of establishing their equilibrium".[70]

Friedrich's idea of federalism as a process led scholars to search for variables that push a system toward centralization or decentralization. Mostly they identified social, economic, and political forces.[71] By contrast, not much light has been shed on institutional instruments as drivers for change. Simeon observed that constitutions are both dependent and independent variables. For example, variations in space and time are the result of historical, cultural, and political forces; but at the same time, constitutional provisions influence the conduct of political actors, and therefore, cause their own processes of constitutional change.[72] The author's focus was on the constitution as a dependent variable,

65 For this definition of stability see Nathalie Behnke and Arthur Benz, 'The Politics of Constitutional Change between Reform and Evolution' (2009) 39 *Publius: The Journal of Federalism* 215.

66 Michael Burgess and G Alan Tarr, 'Introduction: Sub-national Constitutionalism and Constitutional Development', in Michael Burgess and G Alan Tarr, *Constitutional Dynamics in Federal Systems: Sub-national Perspectives* (Montreal & Kingston, McGill-Queen's University Press 2012) 3.

67 Nico Steytler and Johann Mettler, 'Federalism and Peacemaking: A South African Case Study', (2001) *Publius: The Journal of Federalism* 93. See also André Lecours, 'Federalism and nationalism', in Kincaid (n 20) 143–144.

68 On the debate of whether ethnic federalism is a device for success or failure, see Sujit Choudry and Nathan Hume, 'Federalism, Devolution and Secession: From Classical to Post-conflict Federalism', in Tom Ginsburg and Rosalind Dixon (eds), *Comparative Constitutional Law* (Edward Elgar 2011) 356–357, 364–372 and Palermo and Kössler (n 58) 97–101.

69 See Feargal Cochrane, Neophytos Loizides and Thibaud Bodson, *Mediating Power-Sharing* (Routledge 2018) 5 and 47–48.

70 Roland L Watts, *Comparing Federal Systems* (Queen's University 2008, 3rd ed.) 25.

71 Birch (n 12) 15–33 for one, criticized the focus on social forces and drew the attention to political factors: 15–33.

72 Richard Simeon, 'Constitutional Design and Change in Federal Systems: Issues and Questions', (2009) 39 *Publius: The Journal of Federalism* 242.

but his observation that constitutions are both dependent and independent variable is maintained in the theory of dynamic federalism. Such a theory must therefore examine the instruments that are established as 'hubs' for changes in power relations.

Federal theory, then, shares with constitutional theory an interest in the mechanisms of constitutional change. Constitutional change refers to transformations through the "perpetual interaction of formal and informal mechanisms", which includes legal and extra-legal instruments.[73] Dynamic federalism, however, is not only interested in identifying the factors of change. It also seeks to find out whether, and how, dynamics can be changed. For this reason, it is also interested in 'measuring' power relations, so that the centralization grade of MTSs can be compared across countries and across time.

This justifies the legal-institutional approach this book takes. In the first place, the constitutional setting outlines the default position, against which changes produced by legal and extra-legal instruments can be measured. Secondly, extra-legal forces often use institutional instruments and procedures to produce change, which could be hindered by institutional safeguards. Third, institutional instruments and procedures can be subjected to constitutional engineering, whereas we have less control over extra-legal forces. This does not mean that dynamic federalism is essentially a legal theory. Instead, the mutual influence of legal and nonlegal factors is an important part of the theory's research agenda. This book will certainly take notice of insights from other disciplines. However, consistent with my field of expertise, the book will concentrate on the legal framework: the institutional set-up, and the institutional hubs for change. Interdisciplinary research is essential to complete the theory and is the next analytical step.

2.2.2 A categorization of forms of state

In a dynamic approach, forms of state are distinguished based not on qualifying features, but on indicators. Since MTSs aim to strike a balance between subnational autonomy and overall cohesion, the indicators will measure push and pull factors in two dimensions: one set of indicators to measure cohesion, another to measure autonomy.

Friedrich's metaphor of a gliding scale is appropriate to display centralization and decentralization processes, but less adequate to illustrate federalism processes. This is because cohesion is not the opposite of autonomy, and the balance between both is not a trade-off.

On a de/centralist gliding scale, the most centralist systems are placed on the left: these are systems where power is concentrated in the center and, consequently, autonomy remains limited. The most decentralist systems are placed on the right, and systems with medium levels of centralism and moderate subnational autonomy are placed in the middle. Systems glide from one end of the

73 Xenophon Contiades, 'Constitutional Change Engineering', in Contiades (n 57) 1.

	SUBNATIONAL AUTONOMY →		
COHESION ↑	**High – Low:** Integrationist MTS	**High – Medium:** Federation type 1	**High – High:** Federation type 2
	Medium – Low: Consociation-based MTS	**Medium – Medium:** Regionalized system	**Medium – High:** Confederation
	Low-Low: Deconcentrated unitary system	**Low – Medium:** Decentralized system	**Low – High:** Political Association

Figure 2.1 Forms of state

scale to the other, but what they win in autonomy they lose in power concentration, and vice versa.

However, when cohesion (not centralism) is measured, the picture becomes much more complex. Systems can simultaneously achieve high or low scores for autonomy and cohesion, and any other combination of results. This means that they do not necessarily move from the left to the right side or vice versa. They can move up or down, toward more or less cohesion, to the left or the right, toward less or more autonomy, or in two directions at the same time. In this system, forms of state are defined by their combined scores on the cohesion index and the autonomy index, visualized in Figure 2.1.

In the lowest row, we find systems that score low for cohesion, but glide as follows on the subnational autonomy dimension:

- deconcentrated unitary systems are systems that score low on cohesion and low on subnational autonomy. They can score low on both dimensions because cohesion and subnational autonomy are not mirroring concepts: cohesion measures partnership, not central dominance. These systems, while allocating decision-making power to territorial units, are very centralized, but not according to the 'federal spirit';
- decentralized systems are systems that score low on cohesion and moderately on subnational autonomy. Here, SNEs can have some recognition and enjoy a reasonable number of powers, but there is no sense of equal partnership;
- political associations are systems that score low on cohesion and high on subnational autonomy. 'Association' is the term Friedrich used to denote the organization of loose federal relationships.[74] For example, intergovernmental international organizations would fall under this category;

In the highest row, we find systems that score high for cohesion, and glide as follows on the subnational autonomy dimension:

- integrationist MTSs score high on cohesion and low on autonomy. Here, preference is given to partnership and co-government rather than to autonomy;

74 Friedrich 1968 (n 2) 89.

- federations are systems that ideally score high on both cohesion and autonomy, or at least high on cohesion and medium on subnational autonomy. This is what Watts considers the common feature of successful federations to be: the combination of a strong integrative consciousness with an equally strong regional consciousness.[75] Yet, cohesion is even more important than autonomy because the idea of partnership prevails as the 'federal spirit';

In the middle row, we find systems that score moderately for cohesion and move on the subnational autonomy dimension:

- consociation-based MTSs have some partnership arrangements with SNEs, but these arrangements are less cohesive than is the case in integrationist systems. This is because they are not based on community-transcending instruments. Instead, it is considered essential for the construction of 'federal trust' to let national groups participate on the basis of their singular character as a subnational entity. Meanwhile, instruments can be built in, such as veto rights and opting-out procedures, to protect national groups from 'the tyranny of the majority'.[76] Like consociations,[77] consociation-based MTSs are interested in giving voice rather than autonomy. In 'consociation-based MTSs', however, some territorial power division is nevertheless implied, which is not necessarily the case in consociations;
- regionalized systems are systems that score moderately on both cohesion and subnational autonomy;
- confederations are systems that score high on the subnational autonomy dimension and moderately for cohesion.

The terms 'integrationist systems' and 'consociationalist systems' are borrowed from the power-sharing literature. They represent two schools of thought with different recipes for accommodating ethnic groups in divided societies.[78] Centripetalists favor an integrative, cross-community model, whereas consociationalists argue for guaranteed group representation and prefer a model where the members of the governing bodies remain firmly rooted in their separate subgroup. The second model is considered less cohesive in Figure 2.1 because it encourages group mobilization. In divided societies, these subgroups are not necessarily concentrated within a specific territory.[79]

75 Watts (n 70) 63.

76 Ferran Requejo, 'Federalism and democracy. The case of minority nations: a federalist deficit', in Michael Burgess and Alain-G Gagnon (eds), *Federal Democracies* (Routledge 2010) 290. See also Ferran Requejo, 'National Pluralism, Recognition, Federalism and Secession (or Hegel Was a Clever Guy)', in Gagnon, Keil and Mueller (n 30) 164.

77 Rubin (n 30) 127.

78 For an effort to overcome this dichotomy, see Cochrane, Loizides and Bodson (n 69) 2–4, 105–108.

79 As Livingston (n 30) 2 pointed out, this is what distinguishes federalism from "functionalism, pluralism or some form of corporatism".

Considering that this scheme is only concerned with territorial divided MTSs, it only addresses those systems where the main groups largely overlap with territorial delineations.

In terms of traditional concepts of federalism, type 1 federations show resemblance to forms of administrative federalism, where the subnational and federal level are entwined to the cost of subnational autonomy. Type 2 federations, in turn, are advanced forms of cooperative federalism.

All this means that systems can evolve from one category to another, but in more than one direction. The difference between forms of state is more than a matter of degree, since scores depend upon variables that also relate to status: the constitutional recognition of an entity, its self-organizing powers, and its representation in central institutions. This suggests that throughout the process from one form of state to the other, the system transforms in a more substantial way. My perception is that institutional and noninstitutional dynamics change along with this change of form. This might lead to an acceleration in the case of an ongoing process toward increasing autonomy that is combined with decreasing cohesion. However, this is a hypothesis that needs to be tested empirically.

The proposed terminology is open to debate. The definitions are what matters in terms of how the systems relate to cohesion and subnational autonomy. In this scheme, confederations are not a synonym for international organizations. Instead, loose intergovernmental international organizations will most probably fall under the category of 'political association'. In contrast, more integrated international organizations such as the European Union (EU) will presumably qualify as a confederation instead.

By a 'political association', I do not mean to imply that the component units are necessarily independent states. For example, the Flemish-nationalist N-VA proposes a reform of the Belgian state in which all powers reside with the component units, except for a few very basic matters that are jointly regulated at the Belgian level and are governed by the SNEs.[80] Under such a reform the Belgian state would still exist – enabling the SNEs to maintain EU membership without having to open new negotiations – but the state structure would be emptied of all meaning.

2.2.3 The development of indicators

A crucial aspect for the operationalization of this theory is the development of indicators that can measure both subnational autonomy and cohesion. The first concept calls for a set of indicators that regards the SNE as the unit of analysis, whereas the second concept uses the central government as the unit of analysis.

80 N-VA, Congress paper, *Verandering Voor Vooruitgang* (2014) https://www.n-va.be/sites/default/files/generated/files/dossier/definitieve_congresbrochure.pdf.

Hooghe et al. have distilled the process of constructing an index into six steps:[81] (1) Defining the background concept; (2) Specifying the measurement concept; (3) Unfolding the concept into dimensions; (4) Operationalizing the dimensions; (5) Scoring cases; and (6) Adjudicating scores.

The first two steps were completed in Chapters 1 and 2. The dimensions in step 3, have been identified as 'cohesion' and 'subnational autonomy' for three categories (status, powers, and fiscal arrangements). They provide the basis of the next three chapters, which will further disaggregate the dimensions and operationalize them (step 4) into indicators. For the scoring, I will rely on primary and secondary sources: constitutions, legislation, and doctrine. The last step is about adjudicating scores: how will we interpret gray cases? The Belgian test case is used to deal with steps 5 and 6. This example will provide information on how I interpret and evaluate specific data. Each chapter will propose a set of options, on the basis of which a score can be given from 0 to a maximum of 10. More case studies are needed to refine the index. The present study will therefore only result in a first proposal that needs further adjustments.

In the (mostly nonlegal) literature, we already find some scaling of political systems on the basis of indicators. The indicators used in these studies give us important starting points, but are not sufficient for our purpose. Mostly, these scholars are interested in autonomy rather than cohesion, and they tend to ignore the role of courts. In the next sections, I review some of the relevant literature to identify useful indicators for the subsequent chapters and to identify weaknesses that need to be taken into account. The review is not exhaustive; it only selects authors that are representative for a specific approach. Mueller is not included in this selection, because in his measurement of de/centralization, he uses the dimensions of policy, polity and politics,[82] and only develops new indicators for the latter dimension. These are not useful for an institutional assessment but may later serve for the construction of a model to measure federalism in action, i.e. the 'actual federalism score' as defined in Chapter 7.

2.2.3.1 Aubert: an inventory of institutional arrangements

Aubert was a Swiss constitutionalist who, in the same period as Friedrich, criticized traditional theory for being too focused on institutional features. To him, taking stock of the different ways in which territorial groups are managed within one political system was more interesting than whether or not a particular political system qualified as a federation.[83] To this end, two sets of inventories were proposed. One took stock of how political systems organize themselves internally,

81 Liesbeth Hooghe, Gary Marks, Arjan H. Schakel, Sara Niedzwiecki, Sandra Chapman Osterkatz, and Sarah Shair-Rosenfield, *Measuring Regional Authority: A Postfunctionalist Theory of Governance. Volume 1* (Oxford University Press 2016) 7–8.

82 *Ibid* 36–48.

83 Aubert (n 30) 403, 414.

and the other considered how they connect externally.[84] Such inventories allowed Aubert to categorize political systems as more or less decentralized.[85]

The first inventory examines the mechanisms of decentralization.[86] For this purpose, the author inquired into guarantees for the existence of territorial groups; the entrenchment and the technique of the distribution of powers; the location of residual powers and the procedure to amend this distribution; the financial arrangement; the involvement of territorial groups in the conclusion of international agreements; their power to organize themselves; and central control or supervision.[87]

The second inventory assesses the predictability of the sacrifices that political systems make by joining a more global political entity.[88] The more specific the domains for joint action and the costs to be paid, the more predictable these sacrifices are. This inventory is much less detailed than the first one. It serves, in particular, to point out that in the Coal and Steel Community, which was at that time a new type of 'supranational' organization, the sacrifices were unpredictable. On that basis, Aubert envisioned that the organization would create its own power-increasing dynamics.[89]

Aubert's approach is inspirational for our purpose of building indexes because he covers the categories of status, power, and financial arrangements. Further, he pays proper attention to how international treaties may influence the position of territorial entities within a political system. However, his questions are directed at the description of institutional arrangements and do not involve scores, which may complicate the comparative exercise in terms of ranking. Further, the second inventory is too vague to be operational. Also, his method is not concerned with measuring cohesion.

2.2.3.2 Baldi, Requejo: unitary/federalism and de/centralisation axes

In this group of literature, (de)centralization processes and federalism processes have been separated, each with their own set of variables. Two authors are selected, representing an economic approach and a political approach respectively. This is to give an idea of how these axes are built.

Baldi discerns, for the centralism/federalism continuum, two sets of variables that have center-constraining potential: constitutional variables, and 'para-constitutional' variables. The author distinguishes two sets of constitutional variables, for which more detailed indicators are proposed. The first variable is the allocation of power, operationalized as: (1) the distribution of lawmaking

84 *Ibid* 414.
85 *Ibid* 420–421.
86 *Ibid* 415–416.
87 *Ibid* 416–420.
88 *Ibid* 444.
89 *Ibid* 449.

competences; (2) residual powers; (3) criteria for the allocation of competences (exclusive or shared); and (4) territorial diffusion (symmetry/asymmetry). The second variable is representation in the Second Chamber, operationalized as: (1) the extension of the territorial representation within the Chamber (exclusive/partial); (2) the policy scope (in relation to the First Chamber); (3) the degree of overrepresentation; and (4) the method of selection of representatives (direct or indirect election by citizens versus appointment by subnational executives).[90] Para-constitutional variables are intergovernmental relations and the party system. For the purpose of setting the institutional blueprint, I am primarily interested in the constitutional variables.

For the centralization/decentralization continuum, lawmaking powers, administrative powers, and financial (or fiscal) powers are selected.[91] Indicators for administrative powers are: (1) the legal allocation of functions among levels of government; (2) the size of administrative structures (public employment at each level as a percentage of the total); and (3) the government expenditure at each level as a percentage of the national expenditure. Indicators for fiscal powers are proposed with reference to central and noncentral taxation: (1) regional and local taxes; (2) central taxes collected by the subnational government for their use; (3) additional regional or local rates on central taxes; and (4) the relationship between expenditures and revenues per level of government.

Again, some of these indicators are useful for our purpose, as they coincide with the categories of 'status' and 'powers'. However, there are some problems attached to this toolbox. First, Baldi only pays attention to variables that measure the extent of subnational autonomy, ignoring instruments with cohesive potential. Second, the institutional indicators within the category of 'status' are limited to only one aspect, namely parliamentary representation.[92] This excludes the executive and the judiciary. Also, Baldi does not pay attention to the relevance of how electoral districts are delineated. While the indicator 'intergovernmental relations' takes into account the executive level, it ignores the composition of the federal executive, and loses sight of the fact that intergovernmental relations can also have an institutional basis. Third, the exclusive focus on bicameralism as a parliamentary representation method ignores possible alternative mechanisms. These might include territorial representation in a unicameral system or direct involvement of individual SNEs in the parliamentary process. Fourth, there is an assumption that asymmetry has less center-constraining power. However, this is difficult to confirm, considering the varying ways in which constitutional asymmetry is institutionalized. The indicator leads us astray from the fact that in asymmetric arrangements, there are different power relations between the center

90 Baldi (n 23) 8.–9. This distinction finds support in Friedrich's writings, see Friedrich 1968 (n 2) 6.

91 Baldi (n 2) 13.

92 Where Baldi discusses 'administration', this concerns administrative powers, not representation of subnational entities in administration.

and various SNEs. These power relations must therefore be assessed separately. Fifth, 'regional' or 'local' tax is a vague indicator. The author does not specify whether she means the proportion of taxes or the power to raise taxes. If the former, then the picture may be distorted by the extent to which SNEs make use of their taxation powers. If the latter, then no thought is given to the fact that the central authorities may have the power to put limits on these taxes.

Requejo proposes a more comprehensive model. He presents four axes: the uninational-plurinational axis, the symmetry-asymmetry axis, the unitarianism-federalism index, and the centralization-decentralization axis.[93] For the purposes of this book, I only discuss the latter two axes.

The unitarianism-federalism axis takes the perspective of the federated units.[94] Indicators are the existence or absence of: (1) federated polities as constituent units; (2) constitutional guarantees of self-government; (3) agreement for constitutional reform; (4) institutional dualism in relation to the executive, legislative, and judicial power; (5) a model of fiscal federalism; (6) an upper chamber with representatives appointed by the institutions of the federated entities and (7) with seats distributed along territorial lines instead of proportional to the population; (8) powers of the upper chamber within the institutional system; (9) the allocation of unallocated powers to the federated units; (10) a court to arbitrate in disputes with (11) the sub-entities having a say regarding to who is appointed to it; and (12) the right of secession of (some of) the federated units.[95]

The centralization-decentralization axis is measured by: (1) the kind of legislative powers enjoyed by the subunits, subdivided into the areas of (i) economy, infrastructures, and communication, (ii) education and culture, (iii) welfare, (iv) internal affairs, penal and civil codes, and others; (2) executive and administrative powers; (3) the right of subunits to conduct their own foreign policy, taking into account both the scope of the matters and agreements with federal support; and (4) economic decentralization, calculated according to a single average index obtained by taking into account the distribution of the public revenues and the public expenditures (GFS/IMF indexes) in each country.[96]

Here as well, both axes combined give a picture of subnational autonomy, conceived as self-rule and shared rule. This model is more interested in the institutional set-up than Baldi's model, which takes a more economic perspective. Requejo's model has the advantage of elaborating on the status component in more detail and of taking the role of the courts into account. Unlike other indexes, it also includes the right of secession as a variable to measure autonomy. This is conceived as a right to self-determination.[97] The index is applied at the country level, as shown in the rankings that are found in the appendix. A separate

93 Requejo 2010 (n 76) 285–286. See also Requejo 2015 (n 76) 161–163.
94 Requejo 2010 (n 76) 285.
95 *Ibid* 285.
96 *Ibid* 285.
97 *Ibid* 285, 291.

index is built to measure symmetry and asymmetry, but this is not combined in a way that measures the autonomy grade of particular SNEs. However, nothing prevents the axis from being used at the level of a particular SNE. Regrettably, this model focuses on upper chambers and neglects the important position of the executive. Moreover, the model is only interested in autonomy, not cohesion.

2.2.3.3 Hooghe et al.: the Regional Authority Index

Hooghe et al. undertook the task of building "a reasonably valid measure of subnational government structure that is sensitive to cross-sectional and temporal variation".[98] A first version appeared in 2010,[99] the latest updated version was published in 2016.[100] The authors were not interested in concepts of federalism, but in measuring the authority of subnational governments in any form of state: the capacity to make legitimate and binding decisions for a community.[101] However, they borrowed the 'self-rule – shared rule' dichotomy from the federalism literature.[102]

Based on this structure, Hooghe et al. have developed the Regional Authority Index (RAI). This is to measure the authority of regional governments, conceived as the combination of self-rule and shared rule.

Indicators to measure self-rule are: (1) institutional depth (how independent is a regional government from central state control?); (2) policy scope, i.e. the breadth of regional self-rule over policing, its own institutional set-up and local governments, whether it has residual powers, and competences over economic policy, cultural-educational policy, welfare policy, immigration, or citizenship; (3) fiscal autonomy; (4) borrowing autonomy; and (5) representation, covering both the election of the legislature and the appointment of the executive.[103]

Indicators to measure shared rule are: (1) law-making in the second legislative chamber (representation and scope); (2) executive control, indicated by 'routine meetings with the central government', with advisory or veto power; (3) fiscal control; (4) borrowing control; and (5) involvement in constitutional reform.[104]

Several of these indicators are useful for our purpose, especially since they are situated in the three categories of status, powers, and fiscal arrangements.

98 Liesbeth Hooghe, Gary Marks, Arjan H Schakel, Sara Niedzwiecki, Sandra Chapman Osterkatz and Sarah Shair-Rosenfield, (further Hooghe *et al.*) *Measuring Regional Authority: A Postfunctionalist Theory of Governance. Volume 1* (Oxford University Press 2016), 4.

99 Liesbeth Hooghe, Gary Marks and Arjan H Schakel, *The rise of regional authority: a comparative study of 42 countries (Routledge 2010).*

100 Hooghe *et al.* (n 98). See also the project's website, with a ranking of countries: http://garymarks.web.unc.edu/data/regional-authority/. For an appreciation of the RAI, see Mueller (n 27) 169–172.

101 Hooghe *et al.* (n 98) 16.

102 *Ibid* 18.

103 *Ibid* 25.

104 *Ibid* 26.

Their dimensions of 'self-rule' and 'shared rule' match with the terminology of federal theory. In this book, they can be considered subdimensions of subnational autonomy. Also, like the approach taken in this book, the regional level is selected as the unit of analysis. Moreover, the index is only interested in formal rules, to the exclusion of informal arrangements. Finally, the authors provide a detailed scoring mechanism that can be used as a model.

Regrettably, the RAI only measures regional authority and does not examine cohesive instruments for maintaining state integrity. The role of courts is also neglected, and representation at the parliamentary level is only concerned with second chambers. Further, the authors have taken a minimalist approach, distilling their indicators to the essential features.[105] For this book, however, I am not merely interested in the ranking of countries. Instead, I want to develop a theory of federalism, which means that I need to tackle all aspects that affect federalism in any given MTS. In this first phase, I concentrate on the institutional aspects. In later phases, noninstitutional dynamics should be included.

2.2.3.4 Ivanyna & Shah: the World Bank's Fiscal Decentralization Index

Ivanyna and Shah have developed indicators to measure centralization, which have evolved into the World Bank's Fiscal Decentralization Index.[106] These authors are interested in measuring how close decision-making is to the people. For this purpose, they use the local governments as a unit of analysis. They claim that using regional governments as a unit of analysis would be indefensible. This is because some sub-states in large countries, (e.g., in the United States of America, Canada, India, or Russia) are larger than some small countries such as Liechtenstein and Singapore. The latter "would be mistakenly rated as having decision making far removed from the people".[107] They then developed indicators on two dimensions: significance of local governments, and local government empowerment. Finally, the indexes are adjusted for variances in, for example, population and area.[108]

The significance of local government is measured by the indicators of relative importance and security of existence. The first indicator is measured by the share of local government expenditures in consolidated general government expenditures for all orders of government.[109] The second indicator is measured by the constitutional and legal restraints on the arbitrary dismissal

105 *Ibid* 20.

106 Maksym Ivanyna and Anwar Shah, *How Close is Your Government to Its People? Worldwide Indicators on Localization and Decentralization*, World Bank Policy Research Working Paper 6138, 2012.

107 *Ibid* 4.

108 *Ibid* 23.

109 *Ibid* 10.

of local governments.[110] Local government empowerment is measured by three formulas that use indicators of, respectively, fiscal, political, and administrative decentralization. Variables to assess fiscal decentralization are: (1) the vertical fiscal gap, i.e. fiscal dependence of local government on higher-level financing; (2) taxation autonomy, i.e. the local government's ability to determine local taxes, including bases and rates, as well as autonomy in tax collection and administration; (3) unconditional transfers; (4) expenditure autonomy; and (5) borrowing freedom.[111] Political decentralization is measured by: (1) legislative elections (elected, appointed, or a combination); (2) executive elections (idem); and (3) direct democracy provisions.[112] Administrative decentralization is measured in terms of human resources (HR) policies: are local governments able to conduct their own policies regarding hiring, firing, and setting terms of local employment?[113]

Again, the indicators are useful starting points. They cover aspects of status and fiscal arrangements and provide a sophisticated measuring model for this latter dimension. Also, by taking the local government as a unit of analysis, they are not biased by model institutional arrangements such as second chambers. The index was criticized for taking local governments as the unit of analysis and for giving a distorted picture of regional autonomy. Belgium, widely considered to grant broad autonomy to its Communities and Regions, is now ranked as one of the most centralized countries in the OECD.[114] However, as I explained above, a political system can be different things at the same time, depending on which tier is measured. In this case, it can be decentralized in its relation to Communities and Regions and centralized in its relation to local governments.

Nevertheless, the index is in other aspects too limited to serve our purposes. First, the index does not measure cohesion. Second, the indicators do not measure the scope of policy powers, other than the autonomy to determine the employment of their own staff (which can be considered an aspect of subnational constitutional autonomy). Third, the index ignores several aspects that are relevant for examining the broader state structure, such as constitution-making, or the role of the courts. Fourth, there is a dispute about whether the share of government expenditures is a valid measure of decentralization. Sometimes, federal scholars are also tempted to determine the scope of sub-state power as a proportion of federal and sub-state expenditures after intergovernmental transfers.[115] However, expenditures do not necessarily involve the authority to make

110 *Ibid* 11.
111 *Ibid* 12–13.
112 *Ibid* 15–17.
113 *Ibid* 17–18.
114 Hooghe et al. (n 98) 12–13. However, in Ivanyna and Shah's list Belgium is ranked 25th in the decentralization ranking, 23th in the relative importance ranking, and seventh in the security of existence ranking.
115 Ronald L Watts, 'Typologies of federalism', in Loughlin, Kincaid and Swenden (n 48) 31–32.

decisions[116] and are influenced by the government's political stance – for example, left-wing governments are expected to result in more public spending.[117] Fifth, the index does not measure asymmetry – it relies instead on average variables.

2.2.3.5 *Sahadžić: measuring constitutional asymmetry*

In her book on constitutional asymmetry, Sahadžić measured a wide sample of MTSs to conclude that constitutional asymmetry is typical for multinational systems and of little relevance in non-multinational systems.[118] She measured constitutional asymmetry in three categories: status, powers, and fiscal arrangements.

To measure variation in the status of SNEs, she examined: (1) formal recognition, i.e. whether the status of a specific subnational entity is recognized in constitutional or legal acts; (2) institutional autonomy, i.e. the power to organize its own legislative and executive bodies; (3) representation in central institutions; (4) involvement in constitutional revision procedures; (5) involvement in central decision-making procedures; (6) veto powers in central institutions; (7) locks for the protection of autonomy at the central level; and (8) central oversight. The indicators to measure variance in the distribution of powers are: (1) the scope of competence, i.e. whether they are broad or narrow; (2) the technique of the allocation of powers (exclusive, concurrent, or shared); (3) differences in the policy domains for which the subunits have competence; (4) possibilities to opt-in or opt-out; (5) differences in speed in which autonomy is granted; and (6) the power to formulate measures enforced in the subnational entity. Finally, variance in fiscal arrangements is measured by: (1) to power to raise taxes; (2) the discretion to set bases and rates for major taxing powers; (3) the power to raise revenues; (4) reliance on conditional and unconditional transfer; and (5) budgetary control over borrowing.[119] These indicators were incorporated into a questionnaire sent to country experts. These experts were asked, for some indicators to reply with yes or no, and for other indicators to give a value on an 11-point Likert scale.

These indicators are especially useful because they overlap with the three categories of status, power, and financial arrangements. They also helpfully cover the constitutional, the legislative, and the executive levels. Further, they are neutral as to the specific institutional arrangements.

However, the author was measuring constitutional asymmetry and not federalism. The study therefore does not cover all the aspects that this book investigates. For example, the role of courts is not explored in the questionnaire.

116 Paolo Dardanelli, 'Decentralization', in Kincaid (n 20) 111; Hooghe *et al.* (n 97) 13; Paul B Spahn, 'Measuring decentralization of public sector activities: Conceptual issues and the case of Germany', in Junghun Kim, Jorgen Lotz and Hansjörg Blöchliger (eds), *Measuring Fiscal Decentralization: Concepts and Policies* (OECD Publishing 2013) 90.

117 Hooghe et al., *Measuring Regional Authority* 13.

118 Sahadžić (n 43) 83, 88, 95–96.

119 *Ibid* 76–79.

Also, cohesion is discussed as a theoretical concept but is not measured – although her definition of institutional cohesion as the creation of "arenas for partnership between and among the central level and SNEs through established bargaining instruments and mechanisms"[120] will prove useful for our cohesion indexes. Further, the choice for the Likert scale implies some subjective judgment. For example, for the question: 'how would you rate the assigned set of competences to the SNE, as specified in the constitution or other legal act(s) at the central level?', the choice for a value between 0 (narrow) and 10 (broad) is possibly influenced by the respondent's normative account of how broad or narrow this 'should' be. For the purpose of Sahadžić's research, this is not problematic, because she was measuring asymmetry within the different countries. As the same expert was supposed to assess the scores for the various SNEs, the same point of reference applied for the scoring of all SNEs within one country. However, for the purpose of comparison and ranking of different countries, with different experts to examine each political system, the index must avoid such scaling. The check-the-box method used by Hooghe et al. seems more appropriate for that purpose.

2.2.3.6 Conclusion

In the following chapters, a broad set of indicators to measure autonomy and cohesion is proposed. These build on the indicators that have been discerned from the existing literature in the previous paragraphs. It logically follows that I will take the subnational level as a unit of measurement for the autonomy index, and the central level for the cohesion index. 'Subnational' is defined in a broad sense. It is dependent upon the purpose of the research, meaning one can take a sub-state, region, or local government as the unit of analysis. For example, when applied to Kenya, the indexes should be able to reveal in which ways the devolution reform strengthened the position of local governments, and where this type of state structure differs from regional entities in federations.[121]

As the goal is to develop a theory of dynamic federalism, I will take a maximalist approach. This may invoke the critique that one variable can compensate for the other, with an aggregate total picture rather than an unambiguous qualification.[122] Yet, the fact that one variable can compensate for another gives a more accurate picture and enables us to avoid fixating on specific instruments that are typical for a particular model. Follow-up research may reduce the index to a more practical toolbox. The more case studies are developed, the more we will be able to discern the most essential features for a minimalist approach.

120 *Ibid* 225.

121 For this development: Conrad M. Bosire, 'The Courts and Devolution. The Kenyan Experience', in Yonatan T. Fessha and Karl Kössler (eds), *Federalism and the Courts in Africa* (Routledge 2020) 124–127.

122 Bernard JS Hoetjes, 'Federaties en federalisme. Een raamwerk voor theorie en onderzoek', (1978) 20 *Res Publica* 569.

Still, we need to be careful. For example, we might discover that subnational representation in Parliament is in most cases not so essential to measure subnational impact on central decision-making. However, if we omit it altogether we miss important contributions to subnational authority in states such as Germany and the United States of America.

2.3 The theory of dynamic federalism put to the test

Chapter 1 concluded with three tests to assess the validity of federal theory: a specificity test, a universality test, and a flexibility test. In this section, I will assess dynamic federalism against these criteria.

2.3.1 The specificity test

The condition of specificity requires that:

1 the definition of federalism as a value, MTSs as political organizations, and the categorization of forms of state all derive from the idea of power relations between territorial levels of authority, and
2 definitions must be sharp enough to distinguish and compare forms of state in a meaningful way.

The first condition of specificity is met, in the sense that federalism as a value is defined as the search for a proper balance between the autonomy of SNEs and the cohesion of the entire system. Federalist political organizations are called MTSs, defined in terms of power relations between the central entity and the territorial tiers. Forms of states are distinguished in terms of how autonomy factors relate to cohesive factors. This means, however, that the table for forms of state only covers a specific type of centralist system and consociation, namely the ones that have at least a minimum form of territorial division. It also means that it only identifies those consociations where the power-sharing instruments are used for groups that have at least some coincidence with the territorial division, even if they do not necessarily overlap entirely.

The second condition is met, in the sense that nine different forms of states are distinguished, along with their different qualities. The precision of the delineation depends upon how precise the measuring indicators are. If they are too rough, it will not always be possible to qualify a system as, for example, either a regionalized system or a federation type 1; or either a federation type 2 or a confederation. In the end, this is not necessarily a problem, because we will nevertheless be able to approximately situate the system in comparison with other systems. Moreover, the precise location is only a snapshot in time. States move on the checkerboard, and the direction in which they move is more interesting than their precise location at any given moment. In addition, meaningful comparisons are possible because the model can be applied to the entire system, parts of a global system, or specific tiers within the system. I will return to this point later.

2.3.2 *The universality test*

The universality test requires that:

1 the theory covers very different institutional arrangements. This means that it does not put forward specific institutional mechanisms as defining features, or specific states as model federations. It also means that no allowance must be made for *sui generis* qualifications.
2 the theory does not give particular value to any particular form of state but sees every form as valuable in itself. This means that no distinction is made between 'mature' or 'complete' federations and 'immature' or 'transitionary' federations.

The first condition is met because the indicators do not point to particular institutions, mechanisms, or procedures. Rather, the indicators address categories of status, powers, and fiscal arrangements that translate the power relationship between the central government and the subnational authorities. Any institution, mechanism, or procedure in a given MTS qualifies for examination about how it enhances subnational autonomy or cohesion.

The second condition is also met. The theory does not take a particular model state as a point of departure. It classifies forms of state according to the balance they institutionalize between cohesion and subnational autonomy. This is the 'proper' balance if it conforms to a constituent consensus. This depends, initially, on what was laid down in the constitution. However, the political consensus may change over time, because what amounts to a proper balance is a perpetually contested concept. As soon as political consensus is reached for a new form of state, institutional reform is warranted. This does not imply that the future form is a superior model; it only means that for this particular state, in this specific context and at this specific moment, it is the preferred model.

2.3.3 *The flexibility test*

The flexibility test requires that:

1 the model can cover innovative institutional arrangements and new developments that impact on state structures, including their relationship with internal tiers of government and with global political systems, and
2 the model incorporates adaptations over time, considering noninstitutional contextual factors and new preferences as to the balance of power relations.

The first condition is met. It already follows from the universality test that the theory covers different institutional arrangements. Moreover, the system manages the complexity that results from a multiplication of levels of authority, and from constitutional asymmetry. This is because relationships can be measured with respect to any tier within any part of a global political system. For example, the theory can be used to examine the relationship between the EU and its member states. However, it may also include a criterion that examines the involvement of the subnational level in EU decision-making, as part of the relationship between the national and the subnational level. Or it can focus on the relationship between the subnational level and the local level. As a result, an MTS with multiple (local and regional) tiers can be qualified as a mixture of systems. Depending on which relations are measured, it can be both an administrative decentralized system and a federation, or both a regionalized system and a federation.

Also, the theory takes into account that MTSs have a vertical and a horizontal dimension, pointing to the central and subnational levels of authority and the relation between SNEs respectively.[123] The institutional analysis focuses on the vertical relationship, but fiscal arrangements reveal horizontal (im)balances, and the fact that particular SNEs are selected as units of analysis for the autonomy indexes, allows us to grasp constitutional asymmetries at the same geographical level. Constitutional or *de jure* asymmetry addresses varieties in status, powers, and fiscal autonomy of SNEs within one legal system.[124] As a result, the system can be qualified as a federation in its relationship with some SNEs and at the same time as a regionalized system in its relationship with others. The model also allows the measurement of constitutional asymmetries within one system and comparison with asymmetries in other systems.[125] This is further explained in Chapter 7.

The second condition is also fulfilled. The 'proper balance', as a value of federalism, is an essentially contested concept. This means that the theory allows room for change in the preferred balance of powers. It is not only interested in extra-legal drivers for change but incorporates institutional 'hubs' for change within the institutional arrangement itself.

2.4 Conclusion: setting the scene

In the previous sections, the contours of a theory of dynamic federalism were drawn. This theory is dynamic in three ways.

First, it does away with the static categorization of forms of state, in which systems are disqualified by the absence of one of the defining institutional features. For example, the use of concurrent powers led to the erosion of *Länder* competences in Germany, but at the same time, the position of the *Bundesrat* was strengthened. In the literature, this is called 'compensation through

123 Arthur Benz and Jorg Broschek, 'Federal dynamics: Introduction', in Benz and Broschek (n 28) 4.

124 Popelier and Sahadžić (n 36) 6; Sahadžić (n 43) 28–41.

125 For this exercise, see Sahadžić (n 43) 84–88.

participation'[126] or 'compensatory federalism'.[127] Likewise, if a system does not give full constitutional autonomy to SNEs, then this lowers the autonomy score but this does not necessarily mean that it cannot be called a federation. The low score for subnational constitutional autonomy may be compensated by a higher score for another indicator of autonomy. For example, Belgian Communities and Regions have only limited subnational constitutional autonomy, but they score very high on the indicator that measures their powers to conclude international treaties.[128] This also means that the theory allows us to make comparisons at the level of systems as well as at the level of specific instruments. As a result, the theory is apt for dealing with the multiplying dynamics that result from the complexity of systems with multiple tiers, both within and beyond the national state.

The second dynamic has to do with the difference between institutional design and practice. The model shows where the institutional design situates a system, but noninstitutional factors may reveal a different picture. For example, in Ethiopia and South Africa, subnational autonomy is reduced in practice because of the dominance of the same political party at the central and the provincial level.[129] However, this may change as soon as the party-symmetry disappears, as happened in Cape Town.[130] Economical changes may, again, change this picture. However, we need this starting point of the institutional design to find which extra-legal forces have centralizing or decentralizing power. Also, the difference between the location of a system in terms of institutional design, and how it works in practice, may predict how the system will evolve institutionally over time. This is because extra-legal factors can be drivers for institutional change.

This brings us to the third dynamic. Like Friedrich's concept of federalism as a process, the theory emphasizes evolution over time. The model is interested in the direction that systems take. This may be a pendulum for some systems, with push and pull factors that, over time, keep the system stable. This is the case even if at particular moments the system is more centralized and at other moments more decentralized, or more or less cohesive. For other systems, the dynamics may inevitably point to one end of the spectrum. Belgium, for example, started as a decentralized unitary system. Now, after six state reforms that pushed it toward the central-right end of the de/centralism scale, Belgium is

126 Carolyn Moore, Wade Jacoby and Arthur B Gunlicks, 'Introduction: German Federalism in Transition?', (2008) XVII *German Politics* 395.

127 Markus Kotzur, 'Federalism and Bicameralism – The German 'Bundesrat' (Federal Council) as an Atypical Model', in Jörg Luther, Paolo Passaglia and Ronaldo Tarchi (eds) *A World of Second Chambers* (Giuffrè Editore 2006) 280.

128 See Appendix, the Belgian showcase.

129 J Tyler Dickovick, 'Federalism in Africa: Origins, Operation and (In)Significance', (2014) *24 Regional & Federal Studies*, 555, 562.

130 Although Jan Erk, 'Federalism and Decentralization in Sub-Saharan Africa: Five Patterns of Evolution', (2014) *24 Regional & Federal Studies*, 542–543 notices that this also due to the fact that the Western Cape is a 'have' Province, with the institutional capacity to use its autonomy.

considering confederalism. The million-dollar question in these cases is whether these dynamics can be changed, or whether they are inevitable. If they are inevitable, where is the point of no return?

In this way, Chapter 2 has set the scene for a theory that is further developed in the subsequent chapters. First, the tricky exercise to develop indicators is commenced with regard to status (Chapter 4), powers (Chapter 5), and fiscal arrangements (Chapter 6). Chapter 3 offers guidelines for the interpretation of the indexes and discusses the results of the Belgian case. Next, I will examine the institutionalization of hubs for change (Chapters 7 and 8).

As mentioned, I do not regard what is presented in this book as the perfect toolbox: it takes an entire scientific community to build a theory. My aim is to discuss possible indicators and to test them by applying them to one case study. Belgium has been selected for two reasons. The first reason is a very pragmatic one: it is the system that I am most familiar with. It does not serve as a model state for the theory of dynamic federalism: any other system could have been selected. What matters is that applying the indicators to a specific case gives us some idea of the strengths and weaknesses of the proposed indicators, and an opportunity to refine them. The second reason is that Belgium is the perfect showcase for the dynamics of federalism. In only five decades it transformed from an administratively decentralized state over a regionalized system into a federation. It has traits that presumably make it a confederation in our table, and with current proposals to transform it into a very loose system, close to what I have labelled a 'political association'. So far, it manifests itself as a system that has crossed several boxes in the checkerboard and is possibly about to enter the final ones.

In follow-up research, especially the relations and dynamics between the local, regional, national, and supranational as a whole should be disentangled. I will come back to this in the concluding chapter, where I present a research agenda for dynamic federalism.

Part II

Measuring cohesion and autonomy

3 Preliminary notes: representation, and the Belgian case study

In the next three chapters, indicators are developed to measure cohesion and autonomy for the categories of status, power, and fiscal arrangements. References are made to various jurisdictions to explain these indicators. Belgium is an important reference point because it showcases a number of indicators and allows them to be tested. The appendix only shows the individual and aggregate scores. Chapters 4, 5, and 6 will further elaborate on how the index is applied

In order to measure cohesion, the indexes seek proxies for solidarity, the shaping of a sense of community, and intergovernmental dialogue. To measure autonomy, both self-rule and shared rule are examined. Self-rule is the most obvious expression of subnational autonomy.[1] The idea that political systems can pursue policies in a completely autonomous manner is becoming increasingly utopian. Political systems are increasingly embedded in complex multilevel networks. This puts forwards the question of how SNEs can voice their interests at (various) upper levels

For this reason, intergovernmental decision-making and subnational representation reappear as important indicators throughout the indexes. Specific terminology is used to refer to varying degrees of involvement. This chapter clarifies what is meant by terms such as the representation of the national electorate, of the SNEs, or the SNEs' electorate (section 3.1).

Importantly, subdivisions within indexes have the same weight. No prior assumption is made that one aspect is more important than another. For this reason, the scores for each subdivision must be reduced to the same denominator. In the end, the scores for each category are put on an equal level by converting them to a value between 0 and 1.

Finally, this chapter anticipates the building of the indexes. This is through Belgium being used as a showcase of indicators (section 3.2). In this way, it will be immediately clear which insights the indexes can give and how useful they are for further research.

1 Francesco Palermo and Karl Kössler, *Comparative Federalism* (Hart 2017) 125.

3.1 Which interests are voiced?

The indexes frequently refer to 'representation of the SNEs'. This points to an institutional link.

The link is strong if members are appointed by the governments of the SNEs. This is the case in the so-called 'Council' or 'Ambassadorial model'.[2] An example is Germany, where members are appointed by the governments of the Länder.[3] Another example is the EU, where the Council of Ministers represents member states' governments.

In some cases, SNEs are not part of the federal legislative body, but they are included in the lawmaking (or constitutional amendment) procedure. This also provides a strong institutional link. SNEs' impact on federal decision-making is especially notable when they have a (collective) veto, for example, if the approval of a majority of the SNEs is required. In other cases, they have no decisive say and merely have informal power. For example, the Italian Standing Conference for the Relations between the State and Regions must be consulted for measures that affect regional competences.[4]

More often, institutional delegates in the central legislative chamber are representatives of the subnational parliaments. This is the case in India, where the majority of members of the Council of States represent the States and the Union Territories, and representatives of the States are elected by the elected members of the Legislative Assembly of each state.[5] In Belgium as well, (most) Senators are appointed by the subnational Parliaments. In the so-called 'hybrid models',[6] the chamber consists of representatives of the subnational executive as well as representatives of the subnational parliaments. Examples of these hybrid models can be found in South Africa[7] and Russia.[8] Delegates appointed by subnational parliaments have a weaker institutional link than representatives of the executives. If the delegations are large enough, they may include subnational opposition parties. This is not the case in Russia, where only one representative from the subnational legislative is appointed.[9] By contrast, participation of minority parties in South Africa's subnational delegations is a constitutional requirement.[10]

What matters for the purpose of the indexes is that there is a link with substantial institutions. The nuanced distinctions between the representation of the subnational parliaments, executives, or both, are not made.

In some states, there is only a partial institutional link. In Spain, the Senate is primarily composed on the basis of cities and provinces, whereas the

2 Giancarlo Doria, 'The Paradox of Federal Bicameralism', (2006) 5 *European Diversity and Autonomy Papers* 7; Palermo and Kössler (n 1) 172.
3 Art. 51 German Constitution.
4 Palermo and Kössler (n 1) 178.
5 Art. 80 Indian Constitution.
6 Palermo and Kössler (n 1) 176.
7 Art. 60 and 61 South African Constitution.
8 Art. 95(2) Russian Constitution.
9 Art. 95(2) Russian Constitution.
10 Art. 61(3) South African Constitution.

Self-Governing Communities' Legislative Assemblies appoint only a small portion of the chamber's members.[11] As a result, the Spanish Senate should be viewed mainly as a chamber representative of local entities. This is just like the members of the Dutch upper house, elected by the members of the provincial assemblies, who represent the local entities in the Netherlands.[12] If regional entities are the unit of analysis, the representation should be substantial enough to weigh on decision-making. This requires at least a 30 percent threshold.

There is no institutional link in the so-called 'Senate model', where representatives of the SNEs are directly elected. This is the case in Australia, Nigeria, the United States of America, and many other countries. Scholars argue that this so-called 'compound majoritarianism', with the representation of the electorates of the SNEs, has "little if anything to do with federalism".[13] It is argued that in the Senate model, the upper house represents the SNE's electorates: "the specific community of the region from which the members of the federal chamber" come.[14]

In reality, it is not always clear which electorates individual Members of Parliament (MPs) represent, and whether this necessarily takes place in a second 'federal' chamber. Interestingly, in other countries, the first chamber is organized in the same way, where it is supposed to represent the national electorate. For example, in Switzerland, the Federal Assembly is composed of a National Council and a Council of States.[15] The National Council is composed of representatives of the Cantonal electorates rather than the national electorate because each canton constitutes an electoral constituency.[16] In Belgium, the Senate is (mainly) composed of representatives of the subnational parliaments, but the House of Representatives consists of members elected in constituencies that coincide with the provinces and remain within regional borders.

The question, then, is whether this qualifies as a representation of the SNE's electorate, and therefore, a weak representation of the SNEs, or as a weak representation of the national electorate. Further, in the case of the Belgian House of Representatives, would this mean only the electorate of the local provinces, or also the Region's electorate? This question is especially relevant where the cohesion index prefers a dialogue-fostering mixed body in which both national and regional interests are voiced.

Where the representation of the SNEs or their electorates is weak in the upper chamber, the lower chamber may compensate for this. For example, Canada has

11 Art. 69 Spanish Constitution. See Victor Ferreres Comella, *The Constitution of Spain* (Oxford, Hart 2013) 96–97.

12 Art. 55 Dutch Constitution.

13 Thomas O. Hueglin, 'Comparing Federalisms: Variations or Distinct Models?', in Arthur Benz and Jörg Broschek, *Federal Dynamics. Continuity, Change, & the Varieties of Federalism* (Oxford University Press 2013)43.

14 Doria (n 2) 10.

15 Art. 175(2) Swiss Constitution.

16 Art. 149(3) Swiss Constitution.

been named 'a case of pseudo-bicameralism',[17] with Senators appointed for life by the Governor-General.[18] For the indexes, however, what should be considered is the representation of the provinces' electorates in the House of Commons. This is because Art. 37 of the Canadian Constitution explicitly allocates several seats to each Province.

In Ethiopia, it is up to the SNEs to either appoint representatives or have them elected by the people.[19] In that case, the arrangement qualifies as a representation of the SNE. The reason is that there is a potential to have an institutional link, and it is up to the particular SNE whether it makes use of it or not.

An additional complication follows from the strong link between consociationalism and federalism. This occurs if power-sharing mechanisms are in place to protect the interest of national or minority groups that are situated within the boundaries of specific territorial SNEs. Ignoring this link leads to misconceptions. For example, the contention that Belgium is a decentralized system where regions do not participate in nationwide decisions[20] is far from the truth. Even if we disregard the point that representatives are linked with region-based parties, the fact remains that they are elected in districts that remain within the boundaries of the territorial SNEs. This determines their belonging to one of two language groups that largely overlap with the SNEs.

In practice, much will depend on the political party constellation. For example, representatives are bound to defend their electorates' interests, as defined by their political party, rather than the level where they are elected.[21] Thus, representatives of the regional electorate are less inclined to defend the SNEs' interest, if they have to account to central party leaders.[22] Conversely, if national representatives are elected on lists submitted by region-based parties, they are bound to be more receptive to subnational interests. However, the impact of external variables such as political parties should only be measured after the establishment of institutional cohesion and autonomy grades. This is discussed in Chapter 7. In this chapter, the basic institutional set-up is examined, which means that only institutional mechanisms will determine whether national, regional, or local interests are (supposed to be) voiced. To determine this, I use the following criteria:

1 Constituencies of cross-border SNEs: the assembly represents the central interest.
   To qualify as cross-bordering, a substantial number of constituencies must cross-border subnational territories. This was not the case in Belgium

17 Thomas O. Hueglin and Alan Fenna, *Comparative Federalism: A Systematic Inquiry* (Broadview Press 2006) 190.
18 Art. 24 and 29 Canadian Constitution.
19 Art. 61.3 Ethiopian constitution. However, it should be kept in mind that the Ethiopian House of Federation represents ethnic groups, not SNEs in themselves: Alem Habtu, 'Multiethnic Federalism in Ethiopia: A Study of the Secession Clause in the Constitution', (2005) *Publius: The Journal of Federalism* 330.
20 Mueller, 'Federalism and the politics of shared rule', 167–168.
21 Jean-François Aubert, 'Essai sur le fédéralisme', (1963) 80 *Revue de droit public* 412.
22 Palermo and Kössler, *Comparative Federalism*, 142.

BOX 3.1

Rules of thumb: central and subnational representation

Rules of thumb: an overview

I Institutional link: representation of the SNE

- representation of subnational executives in the central legislative assembly;
- representation of subnational parliaments in the central legislative assembly;
- involvement of the SNEs (parliaments or executives) in the procedure;

II Elections: representation of the national or the SNEs' electorates?

1 constituencies of cross-border SNEs: the assembly represents the central interest.
2 (most) constituencies coincide with subnational borders: the assembly represents the interests of the subnational electorate.
3 constituencies do not coincide with, but remain within subnational borders:

3.1 if there is an additional institutional factor that amplifies the subnational presence, the assembly voices the interests of the subnational electorate.
3.2 if there is an additional institutional factor that amplifies the central presence, the assembly voices the central interest.
3.3 if there are no additional factors, or they outweigh each other, the constituent's intent counts.

even before the electoral district Brussels-Halle-Vilvoorde was split, because this district was the only exception to the rule that electoral districts respect regional borders. In case of doubt, criteria 2 and 3 apply.

If local entities are the unit of analysis, this means that constituencies that cross local borders but remain within regional boundaries voice the central interest.

If regional entities are the unit of analysis and constituencies cross local borders but remain within regional boundaries, criterion 3 or 4 applies.

2 (most) constituencies coincide with subnational borders: the assembly represents the interests of the subnational electorate.

This is the case in Switzerland (mentioned above).

3 Constituencies do not coincide with, but remain within subnational borders:

3.1. If there is an additional institutional factor that amplifies the subnational presence, the assembly voices the interests of the subnational electorate.

Example 1: the assembly is divided into groups, with collective group rights or vetoes, that have traits that characterize the SNEs or largely overlap with their territories. In Belgium, both the House and the Senate are divided into a French- and a Dutch-language group.

Example 2: the subnational entities determine the electoral law and organize the elections. This is the case for the European Parliament.

Example 3: the electoral districts are mixed, which means that apart from smaller electoral districts, additional constituencies are established that coincide with the territory of the SNE as a whole. This is the case in Bosnia and Herzegovina, where the House of Representatives consists of two-thirds of members elected in the territory of Bosnia and Herzegovina, and of one-third of members elected in the territory of Srpska.[23] Within these territories, there are smaller constituencies, as well as an electoral district that coincides with the entire territory. For the Federation of BiH, seven out of 28 members are elected in the regional constituency; for Srpska five out of 14.[24]

Example 4: there is a fixed number of seats for each SNE, with (mostly) an equal number of representatives for each entity. This is an indication that the entities are represented because no regard is taken of the size of their populations.[25] For example, in the United States, the Senate is composed of two senators from each state.[26] This also applies in Switzerland, even though six cantons (formerly called half-cantons) for historical reasons are represented by one instead of two members.[27]

3.2. If there is an additional institutional factor that amplifies the central presence, the assembly voices the central interest.

This is, for example, the case if seats in the upper house are distributed on the basis of the outcome of national elections for the lower house. These are in turn based on cross-bordering electoral districts, or take place at an earlier moment in time. In Belgium, before 2014, seats in the Senate were allocated on the basis of elections for the House of Representatives. Electoral districts, however, reamined within regional borders. One exception was the electoral district Brussels-Halle-Vilvoorde. As argued above, however, one small exception is not enough to qualify as a representation of the central interest.

3.3. If criteria 3.1. and 3.2. do not solve the problem – there are no additional factors, or they outweigh each other – the constituent's intent counts. For example, if in bicameral systems the upper house is intended to serve as an upper chamber, then this is decisive.

23 Art. IV.2 Constitution of Bosnia and Herzegovina.
24 Art. 9.1. Election Law of BiH.
25 Palermo and Kössler, *Comparative Federalism*, 171.
26 Art. 3(1) US Constitution.
27 Art. 150(2) Swiss Constitution.

3.2 The Belgian case

3.2.1 Context

The reasons for selecting Belgium as a showcase for the indexes are explained in Chapter 2. Here, it is important to remind ourselves that Belgium is a fragmenting system. Over more than two decades (1970–1994), it evolved from a decentralized system with local entities, to a federal system consisting of regional entities (Communities and Regions) as well as local entities. Since then, two subsequent state reforms reinforced the devolving dynamics.[28] Two Flemish political parties, N-VA and Vlaams Belang, strive for independence. The N-VA's strategy is to do this gradually, with confederalism as the next step. The regional entities are selected as the units of analysis because of these developments.

Belgium is a multinational state, consisting of two major groups, the Dutch-speaking Flemings, and the francophone people in Wallonia and Brussels. There is also a minority German-speaking group, which makes up less than 1 percent of the population. Officially, Belgium consists of six entities, the Communities and Regions,[29] each with their own set of competences. The Flemish Community, the French Community, and the German-speaking Community were established to accommodate the Flemish demand for autonomy to protect their language and culture. The Flemish Region, the Walloon Region, and the bilingual Brussels Region were established following Walloon demands to take control over their economy. The territories of the Flemish Community and the Flemish Region largely overlap, and so do the French Community and the Walloon Region. The territory of the German-speaking Community is under the jurisdiction of the Walloon Region, and the French-speaking Community and the Flemish Community both have jurisdiction over unilingual (French and Dutch, respectively) institutions in Brussels territory. The institutions of the Flemish Community and the Flemish Region have merged, bringing some simplification. By contrast, the overlap of entities on Brussels soil has led to institutional complexity.[30]

Belgium is an example of distrust federalism. Federalism serves to manage multinational conflicts. Its institutional set-up in Belgium therefore revolves around the antagonism of the two major language groups. These groups largely overlap with the territories of the SNEs. The French-speaking group overlaps with the French Community but to a large extent also with the Walloon Region.[31] The Dutch-speaking group overlaps with the Flemish Community.

28 For an overview, see Patricia Popelier and Koen Lemmens, *The Constitution of Belgium. A Contextual Analysis* (Hart 2017) 15–32.

29 Art. 1 Belgian Constitution.

30 In more detail: Popelier and Lemmens (n 28) 97–100.

31 The Walloon Region, however, also has jurisdiction in the territory of the German-speaking Community and no jurisdictions in bilingual Brussels.

For the showcase of indexes, the Flemish Community and the German-speaking Community are selected. The first because it is the largest entity, due to the merger of institutions and competences of the Flemish Community and the Flemish Region; and because it overlaps with the largest language group. The German-speaking Community is selected because it is one of the smaller entities. This combination allows us to show how the indexes lay bare the characteristics of constitutional asymmetry, which is typical for more recent forms of multinational MTSs.

3.2.2 Results

The appendix shows the scores for the Flemish Community (FLC) and the German-speaking Community (GSC) for each index, as well as overall scores. These scores are converted to a value between 0 and 1, for easy comparison. Percentiles are used to qualify systems as low (0.0 to 0.33), medium (0.34 to 0.66), or high (0.67 to 1).

- forms of state
  The results in the appendix show that the Belgian institutional design is more interested in subnational autonomy than in cohesion. At the same time, it takes a different form when viewed from the angle of the FLC compared to the GSC.
  In its relation to the FLC, the system overall achieves a medium score for cohesion (0.58) and a high score for subnational autonomy (0.84). In the model presented in Chapter 2, this turns the system into a confederation. This is not quite the same as the confederal model presented by the political party N-VA.[32] That party's model, with almost all powers conferred to the major SNEs and the Belgian state remaining as a formal packaging, has more resemblance with a 'political association' (low cohesion, high autonomy).
  In relation to the GSC however, subnational autonomy is still the dominant factor. Subnational autonomy and cohesion achieve a medium score – although the GSC verges on a high autonomy score (0.58 for cohesion, 0.64 for autonomy). This means that Belgium is at the same time a confederation and a regionalized system, depending on the unit of analysis. This is true even if entities at the same (here: the regional) level are analyzed;
- constitutional asymmetry
  The different scores for autonomy allow us to calculate the asymmetry score. The spread between the autonomy scores is 0.20. It is the smallest in the category 'status' (0.13) and the widest in the category 'fiscal arrangements' (0.28).
  In follow-up research, the asymmetry-spread in other asymmetric MTS can be measured. This will allow us to assess how substantial this spread

32 https://www.n-va.be/sites/default/files/generated/files/dossier/definitieve_congresbrochure.pdf.

really is, compared to the average. The asymmetry spreads, in combination with the cohesion scores, will enable us to examine at which point the spread (and in which category) becomes so wide that constitutional asymmetry endangers constitutional stability;[33]

- indicators
  The detailed score tables show how low subnational autonomy for one indicator can be compensated by high subnational autonomy for another indicator. The indexes bring every indicator down to a value between 0 and 1, thereby giving each indicator equal weight. Follow-up study that analyzes the functioning of the system in practice, taking into account noninstitutional factors, will give us more insight into which indicators are the most relevant. If clear patterns emerge, this might enable us to reduce the model to a more practical size.
  For now, the indexes show which institutional features are the most dominant in the aggregate scores. This is useful for institutional engineering.
  For example, if one would like to make Belgium more stable, it is advisable to work on indicators where cohesion is low. In the category 'powers', this is clearly the allocation technique, based on the principle of exclusivity.
  For those who are mostly interested in subnational autonomy, the indexes show that there is still much growth potential for the GSC. For the FLC, autonomy is quite high for every aspect, except for subnational constitutional autonomy. The details within each index, however, reveal that the high score is often due to the strong involvement of the FLC or its electorate at the central level. If the idea is for each SNE to take everything in their own hands, then work can be done on matters such as fiscal arrangements. The weak representation of the GSC at the central level, examined in the category 'status', is also reflected in the other categories.
  Finally, Flemish nationalists that strive for Flemish independence will likely focus on institutions that have a high score for cohesion. The score is already low in the category 'status'. In the category 'powers', the cohesion score for allocation principles stands out. This, however, is largely due to the jurisprudence of the Constitutional Court and is, therefore, more difficult for political actors to change. For these actors, 'fiscal arrangements' is the most eye-catching category. It is the only category where the cohesion score outweighs the autonomy score, for both the FLC and the GSC. This brings us to the topics of categories and dynamics;
- categories
  The appendix shows the aggregate scores of these indicators per category. It is noteworthy that these categories show different patterns. Autonomy scores highest in the category of 'powers', whereas cohesion scores lowest in the category of 'status'. Cohesion achieves a medium score for 'status' and

33 For this risk: Maja Sahadžić, *Asymmetry, Multinationalism, and Constitutional Law* (Routledge 2020) 135–157.

'powers', but a high score for 'fiscal arrangements'. If fiscal arrangements are the only object of study, then Belgium indeed qualifies as a federation (type 2 for the FLC, type 1 for the GSC);

- dynamics
  The Belgian case only gives a snapshot of the Belgian institutional set-up at the current point in time. It does not consider how the system functions in practice. For example, subnational tax autonomy is hardly used in Belgium. The GSC has no need for it, with all the contributions coming from the central level. There was a strong belief that the French and Flemish Communities were not able to levy taxes, based on an erroneous opinion of the Council of State,[34] and the Special Finance Act is still based on that premise. Also, the evolution in the political party landscape, with the splitting of national parties into regional-based parties and the emergence of regionalist parties, strengthens the fragmenting dynamics.

  We need to study how the system works in practice, to assess which factors determine whether institutional mechanisms live up to their potential. These factors, however, will most likely also induce institutional change. A series of 'snapshots', then, will show the evolution of the system over time, and enable us to pinpoint which institutional features have been most crucial to effect these dynamics. This is further explained in Chapter 7.

34 The Council of State claimed that it would be contrary to the representation principle to raise taxes, because it is not clear whether persons residing in Brussels belong to the French or the Flemish Community, and it was contrary to the equality principle to exempt Brussels: Advisory Opinion of the Council of State, Division Legislation, No 21.104/2/V of 28 August 1991. However, these Communities only have jurisdiction over unilingual institutions in Brussels.

4 Status

'Status' concerns the identification of the SNEs. This includes their territorial boundaries, their involvement in central and intergovernmental decision-making bodies and procedures, and their powers of self-organization. It also includes the representation of the central government in governing institutions and procedures for voicing the general interest.

In this chapter, indicators are developed for all elements that determine the status of SNEs. First, I will develop indicators related to self-identification: how the constitution presents the form of state and the relation between the central government and the different tiers (section 4.1). The next sections focus on the different levels of public authority. At the constitutional level, both the actors and the procedures for federal constitution-making and the autonomy to adopt subnational constitutions are examined (section 4.2). At the legislative and the executive level, representation and voice in the central decision-making procedures are at stake (sections 4.3 and 4.4). This is also the case for international and supranational decision-making. Here, a general index for the conclusion of international treaties is followed by a specific index for EU Member States (section 4.5). These indexes measure the subnational voice in international and supranational decision-making and thereby cover three different levels of authority. The second index is relevant to all systems of multilevel governance. Presently, however, no supranational system is in place with a scope and impact comparable to that of the EU. For example, the African Union sometimes acts as a supranational organization, but lacks institutional embedding.[1] Therefore the index, for now, is designed for the specific situation of the EU. The last section is dedicated to the judiciary (section 4.6).

4.1 Constitutional self-definition

Constitutional self-identification may not be considered the most essential feature in the federalism index. More important is how the constitutional design facilitates the operation of the MTS. Yet, it is a meaningful aspect of dynamic

1 Thomas Kwasi Tieku, 'African Union: from practical federalism to fantasy union', in John Loughlin, John Kincaid and Wilfried Swenden (eds), Routledge Handbook of Regionalism and Federalism (Routledge 2013) 573–574.

federalism for at least three reasons. First, it has important symbolic value as an expression of the type of 'federal agreement' that the community envisages. For example, Requejo identifies constitutional recognition of national pluralism instead of an emphasis on unity as a basic feature of plural federalism that is necessary to accommodate multinationalism.[2] This is why recognition of the plurinational character is a variable in his unitarianism-federalism index, presented in Chapter 2.[3] Further, it provides courts – and other adjudicators – a legal basis to guide their decisions in federalism disputes. Finally, it constrains the legality of constitutional amendments and the scope for constitutional change through other means. Such changes have to conform to the basic structure that can be considered to be a core aspect of the State's constitutional identity.[4] This way, the constitution puts boundaries on how far along the gliding scale constitutional change may occur.

At the same time, self-definition is a difficult indicator for several reasons. One reason is that not all constitutions explicitly define the form of state. Some explicitly mention that they are federal states. Examples can be found in Argentina (Art. 1), Austria (Art. 2(1)), Belgium (Art. 1), Brazil (Art. 1), Ethiopia (Art. 1), Germany (Art. 20), Pakistan (Art. 1(1)), Russia (Art. 1), and Venezuela (Art. 4), amongst several others. Other systems do not explicitly define the structure of the political system in an entrenched constitutional text. The United States of America is one example. Other MTSs do not even have a written constitution – for example the United Kingdom. Next, constitutions sometimes use different or ambiguous terminology. In Chapter 2 it was discussed how 'federalism' can have different meanings for different people. Also, MTSs that are not considered to be 'true' MTSs were labelled 'hybrids' or 'regionalized systems', but these are not terms that constitutions generally use. Terms may also be country-specific, such as the 'Federal Commonwealth' in the preamble to the Australian constitution. Finally, the self-definition may appear contradictory. For example, several constitutions use the words 'federal' and 'unity' in one word. Art. 1 of the Iraqi Constitution states that the Republic of Iraq is 'a single federal' state, and the Constitution is 'a guarantor of the unity of Iraq'. Art. 2 of the Mexican Constitution refers to itself as a federation and as an indivisible Nation at the same time. The same kind of description is used in Art. 2 of the Nigerian Constitution.

For our purposes, however, these are not insurmountable problems.

First, preambles or case law may compensate for the absence of an explicit self-definition. For example, in Australia, the preamble refers to 'one indissoluble Federal Commonwealth'. Even though the preamble is not considered part

2 Ferran Requejo, *Multinational federalism and value pluralism* (Routledge 2005) 72–73.

3 Ferran Requejo, 'Federalism and democracy. The case of minority nations: a federal deficit', in Michael Burgess and Alain-G. Gagnon (eds), *Federal Democracies* (Routledge 2010).

4 In this sense: Markus Kotzur, 'Constitutional Amendments and Constitutional Changes in Germany', in Xenophon Contiades (ed), *Engineering Constitutional Change* (London, Routledge 2013) 127.

of the constitution, the High Court has – even if only reluctantly and secondary to other arguments – used it as a tool for constitutional interpretation, in order to protect both the Commonwealth and the States.[5] While the Canadian Constitutional Act 1867 does not explicitly define its structure, the preamble underlines the desire of the provinces to be 'federally united'. Moreover, federalism is read into the Constitution as a basic principle,[6] to guide the interpretation of constitutional provisions and to fill in gaps.[7] In Kenya, the Supreme Court has clarified that devolution rests on a unitary, rather than a federal system of government.[8]

More importantly, what we need to identify for the dimension of autonomy is whether the constitution in any way secures the autonomy of SNEs as a constitutional principle. Further, for the dimension of cohesion, it is necessary to identify whether it stresses unity or integrity as a whole, with respect for subnational autonomy. For example, the US Constitution does not define the United States of America as a federation, but it has been advocated that the duty to guarantee to every State a republican form of government[9] articulates the federalism principle. This is because this duty is considered to imply sufficient autonomy for self-organization.[10] From this perspective, it is not problematic if the Constitution stresses both autonomy and integrity. One is an indicator for the autonomy dimension, the other for the cohesion dimension, and both will have to be taken into account by the court.

Systems that self-define as federations often give constitutional status to the federated entities, as an essential component, or even identify (all or some of) the specific entities. However, elected local governments can be referred to as essential components of the state structure.[11] Art. 151 of the South African Constitution explicitly states that the South African government is "constituted as national, provincial and local spheres of government which are distinctive, interdependent and interrelated". Such clauses are more important than the precise term used by the Constitution.

5 Mark McKenna, Amelia Simpson and George Williams, 'First Words: the Preamble to the Australian Constitution', (2001) 24 *U. N. S. W. L. J.* 388–389.
6 Tsvi Kahana, 'Canada', in Dawn Oliver and Carlo Fusaro (eds), *How Constitutions Change: A Comparative Study* (Oxford, Hart 2011) 12–13, 37.
7 Eugénie Brouillet, 'The Supreme Court of Canada: The Concept of Cooperative Federalism and its Effect on the Balance of Power', in Nicholas Aroney and John Kincaid (eds), *Courts in Federal Countries: Federalists or Regionalists?* (University of Toronto Press 2017) 151.
8 Conrad M. Bosire, 'The Courts and Devolution. The Kenyan Experience', in Yonatan T. Fessha and Karl Kössler (eds), *Federalism and the Courts in Africa* (Routledge 2020) 134.
9 Art. 4(4) Constitution.
10 Deborah J. Merritt, 'The Guarantee Clause and State Autonomy: Federalism for a Third Century', (1988) 88 *Columbia Law Rev.* 2.
11 E.g., Art. 162 Belgian Constitution; Art. 7 Nigerian Constitution.

Measuring cohesion

Index 1.1 Cohesion index – self-definition

The constitutional act stresses the autonomy of the constituent entities, not integrity or co-government	0
The constitutional act stresses integrity, not co-government	1
The constitutional act defines the system as a form of co-government	2
The constitutional act defines the system in terms of both unity and co-government	3
Co-government is locked by an eternity clause	+1

To measure cohesion, we are interested in the extent to which the constitutional arrangement emphasizes the importance of the integrity of the entire system, with recognition of the autonomy of the SNEs. From the viewpoint of cohesion, the constitution ideally emphasizes the integrity of the system, but at the same time values co-government as a basic principle. Constitutions that use the term 'co-government' usually refer to the relationship between national, regional, and local entities. In the index, the term is used in a broad sense, regardless of the nature or number of entities involved. This means that it also applies if the constitution identifies the system as 'federal'. An emphasis on national integrity or indissolubility alone points to a centralist position, but is ultimately less cohesive, even if the constitution also operationalizes autonomy for SNEs.

An extra score is given if self-definition as a form of co-government is locked in an eternity clause. This means that this form is considered a basic value, or part of the constitutional identity,[12] and cannot be altered under this constitution. For example, in Brazil, Germany, and Russia, the basic federal form of state is shielded from revision by an explicit eternity clause.[13] In Germany, this also applies to the division of the Federation into Länder and their participation (in principle) in the legislative process.[14] There, the eternity clause ensures the apportionment of SNEs with state quality, minimal material and institutional autonomy, and financial independence.[15]

The term 'eternity clause' is used to include both codified and interpretative unamendability. The first refers to an explicit constitutional provision, the second to construction through courts or convention in the absence of an explicit clause.[16] For example, the Indian Constitution does not contain an express eternity clause, but the Indian Supreme Court developed the basic structure doctrine to invalidate amendments that change the basic structure of the Constitution.[17] It has not yet

12 Constance Grewe, 'Methods of Identification of National Constitutional Identity', in Alejandro Saiz Arnaiz and Carina Alcoberro Llivina (eds), *National Constitutional Identity and European Integration* (Cambridge, Intersentia 2013) 40.

13 Art. 60 para 4 Brazil Constitution; Art. 20 para 3 German Constitution; art. 135 Russian Constitution.

14 Art. 20 para 3 German Constitution.

15 Kotzur (n 4) 132; Jens Woelk, 'Germany' in Oliver and Faruso (n 6)149.

16 Richard Albert, *Constitutional Amendments* (Oxford University Press 2019) 140–158.

17 *Kesavananda Bharati v. State of Kerala* (1973) 4 SCC 225.

been clarified what precisely falls under the 'basic structure', but judges so far have included 'federalism' as an unamendable component of the system's basic structure.[18]

Other constitutions do not have an eternity clause, and some even prohibit a judicial lock. For example, in Pakistan, the Constitution declares "for the removal of doubt", that there is no limitation whatsoever on the power of the federal Parliament to amend any of the provisions of the Constitution.[19]

This extra score only applies when it is uncontested that the MTS's self-definition as co-government falls under an eternity clause. For example in Italy, the eternity clause protects the 'republican form of the state', but it is hotly debated what this 'republican form' involves, whether it includes the unity clause in Part I of the Constitution, and whether it prohibits the introduction of a federal system.[20] It also does not apply if, in multi-track systems,[21] amendment of the self-defining provision may be submitted to a rigid procedure, as is the case in Spain or Austria.[22] However, it does apply if amendments are possible under very strict conditions, but only if it is regarded as a proposal for a new constitution, as is the case in Russia.[23] Further, the extra score only applies if co-government is protected. This is not the case in Indonesia, where the eternity clause protects the unitary character of the system.[24]

Measuring autonomy

Index 1.2 Autonomy index – self-definition

A. Recognition	
The SNEs are not recognized as autonomous constituent parts of the system	0
The SNEs are recognized but the central government can abolish or merge them without constitutional amendment	1
The SNEs are recognized as autonomous constituent parts of the system	2
The particular SNE is recognized as autonomous constituent part of the system	3
Recognition of the SNEs is locked by an eternity clause	+1
B. Secession	
Secession is explicitly prohibited	0
There is no (written or unwritten) secession clause	1
There is a secession option, conditional to intergovernmental approval	2
There is a unilateral secession option, conditional to obstacles imposed by the central government or constitution	3
There is a unilateral secession option, unconditional, or conditional to requirements imposed by the subnational constitution	4

18 Mahendra Pal Singh, 'India', in Oliver and Fusaro (n 6) 20 at p. 183. See also Francesco Palermo and Karl Kössler, *Comparative Federalism: Constitutional Arrangements and Case Law* (Oxford, Hart, 2017) 41.

19 Art. 239(6) Pakistani Constitution.

20 Tania Groppi, 'Constitutional Revision in Italy', in Contiades (n 4) 211.

21 For this category, see Richard Albert, 'The Structure of Constitutional Amendment Rules', (2014) *Wake Forrest L Rev.* 937–942; Albert (n 16) 178–182.

22 In Austria, the procedure for a partial or total revision applies whenever principles of the Constitution, such as the principle of the federal state, are altered or seriously affected, Manfred Stelzer, 'Constitutional Change in Austria', in Contiades (n 4) 17.

23 Art. 135 Russian Constitution.

24 Art. 37(5) Indonesian Constitution.

For subnational autonomy, two sets of indicators are constructed.

The first examines whether the tier is recognized as a constituent part of the entire system. The autonomy of particular entities are even more secure if they are explicitly named. Examples of constitutions that mention (most) SNEs can be found, for instance, in Austria,[25] Belgium,[26] Bosnia and Herzegovina,[27] Ethiopia,[28] Malaysia,[29] Pakistan,[30] Russia,[31] or Switzerland.[32]

Some constitutions only mention some but not all SNEs. This may be the result of expansion over time. This is why the four 'founding' Provinces are mentioned in the Canadian Constitution,[33] while the other Provinces are based on an Act adopted following the procedure set out in Art. 146 of the Constitution. It may also be due to constitutional asymmetry. For example, the Italian Constitution mentions the five 'special' regions by name, but not the ordinary regions.[34] Other constitutions only mention categories of SNEs, but do not secure the existence of specific SNEs. For example, SNEs are not mentioned in Spain, where the Constitution provides for two tracks of creating self-governing Communities.[35] In Iraq, the Constitution defines itself as a federal system made up of a decentralized capital, regions, and governorates, as well as local administrations (Art. 116 Constitution). However, with regard to the Iraqi regions, it only recognizes the region of Kurdistan (Art. 117.1 Constitution). The Constitution provides a procedure for the recognition of other regions, but these have never been established.[36]

Recognition of the constituent parts is least guaranteed if the SNEs are not recognized at all. If they are recognized, the central government can decide to abolish an entity or to merge it with another. This is most often the case for local governments, but also occurs in traditional federal systems. In Germany, for example, the federal structure is protected from change, but the individual Länder are not.[37]

The second set measures the power to secede, which was also a variable in Requejo's unitarianism-federalism axis that was discussed in Chapter 2.[38]

25 Art. 2(2) Austrian Constitution.
26 Art. 2 and 3 Belgian Constitution – although meanwhile two small SNEs with (restricted) lawmaking powers have been established that are not recognized in the Constitution: the French Community Commission and the Joint Community Commission.
27 Art. 3 Constitution of Bosnia and Herzegovina.
28 Art. 47.1 Ethiopian Constitution.
29 Art. 1 Malaysian Constitution.
30 Art. 1(2) Pakistani Constitution.
31 Art. 65 Russian Constitution.
32 Art. 1 Swiss Constitution.
33 Art. 5 Constitution Act 1867.
34 Art. 116 Italian Constitution.
35 Art. 143 and 144 Constitution.
36 Bawar Bammarny, 'Federalism and Decentralisation in Iraq. A Country Study of Constitutional Asymmetry in Iraq', in Patricia Popelier and Maja Sahadžić (eds), *Constitutional Asymmetry in Multinational Federalism*, 256–259, 267–270.
37 Werner Heun, *The Constitution of Germany. A Contextual Analysis* (Hart 2011) 55.
38 Requejo (n 3).

Autonomy is at its strongest if the constitution also contains a secession clause, as this is an exit option that implies the promise of complete self-government. Such explicit secession clauses are more exceptional.[39] At the other extreme, we find those systems that prohibit secession. For example, the South African Constitution demands that all spheres of government preserve national unity and the indivisibility of the Republic.[40] For the same reason, secession is prohibited under the Russian constitution.[41] Sometimes, the prohibition is articulated in a more implicit manner. For example, the German constitution considers political parties that seek to "endanger the existence of the Federal Republic of Germany" as unconstitutional.[42] This is considered to include threats to the integrity of the state, such as activities with the aim of detaching part of the country.[43] Other constitutions remain silent, and courts have not elaborated on the topic. Usually, this means that secession is considered unconstitutional and requires specific constitutional reform. However, in the absence of a prohibition, we may expect that secession is a legitimate topic for public debate. This is the case in Belgium, where two political parties strive for Flemish independence.

Written or unwritten secession clauses can require the approval of the central government, or passively accept unilateral secession.

In one relevant case, the Canadian Supreme Court did not recognize a unilateral right to secession without principled negotiation. It did however recognize – conditional upon "a clear referendum result" – the right of an SNE to pursue secession, and the corresponding duty for the central government to enter into a negotiation process.[44] Written secession clauses also tend to impose consensual secessions, which implies intergovernmental negotiations and the approval of both the SNE and the central government. For example, the Northern Ireland Act declares that a majority of the people of Northern Ireland may vote for Northern Ireland to cease to be part of the United Kingdom and form part of a united Ireland instead. In that case, Parliament is required to discuss proposals to that effect, as agreed between the UK and Irish governments.[45] According to the Act on Greenland Self-Government, the people of Greenland can initiate the acquisition of independence. In this case, intergovernmental negotiations would commence for an agreement that ultimately requires the consent of the

39 For a (historic) overview, see Pau Bossacoma Busquets, *Morality and Legality of Secession* (Palgrave MacMillan 2020) 2012–2016.

40 Art. 41.1 South African Constitution.

41 Elena A. Kremyanskaya, Tamara O. Kuznetsova, Inna A. Rakitskaya, *Russian Constitutional Law* (Cambridge Scholars Publishing 2014) 70.

42 Art. 21(2) German Constitution. For similar provisions, see amongst others Art. 13(5) Russian Constitution.

43 Carl J. Schneider, 'Political Parties and the German Basic Law of 1949', (1957) 10 *Western Pol. Quarterly* 537.

44 Canadian SC, Reference re Secession of Quebec, 1998 CanLII 793 (SCC), [1998] 2 SCR 217, under (2) Question 1.

45 Art. 1 of the Northern Ireland Act 1998 and Schedule 1.

Greenland Inatsisartut as well as the Danish Folketing, after endorsement by a referendum.[46]

More extreme is the right to unilateral secession, but this as well can be conditional or unconditional. Conditional means that the central constitution requires specific thresholds or majorities within the subunit. Ethiopia is an example of this, where the constitution explicitly allows secession. However, it is conditional upon a two-thirds majority in the subnational legislative council to trigger the procedure and a majority vote in a (regional) referendum.[47] Likewise, the constitution of Saint Kitts and Nevis gives Nevis the right to secede, conditional upon a two-thirds majority in the legislative assembly of Nevis and a two-thirds majority in a referendum. This referendum is held after the public are given full details of the proposed new constitution.[48] Unconditional means that the subnational government can declare the unit's independence, by a majority or under the conditions set by its own constitution. For example, Art. 50 of the Treaty of the European Union (TEU) gives any Member State the right to withdraw "in accordance with its own constitutional requirements".[49] The negotiations that follow do not detract from the unilateral nature of the withdrawal, because the agreement concerns the relations with the EU after the withdrawal. The exit from the EU takes effect even if no agreement is reached. However, the Treaty does impose a timeline, which is an obstacle imposed by central rule.

4.2 The constitutional level

The central constitution is the level at which the most basic principles are laid down to determine the relations between the central and the subnational levels. From a cohesion perspective, it is important that these relations are designed by way of a common enterprise, and that the basic principles that underpin the political system are secured throughout the different units. From an autonomy perspective, the self-constituent capacity of the SNEs is at stake. Self-constituent capacity is the power to influence the constitutional arrangements that are applied to subnational governments.[50] This power comprises the involvement of SNEs in the amendment of the central constitution's provisions that affect their

46 Art. 21 of the Act on Greenland Self-Government of 12 June 2009.

47 Art. 39 Ethiopian Constitution. For a discussion, see Alem Habtu, 'Multiethnic Federalism in Ethiopia: A Study of the Secession Clause in the Constitution', (2005) *Publius: The Journal of Federalism* 313–335.

48 Art. 113 Constitution of Saint Kitts and Nevis.

49 Art. 50(1) TEU. This reference has brought secession into a procedural framework, where this was mostly absent in the Member States: Francesco Palermo, 'Federalism and the European Union: asymmetry, policies and some recurring federal dilemmas', in John Kincaid, *A Research Agenda for Federalism Studies* (Edward Elgar 2019) 201.

50 For more detail, and for the definitions, see Patricia Popelier, Nicholas Aroney and Giacomo Delledonne, 'Subnational Constitutions: an Introduction', in Patricia Popelier, Giacomo Delledonne and Nicholas Aroney (eds), *The Routledge Handbook of Subnational Constitutions and Constitutionalism* (Routledge 2021, forthcoming).

status, power, and financial capacity. It also includes the power to adopt their own subnational constitutions. This means that the constitutional amendment procedure as well as subnational constitutional autonomy are examined for this dimension.

What counts as the (relevant) central or subnational constitution is sometimes a grey zone. Not all MTSs have a supreme, written constitution – the United Kingdom is an example of this. Some MTSs defer the allocation of powers to other instruments, as discussed further in Chapter 8. This enables a more tailored form of subnational involvement, often resulting in constitutional asymmetry.

In the United Kingdom, three different models of devolution were created this way, with varying degrees of subnational autonomy. The degrees of autonomy reflect the different historical tracks and national sentiments in Scotland, Wales, and Northern Ireland.[51] The central administration's grip on the state structure is substantial, as the UK Parliament retains the power to legislate in devolved matters. Further, the Acts themselves may be amended by an Act of Parliament, with no institutional representation of the devolved entities.[52] This is put in perspective by the Sewel Convention, according to which the UK Parliament will not 'normally' legislate without the consent of the Scottish Parliament.[53] The Convention is only a political agreement, but the rule was added to the Scotland Act.[54]

In Belgium, the Constitution defines four categories of Community powers, but an organic law specifies which particular powers are transferred to the Communities and the Regions.[55] The organization of the Communities and Regions is also, for the most part, deferred to organic laws. For most Communities and Regions a special majority law is required, but the institutions and powers of the German-speaking Community (GSC) are regulated in an ordinary law adopted by a simple majority in the House and the Senate, where this entity is represented by only one senator. This illustrates the subordinate position of the GSC, which has no decisive voice in the regulation of its status and competences, in sharp contrast to the veto powers of the Flemish and French-speaking entities.

In Spain, the Constitution allows the State to transfer powers to Self-governing Communities by an Organic Act.[56] This was used in a symmetrization process for fast- and slow-track autonomous communities.[57] A transfer of

51 Stephen Tierney, 'Giving with one hand: Scottish devolution within a unitary state', (2007) 5 Int. J. Const. Law 741–742.

52 More so, with the adoption of the Scotland Act 1998, the previous overrepresentation of the Scottish people was corrected, *ibid* 748.

53 Although Scottish practice has turned this into a mechanism with centralizing effects, see *ibid*.

54 Art. 28(8) Scotland Act 1998 as amended by Art. 2 Scotland Act 2016.

55 Art. 127–130 Belgian Constitution.

56 Art. 150(2) Spanish Constitution.

57 Carles Viver, 'Spain's Constitution and Statutes of Autonomy: Explaining the Evolution of Political Decentralization', in Michael Burgess and G. Alan Tarr (eds), *Constitutional Dynamics in Federal Systems. Subnational Perspectives* (McGill-Queen's University Press 2012) 229.

powers through this channel leaves the central authority in control, as it may unilaterally withdraw such act.[58]

In cases such as Belgium, the question is which act is the unit of analysis for the central level dimension: the actual constitution, or the act to which a constitutional arrangement is deferred. A similar problem arises in multi-track systems, where the constitution provides different procedures for amending specific provisions. Hooghe *et al.* solve this by choosing the most authoritative track, i.e., the track that leads to the highest score for regional authority.[59] Here, however, we are also concerned with measuring cohesion. Therefore we choose the most important track or document, i.e., the one that applies to most (or the most important) provisions that determine the relationship between the central and subnational government on the issues of status, powers, and fiscal arrangements.

In Belgium, both the Constitution and organic laws are eligible for analysis. There are undoubtedly arguments to select the Constitution: it establishes the Communities and Regions, determines the policy domains in which competences can be assigned to the Communities and lays down the basic principles about their organization. The organic laws, however, determine how the Communities and Regions are organized and what powers they have. For the Regions, the Constitution merely states that regions are established, leaving everything else to organic laws. The Constitution assigns education, language, culture, and person-bound competences to the Communities, but the organic laws specify which exact matters within the policy domains of culture and person-bound competences are transferred to them. In 2011, an entire state reform took place through changes in the organic laws, without any constitutional amendment. For this reason, the organic laws are selected as the unit of analysis. These are mostly special majority acts, but in some cases they are ordinary Acts of Parliament. Ordinary acts might relate, for example, to the German-speaking institutions. For the cohesion index, the special majority acts are selected. This is because they apply to most and to the largest SNEs. For the autonomy index, the organic law is selected that applies to this particular SNE. For the Flemish Community (FLC), this is a special majority act; for the GSC it is an act adopted by an ordinary majority.

To identify the relevant act at the subnational level, the definition of a subnational constitution is the starting point. Elsewhere, we have developed the definition of subnational constitutions as "the basic documents for given SNEs which lay down entrenched basic rules on subnational identity, representative structures and organization of powers, fundamental rights and/or policy principles, and require the approval of the people or representatives of the SNE".[60]

58 Pau Bossacoma Busquets and Marc Sanjaume-Calvet, 'Asymmetry as a Device for Equal Recognition and Reasonable Accommodation of Majority and Minority Nations. A Country Study on Constitutional Asymmetry in Spain', in Popelier and Sahadžić (n 36) 450.

59 Our rule is to score the most authoritative route.

60 For this definition, see in more detail Popelier, Aroney and Delledonne (n 50).

In doctrine, an entrenched procedure is often used as a criterion to distinguish subnational constitutions from ordinary legislation.[61] This is not included in the definition, in order to secure maximum institutional flexibility. Instead, the procedural focus is on ownership, which is a more relevant criterion to measure autonomy: the subnational constitution must be approved by the SNE's population, directly or through its representatives.

The definition does not require that constituent power is exclusively in the hands of the self-governing people. It does not exclude fundamental texts that require the approval of the central authorities, which is even the case in a 'model' federation such as Switzerland,[62] or even bilateral negotiated instruments. What is decisive for a subnational constitution is that the act only applies to one particular SNE, and that this SNE, as an entity, has an important say in the act.

The definition, therefore, allows for variety in the involvement of SNEs. This does not mean that the difference between national and subnational constitutions is one of degree, rather than category.[63]

For example, the Spanish Statutes of Autonomy, which are negotiated for the separate SNEs, are considered subnational constitutional acts if they follow the fast-track procedure. In such a case they have to be approved by their Provincial Council.[64] Likewise in Russia, the acts regulating the 'status' of SNEs are adopted in mutual agreement between the federal and the subnational authorities.[65] By contrast, the UK devolution acts for Scotland and Wales are considered at the central level. The statutes are bilateral, but the devolved entity has no formal say, although it is consulted. The Sewel Convention has also been applied to the Scotland Act.[66] According to this convention, the UK legislator will only legislate in devolved matters with the consent of the Scottish Parliament. It remains for UK scholars to decide whether this convention is sufficiently solid to qualify as positive law. The Belgian laws on the institutions and powers of the Communities and Regions, on the Brussels institutions, and on the GSC, are considered central, not subnational constitutional arrangements. None of these entities are formally involved in the procedure.

When examining subnational constitutions, two systems are distinguished. The first category consists of systems that permit SNEs to create their own constitution based on their residual competences or as an inherent part of their autonomy. The United States is a prominent example. In the other category, SNEs are organized in a central act and may deviate from the blueprint on

61 For example Palermo and Kössler (n 18) 128.

62 Art. 51(2) Swiss Constitution.

63 As implied by Michael Burgess and G. Alan Tarr, 'Introduction: Sub-national Constitutionalism and Constitutional Development', in Burgess and Tarr (n 57) 6.

64 Art. 151 Spanish Constitution. See Gonzalo Gabriel Carranza, 'Subnational constitutionalism in Spain', in Popelier, Aroney and Delledonne (n 50).

65 Art. 66 Constitution. Kremyanskaya, Kuznetsova and Rakitskaya (n 41) 71–72.

66 Nikos Skoutaris, 'Subnational constitutionalism in the UK', in Popelier, Aroney and Delledonne (n. 50).

specific points. Belgium and South Africa are examples of this category. It is argued that in the latter case, SNEs have some constituent autonomy, but no subnational constitutional act or constitutional autonomy.[67] In the next section, in order to accommodate a wide institutional variety, this categorical distinction is not made but is merely reflected in the measurement of subnational constitutional autonomy.

Likewise, no distinction is made between systems that adopt one clearly identifiable constitutional act, and systems such as Canada's, with constitutional arrangements spread over multiple sources. This can include constitutional acts, acts of parliament, and unwritten conventions.[68] In the end, such distinctions are merely a matter of degree, since every written constitution is to some extent complemented by other sources. What matters is whether SNEs have some control over the constitutional rules and principles that govern their jurisdiction.

4.2.1 The central level: constitutional reform

Constitutional amendment procedures are designed to enable adjustments to new developments while safeguarding constitutional stability. This is usually translated in constitutional rigidity: constitutional change through amendments is possible, but a difficult procedure is in place. This balance has specific importance in federal systems, where flexibility is required to adjust the system to political power shifts. However, as Halberstam put it, the procedure must 'be stable enough to prevent radical centripetal or centrifugal shifts of power that undermines the principle of shared rule'.[69] This is further discussed in Chapter 8.

As mentioned in Chapter 2, federalism literature was traditionally mostly concerned with rigidity safeguards. In a theory of dynamic federalism, where the balance of powers is essentially a contested concept, the ability to change the constitution is equally important. For this index, we are therefore not so concerned with rigidity safeguards. Rigidity protects the status quo, which may benefit the integrity of the whole, the interests of the SNEs, or those of the central government. This depends on the current balance, and which changes are proposed. SNEs benefit from the flexibility to gain more powers, and from rigidity to protect acquired powers. At this point we are instead more concerned with the actors that have the power to change the constitution, and whether or not this is a common enterprise.

67 Patrick Peeters, 'The Constitutional and Institutional Autonomy of Communities and Regions in Federal Belgium', in Burgess and Tarr (n 57) 167, 170.

68 Gerald Baier, 'Canada: Federal and sub-national constitutional practices', in Burgess and Tarr (n 57) 175–176.

69 Daniel Halberstam, 'Comparative Federalism and the Role of the Judiciary', in Keith E. Whittington, R. Daniel Kelemen and Gregory A. Caldeira, *The Oxford Handbook of Law and Politics* (Oxford University Press 2010) 143. See also Ronald L. Watts, *Comparing Federal Systems* (Queen's University 2008) 161–162.

Measuring cohesion

Index 2.1 Cohesion index – constitutional reform

As a rule, the constitution is amended without direct or indirect involvement of SNEs	0
As a rule, the constitution is amended by institutional representatives of the SNEs only, or by representatives of the electorate of the SNEs only	1
The constitution is amended by the central authority after intergovernmental negotiations	2
The constitution is amended by a special majority, or by a central assembly in a mixed composition	3
Constitutional change requires a double majority	4
Constitutional change requires a double special majority	5
All SNEs are adequately involved in the constitutional amendment procedure	+1

Cohesion is not about central influence over constitutional change, but is concerned with creating a commitment to the stability of the system as a whole.[70] This means that negotiated change is more cohesive than unilateral change. In turn, unilateral change by SNEs is considered more cohesive than unilateral change by central representatives. This is because this requires, at least, horizontal intergovernmental dialogue. This can for example be the case in treaty-based political systems.

A special majority is considered more cohesive than a simple majority, because a simple majority may (almost or entirely) coincide with one particular group or a small coalition of groups. Cohesion is also promoted if the decisive body has a mixed composition, which means that it is composed of representatives of the national electorate, and a substantive number of representatives of (most of) the SNEs or their electorates.

A double majority implies: (1) a majority that voices the central interest; and (2) a majority that voices the subnational interest. A double majority is considered the most cohesive method. This is because it gives a veto right, and therefore, gives strong negotiating powers to all parts.

To decide whether the central or the subnational level is represented, or whether the central or subnational interests are voiced, I refer to the criteria in Chapter 3. For the Belgian showcase (see Appendix), this means that the extra score does not apply, even though constitutional revision requires a special majority in both the House of Representatives and the Senate.

These mechanisms, however, do not guarantee that a dialogue is in place in which all SNEs are adequately represented. Especially small SNEs risk being pushed aside. This is especially the case if the organization of the SNE is decided on a bilateral basis, as is the case in Spain. In Belgium as well, separate organic laws apply to the major entities (FLC, French Community, and Walloon Region), the Brussels Region, and the GSC. With only one representative in the Senate, the

70 'Federal togetherness', as Michael Jewkes, 'Theorising federal togetherness in multinational states', (2015) 15 *Ethnicities* 327–328 puts it.

GSC is not formally involved in the procedure, even where its own organic law is concerned. Even if the Constitution were taken as the relevant act, the situation would be the same. Therefore, an additional score applies if all SNEs are involved in the procedure. This gives them at least some weight in the decision-making process.

Measuring subnational autonomy

Index 2.2 Autonomy index – constitutional reform

The central government or national electorate can unilaterally change the constitution	0
The subnational electorate or their representatives can delay constitutional reform or create an extra hurdle	1
The SNE can, through a collective vote, propose or delay constitutional reform or create an extra hurdle	2
The individual SNE can propose or delay constitutional reform or create an extra hurdle	3
The subnational electorate or their representatives can veto constitutional reform	4
The SNE can, through a collective vote, veto constitutional reform	5
The individual SNE can veto constitutional reform	6
For hypotheses 1-6: the individual SNE can veto reform that applies to this particular SNE or can veto a very specific piece of reform that has an impact on the SNEs	+1
The individual SNE can exclude certain reforms from taking effect in its jurisdiction	+1
The SNE can, individually or through collective vote, propose constitutional reform	+1

For measuring subnational autonomy, the index focuses on the involvement of SNEs in the revision of the central constitution. This is especially important where the central constitution arranges in detail how the subnational public authorities are organized, as is, for example, the case in Belgium, India, and South Africa.

The Regional Authority Index serves as a starting point, but it is adapted for two reasons. First, the present index does not use the RAI's distinction between multilateral and bilateral control. Instead, the index distinguishes between central and subnational constitutions. This means that several bilateral instruments will be considered under the subnational dimension. For what remains, the same index applies to both multilateral acts and bilateral instruments, but there is a distinction made between collective and individual control. Individual control secures the entity's autonomy better than collective control and will more often occur in (negotiated) bilateral instruments. Second, the index is indifferent as to whether control takes place in the first or a second chamber, in order to remain as neutral as possible about institutional design.

Like the RAI, and as explained in Chapter 3, I make a distinction between regional vetoes: the SNE has more control if there is an institutional link. This means that the SNEs in Argentina, where constitutional reform requires a two-thirds majority in both Houses and Provinces are represented through direct elections,[71] have less control than the SNEs in systems that provide for an

71 Art. 30 Argentine Constitution.

institutional link. An example of this is Nigeria, where constitutional reform has to be approved by both Houses in Congress but also by two-thirds of the legislative assemblies of the States;[72] or in Russia, where all amendments to the federal structure in Chapter 3 of the Constitution need the approval of the legislative assemblies of at least two-thirds of the SNEs.[73]

If the veto is in the hands of the electorate, it does not matter so much whether this takes place through a referendum, or in the first or in a second chamber. What is important is that the criteria explained in the introduction to this chapter are used.

In the case of collective votes by the entities, I make no distinction between votes by institutional representatives in a chamber of the central Parliament or a majority vote of the separate entities. This means that the autonomy score for Germany and Nigeria is equal, even though in Germany, the SNEs exercise the collective vote (two-thirds majority) in the Senate that is composed of members of the Land governments,[74] whereas in Nigeria the legislative assemblies of two-thirds of the States have to give approval.

The SNE's ability to delay constitutional reform or create extra hurdles may come in different forms. One example is the possibility for five regional councils in Italy to trigger a popular referendum.[75]

The index distinguishes between three types of individual vetoes. One category concerns vetoes for reforms that concern this particular SNE. For example, territorial changes usually require the consent of the concerned entities.[76] In a second category, the amendment is adopted, but the new provision will not take effect in the SNE's jurisdiction. Both categories apply in Canada.[77] The third category gives the SNE a veto for reforms with a general scope.

In Belgium, the FLC is in the same position. Here, a special majority act is the relevant act. This requires a majority in each language group in the House of Representatives and the Senate. These language groups have traits that characterizes the FLC, and the overlapping French Community and Walloon Region respectively. This veto is given to the subnational electorate rather than the SNE itself. However, in the Senate, where the SNEs are represented, the Dutch language group consists of 35 Senators. The majority of these senators are representatives of the Flemish Parliament. As a result, the FLC cannot force institutional reform, but it does have the power to veto any change.

Finally, the index considers the right to initiate constitutional reform. This allows SNEs to take a proactive stance, instead of a defensive one. This can take three forms.

72 Art. 9.2. Nigerian Constitution.
73 Art. 136 Russian Constitution.
74 Art. 79(2) and 51(1) German Constitution.
75 Art. 138(2) Italian Constitution.
76 Palermo and Kössler (n 18) 186.
77 Art. 43 and 38(3) Canadian Constitutional Act 1982.

SNEs have an individual right to propose constitutional amendments in Canada and Russia.[78] In Italy, the Constitution is not explicit, but the Constitutional Court acknowledged the right of each subnational parliament to introduce constitutional law bills on subnational issues.[79]

In other systems, this is a collective right. For example in Ethiopia, where one-third of the subnational Councils can propose an amendment by a majority vote in each Council.[80] Another example is the United States of America, where two-thirds of the State legislatures can call a Convention for proposing amendments.[81] In Spain, the legislative assemblies of the Autonomous Communities may ask the Government to propose a bill or send a proposal to the Board of the House of Representatives, and then delegate a maximum of three Assembly members to defend it.[82] Considering that it is up to the central authorities to take the initiative into consideration, this has been called a 'mere proposal of initiative'.[83] The index does not apply to this case.

Finally, SNEs can have a right of initiative through the upper house. Examples can be found in Belgium, Ethiopia, and Pakistan.[84]

4.2.2 The subnational level: constitutional autonomy

At the subnational level, the question is whether the SNEs have the autonomy to decide on the basic rules that determine their functioning by adopting their own acts. Subnational constitutions were defined in the introduction to section 4.2.

Measuring cohesion

Index 3.1 Cohesion index – subnational autonomy

There is no homogeneity clause	0
There is no or no binding compliance check with the homogeneity clause	1
The central political or judicial authority executes a binding compliance check with the homogeneity principle, upon request or under specific conditions, and after the act has taken effect	2
The central political or judicial authority executes a binding compliance check with the homogeneity principle, upon request or under specific conditions, and before the act has taken effect	3
The central political or judicial authority automatically executes a binding compliance check with the homogeneity principle, after the act has taken effect	4
The central political or judicial authority automatically executes a binding compliance check with the homogeneity principle, before the act has taken effect	5

78 Art. 46(1) Constitution Act 1867; Art. 134 Russian Constitution.
79 Groppi (n 20) 207.
80 Art. 104 Ethiopian Constitution.
81 Art. V. US Constitution.
82 Art. 87(2) Spanish Constitution.
83 Abraham Barrero Ortega and Irene Sabrino Guijarro, 'Constitutional Change in Spain', Contiades (n 4) 304.
84 Art. 195 Belgian Constitution; Art. 104 Ethiopian Constitution; Art. 239(1) Pakistani Constitution.

To measure cohesion, we are concerned with uniformity or homogeneity clauses that require compliance with (central) constitutional provisions and principles that are deemed essential for the integrity of the federal entity, or its identity of the entire political system. We are also concerned with the mechanisms – political or judicial – that control compliance, before or after they take effect. This dimension is not about which system puts subnational constitutions in the most restrictive harness. Instead, homogeneity clauses have the purpose of fostering a coordinate relationship between the federation and the SNEs.[85] For this reason, the cohesion perspective is not so concerned with the detailed provisions which subnational constitutions need to adopt or may not deviate from. Rather, it is interested in the basic values and principles that underpin the political system, and that would be undermined if territorial subunits relished other principles. So, where the autonomy index assesses subnational constitutional space, the cohesion index assesses value homogeneity.

Examples of homogeneity are numerous. The US Constitution requires a 'Republican form of government',[86] which is not further specified, but seems to come down to a type of representative democracy.[87] Similarly, the Argentine Constitution imposes a 'republican, representative' form of government.[88] The Ethiopian Constitution goes somewhat further where it requires subnational constitutions to advance self-government and a democratic order based on the rule of law.[89] The South African Constitution is more detailed, where it refers to values of integrity, representative democracy, human dignity and human rights, constitutionalism, the rule of law, and cooperative government.[90] Likewise, the German Constitution requires the Land Constitutions to conform to the principles of a republican, democratic, and social state, governed by the rule of law. Even the EU is founded on basic values that the Member States must adhere to, enumerated in Art. 2 TEU, which are backed up by an enforcement mechanism laid down in Art. 7 TEU.[91]

Cohesion is least protected, if there is no homogeneity clause, or when compliance with such a clause is not secured. For example, both the US Supreme

85 Anna Gamper, 'Homogeneity and Democracy in Austrian Federalism: The Constitutional Court's Ruling on Direct Democracy in Vorarlberg' (2003) 33 *Publius: The Journal of Federalism* 46.

86 Art. 4, Section 4 US Constitution.

87 See James Madison in *The Federalist*, Paper No. 39. See also, amongst others, James Gardner, 'Subnational Constitutionalism in the United States', in Popelier, Aroney and Delledonne (n 50). Some scholars have argued in favor of a broader scope, for example by including the protection of basic individual rights, see Erwin Chemerinsky, 'Why Cases Under the Guarantee Clause Should Be Justiciable', (1994) 65 *U. Colo. L. Rev.* 851.

88 Art. 5 Argentine Constitution.

89 Art. 52(2)(a) Ethiopian Constitution.

90 Art. 143.2. South African Constitution, with reference to Art. 1 and Chapter 3.

91 For a discussion, see, amongst others, Oliver Mader, 'Enforcement of EU Values as a Political Endeavour: Constitutional Pluralism and Value Homogeneity in Times of Persistent Challenges to the Rule of Law', (2019) 11 *Hague J. on the Rule of Law* 133–170.

Court and Congress have shied away from enforcing the 'guarantee clause' for republican government.[92] In other MTSs, weak subnational constitutional autonomy explains the absence of a homogeneity clause, for example in Belgium. At the same time, there is a missed opportunity to develop a constitutional narrative appropriate to the creation of a constitutional identity that binds the different tiers.

Cohesion is best protected where a homogeneity clause is present and enforced through an automatic and binding *ex ante* check. The index does not distinguish between political and judicial control; what counts is whether the outcome is binding. 'Binding' also means that political intervention by the government to secure homogeneity is considered valid. For example, the Argentine Constitution allows the federal government to intervene in the territory of the Provinces to guarantee the republican form of government.[93] An automatic check means that no clause can escape control and is, therefore, more cohesive than control upon request, or under certain circumstances. For example, in South Africa, all subnational constitutions and constitutional amendments need the Constitutional Court's certification before they can take effect.[94] *Ex ante* control is considered more cohesive than *ex post* control because it avoids clauses that potentially undermine the system's cohesion taking effect.

Measuring autonomy

Index 3.2 Autonomy index – subnational autonomy

A. Content	
The SNE has no subnational constitutional autonomy	0
The SNE can make non-substantial arrangements in some of the four categories	1
The SNE can make non-substantial arrangements in all four categories	2
The SNE can make substantial arrangements in one of the four categories	3
The SNE can make substantial arrangements in some of the four categories	4
The SNE can make substantial arrangements in all of the four categories	5
B. Procedure	
The SNE cannot adopt its own constitution	0
The SNE can adopt its own constitution, but the central or other external authorities have a discretionary veto power	1
The subnational constitution can only take effect after a legality test by a central body or the central government can refer it to a central body for a legality test before it takes effect	2
The SNE can adopt its own constitution without central interference according to a procedure designed at the central level	3
The SNE can adopt its own constitution without central interference according to the amendment procedure decided by its own bodies	4

92 Luther v. Borden, 48 U.S. 1 (1849). See Gardner (n 87). For advocates of judicial enforceability in legal scholarship, see amongst many others: Chemerinsky (n 87) 849–880.

93 Art. 6 Argentine Constitution.

94 Art. 144.1 South African Constitution.

To measure the strength of the power to adopt subnational constitutions, two indicators are used: content and procedure.[95] The first one measures the scope of constitutional autonomy: to what extent SNEs can decide how to organize themselves. The second one measures to what extent SNEs can take these decisions autonomously. What is measured is the constitutional space that SNEs have, not the use they make of that space. Usage will mostly depend upon external, noninstitutional variables. For example, in countries such as Ethiopia subnational constitutional space is broad, but the SNEs make little use of it.[96] The 'constitutional space' is determined by the legal framework. It consists of constitutional provisions as interpreted or completed by other legal sources. For example in Brazil, the Supreme Court has reduced subnational constitutional autonomy beyond the explicit provisions of the federal constitution through the 'symmetry principle'. It held that state constitutions should make institutional arrangements that reflect those that apply at the federal level.[97]

For content, the indicators refer to the definition of subnational constitutions, which distinguishes four categories of constitutional matters: identity clauses, representative structures and the organization of public authority, fundamental rights, and policy principles.[98] Autonomy is strong if SNEs can make substantial provisions for all of these aspects of substantive constitution-making. Autonomy is weak if they can only act in some of these categories and only in a fragmentary way, for a limited number of minor issues.

In the United States for example, States have the residuary competence to adopt and revise constitutions, limited only by the republican guarantee clause.

By contrast, Belgian Communities and Regions are only allowed to deviate from central provisions for a limited number of issues, related to elections, the Parliament, and the Executive. These deviations are enumerated in a federal special majority law and generally have specific conditions and limitations.[99] The FLC has coordinated all punctual deviations in one 'Special Decree'. This Act, with barely 28 articles on the Flemish Parliament and Government, shows how meagre and dispersed subnational constitutional autonomy in Belgium really is.

In India, with the exception of Jammu and Kashmir, subnational constitutional autonomy is reduced to the decision to change the parliament into a unicameral or a bicameral system.[100] This does not pass the threshold for subnational

95 See Popelier, Aroney and Delledonne, (n 50). What follows in this paragraph, is based on the indicators used in that chapter, but is further elaborated here.

96 Yonatan T. Fessha, 'Constitutional Déjà vu: Reading Subnational Constitutions in Ethiopia', in *ibid.*

97 See Marcelo Labanca Corrêa de Araújo, 'Subnational constitutionalism in Brazil', in *ibid.*

98 Section 3.2., introduction paragraph.

99 Compare the US chapter (by J. Gardner) and the Belgium chapter (by myself) in Popelier, Aroney and Delledonne, (n 50).

100 Art. 169(1) Indian Constitution.

constitutional autonomy, apart from one minor aspect in one category. More significant is the authorization for Scotland and Wales to make provisions about, for instance, elections and officeholders.[101]

In South Africa, Provincial Constitutions must remain consistent with the central Constitution. The central Constitution organizes the Provincial institution in extensive detail. The Provinces can only deviate from the constitutional provisions regarding legislative and executive structures and procedures and they may provide for a traditional monarch.[102] They can also adopt a Provincial Bill of Rights, but only within the range of their own competences, and such a document must be consistent with the national constitution.[103] Further, they can add some provisions related to Provincial identity (such as a flag) and incorporate policy principles within their range of powers.[104] According to the South African Constitutional Court, the mandate to organize their own governments gives the Provinces 'significant' constituent powers.[105] At the same time, the Court accepts deviations of 'form', not of 'substance'.[106] It is up to the Court to interpret whether this amounts to 'substantial' arrangements or not. For example, it argued that the Provincial Constitution can regulate the number of the Members of a Provincial Legislature, but that the electoral system goes beyond 'form' and affects the 'substance'.[107] Scholars hold that this narrow interpretation has turned subnational constitutional autonomy into 'an empty shell'.[108]

Procedural power is at its strongest where SNEs can take the initiative and adopt the constitution with little or no involvement of the central authorities. This is the case in the United States of America, for example.

An intermediate form applies where the SNEs can adopt and amend their own constitution without the involvement of the central authorities, but following a procedure laid down in a central act. For example, in Belgium, the constitution requires a two-thirds majority for subnational constitutional provisions, provided that a majority of the members of the Parliament are present. The central government cannot interfere in this process.[109]

Procedural subnational autonomy is weak when external authorities must give preapproval, and therefore, exercise a veto right. This is more likely to occur in

101 Skoutaris (n. 66).
102 Art. 143 South African Constitution. See Nico Steytler, 'Provincial Constitutions in South Africa: an Empty Promise', in Popelier, Aroney and Delledonne, (n 50).
103 Ex Parte Speaker of the KwaZulu-Natal Provincial Legislature: In Re Certification of the Constitution of the Province of KwaZulu-Natal, 1996; 1996 (4) SA 1098 (CC); 1996 (11) BCLR 1419 (CC), par. 24–26.
104 See Steytler (n 102).
105 *Certification of the Constitution of the Western Cape, 1997* [1997] ZACC 8, par. 8.
106 *Ibid* par. 39. See Steytler (n 102).
107 *Certification of the Constitution of the Western Cape, 1997* [1997] ZACC 8, par. 49 and 51.
108 Steytler (n 102).
109 Art. 118, par. 2 and art. 123, par. 2 Constitution.

holding-together federations: it presupposes that constitutions do not preexist.[110] Here, a distinction is made between discretionary veto powers and judicial oversight. The latter is less intrusive because it will only hinder a subnational constitutional provision to come into force because of legal arguments, even if this leads to intense scrutiny. The South African Constitutional Court can give certification after examining whether the text was adopted by at least two-thirds of the members of the provincial legislature and complies with Art. 143 of the Constitution. This kind of certification implies that the provision is consistent with the constitution and the values enshrined in it.[111] The consistency test enabled it to reject the entire draft constitution that was drafted by the Province of KwaZulu-Natal.[112] The index only takes into account judicial oversight by a central judicial body. If judicial review is exercised by a subnational constitutional court, then this forms part of the entity's constitutional autonomy.

4.3 The legislative level

Representation of SNEs in the central legislative assembly is usually examined from the perspective of shared rule, to assess subnational autonomy that influences nationwide decisions. If SNEs have a say in the parliamentary procedure, they can impact on central decisions that affect them. Usually, the second chamber is the focal point of activity here. However, in some countries, SNEs can intervene in the parliamentary procedure without the involvement of an upper chamber, or they have some representation in the unicameral Parliament. Representation of SNEs in the central parliament is less frequently considered from a cohesion perspective, other than to point out the inefficiency of upper chambers for sub-state representation.[113] Yet, as Mueller remarks, "representation may force the SNEs to think beyond their regional boxes and consider the interests and sensibilities of other regions, too. A single region can only very rarely hold its national government accountable on its own, so horizontal alliances will emerge. Ideally, this contributes to inter-regional solidarity and strengthens societal cohesion".[114]

To measure autonomy, indexes are developed for both the central and the subnational authorities, as was the case for the constitutional level. By contrast, there is no separate cohesion index for the subnational level. These safeguards overlap with the ones that are included in other indexes.

The index is mostly interested in the body that has lawmaking capacity, which means that it adopts decisions with a general scope that are not merely the

110 Burgess and Tarr (n 57) 8.

111 Art. 144 South African Constitution.

112 *Certification of the Constitution of the Western Cape, 1997* [1997] ZACC 8. See Steytler (n 102).

113 Francesco Palermo, 'Beyond Second Chambers: Alternative Representation of Territorial Interests and their Reasons', (2018) 10 *Perspectives on Federalism* 49–70.

114 Sean Mueller, 'Federalism and the politics of shared rule', in Kincaid (n 49) 162.

implementation or execution of laws adopted elsewhere, without any discretion. We are, however, not yet concerned with the nature of legislative powers: administrative federalism and administrative decentralized systems are discussed in Chapter 5, under Indexes 12.1 and 12.2.

Usually, laws are adopted by elected parliaments that give legitimacy to these decisions. However, this is not always the case or does not always happen exclusively. For example, Germany's Bundesrat, as part of the German Parliament, is composed of representatives of the Länder executives.[115] Another example is the EU, where the Council of Ministers consists of members of the national governments.[116]

In the EU, the Member State can also decide to send a member of the subnational government. In this index, this applies as a representative of the SNE (the Member State in this case). Members of subnational governments are there to represent the Member State as a whole, and usually have a mandate for this purpose. What this means for the relations between the central and subnational governments of the Member State, is examined further in Indexes 9.1 and 9.2.

'Hybrids' also exist, with mixed compositions representing both the executives and parliaments of the SNEs.[117]

At the central level, no distinction is made between representatives of subnational parliaments and representatives of subnational executives. The reason is that the indexes measure cohesion and autonomy, not legitimacy. By contrast, electoral representativeness is considered at the subnational level. This is because the legitimacy provided by the popular vote puts SNEs in a stronger position towards the central government. Further, elections give protection against central government interference in the composition of the subnational body.

Finally, the legislative procedure may involve intergovernmental bodies. In many systems, they compensate for the inadequacy of second chambers.[118] For example, in Italy, there is a duty to consult the Standing Conference for the Relations between the State and Regions for measures that could affect regional competences. This body consists of the Italian Prime Minister and the Presidents of the regional executives.[119]

Next, the procedure can involve several bodies. For example, even if the central Parliament consists of two houses with one representing the SNEs, separate subnational legislatures may also interfere in the lawmaking procedure. This is the case in Belgium.[120] In the EU, laws are, as a rule, made by the Council of Ministers and the European Parliament jointly.[121] However, proposals are

115 Art. 51 German Constitution.
116 Art. 16(2) TEU.
117 Art 95 Russian Constitution; art. 60–61 South African Constitution. See Palermo and Kössler, (n 18) 176–177.
118 Palermo and Kössler, (n 18) 177.
119 *Ibid* 177.
120 Art. 143, §2 Belgian Constitution and art. 32 Ordinary Law on the Reform of the Institutions.
121 Art. 289 and 294 Treaty on the functioning of the European Union (TFEU).

initiated by the European Commission, and national parliaments can intervene through the Early Warning Mechanisms. These mechanisms can be used by national parliaments to create an obstacle in the procedure if they find the proposal to contravene the subsidiarity principle.[122] In these cases, the most relevant procedure is chosen, i.e., the one that applies as a rule. For example in Belgium, the Senate hardly has any legislative powers left. Therefore, the unicameral procedure is examined, with the possibility for subnational parliaments to interfere with a motion of conflict of interest, except if the bill concerns personal taxes. If several modes of intervention apply as a rule, what counts is the one that is most relevant for the index. For example, in the autonomy index, the autonomy of the Member States is better guaranteed by the Council of Ministers than by the national parliaments under the Early Warning Mechanism.

Measuring cohesion

Index 4.1 Cohesion index – the legislative level

As a rule, laws are adopted by representatives of the national electorate only	0
As a rule, the constitution is amended by institutional representatives of the SNEs and/or representatives of their electorates only	1
One of both, but representatives of the SNEs or their electorates (hyp. 1), or respectively, representatives of the national electorate (hyp. 2) have to be consulted, have suspensive veto rights or can create other hurdles	2
As a rule, laws are adopted by representatives of the national electorate and representatives of the electorate of the SNEs	3
As a rule, laws are adopted by representatives of the national electorate and institutional representatives of the SNEs	4
Important matters are adopted by a mixed body, with representatives of the national electorate as well as representatives of the SNEs or their electorates	+1

Participation of SNEs in the central decision-making procedure can increase legitimacy and cohesion if it enables a multilateral dialogue. The Swiss constitution is very outspoken in this respect. That constitution clearly states the participation of the Cantons in the legislative process as a principle, as well as the duty to inform and consult them. Cohesion, then, is not only about the participation of the SNEs in the legislative process; it also requires that all parties enter into a dialogue based on mutual respect. This then means that all parties are fully informed, attentive to particular entities' needs, but also committed to the common interest. Hence, to provide "the glue to hold the federation together", the central representative institution should enable effective common action while also representing the internal diversity within the MTS.[123] At the same time,

122 Art. 6–7 Protocol No 2 on the application of the principles of subsidiarity and proportionality.

123 Watts (n 69) 135.

the central bodies also need representation. If not, so-called 'state capture' occurs, where SNEs use their power to shift costs upwards.[124]

A more difficult question is how to organize this at the lawmaking level. Again, centralism is not a synonym for cohesion. The most centralist option, where representatives of the national electorate decide, is not cohesive. This is because it leaves no room for a discussion that takes account of the specificity of subnational interests. The opposite hypothesis, where representatives of the SNEs' institutions or electorate make the decisions, is only slightly more cohesive: it ensures horizontal intergovernmental dialogue, but the general interest is ignored. For example, in Venezuela, the National Assembly consists of representatives of the SNE's electorate – they are elected in each federal entity – as well as institutional representatives of each SNE.[125] The president can create hurdles, for example by asking the National Assembly to reconsider, or by requesting a ruling from the Supreme Tribunal of Justice. However, the president cannot veto the law.[126]

Cohesion is not merely the opposite of autonomy. For autonomy, it is sufficient that subnational representatives have a say in matters that affect SNEs. For cohesion, it is more useful to involve them in every central lawmaking activity, so that they appreciate the central perspective. Then again, there is a risk that they start to sympathize more with the central government and lose perspective of subnational interests.[127] It is, therefore, crucial to safeguard an institutional link with the SNEs. National representation combined with the institutional representation of the SNEs is therefore the best device for facilitating cohesion. Again, to determine whether the central or the subnational interest is represented, the rules of thumb presented in Chapter 3 apply.

A permanent dialogue is more cohesive than one limited to those matters that directly affect SNEs. Therefore, the relevant procedure is one that applies to most legislative matters. This means that symmetrical bicameralism, where, as a rule, all matters are decided by both houses, is more cohesive than asymmetrical bicameralism, where the second chamber only interferes in specific matters. Veto rights that give SNEs the possibility to interfere in the legislative process are less cohesive than co-legislating. As a rule, such veto rights start an intergovernmental discussion. However, interference in the middle of the legislative process is more conducive to conflict than constructive lawmaking, where the SNEs are informed and involved from the start. Finally, joint intergovernmental discussions are preferable to separate discussions by representatives of the different levels, as the former enables a more direct dialogue. For example, in Germany, a joint committee that consists of members of the Bundestag and the Bundesrat can be convened for joint consideration of bills.[128]

124 Mueller (n 114) 162.

125 Art. 186 Constitution of Venezuela.

126 Art. 214 Constitution of Venezuela.

127 Eghosa Osoghae, 'Purpose and functioning of the Senate', in Bertus De Villiers, Frank Delmartino Frank and André Alen (eds), *Institutional Development in Divided Societies* (Human Rights Research Council, 1998) 219–220.

128 Art. 77(2) German Constitution.

Measuring autonomy

Index 4.2 Autonomy index – the legislative level

A. Representation in the central lawmaking body	
The SNE or its electorate has no voice in the central lawmaking procedure	0
The electorate of the SNE can initiate laws or create hurdles	1
The SNEs can initiate laws or create hurdles through collective vote	2
The SNE alone can initiate laws or create hurdles	3
The electorate of the SNE can veto the law	4
The SNE can veto the law through a collective vote	5
The SNE alone can veto the law	6
The SNE is consulted in matters that affect its interests or competences	+1
The SNE's representatives are bound by the instructions of the SNE	+1
B. Subnational representation	
The SNE has no lawmaking assembly, or an assembly appointed by the central government	0
The SNE has an assembly partly appointed by the central government	1
The SNE has an indirectly elected assembly	2
The SNE has a directly elected assembly	3
For all except the first hypothesis: The subnational assembly, as a rule, makes laws without prior central oversight, but with central oversight *ex post*	+1
For all, except the first hypothesis: The subnational assembly, as a rule, makes laws without central oversight	+2
The SNE's lawmaking assembly cannot be dissolved by a central body, unless in exceptional circumstances	+1

To measure autonomy, two indexes are represented. One is for shared rule, and the other for self-rule.

For shared rule, the Regional Authority Index distinguishes between multilateral and bilateral lawmaking. Here, this distinction is not made. For either procedure, what matters is whether the SNE is involved, and whether it has a decisive voice. The relevant procedure is the one that applies as a rule in matters that affect SNEs, but over which they have no exclusive competences.

The index refers to the representation of the SNE in itself, its electorate, or the national electorate, according to the rules of thumb explained in Chapter 3. Autonomy is better safeguarded if there is an institutional link with the SNEs. An additional score applies if representatives are bound by the instructions of the SNE. In Germany, this rule is enforced by the Constitutional Court.[129]

Another distinction concerns the type of involvement. In some systems, SNEs can intervene in the procedure and create hurdles. For example, the subnational parliaments in Belgium can submit a motion that signals a conflict of interests, leading to a negotiation procedure.[130] In Germany, the Bundesrat has (in principle) suspensive veto powers. Moreover, a suspensive veto that is passed by a

129 106 BVerfGE 310, 328. See Heun (n 37) 69.

130 Art. 32 Ordinary Law on the Reform of Institutions.

two-thirds majority can only be overruled in the Bundestag by a two-thirds majority.[131]

At best, the SNE has decisive veto power. According to the German Constitution, the suspensive veto is the rule, but the Constitutional Court has interpreted constitutional provisions in such a way that a decisive veto has become the rule.[132]

In other cases, SNEs are consulted in matters that particularly affect their interests or competences. Explicit provisions may express a duty to consult the SNE on matters that affect subnational policies. However, courts may also lay down a general duty to consult. For example, the Belgian Constitutional Court imposes a general duty to involve other entities in the lawmaking procedure, if the law would make it impossible or excessively difficult for these entities to exercise their own powers.[133] This principle returns as a measure of cohesion in Index 13.1. In reality, the Constitutional Court is usually satisfied if the other entity is consulted.

For self-rule, both representation and a decisive voice also matter.

A directly elected assembly is more autonomous, for the reasons stated above. Next, the assembly is most autonomous in the absence of any central oversight, and when it cannot be dissolved by a central body. For example, in Austria and Portugal, the President can dissolve the legislature of, respectively, a Land or autonomous region.[134] In some systems, the central authority can dissolve subnational legislative assemblies only in exceptional circumstances, e.g., in the case of grave violations of the law or for reasons of national security, or to disentangle political deadlock.[135] This specific case is removed from the present index, but will return in Index 13.2.

By 'central oversight' the index does not refer to those situations where the central authority preempts subnational laws on the basis of its concurrent powers. Instead, it refers to systems where the central authority can exercise opportunity control (as opposed to legality control) to approve or annul a decision. Here, a system of prior oversight is more intrusive than a system of oversight *ex post*, which does not prevent laws from taking force and will most probably take place on request, although not on a routine basis.

Central oversight does not count if it is limited to a particular type of laws and not to the bulk of subnational laws. It does apply if subnational laws must be approved by a body that is appointed by, or otherwise representative of, the central government, or if such body can veto the law. This is, for example, the case in Canada, where lieutenant governors, appointed by the

131 Art. 77(4) German Constitution.

132 Heun (n 37) 70–71.

133 E.g., Const. Court No 70/96, 11 December 1996; Const. Court No 173/2004, 3 November 2004; Const. Court No 91/2014, 12 June 2014.

134 Art. 100(1) Austrian Constitution; Art. 234 Portuguese constitution.

135 Art. 126 Italian Constitution; Art. 112 Pakistani Constitution.

Governor-General and paid as provided by the Parliament of Canada,[136] give the Royal Assent. This means that (s)he can give force to the subnational law, suspend it, or veto it.[137]

For the index, it does not matter whether much use is made of oversight rights or not.[138] What matters is the institutional setup. External factors will determine the use that is made of instruments that provide autonomy, centralization, or cohesion. Moreover, even if veto rights are not used, they can still give this body an influential role to avoid being vetoed afterwards. Here especially, the representative quality of the subnational assembly is important: arguably, the central government will show more restraint if the law is voted by an assembly elected by the people.

4.4 The executive level

In a globalized and industrialized world, policymaking has become increasingly complex. This has put the executive in a dominant position. In the previous category, intergovernmental negotiations were already taken into account as part of the parliamentary procedure. Here, the focus is on the executive that takes decisions with a general scope, without the involvement of legislative assemblies.

The index applies to both Presidential and parliamentary systems.

In the index, '*President*' points to the head of state that is also the head of government. This means that the index only applies to Presidents with actual power, not what Friedrich calls mere 'figureheads'.[139]

Often such a President has his or her own legitimacy based on elections, but this is not necessarily so. For example, in Iraq, the President is elected by the Council of Representatives.[140] For the indexes, however, the Iranian Council of Ministers, not the President, is the relevant body. This is because it is the Council that plans and executes the general policy and implements laws.[141]

The '*executive council*' covers both governments and presidencies consisting of several Presidents. For example, the presidency of Bosnia and Herzegovina is composed of three members, one Bosniac, one Croat, and one Serb.[142] Here again, the Council of Ministers is the most relevant body, but the Presidency plays a role as the nominating body.[143]

136 Art. 58 and 60 of the Constitution Act 1867.

137 Art. 55, 56, 57, and 90 Constitution Act 1867.

138 For Canada in particular, it has been held that the role of the lieutenant governor is more important than is usually stated, see Alfred T. Neitsch, 'A Tradition of Vigilance: The Role of Lieutenant Governor in Alberta', (2007) *Canadian parliamentary Review* 19–28.

139 Carl J. Friedrich, *Constitutional Government and Democracy: Theory and Practice in Europe and America* (Blaisdell Publishing Company 1968) 207.

140 Art. 70 Iraqi constitution.

141 Art. 80 Iraqi constitution.

142 Art. V Constitution of Bosnia and Herzegovina.

143 Art. V(4) Constitution of Bosnia and Herzegovina.

By 'appointed or elected by a body, or accountable to', the index covers the entire process of nomination, appointment, or election. Where applicable, it also covers accountability, including the vote of confidence. A mixed body is one where both subnational and central-level bodies are involved in the entire process, in a meaningful way. In several monarchies, the King appoints the Ministers according to the Constitution. If this is only a formal act and what really counts is the vote of confidence by the House of Representatives, then only the House of Representative is taken into account.

The role of political parties in the selection of executive members is not covered by the index, unless legal texts explicitly involve them. Again, the impact of political factors on the institutional design is only measured in the second step.

Measuring cohesion

Index 5.1 Cohesion index – the executive level

The central executive President or executive council is elected by the national electorate or appointed by or accountable to a central body representative of the national electorate only	0
The executive President or executive council is elected by a majority of the subnational electorates, or appointed by or accountable to bodies representative of the SNEs or their electorates	1
The executive President or executive council is appointed by or accountable to a mixed body representing both the national electorate and the SNEs or their electorates	2
The executive council is composed in such a way that there is a geographical spread that is representative for particular SNEs only; or in such a way that only particular groups with traits characteristic of SNEs are represented; or consists of representatives of particular SNEs only	+1
The executive council is composed in such a way that there is a geographical spread that is representative for all SNEs; or in such a way that all groups with traits characteristic of SNEs are adequately represented; or consists of representatives of all SNEs	+2
The executive council is a mixed body, composed of representatives of the national electorate as well as representatives of the SNEs or their electorates, or of members of groups with traits characteristic of SNEs	+3
SNEs are consulted for or co-decide in matters that require intergovernmental coordination	+1

Cohesion is assumed to prosper most if decisions are taken in an open dialogue between representatives of the different tiers.

There is no such dialogue if executive measures are issued by a central-level body only. This is the case if the President or an executive council is appointed by or accountable to a central body or elected by the national electorate. Such an executive council is not composed in such a way that the SNEs are represented, directly or indirectly.

There is more potential for dialogue if the President or executive council is elected based on electoral districts that coincide with the SNEs. For example, according to Friedrich, the US President is not elected by a majority of the whole people, but by a majority of state majorities, and this impacts upon the composition of the government. The President will select persons to government that are satisfactory to the Senators of his or her political party.[144]

Dialogue is promoted on a continuous basis if the executive body consists of members that are representative of the SNEs or have identity traits that largely overlap with the SNEs. For example, in Belgium, the Constitution imposes language parity upon the federal government.[145] In Switzerland, care must be taken that the Federal Council appropriately represents the various geographical and language regions.[146]

From a cohesion perspective, it is preferable that the executive council does not consist only of representatives of subnational executives, but also includes representatives of the central level, in order to defend national interests. In Switzerland, the members of the Federal Council are elected by the Federal Assembly,[147] which is composed of a National Council and a Council of States.[148] This, however, does not come down to an appointment by a mixed body, because the National Council itself is composed of representatives of the Cantonal electorates: each canton constitutes an electoral constituency.[149]

In some cases, cabinets are not composed as mixed bodies for day-to-day decisions but convene in that way or in conferences with representatives of subnational executives, to discuss matters that require intergovernmental coordination. For example in South Africa, an 'extended cabinet', including the Provincial prime ministers and representatives of local government in addition to the central government, convenes twice a year. This extended cabinet determines the central government's yearly program of action and reviews progress.[150] In other cases, representatives of subnational executives are involved without a decisive vote. Consultative and co-decision mechanisms can coexist. In South Africa, apart from the extended cabinet, the President's Coordinating Council convenes regularly, and at least twice a year. It considers matters of national interest or effects the implementation of national policy in Provincial and local entities, without a voting procedure.[151]

144 Friedrich (n 139) 206.
145 Art. 99 Belgian Constitution.
146 Art. 175(4) Swiss Constitution.
147 Art. 175(2) Swiss Constitution.
148 Art. 175(2) Swiss Constitution.
149 Art. 149(3) Swiss Constitution.
150 Derek Powell, 'Constructing a Developmental State in South Africa: The Corporatization of Intergovernmental Relations', in Johanne Poirier, Cheryl Saunders and John Kincaid (eds), *Intergovernmental Relations in Federal Systems* (Oxford University Press 2015) 325.
151 *Ibid* 325.

Measuring autonomy

Index 5.2 Autonomy index – the executive level

A. Representation in the central executive body	
The SNE is not represented in the central executive body and is not involved in its appointment	0
The SNE's electorate is indirectly represented in the central executive body through geographical or identitarian criteria that overlap with the SNE	1
The SNE is not or indirectly represented in the central executive body, but is involved in its appointment through collective subnational vote	2
The SNE is not or indirectly represented in the central executive body, but is involved in its appointment with an individual veto	3
The SNE in itself is substantially represented in the central executive body	4
The SNE is consulted for matters that affect its interests or competences	+1
The SNE co-decides in matters that affect its interests or competences	+2
B. Subnational representation	
The SNE has no executive of its own or an executive appointed by the central government	0
The SNE has an executive appointed by the central government and by, or accountable to, a subnational assembly	1
The SNE has an executive appointed by a subnational assembly or directly elected	2
The subnational executive, as a rule, makes decisions without prior central oversight, but with central oversight *ex post*	+1
The subnational executive, as a rule, makes decisions without central oversight	+2

As was the case for the legislative level, the autonomy index distinguishes between representation in the central executive body and representation at the subnational level.

Here, the concern is not so much with wide and multilateral conversations, but with the decisive power that the particular SNE (as a single unit of analysis) has on central decision-making. The more impact it has, the more autonomous it is. 'Substantial' representation means that the SNE weighs on the decision-making, which usually implies a 30% threshold. However, this can be less if the executive council must decide by consensus.

Indirect representation through identity marks is not as strong as direct representation of the SNE but is nevertheless important. For example, the Belgian Constitution requires language parity in the council of ministers: half of the ministers must be French-speaking and the other half Dutch-speaking.[152] The language communities are concentrated within the geographical boundaries of the French and the Flemish Community, and were decisive for their establishment. As a result, every government decision that is discussed by the council of ministers, and every bill that is submitted to Parliament, is scrutinized from the angle of both major language communities. For the Flemish and French Communities, this is a guarantee that no federal decision is issued that is likely to harm the interests of its electorate.

152 Art. 99 Belgian Constitution.

Here as well, a distinction is made between representation of the SNE in itself, and representation of its electorate. For example, as already mentioned, the US President represents the SNEs' electorates, with his or her election by state-based electoral colleges. This counts as involvement in the central executive body through collective subnational vote.

As the subnational level, the crucial questions are whether the subnational executive is appointed with or without the involvement of the central government and whether the central government has any oversight.

The index is still not measuring administrative federalism as a distinct variable – as mentioned, this will be a matter for the dimension of 'powers'. Subnational executives that (mostly) implement central level decisions are not distinguished from subnational executives that (mostly) take their own decisions, in terms of the execution of subnational laws.

4.5 The international and supranational levels

4.5.1 International treaties

The international level is an important part of the 'status' dimension, because entering into international treaties is an extension of national policymaking. While foreign policy and international affairs has traditionally been located at the core of federal authorities in federalist systems, nowadays sub-state diplomacy is blooming.[153] The topic has mostly been examined from an autonomy perspective, listing the different ways in which SNEs are involved in foreign affairs. Less frequent are approaches from the perspective of the central state. Halberstam, for example, examined what advantages subnational involvement in foreign affairs can have for the central state.[154] Others have pointed out that subnational involvement in matters that range across subnational competences secure better implementation by these SNEs. Their involvement, therefore, benefits the national state that is responsible for compliance under international law.[155]

SNEs are active in foreign affairs in several ways, such as state visits abroad, or representation or trade offices in foreign countries.[156] This index, however, concentrates on the most prominent part, namely the conclusion of international treaties. From an autonomy perspective, the question is to what extent SNEs can conclude their own treaties or be involved in treaties concluded by the central authorities that affect their interests. From a cohesion perspective, the question

153 Daniel Halberstam, 'The Foreign Affairs of Federal Systems: A National Perspective on the Benefits of State Participation', (2001) 46 Villanova Law Review 1027–1028; Nikos Skoutaris, 'Comparing the Subnational Constitutional Space of the European Sub-Entities in the Area of Foreign Affairs', (2012) 4 *Perspectives on Federalism* 241.

154 Halberstam (n 153) 1015–1068.

155 Hans Michelmann, 'Introduction', in Hans Michelmann (ed), *Foreign Relations in Federal Countries* (McGills-Queen's Univ. 2009) 6.

156 For an overview in five legal systems, see Palermo and Kössler (n 18) 424.

is twofold: how to maintain coherency of international affairs if international treaties are concluded by SNEs, and how to make sure that international treaties concluded by the central authorities are based on an internal multilateral dialogue. For this reason, and similar to the constitutional level, the index is divided into two categories. One concerns treaties concluded at the central level, the other concerns treaties concluded by the SNEs.

The distinction between treaties concluded by the central authorities and subnational international agreements depends in the first place on the authority that negotiates, concludes, and ratifies the treaty. However, hybrid forms are possible. For example, the Swiss Constitution states that a 'Canton may conclude treaties with foreign states on matters that lie within the scope of its powers', after informing the Confederation. However, it then specifies that it may deal directly with lower-ranking foreign authorities only, whereas 'in other cases, the Confederation shall conduct relations with foreign states on behalf of a Canton'.[157] These treaties are considered subnational international agreements because the SNE takes the initiative and negotiates the content, the agreement addresses this particular SNE, and the central authority concludes the treaty 'on behalf of' the SNE.

For EU members, this index only applies to international treaties in general. Sometimes, different tracks are in place for treaties that concern the EU. For these procedures, Indexes 8.1 and 8.2 apply.

4.5.1.1 Treaties concluded by the central authorities

Measuring cohesion

Index 6.1 Cohesion index – international treaties concluded by the central authorities

As a rule, international treaties concluded by the central authority are approved without direct or indirect involvement of the SNEs	0
As a rule, international treaties concluded by the central authority are approved by institutional representatives of the SNEs or representatives of their electorates only	1
As a rule, for international treaties concluded by the central authorities, SNEs are consulted, have a suspensive veto or can initiate other hurdles	2
As a rule, international treaties concluded by the central authority are approved by representatives of the national electorate as well as representatives of the electorate of the SNEs	3
As a rule, international treaties concluded by the central authority are approved by representatives of the national electorate as well as institutional representatives of the SNEs	4
As a rule, international treaties concluded by the central authority are approved by representatives of the national and the SNE's electorates jointly	5
As a rule, international treaties concluded by the central authority and approved by representatives of the national electorate and institutional representatives of the SNEs jointly	6

157 Art. 56 Swiss Constitution.

Where international treaties are concluded by the central authority, the index examines if approval is based on an internal multilateral dialogue. This index is structured in a similar way to the index for the legislative level. No distinction is made as to whether the treaties affect subnational interests or not: this is more relevant to measure autonomy.

To create a space for multilateral dialogue, joint deliberations are considered to be more cohesive than separate votes, and approval (directly or indirectly) by SNEs only is considered more cohesive than approval by central authorities only. This is because they at least offer a horizontal multilateral dialogue, and the central authorities' voice is probably heard through its negotiations or ratification power. For example in Venezuela, international treaties are approved by the National Assembly, which consists of delegates of the SNEs and their electorates only. Treaties are then ratified by the President.[158]

In some cases, different tracks apply. For example in Belgium, international treaties concluded by the central level are approved by the House of Representatives. In contrast, in so-called 'mixed treaties', i.e., treaties that deal with matters that do not exclusively fall within the competence of either the federal government or the SNEs, the approval of subnational Parliaments is also required.[159] In Germany, for treaties concluded by the federal government, the Bundesrat' consent is required when its consent would have been mandatory if a federal law were enacted.[160] It is also required if the treaty concerns matters under the Länder's exclusive power.[161] In these cases, the focus is on the track that usually applies, or, if there is no default track, the track that applies to matters in which the SNEs have an interest. This means that the Bundesrat generally does not have to give approval but retains a suspensive veto – i.e., a veto that can be overruled by the Bundestag[162]. For Belgium, the track that applies to mixed treaties is examined.

As mentioned, a separate index is constructed for EU Member States regarding treaties that concern the EU. Also, the index in this section does not apply to the category of treaties that affect the situation of a particular SNE. This is relevant for the autonomy index only.

158 Art. 154 Constitution of Venezuela.

159 Art. 167 Belgian Constitution and Cooperation Agreement of March 1994.

160 Art. 59(2) German Constitution.

161 According to the Lindauer Agreement, see Carlo Panara, 'In the Name of Cooperation: the External Relations of the German Länder and their participation in the EU Decision Making', (2010) 6 *Eu Const L Rev* 63–64.

162 Art. 77(3) and (4) German Constitution.

Measuring autonomy

Index 6.2 Autonomy index – international treaties concluded by the central authorities

As a rule, international treaties concluded by the central authority that affect subnational interests or competences are approved without the involvement of the SNE or its electorate	0
As a rule, international treaties concluded by the central authority that affect subnational interest or competences are approved by central authorities only, but the SNE is consulted, has a suspensive veto or can create other hurdles	1
As a rule, international treaties concluded by the central authority that affect subnational interests or competences are approved by representatives of the SNE's electorate in a collective vote	2
As a rule, international treaties concluded by the central authority that affect subnational interests or competences are approved by a majority of institutional representatives of the SNEs	3
As a rule, the SNE alone can veto international treaties concluded by the central authority that affect subnational interests or competences	4
SNEs are involved in the negotiation procedures for international treaties that affect their interests or competences	+1
International treaties concluded by the central authority that affect the SNE, in particular, are approved with the involvement of this particular SNE	+1

From an autonomy perspective, the SNEs' involvement in those treaties that affect the SNE are of interest. Hence, if different tracks are in place, the index addresses treaties that affect subnational interest in general, e.g., because they regulate matters allocated to the SNE(s). The index is mostly concerned with the approval of treaties, but the SNE has even more weight if it is not just consulted, but actually involved in the negotiation procedure. For example, in Switzerland, the constitution demands that Cantons participate in international negotiations if their powers are affected.[163]

An additional score applies if there is a different track for treaties that specifically concern the SNE, and where the SNE is involved more strongly than usual. For example, the German Constitution states that if the treaty affects 'the special circumstances of a particular Land, then this Land shall be consulted'.[164] Under the usual track, the Bundesrat, with institutional representatives of the Länder, has a suspensive veto – its approval is required only in particular cases. An individual consultation right is stronger than a collective suspensive veto, which justifies an additional score.

163 Art. 55(3) Swiss Constitution.
164 Art. 32(2) German Constitution.

4.5.1.2 *Treaties concluded by the subnational authorities*

Measuring cohesion

Index 7.1 Cohesion index – subnational international agreements

SNEs can conclude international agreements without the interference of the central authorities	0
SNEs can conclude international agreements but the central authorities can interfere to avoid treaties being concluded that jeopardize the coherency of international policy or violate international obligations	1
SNEs can conclude international agreements but the central authorities can interfere to avoid treaties being concluded that jeopardize the coherency of international policy or violate international obligations, conditional upon intergovernmental dialogue	2
SNEs cannot conclude international agreements	3

From a cohesion perspective, no distinction is made between the frequency and the extent to which the central authorities may interfere in subnational treaty-making: what matters is that they have the tools to ensure coherency in international affairs.

For example, to the extent that Austrian and German Länder can conclude international agreements, they have to obtain the prior approval of the federal government in all cases.[165] By contrast, in Belgium, the federal government's approval is not required, but the government can prevent the conclusion of the treaty in four specific cases. These four circumstances are all linked to the concern of maintaining coherency in international policy. Three cases refer to the treaty partner, who is not recognized by the Belgian state, with whom the Belgian state does not entertain diplomatic relations, or with whom Belgian relations have been broken, suspended, or seriously compromised. The last case applies when the treaty violates international or supranational obligations of the Belgian state.[166] This difference between supervision *ex ante* and *ex post* is important from an autonomy perspective, but not so much from a cohesion perspective.

If subnational authorities have no power at all to conclude international treaties, there is no threat to the coherency of international relations policy. For the cohesion of domestic policies, it is preferable to include SNEs in the treaty-making power if the treaties encroach upon their competences, but this was measured in the previous index. For the same reason, it is considered more cohesive if interference in the conclusion of subnational international agreements is based on multilateral dialogue. In the Belgian case, for example, the federal government can only interfere when a consensus is reached in an intergovernmental conference.[167]

165 Art. 16(2) Austrian Constitution; Art. 32(3) German Constitution.
166 Art. 81, § 4 Special law on the reform of the institutions.
167 Art. 81, § 3 Special law on the reform of the institutions.

Measuring autonomy

Index 7.2 Autonomy index – subnational international agreements

The SNE has no power to conclude international agreements	0
The SNE has the power to conclude cooperation agreements with foreign SNEs only, or to conclude administrative agreements only	1
The SNE has the power to conclude international agreements with neighboring countries only and/or in specific matters only	2
The SNE has the power to conclude international agreements in a substantial number of matters	3
The SNE has the power to conclude international agreements in all matters within their competences	4
The SNE has the (additional) power to participate in trans-border institutions	+1
The central authority's prior consent is not required to conclude these agreements	+1
The central authority cannot interfere to hinder the conclusion of a particular agreement for particular reasons	+1

The first question that arises from an autonomy perspective is whether the SNE has any power at all to conclude international agreements. For example, Art. 1(10) of the US Constitution prohibits States to enter into 'any treaty, alliance or confederation'. Constitutional autonomy is strong if SNEs can conclude international agreements in all matters within their competences – even if limited to necessary exclusive competences. In Belgium, SNEs, therefore, have treaty-making powers in all matters that fall within their competences.[168] By contrast in Italy, central laws specify in which cases, within the region's field of competence, the region may establish agreements with foreign states.[169]

In addition, SNEs can be given the power to transfer powers to transborder institutions. In this way, they self-constrain their autonomy and also engage in far-reaching international cooperation separate from the central level. For example, German Länder have the constitutional mandate to engage in supranational cross-bordering cooperation.[170] Even if treaty-making power is limited to agreements with bordering countries, as is the case in Austria,[171] such power can still be important to give a firmer legal basis to sustained cross-bordering cooperation.[172]

A middle ground is found in systems such as the United Kingdom and Switzerland. There, SNEs cannot conclude international agreements with foreign states, but can conclude cooperation agreements with other SNEs.[173] Not

168 Art. 167, § 3 Belgian Constitution.
169 Art. 117(9) Italian Constitution.
170 Art. 24(1a) German Constitution.
171 Art. 16(1) Austrian Constitution.
172 On cross-bordering cooperation, see in particular Luis De Sousa, 'Understanding European Cross-border Cooperation: A Framework for Analysis', (2013) 35 *Journal of European Integration* 669–687.
173 Art. 56(3) Swiss Constitution. For the United Kingdom, see Skoutaris (n 153) 246; 247.

included in the index are instruments without legal effect, such as joint declarations or protocols.[174]

Next, subnational treaty-making powers can be limited by central oversight. The most rigid regime is found where SNEs cannot conclude international agreements without an implication that the central authority gives its consent. This is the case in Austria, where the central authority's (implicit or explicit) approval is required.[175] It is also the case in Switzerland, where the central authority concludes the agreement on behalf of the SNE.[176] A more lenient regime does not require prior approval, but allows the central authorities to interfere in particular circumstances and/or for particular reasons, as is the case in Belgium.[177]

The Swiss case is particularly relevant because the central authority concludes the agreement on behalf of the SNE. Technically, it is the central authority that concludes the treaty, but for this index, it is considered a subnational agreement because it is concluded on behalf of the Canton. However, the fact that the central authority concludes the agreement presupposes its consent. If objections are raised, the decision to conclude the agreement lies with the Federal Assembly,[178] which suggests that as a rule, the central authority will be willing to conclude the treaty on behalf of the Canton. What matters is the central authority's discretion. Art. 56(2) of the Swiss Constitution clarifies that subnational treaties "must not conflict with the law or the interests of the Confederation, or with the law of any other Cantons". This is very broad and implies not only scrutiny of the treaty partner and the legality of the treaty, but also opportunity control of its content. Therefore, the Swiss case should be categorized as falling under the strict regime.

4.5.2 Multilevel governance systems: The European Union

As mentioned, an additional index is constructed for subnational participation in EU decision-making, which only applies to EU member states. However, it can be widened when other supranational systems emerge that are comparable to the EU in scope and depth.

The index does not measure the autonomy of member states' central authorities in the EU: this is measured in the previous indexes, with the EU as the central level of authority, and the national member states as the subnational units of analysis. Instead, particular attention is given to how SNEs within the member states are involved in EU decision-making. This is important because many powers transferred to the EU are located with the SNEs in the member states. If subnational powers are constrained by the EU, and SNEs have a responsibility to implement EU Directives and execute EU Regulations, then it makes sense

174 Palermo and Kössler (n 18) 441–442 report that Spanish SNEs have used such instruments in the absence of any treaty-making power.
175 Art. 16(2) Austrian Constitution.
176 Art. 56 Swiss Constitution.
177 Art. 81, § 4 Special law on the reform of the institutions.
178 Art. 172(3) Swiss Constitution.

to give SNEs some representation at the EU level. This is important for the effectiveness of EU laws as well as the autonomy of SNEs. In this vein, even the local levels are relevant as a unit for analysis. The most prominent example is Germany, where local units have direct or indirect involvement in 80% of the responsibilities to implement or execute EU laws.[179]

Likewise, the index does not measure how cohesive the EU system is. Again, this is measured in the previous indexes. Here, the member states constitute the central level of authority. This is because the member states are the EU's main points of contact. Where the EU allows for the involvement of SNEs, it is mostly for each member state to decide to what extent they actually have a say. This is different for each member state.[180]

Subnational involvement occurs in different ways. A detailed analysis takes into account whether and how SNEs are involved in the approval of EU treaties; represented in the Council of Ministers; or involved in the subsidiarity procedure that allows parliaments to interfere in EU decision-making.[181] One could even go into more detail and include the involvement of SNEs in expert committees that prepare Commission proposals or in other forms of EU decision-making such as the Open Method Coordination. Although this index does not take a minimalist approach, too much detail would undermine the feasibility of the analysis. Therefore, this index concentrates on two aspects: the 'constitutional' moment of EU-treaty approval, and representation in the Council of Ministers, which is the most powerful decision-making body. An index with more dimensions could be developed in follow-up research that has a specific focus on EU decision-making.

4.5.2.1 EU treaties

Several types of treaties can be EU-related. The index is interested in 'constitutional moments' that affect the member state (as the unit of analysis): when the country enters the EU as a member state, and when treaty changes are proposed that determine the principles and institutions that govern the EU system. If different procedures apply to, for example, treaties on another country's membership, then they are not taken into account.

Different tracks are in place to amend EU treaties. According to the ordinary revision procedure, the European Council by a simple majority convenes a Convention to prepare a treaty. This treaty should be ratified by all member states in accordance with their respective constitutional requirements.[182]

179 Volkmar Kese *et al. Steigerung der Europafähigkeit der Landkreise - Notwendigkeit strategischer Steuerung* (Ludwigsburg: Institut für Anpassungsherausforderungen durch europäische Politiken und weltweite Migration, 2018) 5.

180 For a comparison of three different models, with the United Kingdom, Germany, and Belgium as prototypes, see Patricia Popelier, 'Subnational multilevel constitutionalism', (2014) 6 *Perspectives on Federalism* 9–18.

181 *Ibid.*

182 Art. 48 (2–5) TEU.

In addition, various simplified revision procedures are in place for so-called 'piecemeal' revisions.[183] In one case, an EU based procedure, which gives each national parliament a veto right, replaces the member states' "respective constitutional requirements".[184] As this index is interested in more fundamental 'constitutional' changes, it only addresses the ordinary revision procedure.

Measuring cohesion

Index 8.1 Cohesion index – EU treaties

As a rule, EU treaties are approved without direct or indirect involvement of the SNEs	0
As a rule, EU treaties are approved by institutional representatives of the SNEs or representatives of their electorates only	1
As a rule, for EU treaties, SNEs are consulted, have a suspensive veto or can initiate other hurdles	2
As a rule, EU treaties are approved by representatives of the national electorate as well as representatives of the electorate of the SNEs	3
As a rule, EU treaties are approved by representatives of the national electorate as well as institutional representatives of the SNEs	4
As a rule, EU treaties are jointly approved by representatives of the national and the SNE's electorates	5
As a rule, EU treaties are jointly approved by representatives of the national electorate and institutional representatives of the SNEs	6

From a cohesion perspective, the question is how the member states manage to take a coherent approach to EU membership and make sure that subnational involvement in the conclusion of EU treaties does not thwart the national interest. At the same time, the involvement of SNEs may be important for legitimacy reasons.[185]

The index is identical to Index 6.1, which measures cohesion for international treaties concluded by the central authorities. However, the outcome may differ, because often a different track applies to EU treaties. Only a few countries, such as Belgium and the Netherlands, do not have a specific Europe clause. For example, the German Constitution requires the same majorities as the ones that apply to constitutional amendments for the establishment of the EU as well as changes in its treaty foundations. This means that the Bundesrat does not merely have a suspensive vote but has to approve changes with a two-thirds majority.[186]

183 Bruno De Witte, 'The European Treaty Amendment for the Creation of a Financial Stability Mechanism', (2011) 6 *European Policy Analysis* 2. For an overview of revision procedures, see Steve Peers 'European Integration and the European Union Act 2011: An Irresistible Force Meets an Immovable Object?', (2012) 58 *Public Law* 122–123.

184 Art. 48(7) TEU.

185 See Patricia Popelier, 'Europe Clauses and Constitutional Strategies in the Face of Multilevel Governance', (2014) 21 *Maastricht J. of Eu. and Comp. Law* 300–319 for efficiency vs legitimacy strategies.

186 Art. 23(1) and 79(2) German Constitution.

Measuring autonomy

Index 8.2 Autonomy index – EU treaties

As a rule, EU treaties are approved without the involvement of the SNE or its electorate	0
As a rule, EU treaties are approved by central authorities only, but the SNE is consulted and has a suspensive veto or can create other hurdles	1
As a rule, EU treaties are approved by representatives of the SNE's electorate in a collective vote	2
As a rule, EU treaties are approved by a majority of institutional representatives of the SNEs	3
As a rule, the SNE can veto the conclusion of EU treaties	4
SNEs are involved in the negotiation procedures for EU treaties or have to be kept informed	+1

To measure autonomy, Index 6.2 for other international treaties is slightly adjusted. No additional score is needed for treaties that affect a particular SNE. Also, the index does not specify that the treaty must affect subnational interests or competences. It is assumed that EU treaties have that effect by default. Here as well, only the SNE's involvement in the case of the ordinary revision procedure is taken into account.

Subnational autonomy is strong if the SNEs can veto the conclusion of the EU treaty. The index concentrates on the approval of EU treaties, although involvement *ex ante* may even be more important. For example, the representation of the German Länder and the Belgian Communities and Regions in the delegation to the Intergovernmental Conference (IGC) leading to the Maastricht Treaty, helped to secure the introduction of the subsidiarity principle, the establishment of the Council of Regions and the opening up of the Council of Ministers to regional representatives.[187] If such involvement is based on the goodwill of the central government, which is most often the case, it is not taken into account in this index. However, in several systems, legal provisions provide for the duty to keep the SNEs informed during negotiation procedures.[188] This enables the SNEs to take positions and communicate these to the country representatives in the IGC. Therefore, mere information duties are also taken into account.

187 Arthur Gunlicks, *The Länder and German federalism* (Manchester University Press 2003) 366, 367; Carlo Panara, 'Multi-Level Governance as a Constitutional Principle in the Legal System of the European Union', (2016) 16 *Croatian and Comparative Public Administration* 716.

188 For example in Belgium: art. 16, par. 2 Special Majority Act on the Reform of the Institutions.

4.5.2.2 The Council of Ministers

The Council of Ministers is the EU's main decision-making body, consisting of "a representative of each Member State at ministerial level, who may commit the government of the Member State".[189] With the provision being phrased this way, member states can delegate a subnational minister to the Council. However, this minister has the mandate to commit the entire member state. Moreover, Art. 5(3) of the Rules of Procedure allows for extended delegations, which means that a mixed delegation with central and subnational ministerial representatives can attend the relevant meetings.

While this gives SNEs direct access to the EU decision-making procedure, its value should not be overstated: the SNEs are not there to represent themselves, but to represent the state. This means that they act only on the basis of a prior agreement.[190] It is therefore important to examine how SNEs impact these negotiations. SNEs may also impact EU decision-making if they have no direct representation, but influence or even bind the central government's position in the Council. Nevertheless, the mere presence of a subnational Minister in the Council meeting gives the SNE an important extra opportunity to make its point of view heard.[191]

The member states have used these options in different ways, with the Belgian SNEs having taken the strongest position.[192] Usually, these variations are examined to assess the subnational impact on EU decision-making, and thus form an autonomy perspective. The present index also examines them from the viewpoint of cohesion.

Different tracks are possible, depending on the matter that is discussed in the Council. For example, the German government has to take the position of the Bundesrat into account when matters are discussed in the Council that remain within federal competences but affect the interests of the Länder. It has to give the Bundesrat's position 'prime consideration' when the matters lie within the legislative powers of the Länder. Representatives of the Länder are delegated to the Council whenever school education, culture, or broadcasting are discussed. Further, the consent of the federal government is required if the matter may have a budgetary impact for the German federation.[193] From an autonomy perspective, what matters most is whether SNEs are involved whenever there is a discussion of topics that are within their range of competences. From a cohesion perspective, intergovernmental dialogue is also relevant when matters are discussed that are normally allocated

189 Art. 16(2) TEU.
190 Michaël Tatham, 'Going Solo: Direct Regional Representation in the European Union', (2008) 18 *Regional & Federal Studies* 499–500.
191 *Ibid* 500–501.
192 For an overview, see Popelier (n 180) 9–18; Skoutaris (n 153) 258–261.
193 Art. 23(5)(6) German Constitution.

to the central level. What is relevant here is the default track or the track that is most often used.

Measuring cohesion

Index 9.1 Cohesion index – Council of Ministers

The SNEs are not involved in determining the member state's position in the Council	0
The member state's position is determined by the central government after a consultation of the SNEs	1
The member state's position is based on intergovernmental agreement, with a veto right for individual entities, resulting in an abstention	2
The member state's position is based on intergovernmental agreement, without a veto right for individual entities resulting in an abstention	3
The member state is represented in the Council by a mixed delegation	+1
There is room for reconsideration of the member state's position after intergovernmental consultation	+1

From a cohesion perspective, what matters is whether the member state's position in the Council of Ministers is the result of domestic intergovernmental agreement.

From that point of view, it is less important which level represents the member state. However, a mixed delegation is preferred over a homogeneous delegation. This facilitates an intergovernmental-based position if the dynamics of the meeting call for reconsideration. This is preferred over a binding mandate that leaves no room for repositioning, even if the domestic authorities might have taken another stance had they been aware of the dynamics of the meeting or the new facts that prompt a reconsideration. Even if such repositioning requires intergovernmental negotiation 'on the spot', as is the case in Belgium,[194] this is still preferred over no reconsideration or reconsideration with no intergovernmental negotiation at all.

An abstention based on the disagreement between the domestic actors that implies individual vetoes, as is the case in Belgium,[195] is considered less cohesive than a position that is based on the collective will of the SNEs, without an individual veto right.

194 See Bart Kerremans, 'Determining a European policy in a multi-level setting: The case of specialized co-ordination in Belgium', (2000) 10 *Regional and Federal Studies* 41–42.

195 Art. 2 Cooperation Agreement of 8 March 1994. See further, under the autonomy index.

Measuring autonomy

Index 9.2 Autonomy index – council of ministers

The SNE is not involved in determining the member state's position in the Council	0
The SNE is consulted in determining the member state's position in the Council for matters that affect its interests or competences	1
The SNE can influence the member state's position in the Council through a weak collective mandate	2
The SNE can determine the member state's position in the Council through a strong collective mandate	3
The SNE alone can strongly impact the member state's position in the Council	4
The SNE is part of the member state's delegation for (most) matters within its sphere of competences, but does not represent the member state	+1
The SNE may represent the member state for matters within its exclusive Competences, but not by default	+2
The SNE represents the member state for (most) matters within its exclusive competences, by default or on a rotation basis	+3
The member state cannot change its position in the Council without consulting the SNE	+1

From an autonomy perspective, the question is how much an individual SNE can influence the member state's position in the Council of Ministers.

To preserve its autonomy, the SNE's concern is not so much whether the member state's position in the Council is coordinated with all SNEs. Rather, it is whether this entity, in particular, is directly involved in the decision-making. Hence, an individual vote that impacts upon the Council's position has more weight. For example in Belgium, the federal and subnational government meet beforehand to agree upon a stance, which is binding in principle. If this would hinder the Belgian state's meaningful participation (considering the dynamics of the Council meeting), efforts are made to consult with the other entities. If this proves impossible or no agreement can be reached, the delegation takes a provisional position that "best fits with the common interest".[196] If the subnational and federal ministers find no consensus in the preceding coordination and concertation meetings, the Belgian representatives in the Council have to abstain from voting.[197]

More often, SNEs can impact the member state's position through a collective vote. To this end, the index distinguishes between weak and strong mandates. It is more difficult for the member state's representative in the Council to deviate from a strong mandate, and relatively easy to deviate in the case of

196 Art. 6 Cooperation Agreement of 8 March 1994. See Kerremans (n 194) 40.

197 Art. 2 Cooperation Agreement of 8 March 1994. This is the case even if an exclusively regional matter is on the agenda. However, in accordance with a gentleman's agreement, an actor that is not competent in the concrete case will not use its veto right, Jan Beyers and Peter Bursens, 'The European rescue of the federal state: How Europeanization shapes the Belgian state', (2006) 29 *West European Politics* 1065.

a weak mandate. In Germany for example, the federal government has to take the position of the Bundesrat "into account" when the interests of Länder are affected in areas within federal competences. Further, the consent of the federal government is required if the matter may result in increased expenditures or reduces revenues for the German Federation.[198] This is a weak mandate. For the index, however, what counts is that the Bundesrat's stance receives 'prime consideration' in matters that affect the Länder's legislative powers, the structure of their authorities or their administrative procedures.[199] This is a much stronger mandate, even if the federal government still has a veto if the federation's financial interests are at issue. Austria provides another example of a strong mandate, where the Länder can issue a binding mandate in matters "in which legislation is the business of the Land". The federal government may deviate from this only for compelling foreign policy and integration policy reasons.[200]

It is important for the SNE to be present in the Council meeting, especially if the delegation has no binding mandate, or is allowed to adapt the member state's position to the dynamics of the meeting. This is possible through mixed delegations and through formal representation. Formal representation is not a panacea – as mentioned, even if a regional minister is delegated, (s)he will still represent the member state and must remain loyal to the agreed-upon position – but it does give SNEs a stronger voice in the negotiation to reach a position.

All multi-tiered member states allow for mixed delegations, but only in Belgium and Germany is formal representation by SNEs a legal right. In Germany this is only the case for three subject-matters. Some other member states enable formal subnational representation, but this remains at the federal government's discretion. For example, the Austrian federal government has the discretion to send a representative named by the Länder to participate in the Council decision-making procedure.[201]

In the United Kingdom (when it was still a member state) there was no legal right for the devolved entities to be involved in the Council meetings, or even in the formulation of a UK policy position. The Concordat on coordination of EU policy issues, however, provided for their involvement on all matters that touched upon devolved matters.[202] The Joint Ministerial Committee was the principal mechanism for the consultation of devolved entities on UK positions in issues that affect devolved matters.[203] Even though the concordats and agreements were political conventions without legal effect, they did lay down a default

198 Art. 23(5) German Constitution.

199 Art. 23(5) German Constitution.

200 Art. 23d(2) Austrian Constitution.

201 Art. 23d(3) Austrian Constitution.

202 Memory of Understanding and Supplementary Agreements, March 2010, Section B.4.3. of the Concordat on coordination of EU policy issues, Common Annex.

203 Memory of Understanding and Supplementary Agreements, March 2010, Section A.1.9 of the Agreement on the Joint Ministerial Committee

procedure that gave the devolved entities a better position than a situation where no involvement was envisaged at all.

4.6 Organization of courts

At this point, the index is not (yet) interested in courts that have the power to resolve federalism disputes. Not all MTSs have such courts, or they have a court that can only partially resolve such disputes. In systems where such courts are present, they may play an important role both as a safeguard and as a hub for change, thus influencing the power relations between the different authorities. This is further explored in Chapter 7. The institutional potential to safeguard existing power relations is measured in Chapter 5, Indexes 15.1 and 15.2.

In the present index, we are interested in the organization of the court system. Courts have lawmaking power by interpreting the constitution, central and subnational laws, and by making judge-made law. There are some serious limitations as to this power: courts, for example, can only act upon petition and within their limits, and have to base their decisions on legal texts and principles. But even so, their decisions can affect personal, subnational, and national interests. This is why courts are examined under the category of 'status'.

In fully integrated systems – Austria, Belgium, and Spain for example – the judiciary is centrally organized. Usually, but necessarily, this is also the case when local entities are selected as the unit of analysis. In that case, again, the question is whether SNEs are involved in the organization of the courts. In other systems, the organization of courts is a matter of constitutional asymmetry. In the United Kingdom, for example, the judiciary is centrally organized. This is except for Scotland which historically has maintained its own judiciary and legal system after the unification with England.[204]

In dual judicial systems, SNEs organize their own courts to apply and review subnational laws and decisions. This safeguards their autonomy because the interpretation of subnational acts lies in the hands of courts that operate within the subnational legal system itself. Also, it reinforces subnational constitutional autonomy, because subnational courts may independently interpret subnational constitutions. This may lead to enhanced protection of rights.[205] At the same time, it can disrupt cohesion where it leads to divergent case law. An example of this would be the interpretation of unwritten principles of law, or the interpretation of subnational constitutional rights and principles that are similar to those inserted in the central constitution. For the sake of cohesion, it is, then, preferable if those cases could ultimately be decided by a central court. This is the case in systems such as Germany, where the courts of first instance and the

204 For an in-depth discussion of the Scottish court system, see Neil Walker, *Final Appellate Jurisdiction in the Scottish Legal System* (Scottish Government 2010).

205 John Dinan, 'State Constitutions and American Political Development', in Burgess and Tarr (n 57) 43, 57.

courts of appeal are organized by the Länder, and the supreme courts by the federal government.[206] In that case, the system is a hybrid.

In practice, many systems are hybrids.[207] One category consists of systems where SNEs have their own courts, but appellate courts are centrally organized. In Nigeria, despite the organization of separate federal and state courts, the court system is qualified as highly integrated because of the binding force of the Supreme Court's decisions.[208] In Ethiopia as well, the dual system is imperfect because state courts have no final authority over state matters.[209] Another category consists of systems where subnational courts have to send preliminary references to a centrally organized court. Here, the Court of Justice of the European Union is a prominent example. In turn, integrated systems may have dual features. For example in Belgium, separate language requirements apply to courts in Flemish or in French-speaking districts.[210] The indexes take account of these variations.

Measuring cohesion

Index 10.1 Cohesion index – organization of courts

Subnational courts can decide cases that involve the interpretation of central legislation or central constitutional law, without the involvement of a centrally organized court	0
As a rule, subnational courts have to send preliminary references to a centrally organized court, whenever the interpretation or application of central legislation or constitutional law is at stake	1
A centrally organized court is the supreme court for all cases directly or indirectly related to central legislation and central constitutional law	2
The centrally organized court is composed of judges appointed by a mixed body, representative of the central and the subnational authorities. Alternatively, it is composed of judges that represent the (major) SNEs in terms of office, geography or identity markers	+1

The cohesion index is interested in mechanisms that ensure that central legislation and constitutional law is interpreted and applied in a uniform way throughout the legal system. This is a concern of judicial integrity,[211] that is by definition better secured in integrated systems. Where SNEs have their own judiciary, the question is whether central courts can interfere in cases decided

206 Arthur Benz, 'The Federal Constitutional Court of Germany: Guardian of Unitarism and Federalism', in Aroney and Kincaid (n 7) 200.

207 Erin F. Delaney, 'Judicial Federalism in Comparative Perspective', in Fessha and Kössler (n 8) 22–23.

208 Rotimi T. Suberu, 'The Supreme Court of Nigeria: An Embattled Judiciary More Centralist than Federalist', in Aroney and Kincaid (n 7) 298; Patrick Ukata, 'Federalism and the Courts in Nigeria', in Fessha and Kössler (n 8) 33–34.

209 Yonatan T. Fessha and Zemelak Ayele, 'Giving "Shape and Texture" to a Federal System? Ethiopia's Courts and its Unusual Umpire', in Fessha and Kössler (n 8) 48, 51, 53–57. See Art. 80(2) and (3) Ethiopian Constitution.

210 See further, where the autonomy index is discussed.

211 Delaney (n 207) 23.

by the subnational courts. This is either by way of preliminary decisions or via a higher court.

Again, cohesion is not a synonym for centralism. This means that the central court that ultimately decides on cases or preliminary questions is more cohesive if it is organized in such a way that it combines expertise in both central and subnational law. In the index, this is translated as a court composed of judges that are appointed by mixed authorities, or of judges that are representative of the SNEs.

In the first case, SNEs have an important say in the appointment of the judges. An example of this is if the appointment needs the approval of Parliament (where SNEs are also represented), or if SNEs are involved in the nomination of judges, either directly or through an external body such as a High Council of Justice. The most prominent example is the Court of Justice of the European Union. The judges of this court are appointed by common accord of the governments of the member states, after the consultation of a special panel.[212]

In the second case, representation is defined in terms of office, geography, or where SNEs converge with group features such as language, religion, or ethnicity, in terms of identity markers. 'Office' means that (some of) the judges are appointed on the basis of their capacity as a judge in a subnational court. For example, the Malaysian Federal Court is composed of ten judges, including the two Chief Judges of the High Courts of Malaysia and Sabah and Sarawak.[213] 'Geography' means that the court is composed of judges that are linked with the different (or major) SNEs, or with geographical districts that converge with the territorial circumscriptions of SNEs. In most cases, however, this is only an informal rule. 'Identity markers' refer to the characteristic features of the groups that are dominant in the different SNEs. For example in Belgium, courts are centrally organized, but in the Supreme Court (called Court of Cassation) language parity is the rule. Language is defined on the basis of whether judges acquired their law degree in Dutch or in French.[214]

In other cases, representation is determined by practice rather than by law. For example, there are no formal criteria to secure subnational representation in the composition of the Brazilian Supreme Federal Court. However, in practice, "a certain balance between federative diversity and population representation in nominations" is respected.[215] In the United Kingdom, a practice has grown to have at least two Scottish members of the Supreme Court.[216] Such informal rules

212 Art. 253 Treaty on the Functioning of the European Union.

213 Asri Salleh, Arnold Puyok and Tony Paridi Bagang, 'Constitutional Asymmetry in Malaysia: A Case Study of Sabah and Sarawak. A Country Study of Constitutional Asymmetry in Indonesia', in Popelier and Sahadžić (n 36) 329.

214 Art. 43 *quater* Law on the use of languages in judicial affairs.

215 Gilberto M. Antonio Rodrigues, Marco A. Garcia Lopes Lorencini and Augusto Zimmerman, 'The Supreme Federal Court of Brazil: Protecting Democracy and Centralized Power', in Aroney and Kincaid (n 7) 119.

216 Walker (n 204) 39.

are included in the index only if they are so established that they have become an unwritten custom.

Measuring autonomy

Index 10.2 Autonomy index – organization of courts

Courts are entirely organized at the central level	0
Courts are organized at the central level, but the SNE is involved in its organization	1
Courts are organized at the central level, but in such a way that they are embedded within the subnational legal space	2
The SNE has its own court system, but supreme courts are organized at the central level	3
The SNE has its own court system, (almost) completely separate from the central level	5
The SNE is represented in central supreme courts, through regional criteria or relevant identity markers, at least in panels that hear subnational cases	+1

From an autonomy perspective, the index enquires into whether SNEs can organize their own courts, with as little interference by the central level as possible.

If courts are organized by the central level, some autonomy is secured if the SNE in itself is involved in the organization of the court. However, the core question is whether the judges that will eventually take judicial decisions, are familiar with the subnational interests, particularities, and legal system. What is at stake, then, is that subnational laws are interpreted and applied by judges that are trained in law from the perspective of the particular SNEs. Even if the law system is centrally organized, SNEs – especially if divided on the basis of language – may develop their own way of dealing with legal principles and interpretation rules. Also, judges that are trained in a particular SNE will be more familiar with the subnational legislation issued in that entity. They will also be familiar with the specific legal system that some SNEs entertain. Examples are Scotland and Québec, which use civil law in a central system that is based on common law. Another example is the Indonesian region of Aceh, which has the power to issue Islamic-based laws.[217] Even if the law system is centrally organized, SNEs – especially if divided on the basis of language – may develop their own way of dealing with legal principles and interpretation rules.

This is mostly secured in dual systems, where SNEs have their own court system, or in systems such as Switzerland where subnational courts enforce both central and subnational law.[218] However, in monistic systems, this is also safeguarded if judges are

217 Simon Butt, 'Provincial Asymmetry in Indonesia: What Is so 'Special' About It? A Country Study of Constitutional Asymmetry in Indonesia', in Popelier and Sahadžić (n 36) 237.

218 For the Swiss system, see Andreas Lienhard *et al.*, 'The Federal Supreme Court of Switzerland: Judicial Balancing of Federalism without Judicial Review', in Aroney and Kincaid (n 7) 414–415.

"embedded in the subnational legal space". This means that they are trained in the legal system particular to the SNE where they take office. For example in Belgium, judges in Flemish districts must have acquired their law degree in the Dutch language, whereas in French-speaking districts, they must have acquired their degree in the French language.[219] This implies that they are trained in law at Flemish and francophone universities respectively, and carry with them a 'Flemish' or 'francophone' frame of reference to understand and interpret the law.

Irrelevant of whether the system is dualist or not, subnational representation in central courts remains relevant if central apex courts act as national courts of last resort. For example, the Canadian Supreme Court was, in its initial stage, criticized for ignoring the particularities of civil law (typical for Québec) for the sake of uniformity.[220] In Ethiopia, the interpretation of the Federal Supreme Court's power of cassation "over any final court decision containing a basic error of law"[221] as including decisions by State courts over State matters has been contested. This is because the federal Supreme Court can then dictate how the State courts should interpret State law.[222]

Representation in the Supreme Court helps to resolve this problem, whether as a rule or when special panels are put in place to hear subnational cases.

Still, much depends on how strongly the 'subnational' judges weigh in. A threshold representation of one-third seems a minimum in that respect. In Canada, one-third of the judges of the Supreme Court are appointed from among the judges of the Court of Appeal or the Superior Court of the Province of Québec, or from among advocates that have at least 10 years standing at the bar of that Province.[223] It has nevertheless been deemed "aberrant" that a body of judges, only one-third of whom are from Quebec, can overrule a Court of Appeal entirely consisting of judges trained in Quebec's civil law.[224]

The most autonomous system is, therefore, a completely dualist system, such as the US system, where the central supreme courts can only decide cases that concern national law. Even in those cases, representation in the central apex courts remains relevant. This is because the interpretation of constitutional or international law by national courts may still impact on the legal development in the subnational jurisdictions.

219 Art. 43 Law on the use of languages in judicial affairs.

220 Catherine Valcke, 'Québec Civil Law and Canadian Federalism', (1996) 21 *Yale J. International Law* 110–113.

221 Art. 80(3)(a) Ethiopian Constitution.

222 Gedion T. Hessebon and Abduletif K. Idris, 'The Supreme Court of Ethiopia: Federalism's Bystander', in Aroney and Kincaid, (n 7) 181.

223 Art. 6 and 6.1 of the Supreme Court Act.

224 Valcke (n 220) 110.

5 Powers

Once it has been established that SNEs have the institutional capacity to make their own constitutional, legislative, executive, or judicial decisions, a question arises about the space in which they can use this decision-making capacity. This is what 'powers' refers to – the policy domains in which the different authorities can act, the techniques for the distribution of competences, and the mechanisms to dissolve conflicts of power. In this chapter, indicators are developed for these three aspects. Once again, separate indexes are created to measure cohesion and autonomy.

First, I will develop indicators related to the policy domains in which the authorities can act, i.e., the scope of their powers (section 4.1). Next, allocation techniques are examined. These techniques are based on well-known categories of shared and exclusive powers, and on tools that enable authorities to encroach upon other competences, or that limit the way that authorities' powers are exercised (section 4.2). The final section examines both political and judicial mechanisms to manage federalism disputes (section 4.3).

5.1 The scope of powers

The scope of powers indicates the range and type of policy domains in which authorities can act. It is not yet concerned with the intensity in which they can act, and whether other entities can preempt their competences. From an autonomy perspective, the question is the breadth of the range of policy domains in which SNEs have authority. From a cohesion perspective, the question of 'which' competences remain under central authority is important, rather than 'how many'.

Measuring cohesion

Index 11.1 Cohesion index – scope of powers

The central level has no substantial powers in any of the categories of security, economic and monetary union, or solidarity	0
The central level has substantial powers in one of the categories of security, economic and monetary union, or solidarity	1
The central level has substantial powers in two of the categories of security, economic and monetary union, or solidarity	2
The central level has substantial powers in all categories of security, economic and monetary union, or solidarity	3

In federalism literature, a tally is often made of which matters are usually allocated to the central level. This comes down to a set of competences that includes defense, international relations, the functioning of the economic and monetary union, interregional transportation, major physical structures, and pensions.[1]

The fact that some matters are usually under central authority in practice does not mean that they 'should' be placed there in order to secure cohesion. Watts requires a central focus on loyalty, to enable the federal government to deal effectively with matters of common interest.[2] To this end, three categories of powers are relevant: (1) security; (2) economic and monetary union; and (3) solidarity. For cohesion purposes, it is not essential that the federal government has complete and exclusive powers in these domains. What matters is that the federal government has important powers, whether shared or not, that enables it to act when needed.

Cross-border activities are not mentioned as a category that, by nature, must be governed centrally in order to secure cohesion. This is because almost all policy domains, in one way or another, have or can have cross-border aspects. To deal with cross-border aspects, intergovernmental relations seem more important. These aspects are discussed in section 5.2.

1 'Security'. The federal level has jurisdiction over the MTS' entire system. For this reason, it falls to the federal government to preserve the integrity of the country against both internal and external threats. Firstly, this means that it needs military powers as well as the powers to control borders, to fight international crime, and to deal with terrorism. The federal government also needs powers to manage crises that may destabilize the entire country, such as health crises or financial crises.
2 'Economic and monetary union'. A common economic and monetary market can foster economic prosperity and national integration.[3] For the purpose of this category, the latter is more important than the former. As a device for cohesion, federal powers to secure an economic and monetary union is not so much economic efficiency and competitiveness in an international market, but interstate harmony: a wide and stable market protects SNEs from protectionist measures. Economic integrity promotes cohesion because it prevents "economic warfare", to the disadvantage of smaller and weaker states.[4] This was why, in the United States, the commerce clause was included in the constitution. This is the legal ground for the federal government's powers for economic integration.[5] In the EU, an economic and monetary union was considered to be an important building block toward a

1 Ronald Watts, *Comparing Federal Systems* (Queen's University 2008, 3rd ed.) 90 and 178.
2 Watts (n 1) 178.
3 John Kincaid, 'Economic policy-making: advantages and disadvantages of the federal model', (2001) 53 *International Social Science Journal* 85.
4 Richard B. Collins, 'Economic Union as a Constitutional Value', (1988) 63 NYU L. Rev. 64.
5 *Ibid* 46, 53, 64.

federalist system.[6] Powers to secure economic integration include the regulation of internal trade, foreign trade, mobility of goods, people and capital, national currency, commerce, banking, and corporations.

3 'Solidarity'. This category envisages tools for creating nation-building and fostering loyalty to the state. Solidarity is therefore concerned with both national and social citizenship, to delineate solidarity circles at the central level. National citizenship is defined as passive and active membership of individuals in a political community with universalistic rights and obligations at a specified level of equality.[7] National citizenship gives access to political participation, whereas social citizenship is about the attribution of social rights and protection to citizens. While social citizenship is generally considered to be the ultimate step to complete national citizenship, it is linked with territory rather than nationality.[8] This focus on territory is especially relevant given the rise of transnational political systems.[9] The link with nationality has also been loosened for political rights, leading to an uncoupling of nation and citizenship.[10] Solidarity circles can therefore be concentric, which means that this is predominantly a category suited to the use of shared powers. Policy domains in this category include social-security policy, labor law and social rights,[11] as well as nationality and political rights.

Measuring autonomy

Index 11.2 Autonomy index – scope of powers

The SNE has no substantial powers in any of the categories of economic purposes, political control, multinational conflict management, territorial management, or the residual category	1
The SNE has substantial powers in one of these five categories	2
The SNE has substantial powers in two of these five categories	3
The SNE has substantial powers in three of these five categories	4
The SNE has substantial powers in four of these five categories	5
The SNE has substantial powers in all five categories	6

6 John Pinder, 'Economic and Monetary Union: Pillar of a Federal Polity', (1996) 26 Publius: The Journal of Federalism, 127.

7 Thomas Janoski and Brian Gran, 'Political Citizenship: Foundations of Rights', in Engin F. Isin and Bryan S. Turner (eds), *Handbook of Citizenship Studies* (Sage Publications 2002) 13–14. I changed 'nation-state' into 'political community' in view of what follows.

8 Ninke Mussche, 'Social citizenship vs. the territoriality principle: lessons for Flanders' solidarity circle', in Bea Cantillon, Patricia Popelier and Ninke Mussche (eds), *Social Federalism: The Creation of a Layered Welfare State* (Intersentia 2011) 172.

9 Maurice Roche, 'Social Citizenship: Grounds of Social Change', in Isin and Turner (n 7) 73, 79.

10 Saskia Sassen, 'Towards Post-National and Denationalized Citizenship', in Isin and Turner (n 7) 277–288; Damian Tambini, 'Post-national citizenship', (2001) 24 Ethnic and Racial Studies 195–217

11 Kees Van Kersbergen, 'The Politics of Solidarity and the Changing Boundaries of the Welfare state', (2006) 5 *European Political Science* 379.

It is difficult to find an adequate measure for the scope of subnational powers.[12] Comparative federalists have pinpointed the policy domains that are typically allocated to SNEs, such as education, social policy, municipal affairs, agriculture, environment, immigration, language, and culture.[13] There is, however, too much variety to discern a real pattern.

Comparing the number of powers allocated respectively to the central and subnational levels may give some insight. For example, when measuring the preponderance of central competences versus subnational competences, countries such as Austria, Brazil, Ethiopia, India, and Nigeria are highly centralist.[14] In contrast, a state like Bosnia and Herzegovina, which has only a few narrow central powers,[15] is highly decentralist.

However, the measure is inaccurate. This is because in some cases the list of competences can be long but related to very detailed parts of a policy domain and with many exceptions. In other cases, the list of competences can be short but encompassing a very broad range of policy domains.

Another indicator that is sometimes used is the proportion of federal and constituent unit expenditures after intergovernmental transfers.[16] According to this measure, we find Belgium, Canada, and Switzerland as being among the most decentralized systems. Venezuela, Mexico, and Ethiopia are among the most centralized. Meanwhile, Austria and Spain fall somewhere in between.[17]

12 Ronald L. Watts, 'The Distribution of Powers, Responsibilities and Resources in Federations', in Ann L. Griffiths (ed), *Handbook of federal countries* (McGill-Queen's University Press 2002) 448–471, reproduced in Kincaid, *Federalism*, Vol 2 (Sage Publications 2011) 216.

13 *Ibid* 218; Watts (n 1) 90–91.

14 See, respectively, Manfred Stelzer, 'Constitutional Change in Austria', in Xenophon Contiades (ed), *Engineering Constitutional Change* (London, Routledge 2013) 29; Gilberto M. Antonio Rodrigues, Marco A Garcia Lopes Lorencini and Augusto Zimmerman, 'The Supreme Federal Court of Brazil: Protecting Democracy and Centralized Power', in Nicholas Aroney and John Kincaid(eds), *Courts in Federal Countries. Federalists or Regionalists?* (University of Toronto Press 2017) 111–112, and Gedion T. Hessebon and Abduletif K. Idris, 'The Supreme Court of Ethiopia: Federalism's Bystander', in *ibid* 174; Rajendra K. Pandey, 'Accommodating Diversity, Consolidating Nationhood. A Country Study of Constitutional Asymmetry in India', in Patricia Popelier and Maja Sahadžić (eds), *Constitutional Asymmetry in Multinational Federalism* (Palgrave MacMillan 2019) 220; Rotimi Suberu, 'The Supreme Court of Nigeria: An Embattled Judiciary More Centralist than Federalist', in Aroney and Kincaid (eds), *ibid*, 294.

15 Maja Sahadžić, 'Mild Asymmetry and Ethnoterritorial Overlap in Charge of the Consequences of Multinationalism. A Country Study of Constitutional Asymmetry in Bosnia and Herzegovina', in Popelier and Sahadžić (n 14) 65; Jens Woelk, 'Bosnia-Herzegovina: Trying to Build a Federal State on Paradoxes', in Michael Burgess and G Alan Tarr (eds), *Constitutional Dynamics in Federal Systems* (McGill-Queen's University Press 2012) 112–113.

16 Ronald L. Watts, 'Typologies of federalism', in John Loughlin, John Kincaid and Wilfried Swenden (eds), *Routledge Handbook of Regionalism and Federalism* (Routledge 2013) 31–32.

17 *Ibid* 31–32

Similar measures were used in the indexes discussed in Chapter 2. There, there was an objection to the fact that expenditures do not always imply an authority to decide. Further, the volume of expenditures may be more indicative of the government's ideology.[18]

Linking clusters of competences with the index's purpose is more difficult when measuring autonomy than it was for constructing the cohesion index. The reason for this is that the essential factors for preserving autonomy flow from the reasons for having a MTS in the first place. These reasons are manifold, which explains the wide variety of subnational competences across countries. Often, a combination of factors underlies the formation of an MTS, and the importance of particular factors may shift over time.[19] We can nevertheless distinguish the most common factors and link them with a set of (sometimes overlapping) competences.

Linking purpose with subnational competences is easier when the reasons for forming an MTS have disintegrative power, e.g., multinational conflict management. This is different when they have integrative power, such as defense against external threats or stimulating economic prosperity. In these cases, any transfer of powers to the central level implies a loss of powers in an otherwise undistinguished, residual set of competences. Therefore, we concentrate on reasons that have disintegrating power and place the remaining competences in a residual category.

1. 'Economic purposes'. Economic purposes can imply integrative as well as disintegrative pressures. This depends on whether significant externalities in consumption and production cross geographical boundaries, whether economies of scale are extensive, or whether there are significant preference variations.[20] For example, the creation of regional autonomy in Belgium was based on differences in economic policy preferences that were linked with differences in economic geography and types of industry.[21] Several African states have turned to decentralization to facilitate economic development.[22] Core competences in the economic purposes category are economic expansion, import and export policy, (regional aspects of) credit policy, natural resources, commerce, tourism, transport, and energy.
2. 'Political control'. This category is about giving individuals political control of their daily lives and over governments that are in close proximity

18 Liesbeth Hooghe, Gary Marks, Arjan H. Schakel, Sara Niedzwiecki, Sandra Chapman Osterkatz and Sarah Shair-Rosenfield, *Measuring Regional Authority: A Postfunctionalist Theory of Governance. Volume 1* (Oxford University Press 2016) 13.

19 Watts (n 1) 63–64.

20 Mikhail Filippov, Peter C. Ordeshook and Olga Shvetsova, *Designing Federalism* (Cambridge University Press 2004) 1–2.

21 Patricia Popelier, 'Asymmetry and Complexity as a Device for Multinational Conflict Management. A Country Study of Constitutional Asymmetry in Belgium', in Popelier and Sahadžić (n 14) 20–21, 23.

22 Karl Kössler and Yonatan T. Fessha, 'Introduction', in Yonatan T. Fessha and Karl Kössler (eds), *Federalism and the Courts in Africa* (Routledge 2020) 1.

to their citizens. Core competences relate to those aspects that impact on the organization of smaller communities. Examples include urban and spatial planning, traffic regulations, local police and public order, public services, establishment conditions, waste management, sports, and recreation. Switzerland, with its deeply rooted culture of local decision-making and direct democracy grown out of small political communities,[23] is a prominent example. However, the same purpose may also explain political decentralization in more unitary systems.

3 'Multinational conflict management'. The aim of this category is to decentralize political conflict that flows from identitarian divides. This is typical for multinational systems such as Belgium, Canada, Ethiopia, India, Malaysia, and Spain. Core competences are linked with the protection of regional identity. Usually, this means culture, religion, education, and language. However, social policy can also be a means of delineating a subnational circle of solidarity based on a shared regional identity.
4 'Territorial management'. This purpose is particularly relevant in vast political systems. In Australia for example, federalism is explained by vast distances and "inhospitable" geography and climate that cannot easily accommodate large populations.[24] This category can contain very diverse competences that often overlap with other categories, such as spatial planning, transport, or natural resources. Some core territory-related competences – that are not already included in other categories – would include environment protection, land policy, agriculture and fisheries, and competence over local administrations.
5 'Residual category'. The aims of strengthening political, economic, or military power are a strong integrative driver. These goals not only explain US federalism, but also the formation of the EU. Here, the logic is that sovereign states unite by transferring to the central level those powers that are essential for these aims, whilst still preserving power in the remaining categories. However, falling-apart MTSs may get caught in a vicious cycle of fragmenting dynamics. This might result in a continued transfer of powers to the SNEs, beyond the set of competences that were linked with their original purpose. Hence, this category includes all the competences that are not already caught by one of the former categories.

Again, it is not crucial that SNEs have complete and exclusive powers in these domains. What matters is that they have important powers in any of these clusters, whether these powers are shared or not. The extent of these powers is measured in another index. Also, no account is taken of whether SNEs actually make

23 This has countered centralizing dynamics over time, according to Paolo Dardanelli, 'Switzerland. Europe's first federation?', in Loughlin, Kincaid and Swenden (n 16) 256.
24 Roger B. Wilkins, 'Federalism: Distance and Devolution', (2004) 50 *Australian J. of Politics and History* 95.

use of the competences they have. What matters here is the institutional setup, and thus the potential to act.

In Belgium, for example, child allowances are a competence transferred to the Communities. This means that they have some (but no substantial) powers in social security, which falls in the residual category. Like the other Communities, the GSC has powers over education, person-related competences, language, and cultural matters. This means it has substantial powers in category 3. In agreement with the Walloon Region, it also acquired competences in the fields of job placement, spatial planning, housing, and agriculture. Arguably, this gave the Community some powers in categories 2 and 4. This is non-substantial in category 2 (only spatial planning). It is more substantial in category 4.

5.2 Allocation techniques

This section first examines the basic allocation techniques. This means the techniques that determine which authorities have, in principle, the competence to regulate a particular subject matter (5.2.1.). Next, there is an analysis of the mechanisms that can be used to deviate from the basic principles (5.2.2.).

5.2.1 Basic allocation techniques

The most basic categories of allocation techniques are exclusive powers and shared powers,[25] each with their own subdivisions. The first category includes parallel powers. The latter category is subdivided into framework powers and concurrent powers.[26] Another categorization focuses on the division of functions and distinguishes between legislative and executive functions. For the sake of simplicity, these techniques are explained in terms of central and regional subnational levels of authority. In reality, powers are usually allocated over more levels of authority – local, regional, central, and supranational. For example, a subject matter can be an exclusive subnational competence in the domestic regime, but also shared with the EU.

Two other categories are not included in the index.

The first distinguishes between assigned and residual powers. Friedrich rightly pointed out that residual powers have erroneously been considered "the decisive test of 'statehood' for the component units", because they are illusory if the central level's powers are all-embracing.[27] For example, it was noticed that in

25 Thomas O. Hueglin, 'Comparing Federalisms: Variations or Distinct Models?', in Arthur Benz and Jorg Broschek (eds), *Federal Dynamics. Continuity, Change & the Varieties of Federalism* (Oxford University Press 2013) 29.

26 Hueglin (n 25) 30.

27 Carl J. Friedrich, *Constitutional Government and Democracy: Theory and Practice in Europe and America* (Blaisdell Publishing Company 1968) 204.

Germany the Länder have residual powers, but that the federal state has used its enabling powers to such an extent that legislation in practice is mostly federal.[28] Mostly, residual powers are located at the subnational level in coming-together systems,[29] and at the central level in falling-apart systems. However, this is only relevant if the lists of assigned powers are short. As residual powers also contribute to the set of subject matters assigned to the central or subnational level, they have already been included in the scope of powers index.

The other category covers 'implied powers'. They allow one tier of authority to encroach upon the policy domain of another tier, whenever this is indispensable to the effective execution of competences. They have a practical function that gives some flexibility to the system of power distribution.[30] In principle, they only have a marginal impact on the other tiers' powers. If their impact in practice is considerable, then this has more to do with the court that resolves competence disputes. This is covered by Indexes 15.1 and 15.2, which is discussed later in this chapter. In of themselves, implied powers are linked with material competences that are assigned to the different tiers of authority. For this reason, they form part of Indexes 11.1 and 11.2 on the scope of powers.

5.2.1.1 Exclusive vs shared powers

In the case of exclusive powers, a matter falls within the ambit of either the central or the subnational authority, to the exclusion of the other. Exclusive powers can relate to a broad policy domain, or to specific subject matters within a policy domain. In the latter case, we observe a fragmentation of powers.[31] Steytler describes this as 'shared' or 'overlapping powers' because they function in the same broad policy domain, with a high degree of overlap where the scope of powers is not clearly delineated.[32] The index does not make this kind of nuance, which is more to do with how the distribution of powers works out in practice. Formally, fragmentation does not detract from the formal qualification of exclusive powers.

A special form of powers are parallel powers.[33] These powers are allocated to both the central and the SNEs, but they can exercise them simultaneously and independently of one another. Usually, these are accessory powers that can

28 Werner Heun, *The Constitution of Germany. A Contextual Analysis* (Hart 2011) 59.

29 Francesco Palermo and Karl Kössler, *Comparative Federalism: Constitutional Arrangements and Case Law* (Oxford, Hart, 2017) 139.

30 *Ibid* 149, 151.

31 Eva Maria Belser, 'Concurrent Powers as Doors to Legislative Innovation, Conditional Powers as Gates to the Blind Alley: Some Swiss Illustrations', in Nico Steytler (ed), *Concurrent Powers in Federal Systems. Meaning, Making, Managing* (Brill Nijhoff 2017) 60.

32 Nico Steytler, 'The Currency of Concurrent Powers in Federal Systems' in Steytler (n 31) 9.

33 'Dualistic autonomous concurrent powers' in Kincaid's terminology: John Kincaid, 'From Dualistic Autonomous Concurrency to Marbleised Permissive Concurrency in American Federalism' in Steytler (n 31) 34.

be exercised by two levels of authority at the same time, without the risk of a clash or incoherency. This is because they are instrumental to their own set of substantive competences. Examples are the power to subsidize fundamental research, to grant subsidies, or to establish public bodies. In a way, substantive subnational powers are also parallel powers, delineated by jurisdiction instead of competences: they are exercised simultaneously and independently by different authorities, but in different territories. This is unless the subject matter is allocated to one privileged SNE only in an asymmetrical design.

In the case of shared powers, both central and subnational levels of authority have governing powers in the same policy fields.[34]

Framework powers are shared powers that distinguish between the general framework and the more detailed regulation of a subject matter.

One level of authority – in principle the central authority – establishes the general principles or basic norms. The other levels of authority regulate a subject matter within the boundaries of the general framework. In some cases, the implementing power is a parallel power. For example, in Germany, the federal legislator enacts 'principle legislation' in the field of public finances. This is framework legislation and is binding on the budgetary activities of both the federal authorities and the Länder.[35]

Framework powers, in turn, are exclusive or concurrent.[36] In the first case, only the central authority can establish the general rules or basic norms. The implication is that SNEs cannot act in the absence of a central framework. In the latter case, SNEs can establish the general principles so long as, or to the extent that, the central authorities have not acted. This is the principle in the EU, where the use of Directives can be viewed as a specific type of framework powers. These directives define the result to be achieved, but leave the national authorities the choice of form and methods.[37]

Partial preemption resembles framework powers but differs on several points.[38] Partial preemption means that the central government issues standards within a concurrent policy domain but leaves room for subnational law. The most important difference is that SNEs can develop their own complementing standards that are similar to or stricter than the national standards. However, framework powers can only issue detailed regulations within the central framework.[39]

34 Steytler (n 32) 1–2 labels this 'concurrent powers', but here we use the term 'shared powers' to cover both concurrent and framework powers.

35 Heun (n 28) 61–62.

36 Steytler (n 32) uses the term 'concurrent powers' as the umbrella term, with framework powers as a subcategory called 'framework concurrency'. However, framework powers can be exclusive. This is why I prefer the term 'shared powers' as the umbrella term.

37 Art. 288 TFEU.

38 Kincaid (n 33) 41.

39 *Ibid* 41–42.

Under concurrent powers, both central and subnational authorities can regulate the same subject matter, both in principle and in detail. To avoid clashes, this system demands priority rules. Usually, federal law preempts subnational law. Only in exceptional cases will subnational rules have priority. For example, in Canada, federal law can regulate old-age pensions and other benefits, but Provincial laws have priority.[40] In Germany, the Länder may deviate from federal law with respect to six specific subject matters.[41] In Ethiopia, in the absence of an explicit priority rule, two theoretical options have been presented. One argues for the priority of central rule, while the other argues that the priority of the central or the subnational law should be decided on a case-by-case basis.[42] However, there is no constitutional review or practice to sustain the latter option.

There are two ways to shape the priority rule. Field preemption means that SNEs cannot regulate a particular policy field once central legislation has been enacted. Contingent concurrency entails a more subtle priority rule that makes subnational laws inoperative only in the case of conflict with central rules.[43] Germany is an example of the first type of priority rule,[44] whereas South Africa and the United States are examples of the second.[45]

The constitutional qualification of powers is sometimes misleading. For example, the South African Constitution enumerates 'exclusive' powers that are assigned to the SNEs. However, the central government can nevertheless intervene when necessary to maintain national security, economic unity, or essential national standards, to establish minimum standards for the rendering of services or to prevent 'unreasonable action' taken by a Province.[46] National security can be seen as a central power that in exceptional circumstances requires intervention in subnational policy domains. Intervention against a particular SNE is discussed below (Index 13.2) and is also meant to take place in exceptional circumstances. By contrast, economic unity and national or minimum standards resemble the necessary requirements that are often used as a condition for

40 Art. 94A Canadian Constitutional Act.

41 Art. 72(3) German Constitution. These policy domains, however, are transferred to the EU, which means that the Länder's discretion is still limited.

42 Assefa Fiseha and Zemelak Ayele, 'Concurrent Powers in the Ethiopian Federal System', in Steytler (n 31) 258–259.

43 For this distinction, see Robert Schütze, *From Dual to Cooperative Federalism: The Changing Structure of European Law* (Oxford, Oxford University Press 2019) 95.

44 Arthur B. Gunlicks, 'Legislative Competences, Budgetary Constraints, and the Reform of Federalism in Germany from the Top Down and the Bottom Up', in Burgess and Tarr (n 15) 65.

45 Derek Powell, 'Constructing a Developmental State in South Africa: The Corporatization of Intergovernmental Relations', in Johanne Poirier, Cheryl Saunders and John Kincaid (eds), *Intergovernmental Relations in Federal Systems* (Oxford University Press 2015) 322; Kincaid (n 33) 35–38.

46 Art. 44(2) South African Constitution. See further, under index 13(2) for the latter exception.

concurrent or framework powers. Arguably, this turns the system of exclusive powers into a system of conditional shared powers.[47]

5.2.1.2 *Legislative vs administrative functions*

In some systems, both legislative and executive functions are assigned to the same level of authority. This is the case in dual systems, where each level executes its own legislation. For example, US federal laws sometimes give administrative instructions to the States, but they are under no duty to obey.[48] By contrast, in so-called 'administrative federalism', the legislative function is assigned to one level and the executive function to another. In Germany, this is a principle that governs the constitutional distribution of powers.[49] Some MTSs have a mixed system. For example, in Ethiopia, the constitution assigns the implementation of federal land laws and criminal laws to the States.[50]

The categorization based on exclusive versus shared powers is analytically different from a categorization on the basis of legislative and executive functions. They are nevertheless closely related.[51] Ultimately, a system that is predominantly based on framework powers may come down to a form of administrative federalism. This is especially the case if the SNEs have broad discretionary powers to implement the legislation, resulting in normative variety. By contrast, if the executive function is limited to technical details or is otherwise left with little discretion, this makes for a completely different picture. This is often the case for local entities,[52] but Austrian Cantons also act on federal instructions, with little discretionary powers.[53] However, even in a system of framework powers, the central level sometimes provides more detail, even if SNEs are left in principle to adopt supplementary legislation.[54] On the other hand, a system of administrative federalism will more easily be coupled to a system of central oversight.[55]

47 Jaap de Visser, 'Concurrent Powers in South Africa' in Steytler (n 31) 225 also describes the concurrent powers in Schedule 4 and the exclusive powers in Schedule 5 as two manifestations of concurrency.
48 Daniel Halberstam and Roderick M. Hills Jr., 'State Autonomy in Germany and the United States', (2001) Annals *AAPSS* 176.
49 Art. 83 German Constitution. See Gunlicks (n 44) 66–67.
50 Hessebon and Idris (n 14) 176. In addition, federal laws sometimes instruct SNEs to execute the act, but this is merely a practice the legality of which has not been tested, *ibid* 174, 176. See also Fiseha and Ayele (n 42) 251–254.
51 Wilfried Swenden, *Federalism and Regionalism in Western Europe* (Palgrave MacMillan 2006) 57, 58. See, in particular, how in Ethiopia the system of administrative federalism pertaining to land laws have been interpreted as framework legislation, Hessebon and Idris (n 14) 176.
52 For example, in Germany, see Heun (n 28) 78.
53 Palermo and Kössler (n 29) 159.
54 Swenden (n 51) 58.
55 See, for example, Art. 84 and 85 German Constitution.

Measuring cohesion

Index 12.1 Cohesion index – allocation techniques

Powers are predominantly allocated on the basis of exclusivity	0
Powers are predominantly situated at the central level, but the application and enforcement is assigned to the SNEs without much discretion	1
Powers are predominantly allocated on the basis of concurrency, with priority given to central legislation in the case of concrete conflicts	2
Powers are predominantly allocated on the basis of concurrency, governed by the principle of field preemption	3
Central powers are predominantly allocated as framework powers, and both the central authority and the SNEs can implement and execute the general framework	4
Central powers are predominantly allocated as framework powers, or under the principle of executive federalism, with both the implementing and executive functions assigned to the SNEs	5
The system of power distribution is predominantly based on a combination of concurrent powers and administrative federalism	6

Scholars have noted that subject matters are increasingly interrelated. This makes it even more important to examine how powers are shared, coordinated, and integrated among levels of authority, rather than focusing on how they are divided.[56] From that perspective, shared powers have greater potential to create cohesion than exclusive powers. By appealing to a cooperative way of governing,[57] they promote a more integrated form of federalism.[58] They also enable national standards to be applied nationwide, but tailored to subnational needs.[59] For the same reasons, 'administrative federalism' is a more cooperative form of federalism.[60]

From this perspective, it makes sense that the Belgian system is based upon exclusive powers. Powers are transferred to the SNEs on the basis of distrust, when different preferences between the two major language communities paralyze decision-making at the federal level.[61] For example, an incident involving the licensing of arms delivery was a controversial issue, and of special interest to the (francophone) Walloons when there was the consideration of plans to locate an armament factory in their Region. To end the dispute, the power to grant permits for arms deliveries was transferred to the Regions. The very ratio of such transfers is to enable the SNEs to each take their own approach, without

56 Francesco Palermo, 'Federalism and the European Union: asymmetry, policies and some recurring federal dilemmas', in John Kincaid (ed), *A Research Agenda for Federalism Studies* (Edward Elgar 2019) 204.
57 Nico Steytler, 'Concurrency of Powers: The Zebra in the Room', in Steytler n 31) 300.
58 Swenden (n 51) 50–57.
59 Steytler (n 32) 3.
60 Swenden (n 51) 57.
61 Wouter Pas, 'A Dynamic Federalism Built on Static Principles: The Case of Belgium', in G. Alan Tarr, Robert Williams and Joseph Marko (eds), *Federalism, Subnational Constitutions, and Minority Rights* (Praeger Publishers 2004) 160.

involvement from the other side of the language border. Creating cohesion is of no importance.

Framework powers can be considered to be more cohesive than concurrent powers because they make central and subnational authorities interdependent: SNEs are limited by the central framework; central authorities rely on SNEs to implement or complete the general framework. The same is true for administrative federalism. This is unless the executive function assigned to SNEs is paired with central instructions that impede on discretionary rulemaking powers, in which case a more hierarchical relationship is in place. A system of framework powers that allows both the central authority and the SNEs to implement the general framework may create confusion and administrative competition – as was the case in Spain[62] – and is therefore considered less cohesive. Finally, field preemption is considered to be more cohesive than priority rules in the case of concrete conflicts. While the latter leaves more autonomy to SNEs, the former enables more coherent policymaking at the central level.

At the same time, shared powers have a strong centralizing effect. This is discussed further below, as part of the autonomy index. For now, it is sufficient to note that shared powers are more cohesive if the central authority exercises them on the basis of intergovernmental dialogue. This is measured in Index 4.1. It shows that specific instruments alone do not determine how cohesive the system is, nor how much autonomy SNEs enjoy: they always function in combination with a more comprehensive set of tools and mechanisms.

Measuring autonomy

Index 12.2 Autonomy index – allocation techniques

The SNE has mostly administrative or implementation powers, without a guarantee for substantial discretionary space	0
The SNE has mostly administrative or implementation powers	1
The SNE has mostly concurrent powers with priority given to central rule	2
The SNE has mostly concurrent powers with priority given to central rule, but central interference is conditional to subsidiarity or necessity conditions	3
The SNE has mostly concurrent powers with priority given to central rule, but central interference is conditional to detailed subsidiarity or necessity conditions	4
The SNE has mostly exclusive powers (or concurrent powers with priority given to subnational rule)	5
There is no political central oversight	+1

Exclusivity is the institutional device for dual states.[63] Ideally, in such systems, each level operates separately from one another. Therefore, exclusivity protects SNEs against interference by the central government better than shared powers. Of course, if most powers are assigned to the central level, exclusivity as the

62 Swenden (n 51) 58; Carles Viver Pi-Sunyer and Mercè Corretja Torrens, 'De Facto Concurrency in Spain', in Steytler (n 31) 119–121.

63 Palermo and Kössler (n 29) 124.

main principle for the allocation of powers may also promote central dominance. Austria is a prominent example, Ethiopia is another. For a nuanced picture, the allocation technique index must, therefore, be combined with the index on the scope of powers which measures the jurisdictional reach.[64] This shows once more that one indicator alone does not give much insight into the nature of a MTS.

By contrast, shared powers have centralizing effects.[65] For example, in the United States, the centralizing effect of the commerce clause has been widely reported upon.[66] Shared powers may even be used in such a way as to encroach upon exclusive subnational powers. In Spain, for example, the Constitutional Tribunal referred to the central competence for "basic rules and coordination of general economic planning" to intervene in exclusive subnational powers.[67]

This means that even if the system is predominantly based on exclusive powers, it takes only one broadly framed concurrent power for the central authority to undermine subnational autonomy. If this allows the central authority to encroach upon a wide range of subnational policy fields, the system is regarded as 'predominantly concurrent'.

However, the centralizing effects of shared powers can be mitigated in different ways. One way is the involvement of the SNEs in central decision-making, giving them an influence on how intensely the central authority uses shared powers.[68] Another addresses the court that arbitrates conflicts of competences and will interpret the central competence in a narrow or a broad way. These are examined in separate indexes. Here, the subsidiarity principle is taken into account.

The subsidiarity principle consists of both a constitutional or substantive and a legislative or instrumental part.[69] The first guides the decision to allocate specific subject matters to the central or subnational level of authority. The latter is a necessity test that helps to decide whether central interference in concurrent policy domains is expedient or justified.[70] In Switzerland, the subsidiarity principle was inserted in the constitution with the precise purpose of protecting cantonal

64 See also Patricia Popelier, 'Exclusive Powers and Self-Governed Entities: A Tool for Defensive Federalism?', in Ferran Requejo and Marc Sanjaune (ed.), *Defensive Federalism* (Routledge, forthcoming).

65 Steytler (n 32) 3.

66 Adrian Vermeule, 'Does Commerce Clause Review Have Perverse Effects?', (2001) 46 *Villanova L. Rev.* 1326–1340. For an overview: Palermo and Kössler (n 29) 142–143.

67 Ramon Maiz, Francisco Caamaño and Miguel Azpitarte, 'The Hidden Counterpoint of Spanish Federalism: Recentralization and Resymmetrization in Spain (1978–2008)', (2010) 20 *Regional & Federal Studies* 70.

68 See Popelier (n 64).

69 Daniel Halberstam, 'Comparative Federalism and the Role of the Judiciary', in Keith E. Whittington, R Daniel Kelemen and Gregory A. Caldeira (eds), *The Oxford Handbook of Law and Politics* (Oxford University Press 2010) 155–156.

70 Anna Gamper, 'A "Global Theory of Federalism'? The Nature and Challenges of a Federal State", (2005) 6 *German Law Journal* 2005, 1300; Werner Vandenbruwaene, 'What Scope for Subnational Autonomy: the Issue of the Legal Enforcement of the Principle of Subsidiarity', (2014) 6 *Perspectives on Federalism* 51.

autonomy against centralization.[71] Again, the effectiveness of the subsidiarity principle depends upon political and judicial safeguards that are examined in other indexes. The German Constitutional Court linked reviewability with the ability to discern more specific criteria and the legislature's discretion to establish facts and make prognoses.[72] Hence, effectiveness can be promoted by defining the subsidiarity principle in a more detailed way, with concrete criteria, and by producing impact assessments or other evidence to explain the reasons for interference.[73] In Germany, however, the constituent power's reaction to the Constitutional review was a restriction of the necessity clause to only a few subject matters.[74]

The Swiss Constitution lays down the duty to observe "the principle of subsidiarity" in the performance of state tasks and specifies that "the Confederation only undertakes tasks that the Cantons are unable to perform or which require uniform regulation by the Confederation".[75]

Under the German Constitution, the federal authority can only legislate on certain concurrent matters "if and to the extent" that this is necessary in the national interest to establish equivalent living conditions throughout the entire territory or to maintain legal or economic unity.[76]

The South African constitution gives priority to central legislation in concurrent matters only if certain conditions are met. These are laid down in detail and come down to a subsidiarity test and a necessity test, or if the central law is aimed at preventing "unreasonable action" by a Province.[77] In this case, however, the number of grounds to justify the prevalence of central legislation is vast, which lowers the protection provided by the conditionality of concurrent powers.[78]

In the EU's establishing treaty, it is specified that "Under the principle of subsidiarity, in areas which do not fall within its exclusive competence, the Union shall act only if and in so far as the objectives of the proposed action cannot be sufficiently achieved by the Member States, either at the central level or at the regional and local level, but can rather, by reason of the scale or effects of the proposed action, be better achieved at the Union level".[79] This gives more concrete guidance to authorities and courts to assess whether the subsidiarity principle has been respected. To evaluate the scale and effects of proposed actions, the Court of Justice of the European Union (CJEU) uses impact assessments. The Commission is under a duty to include impact assessments in the form of a detailed statement to

71 Belser (n 31) 53.
72 Bundesverfassungsgericht (BVerfG), judgment of 24 October 2002, 2 BvF 1/01, C.II.4c. On the tailoring of the justiciability of the necessity test through modifications of the constitutional provision, see Heun (n 28) 61.
73 Vandenbruwaene (n 70) 65–68.
74 Heun (n 28) 61.
75 Art. 5A and 43a Swiss Constitution.
76 Art. 72(2) German Constitution.
77 Art. 146 South African Constitution. See Anna Dziedzic and Cheryl Saunders, 'The Meanings of Concurrency', in Steytler (n 31) 23.
78 De Visser (n 47) 327.
79 Art. 5(3) TEU.

enable a subsidiarity test. This assessment must include, amongst others, the reasons for concluding that the objective can be better achieved by the EU through "qualitative and, wherever possible, quantitative indicators".[80]

Within a system of shared powers, the SNE has the least autonomy if it only or mostly has the power to execute central decisions without substantial discretionary space. Local governments, in particular, are often overburdened with delegated tasks, making them "policytakers, not policymakers".[81] Often, practice will reveal how administrative federalism eventually plays out. The index can only consider institutional safeguards. For example, in Switzerland, the Constitution requires the Confederation to "allow the Cantons all possible discretion to organize their own affairs".[82]

Shared powers are most respectful of subnational autonomy if central rules have priority only in the case of concrete clashes. Of course, its autonomy is even better preserved if subnational rule has priority over central rule. However this is not the general rule in practice, even where it occurs for specific subject matters.

5.2.2 *Constraining allocation principles*

'Constraining allocation principles' refers to principles that interfere with the basic model of power allocation to constrain the range of action of one or all tiers of government. This includes emergency clauses that enable the central government to take over subnational competences, as well as principles that lay down upon each government a duty to consider the other entities' interests, even if the government remains within the boundaries of its competences. Where these principles imply consideration of other entities' interests or even require intergovernmental negotiation, they promote cohesion. By contrast, unilateral overriding powers that impede upon the subnational sphere of (exclusive) competences reduce subnational autonomy.

These kinds of rules and principles come in many different forms. For the feasibility of the index, one type is selected for each dimension. For the cohesion index, the principle of loyalty is selected. For the autonomy index, the focus is on overriding powers that interfere in one particular SNE.

Measuring cohesion

Index 13.1 Cohesion index – constraining allocation principles

There is no federal loyalty principle in place	0
There is a federal loyalty principle in place that comprises one of three components	1
There is a federal loyalty principle in place that comprises two of three components	2
There is a federal loyalty principle in place that comprises all components: a negative duty of self-restraint, a process-bound duty of cooperation, and a positive duty to assist	3
The federal loyalty principle binds both central and subnational authorities, in an asymmetrical way	+1
The federal loyalty principle binds both central and subnational authorities equally	+2

80 Art. 5 Protocol N° 2 on the application of the principles of subsidiarity and proportionality.

81 Palermo and Kössler (n 29) 296, 315.

82 Art. 46(3) Swiss Constitution.

The most cohesion-inducing principles are loyalty principles that oblige all constituent entities to take into consideration each other's interests, even when they remain within the boundaries of their competences. The term 'loyalty principle' is used here to encompass all rules and principles that have similar meanings, even if the underlying assumptions sometimes differ. This is true despite a variety of names such as 'Bundestreue', 'comity', 'mutual consideration', or 'sincere cooperation'. For example, Erk and Gagnon explain that 'federal comity' assumes "an overarching allegiance to the federation and a common purpose between the constituent units". However, 'federal trust' assumes that there is no consensus over issues, but that the different tiers rely on the integrity of one another and are committed to maintaining the partnership.[83]

In some systems, such principles are laid down in the constitution. For example, the Swiss Constitution explicitly mentions that the Confederation and the Cantons owe each other "a duty of consideration".[84] The Belgian Constitution imposes upon the federal state and the SNEs the duty to carry out their competences in consideration of 'federal loyalty'.[85] Meanwhile, the South African Constitution requires all governments to "exercise their powers and perform their functions in a manner that does not encroach on the geographical, functional or institutional integrity of government in another sphere".[86] In some systems, courts play an important role in specifying the loyalty principle, or to recognize it as an unwritten principle. In Spain, it is based on the Constitutional Court's jurisprudence. Even in Belgium, Italy, and Switzerland, the courts had already referred to such a principle before it was explicitly enshrined in the Constitution.[87] Yet, other systems, such as the United States and Australia, do not recognize federal loyalty.[88] Dual systems, in particular, that are interested in competition rather than integration, tend to ignore the existence of a loyalty principle. Else, they reduce it to its negative form as a prohibition against impeding the exercise of central powers or subnational capacity to function.[89]

83 Jan Erk and Alain-G. Gagnon, 'Constitutional ambiguity and federal trust: Codification of federalism in Canada, Spain and Belgium', (2000) 10 *Regional & Federal Studies* 94.
84 Art. 44(2) Swiss Constitution.
85 Art. 143 § 1 Belgian Constitution.
86 Art. 41(1)g South African Constitution.
87 Jean-François Gaudreault-DesBiens, ''Cooperative Federalism in Search of a Normative Justification: Considering the Principle of Federal Loyalty', (2014) 23 *Const Forum*, 7; Palermo and Kössler (n 29) 251.
88 Gaudreault-DesBiens (n 87) 3.
89 Johanne Poirier and Cheryl Saunders, 'Conclusion: Comparative Experiences of Intergovernmental Relations in Federal Systems', in Poirier, Saunders and Kincaid (n 45) 446.

In its broadest sense, federal loyalty has three components.[90] The first component is "a negative duty of self-restraint"[91] and implies a prohibition against acting in such a way that disproportional negative externalities are created. The second component is process bound and requires procedural involvement of other entities if a proposed measure is likely to affect their policies. The last component consists of a positive duty to assist other entities if they encounter problems exercising their competences. For example, the Swiss Constitution explicitly states that the Confederation and the Cantons shall support each other in the fulfilment of their duties, owe each other a duty of support, and must provide mutual administrative and judicial assistance.[92] The Treaty on the European Union states that "pursuant to the principle of sincere cooperation, the Union and the Member States shall, in full mutual respect, assist in carrying out tasks which flow from the Treaties".[93] The South African Constitution obliges all governments to cooperate in mutual trust and good faith, for example, by assisting and supporting one another and coordinating their actions and legislation with one another.[94] Similar duties to assist, support, and cooperate are found in Kenya.[95]

Finally, the loyalty principle may address all tiers or only the subnational ones. Most systems accept federal loyalty as a mutual duty, even if the principle is formulated mostly as a duty falling on the SNEs. In the EU, for example, the principle of sincere cooperation is formulated as a duty to assist that is imposed on both the Union and the member states. However, the treaty only requires the member states to "facilitate the achievement of the Union's tasks and refrain from any measure which could jeopardize the attainment of the Union's objectives",[96] in view of the protection of Union interests.[97] Nevertheless, it is applied as a principle that creates obligations on both the Union and the member states,[98] albeit in an asymmetrical way.[99]

90 Gaudreault-DesBiens (n 87) 4–6.
91 Gaudreault-DesBiens (n 87) 4.
92 Art. 44(1) and (2) Swiss Constitution.
93 Art. 4(3) TEU.
94 Art. 41(1)h South African Constitution.
95 Art. 189(1) Kenyan Constitution.
96 Art 4(3) TEU. This is linked with other, more specific, duties of loyal cooperation that are imposed upon the Member States, see Geert De Baere and Timothy Roes, 'EU Loyalty as Good Faith', (2015) 64 *ICLQ* 834–835.
97 Marcus Klamert, *The Principle of Loyalty in EU Law* (Oxford University Press 2014) 18.
98 De Baere and Roes (n 96) 835–836.
99 Klamert (n 97) 25–28.

Measuring autonomy

Index 13.2 Autonomy index – constraining allocation principles

The central government can assume all powers vested in the SNE to keep the SNE in line	0
The central government can assume all powers vested in the SNE to keep the SNE in line, with some substantial safeguards or exceptions	1
The central government can put the SNE under strict surveillance to keep it in line	2
The central government can legislate in exclusive subnational matters to keep the SNE in line	3
The central government can take sanctions with the purpose of keeping the SNE in line	4
The SNE has the opportunity to be heard before measures are taken to keep the SNE in line	+1
SNEs are, directly or indirectly, involved in the procedure to take measures against the SNE, but with no decisive weight	+1
SNEs have decisive weight in the procedure to take measures against the SNE	+2
The SNE can challenge measures taken against it in court	+1
The central government can only use overriding powers to keep the SNE in line on the basis of legal grounds	+1
The central government has no overriding powers that target a particular SNE to keep it in line	10

To measure autonomy, the index is interested in unilateral overriding powers that upset the normal system of division of powers.

This does not include commerce clauses and similar provisions that enable the central government to encroach upon subnational policy fields. These clauses are part of the normal system of division of powers and are included in the index on allocation techniques. It also takes no account of very specific clauses that do not impact substantially on the normal system of power division. This includes clauses that enable the central government to comply with international obligations instead of SNEs, if SNEs fail to comply.

The most prominent example of clauses or principles that upset the normal system of power division are emergency clauses. They enable the central government to address an emergency situation with measures that are beyond its reach in normal circumstances. They may seriously hamper subnational autonomy if the central authority can declare the state of emergency without (substantial) subnational involvement, as is, for example, the case in India, Malaysia, or Nigeria.[100] Subnational autonomy may be further hampered if these clauses allow the central government to encroach upon exclusive policy domains or even substitute subnational government. In India, the emergency rules were inserted in the Constitution precisely to enable strong Union government.[101]

100 Art. 352, 356, 360 Indian Constitution; Art. 150 Malaysian Constitution; Art. 305(3) Nigerian Constitution.

101 Palermo and Kössler (n 29) 154.

The Canadian P.O.G.G. clause – Peace, Order and Good Government – has been called an 'emergency clause'.[102] However, it does not qualify for inclusion in the index. The reason is that the clause does not allow the central government to impede upon exclusive subnational powers. It also enumerates a set of competences that are assigned to the federal level, and therefore, as a rule, do not fall within the ambit of Provincial competences.[103] Further, the South African Parliament's power to intervene in exclusive subnational competences in certain circumstances[104] does not qualify,[105] for the reasons already explained under the previous section. Rather than upsetting the normal system of power division, it nuances the qualification of exclusive competences under the normal scheme of power allocation.

Emergency powers are necessary for a country's survival in exceptional circumstances and are, therefore, also indicative of cohesion. This is particularly the case if they involve SNEs in the declaration of the state of emergency and the issuing of emergency decrees. This was already partly caught in the previous indexes on the scope of powers (category 1: security) and the allocation technique. However, that did not highlight the risk that they are used as an excuse to centralize with the management of ordinary crises.[106]

This risk is particularly high if the state of emergency can be declared by one central body – mostly the President – and if there is no room for judicial review. However, while the decision is in the hands of the central authority in some systems (such as India, Malaysia, and Nigeria), in other systems (such as Pakistan) the involvement of the SNEs varies depending on the type of emergency.[107]

For these reasons, this index selects only one type of overriding (emergency) powers. These are those that do not address some external threat to the entire country or even to a particular SNE, but target the government performance of a particular SNE, for instance, when it is considered 'rebellious'.

For example, both the Indian and Pakistani Constitutions allow the President to declare a state of emergency in the case of a failure of the constitutional machinery that hinders the SNE from governing according to the constitution.[108] In Ethiopia, it is specified in more detail: the state of emergency can be declared in case of "a breakdown of law and order which endangers the Constitutional order and which cannot be controlled by the regular law enforcement agencies

102 Kenneth Lysyk, 'Constitutional Reform and the Introductory Clause of Section 91: Residual and Emergency Law-Making Authority', (1979) 57 *The Canadian Bar Rev.* 532.
103 *Ibid* 539–540.
104 Art. 44(2) South African Constitution.
105 But see further, for an exception.
106 For this risk: Edward Philips, 'Drastic Solutions: A Comparative Study of Emergency Powers in the Commonwealth', (1990) 5 *Denning Law Journal* 60.
107 Art. 233–235 Pakistani Constitution.
108 Art. 234 Pakistani Constitution; Art. 356 Indian Constitution.

and personnel".[109] In Malaysia and Nigeria, this is not explicitly mentioned as a ground for the state of emergency. However, in Malaysia, it would fall under the general clause that gives the elected monarch the power to declare an emergency whereby the "the security" or "public order" in part of the Federation is threatened.[110] In Nigeria, a catch-all ground of "any other public danger which clearly constitutes a threat to the existence of the Federation" is added to more specific grounds.[111]

Examples that are separate from emergency clauses can be found in, for example, Germany, Spain, Kenya, and South Africa. According to the German '*Bundeszwang*' clause, the federal government can take coercive measures to compel a Land to comply with its duties under the Constitution or other federal laws.[112] In Spain, apart from the clauses that allow the federal government to proclaim a state of alarm, emergency, and siege,[113] there is a separate provision that enables the federal government to intervene "if a Self-governing Community does not fulfil the obligations imposed upon it by the Constitution or other law, or acts in a way that is seriously prejudicial to the general interest of Spain".[114] In South Africa, Parliament can act even in matters that fall under subnational exclusive powers, in order to "prevent unreasonable action taken by a province which is prejudicial to the interests of another province or the country as a whole".[115] Further, the South African executive can intervene if a Province cannot fulfil its obligations.[116] In Kenya Parliament can provide for national government intervention if a county government is "unable to perform its functions" or does not operate a financial management system as required by law.[117]

A special case is the EU, where it can determine that there is "a clear risk of a serious breach" by a member state of values such as democracy, the rule of law, and fundamental rights.[118] This situation does not give the EU the power to take measures in place of the envisaged member state, and therefore, does not upset the normal scheme of power division. However, it can result in the suspension of certain Treaty rights, such as voting rights. This would therefore limit the member state's autonomy that is derived under 'status'. It would have been an option to include this situation in the status indexes, but that would have distorted the picture of status under normal circumstances. Also, by limiting status rights, the central government indirectly instructs SNEs as to how they should act in policy domains under their competence. Therefore, this type of power is included in the present index.

109 Art. 93(1)(a) Ethiopian Constitution.
110 Art. 150 Malaysian Constitution. See Philips (n 106) 62.
111 Art. 305(3) Nigerian Constitution.
112 Art. 37 German Constitution.
113 Art. 116 Spanish Constitution.
114 Art. 155 Spanish Constitution.
115 Art. 44(2) South African Constitution.
116 Art. 100 South African Constitution.
117 Art. 190(3) Kenyan Constitution.
118 Art. 7 TEU.

If one specific SNE is targeted, it is reasonable that this SNE's consent is not required. More indicative of the scope of autonomy, then, is: (1) what triggers the overriding powers; (2) whether the SNE is heard; (3) when the procedure leaves the decision not to one central body, but to a body that includes other SNEs that are more likely to assess the situation from a subnational perspective; and (4) the intensity of the overriding powers.

1 Triggers
There are several reasons that can trigger the use of unilateral overriding powers against one particular SNE.

In India and Pakistan, the constitutional machinery failure emergency, a remnant from colonial times, has been used to keep a strong hold on the SNEs.[119] The President can interfere if he is satisfied "that a situation has arisen in which the Government of the Province cannot be carried on in accordance with the provisions of the Constitution".[120] These are broad terms that leave much scope for opportunity control. For example, in India, the central government invoked article 356 of the Constitution more than 100 times, often inspired by political needs rather than any real emergency.[121]

Opportunity control is also what distinguishes the German and Spanish models of '*Bundeszwang*'.[122] The German trigger is phrased in terms of legality: if a Land "fails to comply with its obligations under this basic Law or other federal laws".[123] In South Africa, Art. 100 of the Constitution is phrased in a similar way.[124] This is also the case in Spain,[125] but another criterion is added that leaves more discretionary power: if the Self-governing Community "acts in a way that is seriously prejudicial to the general interest of Spain".

2 Hearing the SNE's perspective
The first method is explicit in the EU system, where the Council may only determine that there is a clear risk of a serious breach of values after questioning the member state's representatives and that there is in effect a breach after inviting the member state to submit its observations.[126] In Spain, as well, the Government can only establish that a particular Self-governing

119 Panch R.P.D. Sharma, 'In Search Of The Theory Of Constitutional Machinery Failure (Emergency) Models In India And Pakistan: A Comparative Exploration', (2017) 23 *Comp. L. Rev.* 85.
120 Art. 234 Pakistani Constitution. In similar wordings: Art. 356(1) Indian Constitution.
121 Sharma (n 119) 105. See also Palermo and Kössler (n 29) 155 on the use of emergency powers to dismiss state governments controlled by opposition parties.
122 Mariá J. García Morales, 'Federal execution, Article 155 of the Spanish Constitution and the crisis in Catalonia', (2018) 73 *Zeitschrift für Öffentliches Recht* 797.
123 Art. 37(1) German Constitution.
124 "When a province cannot or does not fulfil an executive obligation in terms of the Constitution or legislation".
125 Art. 155 Spanish Constitution: "if a Self-governing Community does not fulfil the obligations imposed on it by the Constitution or other laws".
126 Art. 7(1)(2) TEU.

Community does not fulfil its constitutional obligations or seriously harms the general interest of Spain after lodging a complaint with the president of that Self-governing Community.[127] This gives the SNE an opportunity to respond.[128] Likewise, in Kenya, notice is given to the county government of the measures that the national government intends to take.[129]

It is less explicit in Pakistan, where the President can only act on the basis of the Governor's report on the failure of a particular state's constitutional machinery.[130] The Governor is appointed by the President, and therefore, regarded as a central body. However, considering their proximity, one may assume that the subnational authorities are given the chance to express their views.

In India, the President can act upon the Governor's report "or otherwise" – in practice most often a report by the Union Council of Ministers or the Union Home Ministry[131] – which reduces the SNE's potential involvement.[132] In Nigeria, the President acts upon the request of the State Governor, supported by a two-thirds majority of the State's House of Assembly. This is only if an emergency arises within the boundaries of that State, but even then the President can act unilaterally if the Governor does not make that request "within a reasonable time".[133] The index, therefore, does not inquire whether the SNE 'can' be involved, but whether it is possible for the central government to act 'without' hearing the particular SNE.

3 Procedural safeguards

Ferejohn and Pasquino have developed a typology to distinguish emergency models based on legislative checks and balances on the one hand, and those based on executive dominance on the other.[134] However, the present index does not examine central overriding powers from the angle of constitutionalism, but from the specific angle of federalism. Here, the question is whether SNEs are involved in the assessment that a particular SNE is in a situation that creates central overriding powers and whether they are involved in the use of these powers. Even if the particular SNE is not involved, this would at least ensure that the subnational perspective is taken into account. After all, if one SNE is targeted today, it may be another one tomorrow. Ferejohn and Pasquino's typology is, nevertheless, relevant because subnational involvement is more likely to take place in a legislative model than in an executive model.

127 Art. 155(1) Spanish Constitution.
128 Philips (n 106) 798.
129 Art. 190(5) Kenyan Constitution.
130 Art. 234(1) Pakistani Constitution; Art. 101 Pakistani Constitution.
131 Sharma (n 119) 107.
132 Art. 356(1) Indian Constitution.
133 Art. 305(4)(5) Nigerian Constitution.
134 John Ferejohn and Pasquale Pasquino, 'The Law of Exception: A typology of Emergency Powers', (2004) 2 I.CON 210–239

The strongest safeguards are found in systems that give SNEs (co-)decisive power. For example, in the EU, the Council of Ministers (that consists of all member states) determines the existence of a clear risk via a majority of four-fifths of its members. The Council determines that there is indeed a serious and persistent breach of values by a unanimous vote.[135] The German government needs the consent of the 'Bundesrat' to take coercive measures.[136] The South African Parliament can intervene if a particular Province takes 'unreasonable' action by passing legislation approved by both the National Assembly and the National Council of Provinces. In the case of disagreement, the case is referred to the Mediation Committee. Only if this Committee is unable to agree, then may South Africa's National Assembly pass the bill with a majority of two-thirds of its members.[137] The National Council of Provinces consists of a delegation from each Province.[138] The central executive can intervene in Provinces that are unable or unwilling to fulfil their obligations, conditional upon notice to the National Council of Provinces. This reviews the intervention and can stop it.[139] In Nigeria, the President declares the state of emergency, but the Proclamation ceases to have effect if it is not subsequently approved by a two-thirds majority of the members of both Houses of the National Assembly.[140] This includes the Senate, which consists of three Senators from each State and one from the Federal Capital Territory.[141] In Ethiopia, federal intervention is ordered by the House of Federation – which represents ethnic groups. These ethnic groups are not SNEs, but they, nevertheless, consist of members elected by the State councils.[142] Further, the emergency declaration is approved by the House of Peoples' Representatives, and emergency decrees are scrutinized by a State of Emergency Inquiry Board.[143]

At the other end of the spectrum are executive models such as those in South Asia. In India, it is the President alone that declares the failure of constitutional machinery and that exercises the SNE's executive powers. Legislative powers are exercised by the national Parliament, but this Parliament may delegate this power to the President.[144] In Malaysia, the elected monarch also acts alone. In both cases, Parliament – if in session – may end the state of emergency. However, the Malaysian constitution

135 Art. 7(1)(2) TEU.
136 Art. 37(1) German Constitution. This is, according to García Morales (n 122) (2018) 73 *Zeitschrift für Öffentliches Recht* 795, the essential feature that distinguishes the German from the Spanish system.
137 Art. 44(2) and 76(1) South African Constitution.
138 Art. 60 South African Constitution.
139 Art. 100(2) South African Constitution.
140 Art. 305(2) and (6)b Nigerian Constitution.
141 Art. 48 Nigerian Constitution.
142 Art. 62(9) Ethiopian Constitution.
143 Art. 93 Ethiopian Constitution.
144 Art. 356(1) and 357(1) Indian Constitution.

explicitly states that annulling the Proclamation of the state of emergency or any ordinance will prejudice anything done under that Proclamation.[145]

In between are procedures involving SNEs, but with no decisive weight. For example, the Spanish Government can take measures against a particular SNE after approval is granted by an overall majority of the Senate.[146] The Senate consists mainly of representatives elected in constituencies that coincide with local entities, to which members appointed by the Self-governing Communities are added.[147]

Extra procedural safeguards pertain to judicial control. Even if courts leave a broad discretion to the central government, especially in emergency or crisis situations, there is at least some potential for SNEs to be protected against excessive abuse of overriding powers. For example, in Spain, the Constitutional Court has stressed that Article 155 of the Spanish Constitution can only be used to deal with extremely serious breaches, and is not an instrument of normal supervision to ensure the implementation of central legislation by self-governing communities.[148] In some systems, judicial review in these circumstances is simply forbidden. In Pakistan, for example, the Constitution prohibits the calling into question of the Proclamation of Emergency or any Order made under it.[149]

4 Intensity of the overriding powers

A final question is how deeply the central government can encroach upon the SNE's powers.

The most radical form is when the central government simply takes over. For example, in India, Malaysia, and Pakistan the President and the central Parliament – or even the President alone – can assume (almost) all powers vested in the subnational institutions.[150]

Procedural or substantive safeguards and exceptions can be made, sometimes pertaining to specific SNEs. For example, in Malaysia, even in emergency situations, the central authorities may not interfere with Islamic law or the custom of the Malays. They also may not interfere with any matter of native law or custom in the State of Sabah or Sarawak, and no measure relating to religion, citizenship, or language may be adopted that is inconsistent with the Constitution.[151] In Kenya, the national government can "assume responsibility" for the functions that the county government is unable to perform, but it can only take those measures that are 'necessary'.

145 Art. 150(3) Malaysian Constitution.
146 Art. 155(1) Spanish Constitution.
147 Art. 69(5) Spanish Constitution.
148 García Morales (n 122) 796, referring to decisions STC 76/1983 of 5 August 1983 and STC 41/2016 of 3 March 2018.
149 Art. 236(2) Pakistani Constitution.
150 Art. 356 Indian Constitution; Art. 150(4) Malaysian Constitution; Art. 234(1) Pakistani Constitution.
151 Art. 150(6A) Malaysian Constitution.

The national government must also take measures that enable the county government to resume full responsibility for its functions.[152]

A second category is still intrusive, but less radical. Here, the SNE is still functioning, but under strict surveillance. For example, the Spanish Constitution allows the central government to "take all measures necessary" to compel the Self-governing Community to meet its obligations and to issue instructions to this Community to implement these measures.[153] This is similar to the German model, where the federal government can take "the necessary steps to compel the Land to comply with its duties" and to "issue instructions" to implement coercive measures.[154] In Spain, 'necessary measures' may also imply temporary substitutions, but only for certain specified functions.[155]

Less drastic is a regime that restricts central interference to specific legislative measures, without interfering in the functioning of the SNE. For example, in South Africa, the central Parliament may pass legislation with regard to matters normally falling under the exclusive competence of the SNE, in order to "prevent unreasonable action taken by a province which is prejudicial to the interests of another province or to the country as a whole".[156]

In its mildest form, the central government can only use sanctions to indirectly instruct SNEs how to behave. As mentioned already, in the EU system these sanctions take the form of restrictions on rights related to EU membership.[157] In some systems, the central government may dissolve the subnational legislature to keep a particular SNE in line in a way that seriously violates the constitution or other laws.[158]

5.3 Federalism dispute resolution

The division of powers is never so clear-cut as to prevent federalism disputes from arising: these are conflicts over the question of who has the (overriding) power to regulate any subject matter. A regime of power division is, therefore, in need of a system to resolve this type of dispute.

Such systems can be political (4.3.1.) or judicial (4.3.2.) in nature or combine both. Political and judicial mechanisms may function as communicating vessels: if the political system works adequately, there will be less need to go to court.[159] This is true unless individuals only have access to judicial conflict resolution systems and have the right to challenge an act to invoke a violation of allocation

152 Art. 190(5) Kenyan Constitution.
153 Art. 155 Spanish Constitution.
154 Art. 37 German Constitution.
155 García Morales (n 122) 800.
156 Art. 44(2)(e) South African Constitution.
157 Art. 7 TEU.
158 For example, Art. 126 Italian Constitution; Art. 112 Pakistani Constitution.
159 Palermo and Kössler (n 29) 141.

rules. The South African Constitution even states that courts must refer intergovernmental disputes back to the government body involved, if no reasonable efforts have been made to settle the dispute by political mechanisms and procedures.[160] Similar provisions apply in Kenya.[161] In this index, both political and judicial safeguards are examined, but at this point, their relationship is not explored.[162] The involvement of SNEs in central decision-making was already measured in the status Indexes 4.1., 4.2., 5.1., and 5.2.. Here, attention is given to mechanisms that are specifically created to settle federalism disputes. This is the case if actors that are not part of the normal decision-making procedure can interfere, before or after a decision is taken, and start a political procedure to resolve the issue.

As mentioned in Chapter 2, courts (and other dispute resolution systems) act as both safeguards and hubs for change in power relations. In Chapter 8, dispute resolution mechanisms are discussed as hubs for change. Here, their role as safeguards of cohesion and autonomy rules and principles is measured.

5.3.1 Political mechanisms

Political mechanisms do not only deal with competence conflicts, i.e., conflicts as to whether an authority remains within its legal boundaries. They also resolve conflicts that arise when it is undisputed that one authority has the legal competence to act, but this allegedly harms another tier's interests. Even if SNEs are involved in central decision-making, they may not have any decisive weight to avoid the adoption of acts that create conflicts of competence or conflicts of interest. Also, SNEs may adopt acts that are harmful to other SNEs or to the general interest or exceed their legal boundaries. The question is whether other entities can raise this issue, and how such conflicts are resolved.

The most prominent example of a political mechanism to resolve federalism disputes is found in Ethiopia, where it substitutes for judicial review. Conflict resolution – as with all other constitutional disputes - is trusted to the House of Federations. This is a (nonlegislative) house of the federal Parliament consisting of representatives of ethnic groups elected by the State Councils.[163] The House is assisted by the Council of Constitutional Inquiry, consisting of the President and Vice-President of the Federal Supreme Court, six legal experts appointed by the President of the Federation on the recommendation of the House of Representatives, and three persons designated by the House of the Federation

160 Art. 41(3)(4) South African Constitution. See Nico Steytler, 'The Constitutional Court of South Africa: Reinforcing an Hourglass System of Multi-Level Government', in Aroney and Kincaid (n 14) 344.

161 Art. 189(3)(4) Kenyan Constitution combined with Art. 31(b) and 35 Intergovernmental Relations Act.

162 See further, in Chapter 8.

163 Art. 83 resp. Art. 61 Ethiopian Constitution. The State Councils elect these representatives themselves or hold elections to have them elected by the people.

from among its members.[164] This Council is the first to consider the constitutionality of a federal or state law on the request of any court or interested party, before submitting the case to the House of the Federation for a final decision. Interested parties can lodge an appeal with the House if the Council decides there is no need for constitutional interpretation.[165] Importantly, the incapacity of courts to resolve intergovernmental disputes is not limited to federal-state relations. State courts also have no power of review against state constitutions, which means that they cannot resolve disputes between state and local governments.[166] Such disputes are adjudicated by state constitutional interpretation commissions.[167]

The Ethiopian system is unusual, because it is not complementary to judicial review, but substitutes it instead. Usually, political mechanisms settle disputes that arise between political actors. In the Ethiopian system, courts and private persons may trigger the system, which raises expectations of neutrality, transparency, and coherency that the system is not able to match.[168]

Here, political mechanisms to resolve federalism disputes are not assessed on the basis of neutrality and transparency, but on the basis of whether they promote cohesion and protect subnational autonomy.

Measuring cohesion

Index 14.1 Cohesion index – political federalism dispute resolution

There is no formal political mechanism to resolve conflicts of interest or competence	0
The political dispute resolution mechanisms come down to a procedure where one tier of government is dominant and other parties in the dispute are heard	1
The political dispute resolution mechanism implies unbalanced intergovernmental dialogue, with one tier of government represented in a more prominent manner	2
The political dispute resolution mechanism implies balanced intergovernmental dialogue	3
Political dispute resolution is conditional upon negotiation efforts between the parties	+1
Institutional mechanisms are in place to ensure or assist negotiation between the parties	+1

There is a wide range of political mechanisms available to resolve conflicts of interest and competences. A variety of mechanisms for dispute resolution are sometimes inserted in statutes or cooperation agreements pertaining to specific

164 Art. 82(2) Ethiopian Constitution.

165 Art. 84(2)(3) Ethiopian Constitution.

166 Yonatan T. Fessha and Zemelak Ayele, 'Giving 'shape and texture' to a Federal System? Ethiopia's Courts and its Unusual Umpire', in Fessha and Kössler (n 22) 59.

167 *Ibid* 60.

168 Critical for the lack of visibility, transparency and perceived neutrality, and the briefness of the CCI's opinions: Hessebon and Idris (n 14) 185–191, Assefa Fiseha, 'Constitutional Adjudication in Ethiopia: Exploring the experience of the House of Federation (HOF)', (2007) 1 *Mizan. L. Rev.* 14, 31.

subject matters. In South Africa, it is mandatory to include a dispute-settlement mechanism or procedure in formal intergovernmental agreements.[169] The index takes into account the overall mechanism, if any, that is in place if no specific procedure applies.

Even then, such procedures may involve different steps. For example, in Ethiopia, the Council of Constitutional Inquiry is a filter that selects the cases to be handled by the House of the Federation. In Belgium, the Senate is involved in conflicts that are brought to the agenda by a Parliament, before the matter is sent to the Concertation Committee.[170] Therefore, the index takes account of the entire process, the most prominent body in the procedure, as well as the body that takes the final decision that ends the procedure. A final decision should not be confused with the question of whether the contested act is pursued or not, and can also be an acknowledgement that no solution has been found. For example, in Belgium, the Concertation Committee is the most prominent body. However, if no consensus is reached, the executive or assembly where the conflict arose decides whether to pursue the contested action.

From a cohesion perspective, the core question is whether federalism disputes are resolved through intergovernmental dialogue. This is the case if a dispute is ultimately dealt with by a balanced intergovernmental body that includes representatives of an equal number of central and SNEs. It is unbalanced if the central or the subnational interests are voiced in a more prominent way. For example, in Belgium, the Concertation Committee is composed of an equal number of federal and subnational government representatives.[171] While at first sight, this is a balanced composition, linguistic parity reveals a very prominent representation by the SNEs. Moreover, it gives the Dutch-speaking Community, the Walloon Region, and the (overlapping) French Community a dominant position, as they largely converge with the language criterion. This is not the case for the GSC: it does not coincide with a language group, and its Minister-President is only present if the topic also concerns this Community. In Kenya, the 'Summit' consists of the President (or Deputy President) and the governors of the 47 counties,[172] which means that (on paper) the county perspective dominates. Under the EU infringement procedure, the Commission takes the leading role, inviting the member state to send a detailed reply and take measures to fulfill its obligations. However, in the end, it is the Commission alone that decides whether the case should be brought before the Court.[173]

In some systems, and depending upon the type of conflict, such an intergovernmental body consists of more than two layers. For example, in South Africa, the President's Council consists of five members from the central government,

169 Art. 40(2) Intergovernmental Relations Act.
170 Art. 32, § 1*quater* Law 9 August 1980 on the Reform of the Institutions.
171 Art 31 Law 9 August 1980 on the reform of the institutions.
172 Art. 7(2) Intergovernmental Relations Act.
173 Art. 258 TFEU.

including the President, the Premiers of the nine provinces, and a municipal councilor representing local government.[174] Such structures are appropriate for conflicts that affect all these levels. However, if conflicts only concern the relations between two specific levels, multi-layered negotiation may outbalance one of the relevant levels.

In addition, if procedures and mechanisms are institutionalized to encourage the parties to resolve their differences before they turn into an actual dispute, this promotes an atmosphere of loyalty and good faith. Ultimately this is considered to be more cohesive. For example, in South Africa, a procedure is inserted that makes sure that the parties convene and a 'facilitator' is designated.[175] Even in the absence of a specific institutional setting, institutional encouragement is already in place if intergovernmental dispute resolution is conditional to negotiation efforts between the parties. In Kenya and South Africa, for example, parties must first make "reasonable efforts" and take all necessary steps to amicably resolve the matter, either through direct negotiation or through an intermediary.[176] By contrast, if the procedure merely leaves some time for negotiation between the parties, without any assistance or sanction, this does not qualify. For example, in Belgium, if a Parliament submits a motion of a conflict of interest, the lawmaking procedure is merely suspended to allow negotiations between the relevant parliaments before the matter is brought to the Concertation Committee.[177]

Measuring autonomy

Index 14.2 Autonomy index – political federalism dispute resolution

There is no formal political mechanism to resolve conflicts of interests or competences	0
The SNE is heard if a procedure is initiated against its actions but is not otherwise involved in federalism disputes	1
The political dispute resolution mechanism implies unbalanced intergovernmental dialogue, with a dominant position for the central authorities	2
The political dispute resolution mechanism implies unbalanced intergovernmental dialogue, with prominent representation for SNEs	3
The particular SNE has a dominant position in the political dispute resolution mechanism	4
The SNE can initiate the political dispute resolution mechanisms if the central authorities have harmed its interests or exceeded its competences, or are about to do so	+1

From an autonomy perspective, the question is to what extent the SNE has control over the management of political conflicts. If the conflict concerns the

174 Art. 6 Intergovernmental Relations Act.

175 Art. 42 Intergovernmental Relations Act.

176 Art. 33(1) Kenyan Intergovernmental Relations Act; Art. 41(2) South African Intergovernmental Relations Act.

177 Art. 32 Act of 9 August 1980 on the reform of the institution.

central government's action, the question is whether the SNE can intervene and whether it has a say in the procedure and the final outcome. If its own action is at issue, the question is whether it is sufficiently involved in the procedure and whether it has the final say. This is also relevant where the dispute concerns another SNE's action because the decision will also affect its own maneuvering space.

Similar to the cohesion index, the system scores lowly if there is no formal mechanism in place. In that case, the SNE has no assurance that it will be able to address a conflict other than through judicial proceedings – if a court avenue is available. By contrast, it is more interested in the weight of the subnational perspective rather than a balanced composition of any intergovernmental dispute resolution body. For example, in Germany, the subnational perspective is dominant in conflicts regarding the Land execution of federal laws. In this case, it is the Bundesrat, the representative of the Länder governments that decides whether the Land has violated the law.[178]

5.3.2 *Judicial mechanisms*

According to Dicey, federalism implies "a general willingness to yield to the authority of the law courts", which he considered a weakness.[179] Much depends of course on which systems are considered to be governed by federalism. To him, the United States was the only point of reference, as the "most completely developed" or "perfect" form of federalism, with Germany and Switzerland serving merely as incomplete copies of that model.[180]

Under a wider definition, it turns out that not all MTS have a system of review to safeguard the constitutional distribution of competences. In Ethiopia, there is none.[181] In some other MTSs, such as Switzerland and the United Kingdom, courts can resolve federalism disputes. However, this is only when subnational acts are challenged, whereas central Acts of Parliaments are inviolable. In these cases, other factors may impact the Court's position. However, as an institutional upset, this puts a limit on subnational autonomy because SNEs are not able to launch a court challenge of federal statutes that encroach upon their sphere of competences. Belser finds it "a disruptive fact" that the cantons have no legal redress mechanism against unconstitutional central intrusion into their autonomy.[182]

In Chapter 8, there is a discussion of the widely held assumption that courts by definition have centralizing effects. There, it is noticed that this is not a general truth and that a set of variables determines whether courts have a centralizing

178 Art. 84(4) German Constitution.
179 Albert V. Dicey, An *Introduction to the Study of the Law of the Constitution* (MacMillan, 1915, 8th ed.) xiv.
180 *Ibid* 73–74.
181 See further, Chapter 8.
182 Belser (n 31) 51.

impact. The chapter will examine different types of variables, both legal and nonlegal. For present purposes, we are only interested in institutional variables, because they can be controlled through institutional design.

The courts examined in these indexes are the apex courts that resolve federalism disputes. In some systems, this is entrusted to specific Constitutional Courts, whereas in other systems it is the Supreme Court. The organization and composition of these courts are usually regulated by constitutional acts and organic statutes, with some refinement by court decisions. However, some aspects may be governed by informal rules. For example, there are no formal criteria to secure subnational representation in the composition of the Brazilian Supreme Federal Court. However, in practice, "a certain balance between federative diversity and population representation in nominations" is respected.[183] Such informal rules are included only if they are so established that they have become an unwritten custom, and are, therefore, part of the institutional framework – in other words, they are a constitutional 'custom' rather than a 'convention'.[184] Otherwise, they are the result of a political culture that determines the dynamics of the MTS beyond the institutional setup.

Measuring cohesion

Index 15.1 Cohesion index – judicial federalism dispute resolution

The court is composed of judges appointed by the central authority only	0
The court is composed of judges appointed by the subnational authorities only	1
The court is composed of judges appointed by mixed authorities, in an unbalanced way	2
The court is composed of judges appointed by mixed authorities, in a balanced way	3
The court, as a rule, makes decisions in a mixed chamber	+1
The court is dependent upon both central and subnational authorities to function	+1

Since cohesion is not a synonym for centralism, the present index does not measure the extent to which the court's design has the potential for advancing centralist outcomes – i.e., outcomes in federalism disputes that confirm or strengthen the central authority's power. Instead, the index strives for more balanced outcomes, with regard for both national integrity as well as respect for subnational autonomy. Such outcomes presuppose a dialogue within the court between judges that have some affiliation with the central and the subnational authorities, while remaining independent in legal terms. At the same time, a mixed court will be conceived as being more legitimate, especially in multinational systems. This will help the court to find support for its decisions in the different communities that compose the MTS.

To this end, the rules concerning the selection and the composition of courts are relevant, as well as the way judges make their decisions and the authority that determines the court's functioning.

183 Antonio Rodrigues, Garcia Lopes Lorencini and Zimmerman (n 14) 119.
184 *Ibid*, 81.

Earlier comparative research suggests that a low involvement of SNEs in the selection of judges leads to a more centralist approach by the court.[185] Arguably, courts are more likely to create cohesion if they are appointed in a way that involves both the central and subnational authorities. If not, appointment by SNEs without the involvement of the central government is more cohesive than appointment by the central authority alone. This is because at least some dialogue will emerge between the judges linked with the different SNEs.

By 'appointed by mixed authorities', the index refers to the situation where both the central level and SNEs have an important say. This is the case if, for example, the appointment of the judges has to be approved by Parliament. This Parliament may represent both the national electorate and the SNEs or their electorates, or the SNEs may otherwise be involved in the selection and appointment procedure with a decisive say. To determine whether the national electorate or the SNEs or their electorates are represented, the rules of thumb explained in Chapter 3 apply.

'Mixed authorities' are balanced if all relevant tiers have a decisive say. They are not balanced if the involvement of one tier is weak. For example, the judges of the Spanish Constitutional Court that are appointed by the Senate are selected from candidates nominated by the parliaments of the Autonomous Communities. This is considered to be a strong involvement on its face, but the involvement is made weak by the Constitutional Court's ruling that the Senate must remain free to select other candidates in addition to those nominated by the subnational parliaments. This has rendered the original rule meaningless in practice.[186]

The term 'mixed chambers' points to chambers composed of judges that are representative of the (main) SNEs, through geographical spread or through identity markers such as language, religion, or ethnicity, that largely overlap with the SNEs. When based on identity markers, this reveals the design as being 'power sharing court'.[187] The most radical example is the Belgian Constitutional Court that is composed on the basis of language parity.[188] In other courts, such as the Bosnian Constitutional Court and the Swiss Federal Tribunal, parity on the basis of ethnicity and language, respectively, is merely convention, without a firm legal basis.[189] Judges making decisions in mixed chambers are potentially more cohesion-enforcing that judges deciding alone or in non-mixed chambers. This is because there is a higher chance that the different (central and

185 Patricia Popelier, 'Federalism Disputes and the Behavior of Courts: Explaining Variation in Federal Courts' Support for Centralization', (2016) 47 *Publius: The Journal of Federalism*, 38–40. See further, Chapter 7.

186 Elisenda Casanas Adam, 'The Constitutional Court of Spain: From System Balancer to Polarizing Centralist', in Aroney and Kincaid (n 14) 383.

187 Stefan Graziadei, 'Power Sharing Courts', (2016) 3 *Contemporary Southeastern Europe* 66–105.

188 Art. 31 Special Majority Law on the Constitutional Court.

189 Graziadei (n 187) 82, 83.

subnational) perspectives are included in the balancing of interests. Belgium is a prominent example of how this leads to a balanced approach to federalism disputes.[190]

In doctrine, there is some debate about the desirability of identitarian representation in the organization of courts, given the impartiality of judges, which means that they are expected to decide on the basis of legal arguments only.[191] The index only takes sides in this discussion to the extent that it considers the inclusion of such traits favorable for a balanced outcome in federalism disputes if these traits are more or less congruent with the geographical delineation of SNEs. While empirical scholarship tends to underestimate the merit of legal argument, it has provided abundant evidence that the idea that judges decide cases on the basis of legal merit alone, is a myth.[192]

The index further examines which level of authority the court is dependent upon for its functioning. For example, if the central legislature, without the involvement of the SNEs, determines matters such as salaries, other aspects of the judges' status, the court's budget, or procedures, the 'dependency hypothesis' assumes that the court will be biased in favor of the central government.[193] For this reason, dependency on both central and subnational authorities is considered more cohesive. This is already the case if SNEs or their electorates are involved in the lawmaking procedure.

Measuring autonomy

Index 15.2 Autonomy index – judicial federalism dispute resolution

The SNE has no say in the appointment of judges	0
The SNE is consulted on the appointment of (some) judges	1
The electorate of the SNE is involved in the appointment of judges	2
The SNE is involved in the appointment of judges, through collective vote	3
The SNE is involved in the appointment of judges, with an individual veto right	4
In cases that affect the SNE, the court gives its decisions in a chamber with a judge that is, in terms of geography or identity markers, representative of the SNE	+1
The SNE has a substantial say in the rules that determine the functioning of the court	+1

Where in the cohesion index the focus was on some representation of all or the main SNEs, the autonomy index is only interested in the representation of the particular SNE that is the unit of analysis. As in the cohesion index, the autonomy index examines the appointment procedure, the way courts make

190 See Patricia Popelier and Samantha Bielen, 'How Courts Decide Federalism Disputes: Legal Merit, Attitudinal Effects, and Strategic Considerations in the Jurisprudence of the Belgian Constitutional Court', (2018) 49 Publius: The Journal of Federalism, 587–616.

191 For opposing views see: Graziadei (n 187) 74–76; Kössler and Fessha (n 22) 6; Matthias Kumm, 'On the Representativeness of Constitutional Courts', in Christine Landfried (ed), *Judicial Power. How Constitutional Courts Affect Political Transformations* (Cambridge University Press 2019) 286–287.

192 See further, Chapter 8.

193 Martin Shapiro, *Courts: A Comparative Analysis* (University of Chicago Press 1981) 55.

their decisions and the authorities that adopt the rules on the court's functioning. For the latter aspect, a 'substantial say' means that the SNE – not merely its electorate – influences the outcome, either through a collective vote, or individually. The mere right or practice of being consulted does not suffice.

For example, the Belgian judges of the Constitutional Court are appointed by the monarch after nomination by, alternatively, the House of Representatives and the Senate with a two-thirds majority. The two-thirds majority gives the FLC an individual right of nomination for half of the judges. This is because, in the Senate, which has a total of 60 seats, a nomination can be vetoed by 21 votes. The group of representatives of the Flemish Parliament consists of 29 members. Moreover, the SNE is indirectly represented through the Dutch language group in the Constitutional Court. This language group also has a substantial say in the rules that determine the functioning of the court. They require a special majority in both the House and the Senate, where each language group has a veto right. By contrast, there is much weaker involvement by the GSC, which has only one representative in the Senate and no language group of its own. At least one of the judges must provide proof of sufficient knowledge of the German language,[194] but this in no way requires some link with the GSC or some training in the laws of this Community.

194 Art. 34, par. 4 Special Majority Law on the Constitutional Court.

6 Fiscal arrangements

Fiscal federalism arrangements determine the allocation of taxing and spending powers and the structure of intergovernmental transfers.[1] They are at the core of any MTS and are of crucial importance to both cohesion and autonomy.[2] Interregional disparities potentially diminish solidarity and promote disintegration.[3] Fiscal arrangements, therefore, have cohesive potential if they downplay interregional disparities. They also determine the scope of subnational autonomy.[4] On the one hand, they provide the means for SNEs to pursue their policies. On the other hand, they may constrain subnational policy discretion, for example, through conditional grants.

Fiscal arrangements are usually analyzed alongside three aspects: revenue powers, spending powers, and equalization procedures. However, these aspects easily merge when examined from the perspective of autonomy and cohesion. All three aspects are therefore covered by the same index but reappear in different sections. The cohesion index concentrates on equalization mechanisms and other measures to promote solidarity and partnership. The autonomy index is mostly interested in revenue powers and spending powers. This index is

1 Anwar Shah, 'Introduction: Principles of Fiscal Federalism', in Anwar Shah and John Kincaid (eds), *The Practice of Fiscal Federalism: Comparative Perspectives* (McGill-Queen's University Press 2007) 3.

2 Cheryl Saunders, 'Financial Autonomy vs. Solidarity: A Dialogue between Two Complementary Opposites', in Alice Valdesalici and Francesco Palermo (eds), *Comparing Fiscal Federalism* (Brill 2018) 41. For this balance between cohesion or solidarity and subnational autonomy, see in particular the judgment of the German Constitutional Court of 24 June 1986, 72 BVerfGE 330.

3 Elisabeth Alber, 'Intergovernmental Financial Relations: Institutions, Rules and Praxis', in Valdesalici and Palermo (n 2) 227; Shah (n 1) 37; Alice Valdesalici, 'The peregrinations of fiscal federalism: past, present and future of a research agenda', in John Kincaid (ed), *A Research Agenda for Federalism Studies* (Edward Elgar 2019) 100.

4 Annika Kress, 'Accommodating Diversity While Guaranteeing Stability: The Role of Financial Arrangements', in Valdesalici and Palermo (n 2) 274–275; Francesco Palermo and Karl Kössler, *Comparative Federalism* (Hart 2017) 201.

subdivided into five parts: (A) subnational taxes, (B); borrowing powers; (C) shared tax revenues; (D) conditional grants; and (E) fiscal discipline rules.

In this way, the autonomy index concentrates on self-rule but not on shared rule. Yet, the power to raise central taxes also impacts cohesion and autonomy. Central taxes determine the budget for equalization fees, as well as the scope for SNEs to raise their own taxes or to set additional flat rates. Shared rule, however, is already largely covered by Index 4.2. The indexes set out below will also regularly take into account the involvement of SNEs in central interference. Similarly, the cohesion index focuses on equalization schemes, but consideration of shared rule's cohesive power through the levying of central taxes is left to Index 4.1. The index will nevertheless take into account the power to raise specific taxes that potentially promote cohesion.

A widely held principle of fiscal federalism is that 'finance should follow function': federal and SNEs should have the financial means to implement their policies in the subject matters assigned to them.[5] This does not mean that they should also be able to raise the revenues needed for carrying out their policies. In fact, this is rarely the case.[6] Own revenues are combined with grants. Usually, SNEs receive grants from the central government, but in looser MTSs the reverse is also possible. For example, the European Economic Community started as a supranational organization dependent on the member states' contributions. As it evolved into the EU, it gradually came to rely more on its own revenues.

There are various reasons why SNEs have only partial revenue powers within MTSs. From an economic perspective, it is feared that if SNEs had no responsibility for raising their own revenues, they would have no incentive to act in a cost-effective way.[7] In contrast, if both central and subnational governments have unlimited taxation powers then this may either lead to an overburdening of individuals or *de facto* force the other tier to refrain from raising taxes. Fiscal federalism arrangements are, therefore, guided by several economic principles to secure efficient and fair delivery of public services.[8] Here, we are only interested in arguments that are linked with the autonomy of SNEs, and the cohesion of the overall structure.

A final preliminary note is that fiscal arrangements, in particular, have multilevel dimensions. Revenues are collected, shared, and redistributed among at least three levels of authority: national, regional, and local. Interestingly, in some countries such as South Africa, the local entities enjoy greater fiscal

5 Shah (n 1) 9.
6 Palermo and Kössler (n 4) 201; Valdesalici (n 3) 97.
7 Shah (n 1) 9.
8 See *ibid* 9–37.

autonomy than the regional entities.[9] In EU member states the supranational EU dimension of authority is added. This puts restrictions on member states' national and subnational tax autonomy because the power to set tax bases and minimum rates for Value-Added Tax (VAT) and excise taxes are transferred to the EU level.[10] It also impacts upon domestic fiscal arrangements, because it leaves little room for the decentralization of tax-rate setting.[11] Further, fiscal discipline rules imposed by the Fiscal Compact Treaty triggered intergovernmental negotiation processes within multi-tiered EU member states. Engaging SNEs in these fiscal discipline rules has sometimes come at a cost. In Austria and Germany, it was necessary to issue generous federal grants or subnational veto powers over monitoring and sanctioning procedures; in Spain, it led to a centralization of power and in Belgium, it resulted in more decentralization.[12]

We come back to these multilevel dynamics in Chapter 7. For now, the choice of SNE being used as the unit of analysis determines which arrangements are examined. For example, if the position of local entities within a regionalized system is examined, the cohesion index will only take into account equalization rules that address local entities. However, it will not predetermine whether to consider arrangements at the national or the regional level, or a combination of this. If the EU is the primary unit of analysis then the autonomy index examines the member states as a whole, irrespective of domestic decentralization arrangements.

9 Nico Steytler and Zemelek A. Ayele, 'Local Governments in African Federal and Devolved Systems of Government: The Struggle for a Balance between Financial and Fiscal Autonomy and Discipline', in Valdesalici and Palermo (n 2) 302.

10 See Gisela Färber, 'Taxing Powers of Subnational Entities: Between Domestic and Supranational Constraints', in Valdesalici and Palermo (n 2) 162–165 for this and other examples of EU impact on subnational fiscal autonomy.

11 *Ibid* 162–163.

12 Dietmar Braun and Philipp Trein, 'Federal dynamics in times of economic and financial crisis', (2014) 53 *Eu. J. Pol. Research* 815–816.

6.1 Fiscal equalization and other cohesive arrangements

Measuring cohesion

Index 16.1 Cohesion index – fiscal arrangements

A. Equalization arrangements	
No equalization mechanism is in place	0
An equalization mechanism is in place, based on criteria that take into account subnational fiscal revenue capacity and needs	1
An equalization mechanism is in place, based on criteria that take into account subnational fiscal revenue capacity and needs, as well as overall cohesion concerns	2
Central equalization criteria are determined by the central government or an independent body, after extensive consultation of the SNEs	+1
Central equalization criteria are determined jointly by the central government and SNEs or their electorates	+2
B. Additional arrangements	
The central government does not have the power to raise taxes on mobile factors and tradeable goods and/or to raise progressive redistributive taxes	0
The central government has the power to raise taxes on mobile factors and tradeable goods or to raise progressive redistributive taxes	1
The central government has the power to raise taxes on mobile factors and tradeable goods as well as progressive redistributive taxes	2
Fiscal discipline rules are in place to protect the stability of the common currency	+1
Rules and procedures are in place to constrain horizontal double taxation	+1
Horizontal double taxation is prohibited	+2
Other rules are in place to avoid unfair interregional tax competition	+1
SNEs are prohibited from raising protectionist subnational taxes	+1

Fiscal equalization arrangements are introduced to downplay interregional disparities, and thus create horizontal fiscal balance. This is enshrined as a principle in the European Charter of Local Self-Government: "The protection of financially weaker local authorities calls for the institution of financial equalization procedures or equivalent measures[13] which are designed to correct the effects of the unequal distribution of potential sources of finance and of the financial burden they must support."[14] This presupposes solidarity on the part of wealthier SNEs.

Usually, there is a vertical fiscal gap: central government revenues exceed central government expenditures, whereas SNEs do not have sufficient means to cover their expenditure needs. Horizontal fiscal balance implies that the vertical gap is addressed in such a way that financial transfers benefit SNEs with lower fiscal capacity and/or higher per capita costs of public services.

13 E.g., mechanisms to share tax revenues: Sean Dougherty, Michelle Harding and Andrew Reschovsky, *Twenty years of tax autonomy across levels of government: Measurement and applications*, OECD Working Papers on Fiscal Federalism N° 29 (OECD Fiscal Network, 2019) 7.

14 Art. 9(5) European Charter of Local Self-Government.

Equalization can also take place through horizontal transfers if grants for financially weak SNEs are paid by contributions from wealthier SNEs. In Switzerland, this is upgraded to a constitutional principle, according to which the funds for the equalization of financial resources are provided by the central government and by the Cantons with more resources. In this way, the Cantons make payments of at least two-thirds and at maximum 80 percent of the central government's payments.[15] The index makes no distinction between vertical and horizontal transfers because they are usually determined at the central level. The criteria for redistribution are what matters.

The level of redistribution depends on how much the MTS values either competition or solidarity.[16] Saunders presents the United States as a prototype of systems that favor autonomy, and Germany as a prototype of fiscal federalism based on solidarity.[17] A reason has been given for why the United States is averse to fiscal equalization programs: generous fiscal transfers might keep disadvantaged SNEs in a state of dependency, without any incentives to improve their position.[18] In dyadic MTSs, where one SNE is always the net contributor and the other the net receiver, equalization programs may undermine cohesion in the long term. This will happen if the former feels restraint and the latter threatened because of its dependency, as has occurred in Belgium.[19] Meanwhile, Québec and Catalonia show that equalization can have stabilizing effects if they favor SNEs with strong regional identity. However, this can also reinforce claims for independence in the case of centrally mandated solidarity from such SNEs.[20]

It is, therefore, important that the fiscal equalization mechanisms do not compensate for variations in wealth that result from policy preferences. Instead, they should take into account objective empirical criteria that determine fiscal capacity and per capita costs of public services. For example, elements of economic geography, such as population density and labor mobility, natural resources, or means of transport networks all impact on fiscal capacity. The cost of public services may follow from demographic variations, for example, differences in age structure or other criteria. In Australia, for example, the state of Victoria can deliver public services at a lower cost than the Northern Territory. This is because Victoria has a concentrated population and mild geographic and climate conditions, while the Northern Territory has a small population, many indigenous people living in small communities in remote places, and an inhospitable geographic and climate conditions.[21] Transfers should therefore take

15 Art. 135(3) Swiss Constitution.

16 Palermo and Kössler (n 4) 241.

17 Saunders (n 2) 43–56.

18 Shah (n 1) 30. Saunders (n 2) 45, 47–48 points out several fiscal transfer mechanisms, but stresses that these do not trigger a more general equalization scheme.

19 Despite the symmetrical treatment of the major subunits, ignoring differences in economic strength, see Kress (n 4) 287.

20 *Ibid* 295.

21 Alan Morris, 'Commonwealth of Australia', in Shah and Kincaid (n 1) 60.

into account fiscal capacities and needs based on *de facto* asymmetries between SNEs.[22]

The criteria for this calculation should also be clear and consensual, to avoid disputes or a loss of legitimacy. Both of these consequences may negatively impact solidarity. Therefore, it is preferable for them to be determined by an intergovernmental body, or at least reach an agreement with the SNEs. An intergovernmental example is found in Germany, where the constitution requires the consent of the Bundesrat for laws that implement the constitutional principles regarding shares in turnover tax revenues and financial equalization mechanisms.[23] As the *Bundesrat* consists of representatives of the *Länder* governments that are bound by their governments' instructions, intergovernmental negotiation and consensus are ensured.[24]

The German system, with a strong representation of SNEs in the federal decision-making, is exceptional. In contrast, systems with fiscal watchdogs are on the rise.[25] In these systems, an independent body is established to give recommendations to the national government on the distribution of funds and equalization criteria. In India, the President appoints the members of a Finance Commission, which is populated with experts.[26] Elsewhere, SNEs have a say in the selection of members. In South Africa, for example, the members of the Financial and Fiscal Commission are appointed by the President, but some are nominated by the Provinces and others by the local governments.[27] However, even if such a commission consists of members appointed with the involvement of SNEs, it is not equal to a system where equalization criteria are determined by an intergovernmental body. This because it can only make recommendations. For example, the national legislature has ignored the recommendations of the South African Financial and Fiscal Commission whenever it considered them to be biased in favor of decentralization, even when the Commission made extensive efforts to develop impartial standards.[28]

However, it is relevant if equalization criteria are determined after consultation with the SNEs, either by the central government or an independent body. The Australian Commission exercises its tasks after extensive consultation and interaction with these entities.[29] The index, however, only takes into account consultations that take place on a legal basis. For example, in South Africa, legislation that determines the equitable division of revenues may only be enacted

22 Shah (n 1) 32.
23 Art. 106(3), 106a and 107 German Constitution.
24 Alber (n 3) 250.
25 *Ibid* 260.
26 Art. 180(1) and (3)a Indian Constitution.
27 Art. 221 South African Constitution and Art. 5 Financial and Fiscal Commission Amendment Act.
28 Joachim Wehner, 'Fiscal Federalism in South Africa', (2000) 30 *Publius: The Journal of Federalism* 69–70.
29 Morris (n 21) 62.

after consultation with the provincial governments, organized local governments, and the Financial and Fiscal Commission.[30] In the absence of a legal basis, the consultation practice is examined in a later phase as an indicator of changes driven by noninstitutional factors.

From a cohesion perspective, equalization mechanisms should not only take into account the needs of particular SNEs but also concerns for maintaining overall stability and equality. In Germany, for example, shares in turnover tax revenues must be determined taking into account the necessary expenditures of the Federation and the Länder, fair balance, as well as the uniformity of living standards throughout the federal territory.[31] In South Africa, the constitution lists ten criteria; some related to the needs and fiscal capacities of provincial and local governments, others to the national interest and the needs and interests of the national government.[32]

A subsection completes the equalization mechanism, with additional rules to promote solidarity and partnership.

The second part of the cohesion index examines the type of tax powers allocated to the central level. In fiscal federalism literature, taxes on mobile factors and tradeable goods that have a bearing on the efficiency of the internal common market are generally assigned to the central government as a default economic principle.[33] This is relevant because earlier the economic and monetary union was considered to be an important factor for cohesion.[34] Another rule to safeguard the economic and monetary union is the prohibition of protectionist subnational taxes, such as taxes that have an effect equivalent to that of custom duties.

Also, from a cohesion perspective, progressive redistributive taxes are best located at the central level. This is to avoid competitive policies that attract high-income people and repel low-income people,[35] which might reinforce disparities in wealth. In this way, the cohesion index is also concerned about the horizontal relations between SNEs.

For the same reason, an additional score is added for rules and procedures that prevent double taxation between SNEs. Here, a distinction is made between discouragement and prohibition of horizontal double taxation. For example, the Swiss Constitution prohibits inter-cantonal double taxation and instructs the Confederation to legislate accordingly.[36] In contrast, the US fair apportionment

30 Art. 214(2) South African Constitution.
31 Art. 106(3) German Constitution.
32 Art. 214(2) South African Constitution.
33 Shah (n 1) 20.
34 Chapter 4.1.
35 Shah (n 1) 20.
36 Art. 127(3) Swiss Constitution. So far, measures have not been imposed by the central government, but flow from case law. See Madeleine Simonek, 'Tax Coordination between Cantons in Switzerland – Role of the Courts', in Michael Lang *et al.* (eds), *Horizontal Tax Coordination* (IBFD 2012) 227.

rules to restrict double taxation do not erase the risk of double taxation.[37] In Belgium, the avoidance of double taxation is specified in a special majority law as a fiscal principle, and a negotiation procedure is established to secure compliance.[38] However, double taxation is not prohibited for other taxes than those based on the Special Finance Act. In Canada, there is no rule to prevent or constrain horizontal double taxation, even though Canadian Provinces voluntarily apply a uniform apportionment formula.[39] Of course, it is also important to have a priority rule that avoids vertical double taxation. Usually, this comes down to a priority rule for central taxes, which impedes on subnational tax autonomy and is included in Index 16.2.1. Vertical tax priority rules are mainly concerned with the overburdening of citizens. The cohesion index concentrates on horizontal non-double taxation mechanisms because they have the additional motive of limiting interregional competition. It also takes into account other mechanisms that have the same motive. In Switzerland, for example, cantons have the duty to raise specific taxes to avoid unfair tax competition.[40]

Solidarity is also tested if particular SNEs show undisciplined budgetary behavior, relying on the central government to guarantee their solvency. To discourage SNEs from excessive borrowing that may threaten the value of the currency and overall economic stability, the central government may impose fiscal rules. These might include balanced budget requirements, borrowing restrictions or expenditure limits. Empirical studies suggest that balanced budget rules limit state deficits and reduce state borrowing costs.[41] Fiscal discipline rules constrain subnational autonomy and are, therefore, included in the autonomy index. However, they also determine cohesion to the extent that they protect the entire system against currency and stability threats. They are also a protection against having to bail out irresponsible subnational governments.[42] Therefore, they are also included in the cohesion index, but only if they are imposed by the central government upon SNEs. This is not the case in the United States, where several states have voluntarily inserted balanced budget rules in their constitutions. By

37 Walter Hellerstein, ‘Tax Coordination between the US States – The Role of the Courts’, in Lang (n 36) 282–288

38 Art. 1 *ter* Special Finance Law. See Edoardo Traversa and Barbara Vintras, ‘Tax Coordination between Regions in Belgium – Role of the Courts’, in Lang (n 36) 103.

39 Maximilian Haag, ‘Horizontal Tax Coordination: The Canadian Perspective and a Few General Observations’, in Lang (n 36) 314.

40 Art. 2 Federal Tax Harmonization Statute. See Simonek (n 36) 223.

41 R.R. Daniel Kelemen and Terrence K. Teo, ‘Law, Focal Points, and Fiscal Discipline in the United States and the European Union’, (2014) 108 *Am. Pol. Sc. Rev.* 355, 357.

42 Even if a no-bail out policy is announced, fiscal discipline rules make it more credible that the central government will not have to bail out the SNE after all, see Jan Schnellenbach, ‘Fiscal Sovereignty in a Globalized World: The Pressure of European Economic Governance on Domestic Public Finance’, in Valdesalici and Palermo (n 2) 330–331. See also Braun and Trein (n 12) 808.

contrast, the European Fiscal Compact Treaty requires that the budgetary position of the general government of Contracting Parties is balanced or in surplus.[43] This rule is imposed to prevent Eurozone states from accumulating excessive deficits, in order to safeguard the stability of the euro area as a whole.[44]

6.2 Revenues and spending powers

SNEs obtain their revenues from different sources, such as subnational taxes, revenues from shared taxes, grants, user fees, natural sources, profits from public enterprises, and interests from public borrowing.[45] In this index, social security contributions are considered to be taxes. An example is if they are raised on the basis of income, user fees, or if they are raised within a social care insurance scheme.[46]

From a democratic and accountability perspective, it is preferable if SNEs can raise their own taxes.[47] It is also an important indicator from an autonomy perspective because taxes are important instruments to shape policy – e.g., if environmental taxes are raised to discourage environment unfriendly behavior. It is, however, not a sufficient indicator. In the end, a minimum requirement is that SNEs have financial means to pursue their policies. For example, in South Africa, Provinces have only limited tax autonomy, but federal transfers give them sufficient financial capacity to meet their needs.[48] Moreover, fiscal autonomy concerns both revenues and spending powers.[49] Crucial to SNEs is that they have a say in determining the magnitude of revenues and that they can spend the budget as they wish.

Several indexes have already been proposed but are deemed 'unsatisfactory' to measure the tax autonomy of SNEs.[50] Budget indicators are mostly used

43 Art. 3(1) Treaty on Stability, Coordination and Governance in the Economic and Monetary Union (Further: Fiscal Compact Treaty).

44 Preamble to the Fiscal Compact Treaty.

45 Palermo and Kössler (n 4) 210. For an overview of combinations of taxes and grants in Europe, see Maria F. Ambrosanio, Paolo Balduzzi and Claudia Peiti, 'Accountability and Revenue Assignment across Levels of Government: Rules, Practices, and Challenges', in Valdesalici and Palermo (n 2) 123–128.

46 For example, the Flemish social care insurance system. See several contributions in Bea Cantillon, Patricia Popelier and Ninke Mussche (eds), *Social Federalism: the Creation of a Layered Welfare State* (Intersentia 2011).

47 Haag (n 39) 312–313.

48 Christina Murray and Richard Simeon, 'Promises Unmet: Multi-level Government in South Africa', in Rekha Saxena (ed), *Varieties in Federal Governance: Major Contemporary Models* (Foundation Books 2011) 242 note that deficient government rather than fiscal capacity make it difficult to offer adequate public services.

49 Karl Kössler and Martina Trettel, 'Fiscal Federalism in Times of Crisis: An Iron Law of Centralisation?', in Valdesalici and Palermo (n 2) 348.

50 Ambrosanio, Bulduzzi and Peiti (n 45) 130.

in those indexes, for example, the SNE's share of the country's total tax revenue or public expenditure. However, these give no information about SNEs' discretion to raise taxes, define tax bases and rates, and decide on tax reliefs.[51] Moreover, they measure the actual scope instead of the institutional setup.

In an OECD Working Paper, Dougherty *et al.* provide an interesting measure of tax autonomy in this perspective by developing codes in decreasing order of discretion.[52] They also distinguish between taxes that are determined by SNEs and shared taxes. The latter provide a more nuanced measure of tax autonomy.[53] Codes in category (a) characterize taxes for which SNEs can determine tax rates, exemptions, and other attributes that influence the amount of tax revenue. Codes in category (b) characterize taxes where SNEs can set tax rates, but central governments control some other attributes – e.g., the definition of tax bases. Codes in category (c) refer to situations where SNEs have no control over tax bases or rates but can determine tax reliefs. Category (d) codes refer to tax-sharing schemes, making a distinction according to the individual SNE's say in the revenue split.[54] This scheme, however, still calculates the share of total tax revenue, but in a more differentiated way. It is calculated according to the percentage of taxes in each category.

Hooghe *et al.* also makes distinctions according to the SNE's discretion: whether it can set a base and rate, or only the rate of taxes. They also distinguish between minor and major taxes. Personal income, corporate, value-added, and sales taxes are considered major taxes, whereas others such as property taxes, resource taxes (including royalties on natural resources), excise taxes, and registration taxes are considered minor.[55] In addition, they use a separate index for borrowing powers, taking into account limitations and prior authorizations that put limits on the SNE's discretion. These indexes have the advantage of practicality. However, while the authors use a separate index for borrowing powers, they do not take into account dependency on conditional grants. This kind of dependency may severely affect the autonomy of SNEs. By contrast, Yvanyna and Shaw do take the conditionality of transfers and expenditure autonomy into account.[56]

To measure autonomy, the present index combines these models. The index measures the institutional setup that determines the potential of the SNE to

51 This was discussed in Chapter 2, section 2.2.3.4.
52 Dougherty, Harding and Reschovsky (n 13).
53 Ambrosanio, Bulduzzi and Peiti (n 45) 140.
54 Dougherty, Harding and Reschovsky (n 13) 7–8.
55 Liesbeth Hooghe, Gary Marks, Arjan H. Schakel, Sara Niedzwiecki, Sandra Chapman Osterkatz and Sarah Shair-Rosenfield, *Measuring Regional Authority: A Postfunctionalist Theory of Governance. Volume 1* (Oxford University Press 2016) 71.
56 Maksym Ivanyna and Anwar Shah, *How Close is Your Government to Its People? Worldwide Indicators on Localization and Decentralization*, World Bank Policy Research Working Paper N° 6138 (World Bank 2012) 12–13.

provide for its own revenues through: (1) subnational taxes and social security contributions; (2) shared tax revenues; (3) borrowing powers; and (4) the autonomy to spend grants at its own discretion.

As the final score is the sum of these subcategories, these four elements are given the same weight. In fiscal federalism literature, there is some ongoing debate about the need to apportion different weights to these categories, depending on what they mean to tax autonomy.[57] In this index, however, we are merely exploring the potential to raise revenues that enable SNEs to pursue their policies. We are not yet determining the actual tax autonomy or the extent to which revenues are based on a SNE's own sources or central grants. The SNE may have the power to raise taxes but decide not to exercise it[58] if central grants are sufficient to cover its expenditures. Also, SNEs in countries with limited taxing powers are sometimes better able to finance their expenditures through a high level of shared taxes, compared to SNEs in countries with high taxing powers.[59] The division into subcategories allows us to calculate an overall score for a rough indication of SNEs' autonomy to control revenues and expenditures, and at the same time single out one of the categories for further examination.

The fact that taxes are spread over two indicators – subnational taxes and shared tax revenues – may, at first sight, have some odd consequences. SNEs that combine subnational tax powers and shared tax revenues have a higher autonomy score than SNEs that only have subnational tax powers. This is the case even if the latter have no need for shared tax revenues because they have sufficient revenue. Again, a distinction must be made between institutional potential and practice. For example, under the hypothesis that both SNE X and Y have full subnational taxation powers but SNE X, in addition, enjoys shared tax revenues and Y does not, SNE X will have a better score. X will have potentially more revenues to pursue ambitious policies or have the option to raise no or lower taxes or introduce tax reliefs. If X has limited taxation powers combined with shared tax revenues and Y has full taxation powers but no shared tax revenues, X will have a lower score for the first indicator than Y. If the combined score still equals or outweighs the score for Y, this is because an entity's options to use taxes as a fiscal instrument are simply wider if some minimum revenue is secured through other means.

57 Ambrosanio, Balduzzi and Peiti (n 45) 141.
58 For example, in Belgium the GSC has the power to raise taxes but hardly makes any use of this power.
59 Ambrosanio, Balduzzi and Peiti (n 45) 144.

6.2.1 Subnational taxes

Measuring autonomy

Index 16.2.1 Autonomy index – fiscal arrangements (A) subnational taxes

The SNE has no power to set the base and/or rate of taxes	0
The SNE has the power to set the base and/or rate of minor taxes only, with upper or lower limitations set by the central authority	1
The SNE has the power to set the base and/or rate of minor taxes only, without upper or lower limitations set by the central authority	2
The SNE has the power to set the base and/or rate of at least one major tax (personal income, corporate, value-added, or sale tax) with upper or lower limitations or other constraints set by the central authority	3
The SNE has the power to set the base and/or rate of at least one major tax (personal income, corporate, value-added, or sale tax) without upper or lower limitations or other constraints set by the central authority	4
The SNE has the power to introduce new taxes	+1
The SNE has the power to set tax reliefs	+1
There is no preemption through central taxation	+1
The levying of specific taxes is reserved to the SNE, or other mechanisms are in place to protect the subnational capacity to raise taxes	+1

Even when grants provide SNEs with the financial means to implement their policies, it is still important for SNEs to have tax autonomy. Irrespective of whether they make use of their power to raise taxes, the fact alone of having that power makes them less dependent on decisions adopted by the central government.[60] Also, tax autonomy enables SNEs to achieve policy objectives through both legislation and fiscal instruments. The European Charter of Local Self-Government also applies here. This instrument stresses that at least part of the financial resources of local authorities must derive from local taxes and charges, the rate of which the authorities themselves have the power to determine.[61]

Tax autonomy is best secured if the SNE can raise taxes without substantial limitations. This includes the power to introduce new taxes and to determine the base for taxation and rates. An example of substantial limitations is found in South Africa. There, the constitution prohibits Provinces from imposing income taxes, value-added taxes, general sales taxes, rates on property, or customs duties.[62] Conversely in India, the States cannot issue new taxes; they can only issue those taxes assigned to them by the Constitution.[63]

Intergovernmental instruments may be in place to protect taxpayers against heavy tax burdens, as is the case in Canada,[64] but usually central taxes have

60 Valdesalici (n 3) 97.

61 Art. 9(3) European Charter of Local Self-Government.

62 Art. 228(1) South African Constitution.

63 Indian Constitution, Seventh Schedule, List II, Art. 46–63.

64 Alber (n 3) 237.

priority to avoid double taxation. In this case, field preemption (as exists in Germany) is more intrusive on subnational autonomy than the priority for specific central taxes (as exists in the United States).[65] The index does not include this nuance: it only examines whether there is a priority rule in favor of the central government. Such a priority rule has the potential to strip subnational tax autonomy of its substance. Other mechanisms may be put into place to avoid this. One example is reserving specific taxing powers to SNEs. Another example is found in Switzerland, where maximum tax rates on Confederal taxes are specified in the Constitution. This is to protect Cantons' capacities to raise their own taxes.[66]

In either case, SNEs are protected against preemption if they have the exclusive power to raise taxes in specific subject matters. Also, central government rules may limit the SNE's discretion to determine tax rates, for example, by predetermining the range of rate variations.[67] An alternative is base-sharing taxes. This is where the central government raises taxes, and the SNE then levies supplementary flat rates on the central tax base. In that case, the SNE, as a rule, has no say over the tax base, and its discretion to set rates is usually limited by the central government.

Tax autonomy includes the autonomy to determine tax bases and set rates, but also to decide on tax reliefs. Attributes such as tax reliefs are included in Dougherty *et al.*'s scheme. By contrast, Spahn argues that rate-setting suffices as a proxy for tax autonomy.[68] The power to decide on tax reliefs is included in the proposed index. The reason is that tax reliefs – tax credits, exemptions, or abatements[69] – are important fiscal instruments.

In Belgium, the Constitution lays down a principle that all SNEs – Regions, Communities, and local entities – can raise taxes. The Constitutional Court clarified that this is a shared competence, with priority given to the federal government.[70] The Special Financing Act states that the system is designed specifically to allow the federal government to raise major taxes. However, regions may set the rate of some taxes, such as supplementary flat rates on personal income tax.[71] In addition, Regions have the right to determine the rate, the base, and reliefs of specific taxes. This applies to property taxes, inheritance taxes, mortgage taxes, and specific registration taxes.[72]

65 Daniel Halberstam and Roderick M Hills Jr., 'State Autonomy in Germany and the United States', (2001) Annals *Am. Acad. Pol. & Soc. Sci.* 177.
66 Bernard Dafflon, 'Swiss Fiscal Federalism: New Roads after the Reforms of the Constitution', in Giancarlo Pola (ed), *Principles and Practices of Fiscal Autonomy* (Ashgate 2015, reissued Routledge 2017) 100.
67 Ambrosanio, Balduzzi and Peiti (n 45) 131.
68 Paul B. Spahn, 'Measuring decentralization of public sector activities: Conceptual issues and the case of Germany', in Junghun Kim, Jorgen Lotz and Hansjörg Blöchliger (eds), *Measuring Fiscal Decentralization, Concepts and Policies* (OECD Publishing 2013) 91.
69 Dougherty, Harding and Reschovsky (n 13) 17.
70 Const. Court No. 47, 25 February 1988.
71 This includes the FLC, which has merged the institutions of the Region.
72 Art. 3 Special Finance Act.

6.2.2 Borrowing powers

Measuring autonomy

Index 16.2.2 Autonomy index – fiscal arrangements (B) borrowing powers

The SNE is prohibited from borrowing	0
The SNE has borrowing powers, subject to substantive restrictions and prior authorization	1
The SNE has borrowing powers, subject to substantive restrictions or prior authorization	2
Some of the substantive and procedural restrictions can only be imposed on a temporary basis	+1
All substantive and procedural restrictions can only be imposed on a temporary basis	+2
Most substantive or procedural restrictions can only be imposed after the involvement of the SNE	+1
The SNE has borrowing powers without substantive restrictions or prior authorization	6

A SNE's revenues can also come from loans and obligations. Autonomy is better secured if SNEs can make use of these instruments without the central government imposing substantial restrictions to steer their behavior.

This index relies on the one previously proposed by Hooghe *et al.*, which distinguishes between substantive and formal restrictions. Substantive restrictions are prohibitions against borrowing to cover account deficits (a golden rule), borrowing from foreign institutions or the central bank, borrowing above a ceiling, or limiting borrowing to specific purposes.[73] Temporal restrictions can be added. For example, South African Provinces may raise loans for current expenditure only when necessary for bridging purposes during a single fiscal year.[74] Formal restrictions are in place if SNEs need prior authorization from the central government to borrow. Borrowing or other commitments by local governments may often be subject to government approval.[75] Similar restrictions may apply to regional entities as well. For example, in Belgium, Communities and Regions have to obtain the federal Minister of Finance's approval of public loan conditions and the calendar for repayment.[76]

Sometimes there is a fine line between substantive and formal restrictions. For example, German Länder are prohibited from borrowing funds or issuing surety obligations, guarantees, or other commitments without authorization by a federal law that specifies or permits the computation of the amounts involved.[77] In this index, the term 'authorization' points to the permission to take out a particular loan. A law that generally specifies limits or amounts is considered to impose substantive limits.

73 Hooghe *et al* (n 55) 72.
74 Art. 230(1) and 230A(1) South African Constitution.
75 For example, Art. 34(5) Hungarian Constitution.
76 Art. 49, § 2 Special Finance Act.
77 Art. 115(1) German Constitution.

Restrictions can also be determined for a limited or an undetermined period. For example, the Belgian Special Finance Act recognizes the SNE's borrowing powers, but the borrowing capacity can be limited for a period of two years on advice of the High Council for Finance, and after negotiation with the subnational governments.[78]

6.2.3 Shared Tax Revenues

Measuring autonomy

Index 16.2.3 Autonomy index – fiscal arrangements (C) shared tax revenues

There is no revenue split that benefits the SNE	0
The revenue split is determined by the central government only	1
The revenue split is determined by the central government, but the SNEs are consulted	2
The electorate of the SNE can, through collective vote, veto the law that determines the revenue split	3
The SNE can, through collective vote, veto the law that determines the revenue split	4
The SNE alone can veto the law that determines the revenue split	5

Apart from their own revenues, SNEs can receive contributions from the central government. These can take different forms. The most important are: (1) revenue sharing; (2) contributions from (other) equalization mechanisms; (3) other grants from the central government, for example, to implement specific projects.

Equalization mechanisms were examined under the cohesion index. Revenue sharing and other grants are discussed separately. This is because revenue sharing takes place on the basis of a specific formula, whereas conditional grants are more vulnerable to central interference in subnational policy-making. This subsection discusses shared tax revenues. Grants and other limitations on spending powers are discussed in subsection 6.2.4.

Revenue sharing refers to taxes levied and collected by the central government and raised nationwide or in the jurisdiction of the SNE that are (entirely or partly) assigned to SNEs. These revenues are not subnational taxes, as they are determined by the central government. Yet, like any other grant, they are relevant to subnational autonomy, if SNEs are involved in the determination of the revenue split.[79] The revenue split can be determined in such a way that the SNE's share does not reflect the proportion of revenues generated in its jurisdiction, but redistributes revenues from wealthier SNEs to SNEs with fewer resources.[80] It has been argued from an economic perspective that revenue sharing is not part of tax autonomy if it has equalizing effects.[81] From an institutional perspective, however,

78 Art. 49, §6 Special Finance Act.

79 Spahn (n 68) 92–93. See also Ambrosanio, Balduzzi and Peiti (n 45) 141.

80 Dougherty, Harding and Reschovsky (n 13) 7.

81 Spahn (n 68) 93.

it is relevant to include them in the measurement of subnational autonomy. If SNEs are involved in the decision-making process, it is their decision to assign part of the revenues to SNEs in need.

Dougherty *et al.* make distinctions according to the say that SNEs have in determining the revenue split. The split is either determined by the SNEs themselves; or they have to approve it; or the split is unilaterally determined by the central government on an annual basis or less frequently.[82] The present index follows the scheme presented by Dougherty *et al.*, but in a more differentiated way. It follows the model of Index 4.2 A on central lawmaking. Further, the proposed index does not distinguish between revenue splits according to the frequency with which they are determined by the central government. Frequency here instead refers to the stability or reliability of revenues, rather than to autonomy.[83]

In case there are different systems of shared tax revenues in place, with different levels of subnational involvement, the index is interested in the system that applies to major taxes. Within this category, the index is interested in the system that collects most revenues, such as VAT or income taxes. This is the system where the stakes for autonomy are the highest.

6.2.4 Spending powers: conditional grants

Measuring autonomy

Index 16.2.4 Autonomy index – fiscal arrangements (D) conditional grants

The central government has the power to issue mandatory conditional grants	0
The central government does not have the power to issue mandatory conditional grants, but it has the power to issue voluntary conditional grants, specifying the type of expenditure	1
The central government does not have the power to issue mandatory conditional grants or voluntary grants specifying the type of expenditure. Instead, it can issue voluntary conditional grants based on result, or requiring matching subnational funds	2
The central government does not have the power to issue mandatory or voluntary conditional grants, but it can issue block grants	3
The central government can only issue general-purpose contributions	4
No mechanism is inserted in the finance act that can be classified as a permanent grant conditional	+1
Conditions can only be imposed after the involvement of the SNE	+1

From an autonomy perspective, the SNE's spending autonomy is an important factor. If the central government earmarks transfers for specific purposes, this may strongly impact on subnational policy-making.[84] This part of the index therefore concentrates mostly on grants. It examines whether grants can be

82 Dougherty, Harding and Reschovsky (n 13) 8.
83 Spahn (n 68) 94.
84 Alber (n 3) 226.

made conditional, in order to force the SNE into implementing central government objectives.

Where grants are provided, autonomy is best preserved if these are general-purpose transfers with 'no strings attached'. Again, this is inserted in the European Charter of Local Self-Government as a principle: "As far as possible, grants to local authorities shall not be earmarked for the financing of specific projects. The provision of grants shall not remove the basic freedom of local authorities to exercise policy discretion within their own jurisdiction."[85] It is, of course, possible that SNEs would have used grants for the purposes earmarked by the central government anyway. According to Spahn, this would turn the grant into general revenue.[86] For this index, however, the extent to which the autonomy of an SNE is bound 'in fact' is not relevant. Instead, there is a focus on the extent to which the institutional design allows the central government to interfere in subnational policymaking.

An in-between category is block transfers. These are earmarked for a specific policy domain, but leave much discretion as to how to spend them within this area.[87] Examples are inserted in the German Constitution, where Länder are entitled to an allocation of federal tax revenues for purposes of local public transport. The Federation may grant financial assistance to Länder, or municipalities, for investments in areas such as social housing or education infrastructure.[88] While these grants leave some discretion to the SNE, they have been criticized for displacing priorities in SNE's programs.[89]

Autonomy is least secure in the case of specific-purpose transfers or conditional grants. These grants specify how they must be used, or which results must be achieved. The first are more intrusive than the latter, which leave some discretion as to how to obtain the desired output.[90] Requirements for matching subnational funds restrict the SNE's spending autonomy, but also leave some discretion. Grants can be mandatory or voluntary. Autonomy is most encroached upon if they are mandatory. In practice, voluntary or *ad hoc* conditional grants can have a mandatory effect if the SNE has inadequate financial resources of its own and has, therefore, no choice but to accept the grant. Further, SNEs will not readily pass over conditional grants if their taxpayers have to contribute to the program anyway, to the benefit of neighboring SNEs that do accept the grant.[91] The index, however, only takes into account the institutional setup: how it works in practice is examined in the next phase.

85 Art. 9(7) European Charter of Local Self-Government.
86 Spahn (n 68) 95.
87 Shah (n 1) 25.
88 Art. 106a and Art. 104(b)(c)(d) German Constitution.
89 John Kincaid, 'The Rise and Characteristics of Coercive Federalism in the United States', in Pola (n 66) 66–67.
90 Shah (n 1) 25.
91 Halberstam and Hills (n 65) 178–179.

The precise mixture of contributions may vary per MTS, and over time. For example, in Australia, 'specific purpose payments' are intended to implement national objectives. They constitute 45% of the total federal assistance to the SNEs,[92] but this percentage has evolved over time. In South Africa, conditional grants have gradually eroded local spending autonomy.[93] In the United States, the practice of conditional grants expanded during the 1930s to finance the New Deal social welfare programs.[94] Conditional grants have been an important instrument elsewhere to manage financial and economic crises, by engaging SNEs in national economic recovery policy through financial incentives.[95] The index is not interested in this mixture and how it evolves: that is for a later phase. What matters now is the institutional setup. The index examines whether additional contributions have the potential to limit the SNE's discretion as to how to use its revenues.

For example, in Belgium, the most important fiscal arrangements are included in the Special Finance Act. This Act does not give a mandate to the central government to issue conditional grants. It does, however, include a mechanism that allows a conditional grant for Regions, which makes contributions conditional on meeting certain climate targets.[96] However, these targets are established by the central government with the approval of the Regions.

6.2.5 Spending powers: (E) fiscal discipline rules

Measuring autonomy

Index 16.2.5 Autonomy index – fiscal arrangements (E) fiscal discipline rules

The central government has strong *ex ante* and *ex post* supervisory powers that limit the SNE's spending powers	0
The central government has strong *ex ante* or *ex post* supervisory powers that limit the SNE's spending powers	1
The central government only has weak *ex ante* and *ex post* supervisory powers that limit the SNE's spending powers	2
The central government only has weak *ex ante* or *ex post* supervisory powers that limit the SNE's spending powers	3
The central government has no supervisory powers that limit the SNE's spending powers	4
The electorate of the SNE can, through collective vote, veto central rules that impose fiscal discipline rules	+1
The SNE can veto central rules that impose fiscal discipline rules through collective vote	+2
The SNE alone can veto central rules that impose fiscal discipline rules	+3
The central government cannot impose fiscal discipline rules upon the SNE	8

92 Morris (n 21) 61.
93 Steytler and Ayele (n 9) 304.
94 Kössler and Trettel (n 49) 351.
95 Braun and Trein (n 12) 812.
96 Art. 65 quater Special Finance Act.

Constraints on the SNE's spending powers are not necessarily linked to contributions from the central government. Fiscal discipline rules, mentioned under the cohesion index, may have some cohesive potential. However, they also limit the SNE's discretion with regard to fiscal policy. These rules may consist of budget balance requirements or other conditions.

Here again, the index is only interested in fiscal discipline rules imposed by the central government, not rules that the entities impose on themselves. The distinction is not always clear. For example, in Belgium, budget balance requirements and other fiscal discipline rules are inserted in cooperation agreements concluded between the federal government and the SNEs. These agreements have equivalent standing to central legislation, with a veto power for the SNE.

In this vein, the EU's imposition of balanced budget requirements disregards the fiscal autonomy of the Economic and Monetary Union (EMU) member states more than is usual in federal systems.[97] In turn, some member states have implemented this rule by imposing similar budget requirements on their own SNEs.[98] Where the index examines the autonomy of SNEs, only these budget requirements are calculated. This is because the EU views member states as a whole single entity.

The index does not include limitations on borrowing, or conditions that are attached to grants. They may also contain fiscal discipline rules, but these were already measured in part B and D respectively.

Drastic restrictions on subnational spending powers are imposed if the central government exercises *ex ante* or *ex post* supervisory powers. These restrictions are often combined. Even the EU has both preventive and corrective powers to enforce fiscal discipline rules upon EMU member states.[99]

A strong *ex ante* supervisory power is the requirement that the central government must approve the budget. For example, in Nigeria, several States require the prior approval of a local government's budget.[100] This is not the case if the SNE must merely submit its draft budget to the central government for comments. For example, South African municipalities must inform the Provincial government of their draft budget, but no approval is required.[101] This is considered to be a weak supervisory power: it has no immediate consequences that limit the SNE's spending powers, but it can be used to monitor the SNE.

Strong *ex post* supervisory powers enable the central government to substitute for the SNE or to sanction it financially.[102] Examples of weak *ex post* supervisory powers include monitoring schemes or the requirement for the SNE to draft a financial recovery plan.

97 Federico Fabbrini, 'The Fiscal Compact, the Golden Rule, and the Paradox of European Federalism', (2013) 36 *Boston College Int'l & Comp L Rev* 4.

98 See Art. 109 and 115 German Constitution; art. 135 Spanish Constitution; Art. 119 Italian Constitution.

99 See Schnellenbach (n 42) 334–338.

100 Steytler and Ayele (n 9) 311–312.

101 *Ibid* 304.

102 For an example, see *ibid* 305.

Part III

Measuring change

7 Contours for a theory of change

The study of the dynamics of change has been identified as an important challenge for contemporary comparative federal theory. There is an identified need for more systemic comparative research to examine the changes affecting MTSs, the direction of those changes, and how they can be measured and explained.[1]

These questions are at the core of dynamic federalism. Chapter 2 already stressed that the capacity to respond to change is an important factor for the survival of MTSs.[2] In terms of dynamic federalism, such responses imply either a confirmation or a recalibration of the power balance. The first aims to maintain the power balance. The institutional design reflects a compromise that is based on specific contextual factors. Frictions caused by new evolutions call for readjustments in order to maintain the balance that was initially envisaged. Further, (changes to) institutional designs are conditioned by historical legacies, coincidences, and political bargains. This means that adjustments are needed to correct inconsistencies. In other words: stability is not a synonym for immobility.[3] Secondly, the actors who brought about the compromise may develop different views, or new actors may enter the scene. In this case, change is desirable to modify the initial power balance, not to preserve it. This aligns with Chapter 2's definition, of dynamic federalism as essentially a contested balance between autonomy and cohesion.

1 Arthur Benz and Jörg Broschek, 'Federal Dynamics: Introduction', in Arthur Benz and Jörg Broschek (eds), *Federal Dynamics. Continuity, Change, & the Varieties of Federalism* (Oxford University Press 2014) 3; César Colino, 'Introduction: the study of change in federations', in Jan Erk and Wilfried Swenden (eds), *New directions in federalism studies* (2010) 16.

2 Michael Burgess and G. Alan Tarr, 'Introduction: Sub-national Constitutionalism and Constitutional Development', in Michael Burgess and G. Alan Tarr, *Constitutional Dynamics in Federal Systems: Subnational Perspectives* (Montreal & Kingston, McGill-Queen's University Press 2012) 3.

3 Compare John B. Ruhl, 'Complexity Theory as Paradigm for the Dynamic Law-and-society System: A Wake-up Call for Legal Reductionism and the Modern Administrative State', (1996) 45 *Duke Law Journal* 892 and Maja Sahadžić, *Asymmetry, Multinationalism and Constitutional Law* (Routledge 2020) 148–149, 163. See also Arthur Benz and Jörg Broschek, 'Conclusion: Theorizing federal dynamics', in Benz and Broschek (n 1) 382.

This chapter does not aim to answer all the questions that have been raised about the dynamics of change. It takes an entire research community and a combination of disciplines to answer these questions. The chapter has the more modest purpose of sketching the contours for the study of change. It refers to the indexes presented in Part II to propose a method for measuring change (section 7.1). It then picks up on the question of what the drivers for change are. To this end, this chapter refers to political, sociological, and economic research to stress the importance of noninstitutional drivers (section 7.2). Next, there is an explanation of why institutions are nevertheless important in processes of change (section 7.3). The next chapter will continue with this institutional approach, by identifying hubs for change that are implied in the institutional setup.

7.1 Measuring federal dynamics

The theory of dynamic federalism presented in this book takes institutional design as a starting point for measuring change. In the literature, institutional change is mostly assessed in terms of separate (de)centralization processes and (de)federalization processes. The former point concerns the degree of self-rule, while the latter concerns representation in central decision-making processes.[4] A theory of dynamic federalism still discerns two dynamics, but the self-rule and representation axes are replaced by the more comprehensive autonomy and cohesion axes. Here, the term '(de)centralization' is used to indicate dynamics that lean less or more toward subnational autonomy, and the term '(dis)integration' to indicate dynamics that lean less or more toward cohesion.

Colino pointed out that the usual typologies of change complicate the measurement of variations in federal institutional arrangements. This is because these typologies are too simple and lack a clear theoretical perspective that is linked with the propensity of change.[5] In Chapter 2, I tried to remedy this by distinguishing different forms of state according to the institutional potential to provide subnational autonomy and secure cohesion. I call this the '*federalism potential score*' (FPS). Change can therefore be measured as the difference between the institutional potential and one of three possible situations, and can be used to assess vertical, horizontal, and multi-level dynamics.

In the first situation, the MTS does not live up to its potential. For example, it was observed in Italy that the institutional dimension of federalism is well-developed, but the political dimension is lacking. This results in a large

4 Brunetta Baldi, *Federalism by degree* (Working Paper Institute of Governmental Studies, University of California, 1999); Benz and Broschek (n 1) 8. Ferran Requejo, 'Federalism and democracy. The case of minority nations: a federal deficit', in Michael Burgess and Alain-G. Gagnon (eds), *Federal Democracies* (Routledge 2010) 275–298 adds the uni/pluri-national axis and the a/symmetry axis.

5 César Colino, 'Varieties of Federalism and Propensities for Change', in Benz and Broschek (n 1) 49–50.

discrepancy between 'federalism in the books' and 'federalism in action'.[6] The latter, i.e., the actual use of institutional mechanisms, determines the '*actual federalism score*' (AFS). Change is defined as the difference between the FPS and the AFS (*Informal Change Score icS = FPS – AFS*). This score shows how broad the gap is between 'law in the books' and 'law in action', but also at which points SNEs use their autonomous powers most frequently or infrequently.

In follow-up research, more detailed mirror-indexes can be drawn up to calculate the AFS. Mueller's measurement of the 'politics' dimension in MTS may prove useful.[7] Meanwhile, the indexes can still be used, taking into account the actual situation.

For example, South African Provinces have (some) subnational constitutional space but only the opposition governed Provinces have used it (Western Cape), or have tried to use it (KwaZulu-Natan).[8] Likewise, South African Provinces make little use of their legislative powers.[9] The FPS reflects the extent to which the South African Provinces can legally deviate from the blueprint that is set out in the central constitution. Index 3.2 articulates this as the question of whether a particular SNE 'can' make substantial arrangements in some or most of four constitutional categories. By contrast, the AFS reflects the extent to which they actually deviate from the blueprint. The question is therefore whether this SNE in practice 'makes' (instead of 'can make') substantial constitutional arrangements. As for legislation: a minor legislative activity (an average of one Act per month, mostly of a procedural nature)[10] means that the extra score in Index 4.2.B ("the subnational assembly makes laws") cannot be awarded. Also, where the constitution gives the impression that the distribution of powers is based on a system of conditional concurrency, in practice it has turned it into a system where provincial governments have predominantly implementation powers (Index 12.2.). Likewise, for fiscal arrangements, the AFS is measured by assessing whether the SNE actually 'has' set tax bases and rates and introduced new taxes. There is also an assessment of whether the central government has preempted subnational space for taxes.

In the second situation, actors ignore institutional constraints, leading to new power relations that have no basis in the institutional framework. For example, in India, the central government invoked the emergency clause of article 356 of the Constitution more than 100 times, often on the basis of political needs

6 Francesco Palermo, 'Italy: A Federal Country without Federalism?', in Burgess and Tarr (n 2) 237.
7 Sean Mueller, *Theorising Decentralisation* (ECPR Press 2015) 40–48.
8 Nico Steytler, 'Provincial Constitutions in South Africa: an Empty Promise', in Patricia Popelier, Nicholas Aroney and Giacomo Delledonne (eds), *The Routledge Handbook of Subnational Constitutions and Constitutionalism* (Routledge, forthcoming).
9 Jaap de Visser, 'Concurrent Powers in South Africa' in Nico Steytler (ed), *Concurrent Powers in Federal Systems. Meaning, Making, Managing* (Brill Nijhoff 2017) 229.
10 *Ibid* 329.

rather than a real emergency.[11] This time, the AFS is based on the actual use of power, irrespective of its institutional basis. The fact that in Germany the emergency clause was never used simply means that the central government does not make full use of its potential. By contrast, in the Indian case, central self-empowerment disturbs the institutional balance. This is harder to measure because it requires some interpretation: in the absence of a judicial decision, who is to say whether or not there was an emergency that called for central interference? In this case, change is measured through a comparison of FPS and AFS, as in the first hypothesis, but contested use of powers is earmarked. This way, there is no need to decide whether there really was a violation of competence allocation rules. If scores are heavily or frequently earmarked, this suggests a power change that violates the institutional compromise.

Finally, the initial institutional design may be adjusted, or even replaced, through institutional changes. This may be the result of a revolutionary, extra-constitutional development – for example, the secession of a territorial unit beyond the constraints of the rump state constitution. Most often, it takes place within the contours of the constitution, through institutional 'hubs' for change. Constitutional amendment procedures are just one of these hubs, which are further explored in Chapter 8. In this case, change is the difference between the FPSs (FPS_1 and FPS_2) at two different points in time (*Formal Change Score* $fcS = FPS_1 - FPS_2$).

To capture dynamics as long-term processes of gradual change, a comparison of the FPS at two points in time does not suffice. Instead, a longitudinal study is required, with institutional 'snapshots' taken at different points of time over a longer period. In this way, the indexes can reveal both a-synchronic and sequential developments.[12] Asynchrony means that change and continuity occur simultaneously and with particular patterns over time.[13] The detail of the indexes allows us to single out those institutional features that have been subjected to formal or informal change and those that have not. It also allows us to identify features that were changed in a different direction, and to assess which overall trend this variety of processes has led to. Sequential development means that change at one moment in a specific arena determines processes at later points in that arena.[14]

These scores measure changes that occur in vertical relations, between central and subnational levels of authority. It captures institutional and informal change.

11 Panch R.D. Sharma, 'In Search Of The Theory Of Constitutional Machinery Failure (Emergency) Models in India And Pakistan: A Comparative Exploration', (2017) 23 *Comp. L. Rev.* 105. See also Francesco Palermo and Karl Kössler, *Comparative Federalism: Constitutional Arrangements and Case Law* (Oxford, Hart, 2017) 155 on the use of emergency powers to dismiss state governments controlled by opposition parties.

12 For these terms, see Benz and Broschek (n 3) 373

13 *Ibid* 373.

14 *Ibid* 375.

By combining both it assesses to what extent institutional change reflects prior informal change.

A theory of change, however, also needs to consider a second strand of the architecture of MTSs: the horizontal structure between constituent units.[15] The proposed tool allows us to measure this by comparing scores within a particular system. For example, the Belgian showcase (Appendix and Chapter 3, section 3.2) shows a different outcome for the FLC and the GSC. This difference is the asymmetry score (*Constitutional Asymmetry Score* $caS = AFS_A - AFS_B$). Change in horizontal relations is measured by comparing asymmetry scores at different points in time (*Horizontal Change Score* $hcS = caS_1 - caS_2$).

More complex multi-level dynamics can also be discerned this way. For example, a change in the relationship between the central level and the regional level can be compared with a change in the relationship between the central or regional and the local level. This gives an indication of whether the first dynamics impact upon the second, or *vice versa*.

Measuring change this way is helpful for understanding the dynamics of a given country, but it is also important for comparative study. The scores between the FPS and the FAS will show us whether change (of the entire system or limited to a specific category or mechanism) in a given country is substantial or not, compared to changes in other MTSs. To find cross-country patterns, it may be important to limit the population to MTSs with the same FPS. For example, we may select MTSs that, considering their FPS, qualify as 'federations type 1'. When we assess how they function in practice, political systems in one group may turn out to act as regionalized systems, whilst systems in another group may act as confederations. In another group, changes may be so subtle that they do not impact at all on the form of state. To distinguish country-specific drivers from more general drivers for change, we need to first examine patterns within one group, and then compare these patterns with those identified in the other groups.

7.2 Processes of change

The theory set out in Chapter 2 considers the proper balance between cohesion and autonomy, which is a perpetually contested notion. To accommodate this conflict, the institutional design includes 'hubs for change', which are discussed in Chapter 8. The conflict results from developments and tensions that serve as drivers for change. This section gives a brief overview of these drivers for change. It does not claim to cover all the research that has been carried out in this area or even the most important research points. Instead, its purpose is to give some insight into the nature and importance of these drivers. This is because these drivers will determine how institutional hubs for change will eventually be used.

15 Benz and Broschek (n 1) 4.

To this end, a distinction is made between sources, catalysts, strategies, and actors. Sources refer to the drivers for the construction of an MTS, and for changes of the system. Catalysts are situations or events that accelerate ongoing dynamics. Strategies describe the methods to bring about gradual institutional change. Actors are individuals and groups that take action in order to change the power balance, or with this effect.

7.2.1 Sources

One sociological viewpoint is that "institutions change to reach a better fit with the underlying structural base".[16] This means that frictions that trigger change are inherent to society.[17] As Livingston pointed out, the federal framework is secondary to society itself.[18] The question then is which features that constitute a society's structure are also drivers for change in MTSs.

Livingston looked at the 'federal qualities' of society. 'Diversities' of any kind – such as economic, religious, ethnic, linguistic, and historical – that are territorially grouped and have the potential to produce a demand for self-expression, lend themselves to federal governance.[19] Gradual developments in these social cleavages are likely to trigger institutional adaptations.[20] For Erk and Koning, language is an especially important variable: territorially based heterogeneous linguistic structures result in decentralizing dynamics, whereas homogeneity leads to centralizing trends.[21]

In turn, political scientists have argued that it is "potentially misleading" for any endeavor to explain institutional change without considering political structure.[22]

Riker, in particular, highlighted the importance of the political party system and political bargains to explain (changes in) power relations.[23] Thorlakson also showed how nationalized party systems have an integrated effect. This is in contrast to region-based party systems that lead to conflict in the central legislative

16 Jan Erk and Edward Koning, 'New Structuralism and Institutional Change: Federalism Between Centralization and Decentralization', (2010) 43 *Comp. Pol. Studies* 355. See also Jan Erk, *Explaining Federalism* (Routledge 2010) 1–2.
17 Benz and Broschek (n 1) 2.
18 William S. Livingston, *Federalism and Constitutional Change* (Oxford University Press 1956) 2, 4.
19 *Ibid* 2, 5; William S. Livingston, 'A Note on the Nature of Federalism', (1952) 67 *Political Science Quarterly* 85.
20 Benz and Broschek (n 1) 5.
21 Erk and Koning (n 16) 353–378; Erk (n 16) 6–7. But see Paolo Dardanelli *et al.*, 'Dynamic Decentralization in Federations: Comparative Conclusions', (2018) 49 *Publius: The Journal of Federalism* 211.
22 Anthony H. Birch, 'Approaches to the Study of Federalism', (1966) XIV *Political studies* 15–33, reprinted in J. Kincaid (ed), *Federalism* (Sage 2011, Vol. 1) 323.
23 William H. Riker, *Federalism. Origin, Operation, Significance* (Little, Brown and Company 1964) 11–16, 51, 91–101, 129–135.

arena.[24] There are many examples. In South Africa for instance, the hegemony of the ANC across national and (most) provincial governments explains why the Provinces hardly ever exercise their powers.[25] In Ethiopia as well, one-party dominance explains the centralization of power.[26] In other systems, the accidental convergence of central and subnational coalitions helps to make a system more integrationist. This occurred in the United Kingdom, where the fact that the Labour Party was in power in both London and Edinburgh advanced intergovernmental cooperation that was only based on non-enforceable political conventions.[27]

In addition, more foundational political forces play a role: social narratives, political culture, political discourse, and political self-identification of the demos based on mono- or multinational conceptions of community.[28] Social narratives are developed when new problems emerge for which political elites must find new priorities and legitimation.[29] In Germany, changing social narratives have been deemed essential to understanding the development of German postwar federalism.[30] Changing social narratives, following economic globalization and East-West unification, explain why the 2006 reform broke with the gradual path toward centralization.[31] In turn, political self-identification was an important source for change in countries such as Belgium and Canada. There, nationalist ideas rather than economic interests have generated pressure for the decentralization of social policy.[32]

Economic forces, which are often overlooked in federalism literature,[33] also play a role. Burgess pointed to the nature and distribution of economic power and resources in the state to explain diversity that engenders the territorial

24 Lori Thorlakson, 'Dynamics of Change in Federal Representation', in Benz and Broschek (n 1) 234–237. But see also, conversely, for effects of federal institutional design on party competition *ibid*, 238–244.
25 De Visser (n 9) 232–233.
26 Assefa Fiseha and Zemelak Ayele, 'Concurrent Powers in the Ethiopian Federal System', in Steytler (n 9) 250–251.
27 Stephen Tierney, 'Quiet Devolution: Sub-State Autonomy and the Gradual Reconstitution of the United Kingdom', in Burgess and Tarr (n 2) 209.
28 Benz and Broschek (n 1) 7.
29 Roland Sturm, 'More courageous than expected? The 2006 reform of German Federalism', in Erk and Swenden (n 1) 42.
30 *Ibid* 41.
31 *Ibid* 44.
32 Daniel Béland and André Lecours, 'Federalism, Nationalist Politics, and Social Policy: How Ideas and Institutions Interact to Produce or Prevent Change', in Benz and Broschek (n 1) 224.
33 Luc Turgeon and Richard Simeon, 'Ideology, Political Economy and Federalism: The Welfare State and the Evolution of the Australian and Canadian Federation', in Alain-G Gagnon, Soeren Keil and Sean Mueller (eds), *Understanding Federalism and Federation* (Routledge 2015) 125.

dispersion of power.[34] There are manifold examples of the impact of economic forces. Economic disparity across regions can increase secessionist sentiments, especially if this converges with ethnocultural distinctiveness.[35] Financial constraints may prevent SNEs from making use of their powers – this is another explanation for the inactivity of South African Provinces[36] – or make them dependent upon transfers.[37] On the other hand, groups that have control over large territories and significant resources are in a better position to push for a privileged status, as happened in Myanmar.[38] Overall claims to a share of natural resource revenue have led to increasing pressure and competition among different levels of government.[39] Scholars such as Hueglin maintain that federal theory should, therefore, pay more attention to capitalism as the basic structure for federalism, rather than diversity.[40]

An institutional perspective takes the view that institutions matter: they create a path that reinforces federal dynamics. This is discussed in section 7.3 below.

In all this, history is an important factor that determines the institutional setup, the social structure, and the political culture. However, it may also have a lasting impact on further developments. For example, the coming-together or holding-together formation of a MTS determines the initial institutional design, with long-term consequences.[41] It explains why in some systems the exclusive space of SNEs is better protected and strong constitutional subnational autonomy is awarded, whereas in other systems central government occupies the concurrent space and subnational constitutional autonomy is weak.[42] This initial setup creates a path dependency that determines further developments, with

34 Michael Burgess, *Comparative federalism. Theory and Practice* (London, Routledge, 2006) 144.

35 Jan Erk and Lawrence Anderson, 'The Paradox of Federalism: Does Self-Rule Accommodate or Exacerbate Ethnic Divisions?', in Jan Erk and Lawrence M. Anderson (eds), *The Paradox of Federalism* (Routledge 2010) 8. See also Maja Sahadžić, *Asymmetry, Multinationalism and Constitutional Law* (Routledge 2020) 156–157.

36 De Visser (n 9) 233.

37 Nico Steytler, 'Concurrency of Powers: the Zebra in the Room', in Steytler (n 9) 332.

38 Michael G. Breen, 'Asymmetry or Equality? Ethnic Nationalities in a Bamar-Dominated State. A Country Study of Constitutional Asymmetry in Myanmar', in Patricia Popelier and Maja Sahadžić (eds), *Constitutional Asymmetry in Multinational Federalism* (Palgrave Macmillan 2019) 352.

39 Giorgio Brosio and Juan P. Jiménez, 'Federalism and Oil: The Challenges of Intergovernmental Revenue-sharing in Argentina and Brazil', in Giancarlo Pola (ed), *Principles and Practices of Fiscal Autonomy* (Ashgate 2015, reissue Routledge 2017) 41.

40 Thomas O. Hueglin, *A Political Economy of Federalism* (Queen's University Institute of Intergovernmental Relations 1990) 7–8.

41 Benz and Broschek (n 1) 5; Jörg Broschek, 'Between Path Dependence and Gradual Change: Historical Institutionalism and the Study of Federal Dynamics', in Benz and Broschek (n 1) 99; Steytler (n 36) 326.

42 See also Burgess and Tarr (n 2) 11–12.

new turns mainly occurring through incremental change.[43] Historical claims may also explain constitutional asymmetries, which in turn tend to trigger changes, as discussed below. For example, the political unions that England and Wales formed with Scotland (1707) and Ireland (1801) are at the basis of constitutional asymmetries in the UK devolution system;[44] in Spain, the Basque Country and Navarra enjoy a 'constitutionalized historical privilege' in fiscal matters;[45] and in Myanmar, ethnic groups that already enjoyed large autonomy from British colonial rule had stronger bargaining power to secure a special status, because of their infrastructural capacity and secession threats.[46] The historical account of path dependency, however, has been criticized for mixing contingency and sequence.[47]

It is debatable what the main source for change is ultimately. Since Riker, there has been wide agreement that political factors determine (changes in) forms of state. Then again, Livingston maintained that it is society's social structure that determines political institutions;[48] and still other scholars argue that it is political economy.[49] It is probably a combination of these factors that determine institutional change. Livingston pointed to economic, social, political, and cultural forces that determine the institutional form of federal systems.[50] Empirical studies have tested various combinations of drivers. For example, Esman explained divergent dynamics in Canada and the United States through social and economic modernization along with historical experience, demographic and economic structures, and government institutions.[51] In turn, Muñoz and Tormos gave evidence that identity is a strong indicator of support for secession, that economic expectations play a role, and that the role of political parties and leaders is undeniable.[52] Turgeon and Simeon argue that it is the political economy that determines the contours and functioning of political parties, which in turn contribute to changes in the federal institutional design.[53]

43 For an account of different strands of historical institutionalism applied to change in federal systems: Jörg Broschek, 'Conceptualizing and Theorizing Constitutional Change in Federal Systems: Insights from Historical Institutionalism', (2011) 21 *Regional and Federal Studies* 539–559 and Broschek (n 41) 93–97.

44 Brice Dickson, 'Work in Progress. A Country Study of Constitutional Asymmetry in the United Kingdom', in Popelier and Sahadžić (n 38) 481.

45 Pau Bossacoma and Marc Sanjaume-Calvet, 'Asymmetry as a Device for Equal Recognition and Reasonable Accommodation of Majority and Minority Nations. A Country Study on Constitutional Asymmetry in Spain', in Popelier and Sahadžić (n 38) 454.

46 Breen (n 38) 364.

47 Sturm (n 29) 41.

48 Livingston (n 18) 363.

49 Turgon and Simeon (n 33).

50 Livingston (n 18) 1.

51 Milton J. Esman, 'Federalism and Modernization: Canada and the United States', (1984) 14 *Publius: the Journal of Federalism* 22.

52 Jordi Muñoz and Raül Tormos, 'Economic expectations and support for secession in Catalonia: between causality and rationalization', (2015) 7 *Eu. Pol. Sc. Rev.* 315–341.

53 Turgeon and Simeon (n 33) 125–138.

7.2.2 Catalysts

Catalysts are variables that precipitate changes that were already hidden in the basic structure. These catalysts can take different shapes. Examples are crises, constitutional asymmetries and international developments. The first are "abrupt and order-shattering" critical junctures:[54] they create a moment of fluidity and uncertainty that allows room for radical change. The other two are less visible: constitutional asymmetries are, at first sight, more technical, and international developments are gradual, but both have the potential of accelerating ongoing processes.

'Crises' are preeminent catalysts of political change in general, but this seems, in particular, to be the case in MTSs.[55] Often they create critical junctures that lead to a centralization of power, but economic crises also put a strain on solidarity systems which may lead to a loss of cohesion.[56] In practice, the impact of crises on the system's power balance depends on crisis pressure – i.e., how deeply the system is affected by the crisis – as well as the institutional framework and political behavior.[57]

'Constitutional asymmetry' often reflects political asymmetries, i.e., social, identitarian, or economic disparities. To Livingston, such disparities are essential to federal forms of state.[58] Outspoken disparities, however, may lead territorial groups to aspire to a more advantageous position. For example, in Spain, identity (i.e., ethnic or cultural distinctiveness) as well as economic self-interest (a demand for higher fiscal autonomy, similar to the Basque Country's statute, to address the perceived unfair distribution of resources),[59] explain the development of Catalonian self-determination movements.[60] This translation of political asymmetry into constitutional asymmetry is typical for multinational systems.[61] In turn, constitutional asymmetry may bolster demands for further change. Leyland, for one, has warned that the "extreme asymmetry" characteristic of devolution "has embarked the UK on a journey with an uncertain destination" and that the "lack of constitutional balance created by these extremely diverse

54 Broschek (n 41) 95.
55 Dietmar Braun and Philipp Trein, 'Federal dynamics in times of economic and financial crisis', (2014) 53 *Eu. J. Pol. Research* 803.
56 *Ibid* 803.
57 In Braun and Trein's study of the economic and financial crisis, *ibid*, the EU's influence as well as SNEs opportunistic behaviour played a role. This was combined with crisis pressure (defined as a decrease in economic growth) and an increase in unemployment and gross national debt.
58 Livingston (n 18) 2.
59 See Antoni Castells, 'Catalonia and Spain at the crossroads: financial and economic aspects', (2014) 30 *Oxford Review of Economic Policy* 277–296 and Antoni Castells, 'The Relation Catalonia/Spain: Some Financial and Economic Aspects', in Pola (n 38) 204–216 for an overview of the Spanish and Catalan economic situation and relations.
60 Muñoz and Tormos (n 51) 315–341; Jesús Ruiz-Huerta, 'Spanish Decentralization and Fiscal Federalism', in Pola (n 38) 186, 197–200.
61 See Sahadžić (n 35) 17.

conditions" created a new dynamic.[62] Tierney confirms that devolution in the United Kingdom is a continuous process and that it was only to be expected that Wales was rapidly striving to catch up with stronger models of devolution.[63] Asymmetry may reinforce regional identity, leading to more radical autonomy demands. Moreover, it 'raises the specter of comparison', with the potential to activate the less advantaged groups.[64] This may lead the system into a continuous process of reform, with pro-asymmetry steps being followed by re-symmetrizing steps leading to new asymmetry demands.[65]

'International developments' may also impact on power relations. Steytler points to the interconnectedness of social and economic life in a quickly globalizing world to explain the increasing role of shared powers.[66] The development of the EU, in particular, has impacted vertical power relations within multi-tiered member states.[67] For example, European integration reinforced centralization trends in Germany.[68] This is further discussed in Chapter 8.

7.2.3 Strategies

Critical junctures can trigger radical reforms. Most often, however, changes are incremental rather than radical. Bednar stresses that it is important for political systems to have mechanisms for constraining radical changes. This is because such changes would upset the public, make the government seem unreliable, and create uncertainty and instability.[69] Broschek distinguishes four strategies for gradual change: layering, displacement, conversion, and drift.[70] Strategies of experimentation and delay can be added to this.

'Layering' means that old institutions remain in place, but new institutions are added that incrementally alter their function or impact.[71] The indexes presented in the previous part can be used to single out the instruments that hollow out existing mechanisms. For example, they reveal the impact of conditional

62 Peter Leyland, 'The multifaceted constitutional dynamics of UK devolution', (2011) 9 *International Journal of Constitutional Law* 252–254.
63 Tierney (n 27) 206.
64 Stefan Wolff, 'Cases of Asymmetrical Territorial Autonomy', in Marc Weller and Katherine Nobbs (eds), *Asymmetric Autonomy and the Settlement of Ethnic Conflicts* (University of Pennsylvania Press 2010) 25.
65 Angustias Hombrado, 'Learning to Catch the Wave? Regional Demands for Constitutional Change in Contexts of Asymmetrical Arrangements', (2011) 21 *Regional & Federal Studies* 480.
66 Steytler (n 9) 327–329.
67 Ornella Porchia, 'Sub-national Units, Member States, and the European Union', in Burgess and Tarr (n 2) 286.
68 Werner Heun, *The Constitution of Germany. A Contextual Analysis* (Hart 2011) 56, 75.
69 Jenna Bednar, 'Constitutional Change in Federations: The Role of Complementary Institutions', in Benz and Broschek (n 1) 280.
70 Broschek (n 41) 104–106.
71 *Ibid* 104.

grants. Broschek refers to these grants as an example of layering that enabled federal governments in the United States and Canada to encroach upon subnational autonomy, despite the institutional allocation of powers.[72]

'Displacement' means that old rules are replaced by new ones. Broschek describes this as a process that affects vertical relations. New rules at the central level replace established rules at the subnational level, for example, when interstate trade barriers are abolished for the creation of a common market. Conversely, opting-out provisions enable SNEs to substitute nationwide regulations within their own jurisdiction.[73] This reveals how the allocation of competences can work as a 'hub for change'. For example, concurrent powers allow the central government to preempt subnational rules. However, sometimes the opposite occurs in those rare cases where subnational rules have priority in specific concurrent matters, e.g., pensions in Canada. This was discussed in Chapter 5 and is included again in Chapter 8.

'Conversion' means that old institutions are given new purposes or functions without formal change.[74] Room for conversion is created whenever conflicts arise over the interpretation of rules. This shows the importance of institutional actors with interpretative authority to resolve conflicts of competence and other federalism disputes. Bednar confirms that constitutional change is not merely a matter of periodic constitutional revisions, but "a continuous and dynamic process of constitutional reinterpretation".[75] Again, this is discussed in the next chapter.

'Drift' is a dynamic that flows from the status quo. If status-quo defending actors prevent institutions from adapting to new developments, these institutions remain the same but their impact will change.[76] This should become visible when comparing the federalism potential score FPS with the actual federalism score AFS.

Drift, however, may be controlled if alternative outlets are available for change-demanding groups. For example, subnational constitutionalism allows groups that are unable to achieve their goals at the central level to do so through subnational constitutional processes.[77] This may eventually lead to 'experimentation' as a strategy for gradual change. The strategy is particularly suited to MTSs, where SNEs can serve as experimental laboratories. The idea is that successful institutional innovations that are adopted in one SNE are gradually also adopted in other SNEs, and eventually at the central level. This thought gained global popularity upon Justice Brandeis' remark that "it is one of the happy incidents of the federal system that a single courageous state may, if its citizens

72 *Ibid* 105.
73 *Ibid* 105.
74 *Ibid* 105.
75 Bednar (n 69) 278.
76 Broschek (n 41) 106.
77 John Dinan, 'State Constitutions and American Political Development', in Burgess and Tarr (n 2) 42.

choose, serve as a laboratory, without risk to the rest of the country".[78] However, experimentation can also be a top-down process. For example, in Italy, regionalism started as an experiment that was controlled by the central government.[79]

Finally, 'delay' means that a change is envisaged, but its operation is made conditional upon future arrangements. This is a useful strategy if there is some agreement that change is needed, but trust is lacking to make it operational. For example, the Northern Ireland Act made the transfer of 'reserved matters' in Schedule 3 conditional upon cross-party support.[80] Delay is also used to reconcile parties if there is insufficient vision or agreement to make a detailed arrangement. For example, in Belgium, the Cultural Communities were established in 1970 based on Flemish demands. Meanwhile, Walloon demands for economic autonomy were met by a constitutional clause that envisaged the establishment of 'Regions' but left the conceptual design to a special majority law.[81] The Regions were created ten years later. Likewise, the Belgian Constitution appeased Flemish parties by allocating residuary competences in principle to the SNEs, conditional upon a constitutional amendment to enumerate all federal competences.[82] No further substantial efforts were made to make this provision operational.

7.2.4 Actors

It takes actors to agree on a particular power balance and to actually make use of opportunities to accelerate the dynamics of an underlying structure and bring about a change in power relations. Here, a distinction is made between political, social, and economic actors that "push boundaries"[83] and institutional actors that have the capacity to convert this into institutional change or to resist such pressures. The latter are discussed in section 7.3.

'Political actors', in a wide sense, are all actors that "engage in political decisions". This includes the electorate, political officials, political parties, civil servants, and interest groups.[84] The latter group is regarded as a 'social actor' in the next category. The impact of political parties in particular on the functioning of MTS has been demonstrated numerous times. It was tested empirically and returns in multiple observations. For example, the rise of regional parties in India correlated with a shift in the position of the Indian Finance Commission. This Commission over time increased the share of tax proceeds to the states,

78 *New State Ice Co. v. Liebmann*, 285 U.S. 262, 311 (1932).
79 Palermo (n 6) 239.
80 Nikos Skoutaris, 'Subnational constitutionalism in the UK', in Popelier, Aroney and Delledonne (n 8).
81 Art. 134 (then: *107 quater)* Belgian Constitution.
82 At. 35 Belgian Constitutional.
83 Bednar (n 69) 281, 284.
84 Mueller (n 7) 35.

after having previously favored the Union.[85] The impact of one-party dominance on the functioning of MTSs was already mentioned above (section 7.2.1). In turn, the dominance of region-based parties is likely to intensify disintegrative dynamics, with Belgium as a prominent example of this.[86]

'Social and economic actors' also play a role. For example, economic actors can challenge the federal 'compact' if mobility causes fiscal imbalances.[87] International monetary institutions have demanded decentralized government as a condition for developing states to receive their monetary support.[88] Duchacek noted that interest groups such as labor organizations, mass media, or banks whose activities and organization are nationwide, "may alter the originally federal habits and attitudes more significantly than even the most antifederal political parties".[89] This is illustrated in Belgium, where it is argued that the nationally organized social partners (labor unions and employer associations) have obstructed decentralization of social security, as these organizations are deeply involved in its administration.[90] Conversely, Duchacek argues that because major Australian interest groups were originally organized on a state-basis and have developed state-based vested interests, this makes the Australian MTS more meaningful than we could otherwise have expected.[91] In the United Kingdom, Tierney describes how devolution was a bottom-up process, resulting in a weak model of devolution in Wales (where the civil campaign for devolution was weak), and a strong model for Scotland (pushed by a more powerful mobilization of political and social actors and the population).[92]

Benz distinguishes three mechanisms for these actors to impact on federal systems: exit/entry (i.e., mobility), loyalty, and voice.[93] This way, actors either act as "agents of change or defenders of the status quo". In the end, they bring about institutional change but they are also conditioned by preexisting institutional arrangements.[94]

85 Elisabeth Alber, 'Intergovernmental Financial Relations: Institutions, Rules and Praxis', in Alice Valdesalici and Francesco Palermo (eds), *Comparing Fiscal Federalism* (Brill 2018) 244–245.
86 Kris Deschouwer, 'The Rise and Fall of the Belgian Regionalist Parties', (2009) 19 *Regional and Federal Studies* 559–577.
87 A. Benz, 'Dimensions and Dynamics of Federal Regimes', in A. Benz and J. Broschek (n 1) 79.
88 Jan Erk and Wilfried Swenden, 'The new wave of federalism studies', in Erk and Swenden (n 1) 3.
89 Ivo D. Duchacek, *Comparative Federalism* (Holt, Rinehart and Winston 1970, reissued University Press of America 1987) 343.
90 Béland and Lecours (n 32) 221.
91 Duchacek (n 89) 345.
92 Tierney (n 27) 200–202.
93 Benz (n 87) 78–80.
94 Broschek (n 43) 541; Broschek (n 41) 95.

7.3 Why institutions matter in processes of change

The previous section showed that drivers for change are usually not institutional. They are of a political, sociological, or economic nature, or a combination of these factors. Political, social, and economic disparities, as well as crises and international developments, serve as drivers for change, whereas history explains the direction in which change is taken. This does not mean that institutions are of no importance in processes of change. In fact, as Livingston holds, "the form and the process can never be separated".[95] Duchacek illustrates this where he sees parties as mirrors of the federal constitution and institutions, which were created by them and are then manipulated by them.[96] As a consequence, institutions appear to be a prerequisite for as well as a target of change.[97]

7.3.1 Institutional change as a result of informal change

First, factual changes will often culminate in institutional change, for example, through constitutional amendments.

The relevance of this is often downplayed. It has been noticed that the transformation of Germany into a cooperative federation was formalized through constitutional amendments of fiscal arrangements, but it appears that this merely "legitimized and supplemented developments that had already taken place in practice rather than independently advancing constitutional change".[98] The role of the US Supreme Court in the transformation of the US federal model has been qualified as a mere judicial endorsement of Congressional actions to expand central power.[99] Institutional confirmation of informal changes is, nevertheless, important because it has the potential to reinforce the dynamics at play.

The first reason is that it brings new power relations within the legal realm. This way, the new power relations are given legitimacy and made legally enforceable. This makes it more difficult for new actors that enter the scene to express different views on what should be the proper balance. Livingston pointed in particular to constitutional amendments as a superior form of institutional change because of its "high authority".[100] Benz and Broschek describe this as a locking-in process: institutionalization generates returns for actors operating within the institution and raises the costs of those trying to change it.[101]

The second reason is that institutional changes become part of the constitutional narrative that is used as an interpretative framework for power disputes.

95 Livingston (n 18) 318.
96 Duchacek (n 89) 338.
97 Benz and Broschek (n 1) 6.
98 Heun (n 68) 56.
99 Mark Tushnet, *The Constitution of the United States of America. A Contextual Analysis* (Oxford, Hart 2009) 40, 181, 242.
100 Livingston (n 18) 13, 295.
101 Benz and Broschek (n 1) 16.

An empirical analysis of the Belgian Constitutional Court's stance in federalism disputes showed a significant causal relationship between constitutional change and changes in the Court's centralization grade. With every state reform that turned Belgium into a looser organization with more subnational autonomy, the Court took a more decentralist stance in the adjudication of federalism disputes.[102]

Thirdly, institutionalization creates path dependency. This means, as Broschek explains, that the system's institutional foundations "are reproduced over time and define the basic parameters of the federal trajectory".[103]

7.3.2 Impact of institutional change on noninstitutional developments

Livingston's thesis that institutions follow social dynamics[104] has further support. Erk stresses, on the basis of five country studies, that the institutional framework does not change the social structure, but instead, that the homogeneous or heterogeneous social structure determines institutional change.[105] Likewise, other scholars argue that social cleavages impact on (central or regional) party organization, which in turn paves the way for institutional reform.[106]

Erk's case studies convincingly show that institutional change mostly follows societal dynamics. However, they do not refute the possibility that institutional change, in turn, impacts on these dynamics. The author contends that the Belgian political institutions gradually changed in order to become congruent with the societal structure in terms of linguistic and cultural duality, and that "a satisfactory level of congruence" was attained in 1993 when Belgium officially became a federal state.[107] According to him, Flemings have since then been preoccupied with the contents of their policies more than with further state reforms.[108] Yet, the author neglects a fifth state reform in 2001, which was carried out through special majority laws because the constitution, at that time, was locked against institutional reform. By ignoring the impact of institutions on societal dynamics, he did not foresee the sixth state reform in 2013, nor the subsequent confederal debate. The outcome of the 2019 elections complicated the formation of a federal government. This is because of the unprecedented rise

102 Patricia Popelier and Samantha Bielen, 'How Courts Decide Federalism Disputes: Legal Merit, Attitudinal Effects, and Strategic Considerations in the Jurisprudence of the Belgian Constitutional Court', (2018) 49 *Publius: The Journal of Federalism*, 606–607.
103 Broschek (n 41) 94.
104 Livingston (n 17) 1.
105 Erk (n 16) 2.
106 Wilfried Swenden and Bart Maddens, 'Concluding Observations', in Wilfried Swenden and Bart Maddens (eds), *Territorial Party Politics in Western Europe* (Palgrave MacMillan 2009) 253.
107 Erk (n 16) 13, 33.
108 *Ibid* 33.

of extreme parties, a more driven preference for left-wing parties on the Walloon side and for right-wing parties on the Flemish side. This meant that in 2020, when the Covid-19 crisis emerged, the caretaker minority government had to be transformed into an emergency minority government. Post-electoral research revealed that the division between north and south is a political divide rather than the reflection of a social dichotomy.[109] The different voting results reflected the different mixtures of (mostly regional) political parties that presented themselves to the voters at each side of the language border. However, in reality, both Walloons and Flemings hold mainly centrist political preferences.[110] This suggests that institutional and political dynamics can be mutually reinforcing to the point that they surpass social cleavages.

Elsewhere, Erk admits that institutional design matters, even if in the end external factors seem more powerful than the design of federalism to control secessionism.[111] For example, federalism in multinational systems is supposedly more stable (with multiple constitutional units) than in dyadic systems. This is unless few or just one of the subunits is ethnoculturally distinct. In that case, institutional design does not reduce the 'us vs them' mindset. Instead, it may reinforce secessionist feelings if subunits of the minority culture(s) feel overpowered by the other subunits of the majority culture.[112] Other scholars agree that ethnofederal institutions keep the ethnic conflict alive and create the capacity to secede.[113]

Simeon confirms that constitutions are indeed independent forces that affect federal dynamics.[114] Even Livingston admitted that the very fact that a political system takes the form of a federation may bring about a sense of distinctiveness, and even create diversity where none previously existed.[115] Conversely, the absence of territorial boundaries may prevent regional interests from being mobilized and voiced in central decision-making bodies. For this reason (and in contrast to the devolved entities in the United Kingdom) it has been argued that it is extremely difficult for England to express and advance regional (as opposed to local) interests.[116] Another example was given in the previous section, where constitutional asymmetry was identified as a catalyst for change.

109 Stefaan Walgrave, Jonas Lefevere *et al.* Note based on the RepResent study, 'Vlamingen en Walen stemden voor verschillende partijen maar verschillen van mening over het beleid dat ze willen', 4–11. Unpublished, but authority was given to quote.

110 *Ibid* p. 7.

111 Erk and Anderson (n 35) 11. See also David Cameron, 'The Paradox of Federalism: Some Practical Reflections', in Erk and Anderson (n 35) 116.

112 Erk and Anderson (n 35) 7.

113 Philip G. Roeder, 'Ethnofederalism and the Mismanagement of Conflicting Nationalisms', in Erk and Anderson (n 35)18–19.

114 Richard Simeon, 'Constitutional Design and Change in Federal Systems: Issues and Questions', (2009) 39 *Publius: The Journal of Federalism* 244.

115 Livingston (n 18) 8.

116 Des McNulty, 'Fiscal Decentralization for Scotland: Risks and Consequences for the UK', in Pola (n 39) 174.

Fiscal arrangements also impact on the entities' financial resources and their institutional capacity to exercise autonomy.[117] The institutional design of forms of state – e.g., decentralization of substantive and fiscal powers and the allocation of powers on the basis of exclusivity – shapes the organizational strategy of political parties.[118] This, in turn, may impact on political discourse and reinforce (dis)integrative dynamics.

If institutional engineering can either accelerate or slow down social dynamics, the next question is whether it can also change these dynamics. This is an issue that becomes urgent in systems that are disintegrating at high speed.[119] It can be expected that institutional change will mostly reinforce or accelerate dynamics that were already simmering below the surface. One reason for this is that it will be more difficult for political actors to introduce institutional changes that go against the tide. Hence, there was little political support for a proposal by a group of Belgian political scientists for a nationwide electoral district to resolve disintegrative dynamics.[120] However, if social dynamics are more ambiguous and the balance of power is still in flux or under threat, institutional change may tip the balance in one direction or another.[121] Likewise, new dynamics may emerge if social narratives do not offer an adequate answer to new problems arising from external developments. Even then, institutional path dependency will play a role: changes are more likely to occur in the direction of the dominant trajectory, whereas the reverse is much more difficult to achieve.[122]

7.3.3 Institutional actors

Finally, institutional changes are brought about by institutional actors, such as governments, parliaments, bureaucracies, and courts. Admittedly, they are mostly driven by noninstitutional actors. Moreover, their legitimacy and continuity depend upon political actors or public support. However, this cannot negate their independent role in federal dynamics.

Most of the time institutions are staffed by political actors. For example, the parliaments and governments that make laws and amend constitutions consist of political actors, which, in turn, need their voters' support. As Benz mentioned, reform agendas are discussed in parliament by political actors that pursue

117 A. Benz and J. Broschek (eds), 'Federal Dynamics', 7.

118 Lori Thorlakson, 'Patterns of Party Integration, Influence and Autonomy in Seven Federations', (2009) 15 *Party Politics* 173 and Thorlakson (n 24) 237–244.

119 See, for Belgium, Patricia Popelier, 'Secessionist and Autonomy Movements in Flanders: The Disintegration of Belgium as the Chronicle of a Death Foretold?', in Eva Maria Belser *et al.* (eds), *States Falling Apart? Secessionist and Autonomy Movements in Europe* (Stämpfli Verlag 2015) 244.

120 Report of the mixed parliamentary commission of the House of Representatives and the Senate, *Parl. Doc.* 2013–2015, House of Representatives, 53-3446/1 and Senate, 5-2730/1.

121 Braun and Trein (n 55) 345–348 and 358–360.

122 Broschek (n 41) 107.

their own particular interests instead of a common goal. This means that reform will always be selective and not necessarily responsive to objective needs for change.[123] According to Livingston, constitutions are "creatures of politics", and these politics, in turn, are determined by the societal structure.[124] However, in their capacity as an institutional actor, political actors are constrained by institutional procedures and requirements such as time limits and majorities. For this reason, an institutional perspective is indispensable, and a legal perspective is particularly relevant where noncompliance can be sanctioned by the court.

Courts are therefore another prominent example of institutional actors. As discussed above, they bring about change through conversion. It takes societal and/or political actors to bring a case before the court, and empirical studies show that political structures – in particular, the government in power – influence the court's position in federalism disputes. Nevertheless, legal merit also plays a role, which means that courts can be seen as independent drivers for change. In particular, by issuing judgments that serve as (binding or nonbinding) precedents, they create path dependencies that reinforce structural dynamics. This is further discussed in Chapter 8.

7.4 Conclusion

Scholars have examined constitutional change in federal systems from different angles. These angles are captured in this chapter as sources, catalysts, strategies, and actors. Colino notes that this multifaceted type of analyses results in theories of change being moved between two poles. At one pole, long-term structural changes are described as incremental and driven by social structure. At the other pole, changes are seen as deliberate, actor-driven designs.[125] Arguably, we need a more comprehensive theory that combines these different approaches. The weakness in the approaches so far, according to Colino, is a lack of measurement of change, clear specification of what the objects of change are, and what direction the changes may take.[126] This chapter showed how the indexes, constructed in Part II, can be used for that purpose. They are ready-made to assess institutional change over time but need some adaptation to measure informal change.

The overview in section 7.2 showed how noninstitutional drivers determine institutional change, but also emphasized the importance of institutions in these processes. The role of institutions is especially important in multinational entities because the mutually reinforcing power of institutional, political, and societal dynamics implies that "a satisfactory level of congruence" may never be attained. Where Bednar suggests a "natural pendulum-like swing to the

123 Benz (n 87) 83.
124 Livingston (n 18) 303.
125 Colino (n 1) 17–18.
126 *Ibid* 18.

centralization and decentralization dynamics",[127] she seems to overlook the very clear dynamics over time toward centralization or fragmentation, and how this can be manipulated by political discourse as well as institutional change.

The combination of sources in a given political system will determine the optimal balance of cohesion and subnational autonomy. Whether the system reflects this balance, and whether it does so at once or over time, depends upon the constellation of actors and the robustness of the system's institutions. Catalysts may trigger more radical changes, but the basic societal and economic structure will determine the system's resilience. Most often, changes occur in a more incremental way, through constitutional strategies. This means that dynamics reveal themselves only over time, but also become more robust.

The strategies for gradual change, in particular, highlight the relevance of institutional design to processes of change. The choice of strategies is linked with "the preconditions that make their occurrence plausible",[128] i.e., with the institutional 'hubs for change' that are built in the federal system. If rigid procedures make layering and displacement difficult, more pressure will be put on courts to produce change through interpretation. Insight into political processes is also important for the design of institutional hubs. If the involvement of all interested parties in constitutional reform leads to a deadlock, a way out can be offered by displacement through bilateral agreements or asymmetrical opt-outs. For example, Béland and Lecours show how social security has remained highly centralized in Belgium due to (among other factors) rigid procedures for change in the opposing Flemish and French-speaking parties. In contrast, displacement in Canada took place through asymmetrical decentralization to accommodate Québec nationalism.[129] However, it must be kept in mind that bilateral agreements promote constitutional asymmetry, which in turn serves as an accelerator for change.

All of this helps us to further develop a theory of dynamic federalism. In Chapter 2, nine forms of state were distinguished that are dependent upon nine different relations between cohesion and autonomy. This checkerboard reveals whether systems are stable or not over time. Stability means that despite changes over time, the form of state remains the same. Unstable systems change form through (de)centralization and/or (dis)integration. My expectation is that the stability of MTSs is dependent on two criteria of congruence and non-congruence.

The first criterion is based upon the insight that society structures institutions. According to this criterion, systems must have institutional mechanisms through which institutional power relations can be kept congruent with social power relations. If these mechanisms are lacking, change will be enforced in a more radical and informal way. The second criterion is based upon the contention that

127 Jenna Bednar, 'Federalism theory: the boundary problem, robustness and dynamics', in John Kincaid (ed), *A Research Agenda for Federalism Studies* (Edward Elgar 2019) 35.
128 Broschek (n 41) 106.
129 Béland and Lecours (n 32) 221–2224.

institutional change may create self-reinforcing effects. To mitigate that effect, and thus to stabilize social dynamics, congruence must remain imperfect. For example, the Belgian system became federal as a response to a social-linguistic-cultural divide. In turn, the institutional setup reinforced this divide, leading to a continuous state of reform that seems to bypass the actual social divide. My hypothesis – still to be tested – is that cohesive instruments might stabilize these dynamics to keep the social structure and institutional design congruent.

With regard to the second criterion, it must be kept in mind that a theory of dynamic federalism is neutral on the desired balance of cohesion and autonomy. The theory does not prescribe stability as a normative principle. Whether we prefer a system to remain stable, or strive for a transformation into a new form of state, is a political choice. The theory simply offers the tools to define the form of state and to identify the instruments for autonomy or cohesion that help to either change or maintain the balance of power. Chapter 3 used the Belgian case to illustrate this point.

The first criterion highlights the importance of institutional mechanisms that enable institutional change. These are discussed in the next chapter.

8 Institutional hubs for change

Institutional hubs for change are mechanisms that are built into the institutional architecture in order to facilitate change. In line with Chapters 2 and 7, constitutions are conceived as providing instruments that enable both adjustments to maintain the power balance and recalibrations of power relations when new developments (or new actors) question the federal balance. This chapter identifies five institutional 'hubs' for change: constitutional amendments (8.1); de-constitutionalization (8.2); techniques for the allocation of competences (8.3); judicial and nonjudicial adjudicators of federalism conflicts (8.4); and institutionalization of global governance (8.5). These hubs have been included in the indexes that were developed in Part II. There, their potential for providing autonomy or cohesion was taken into account. In this chapter, they are briefly revisited to discuss the conditions under which they facilitate or curb federal dynamics, and how these hubs relate to each other. At this point, precise data are lacking to fully answer these questions. The purpose of this chapter is, therefore, less ambitious: it merely aims to illustrate the complexity of institutional design as a facilitator of change and give some insights about how constitutional engineering may affect change processes.

8.1 Constitutional amendments

Procedures should be sufficiently flexible to allow adjustments to new developments, whilst also being sufficiently rigid to secure stability.[1] This is a somewhat trite expression that is easy to formulate but difficult to make concrete. In the literature, several formal hurdles have been described that can test the rigidity of constitutional amendment procedures.[2] However, these exercises do not teach

1 Daniel Halberstam, 'Comparative Federalism and the Role of the Judiciary', in Keith E. Whittington, R. Daniel Kelemen and Gregory A. Caldeira, *The Oxford Handbook of Law and Politics* (Oxford University Press 2010) 143.

2 For an overview: Richard Albert, *Constitutional Amendments. Making, Breaking, and Changing Constitutions* (Oxford University Press 2019) 98–101.

us much about the optimal level of rigidity, or about the flexibility to facilitate change without undermining the system's stability.

There are three reasons for this. First, Ginsburg and Melton observe that the validity of these measures is doubtful, considering the poor correlation between the proposed measures.[3] Moreover, extrajudicial factors, such as the demand for constitutional change, political culture and cultural attitudes, or the specificities of the political party landscape may prevail over rigid or flexible formal amendment requirements.[4] For example, supermajorities are more difficult to obtain in polarized two-party systems.[5] In the end, amendment culture – i.e., "the set of shared attitudes about the desirability of amendment, independent of the substantive issue under consideration and the degree of pressure for change" – is a better predictor of amendment rates than formal procedures.[6] For example, in Spain, constitutional amendment is 'a political taboo', implemented only when it is dictated by EU membership.[7] This is why Ginsburg and Melton conclude that "constitutional designers have little influence over the observed flexibility of their product".[8] Finally, and most importantly, measuring formal rigidity misses the point. The real question is whether the constitutional amendment procedure is suitable to institutionalize sustained or new agreements on what is considered the proper balance of powers. This defines 'robust' institutional change in a theory of dynamic federalism.

In a theory of dynamic federalism, robust change is secured if change is based on an agreement between the different tiers. Benz already pointed out that regardless of the form of state, change in MTS has to rely on a model of joint decision-making.[9] Index 2.1 measures this as an indicator for cohesion. The assumption is that if all relevant parties are involved in the procedure, the amendment will be balanced. Cohesion does not require unanimity: what matters is that decisions are made of the basis of an informed discussion that takes all perspectives and interests into account. Still, the procedure implies a number

3 Tom Ginsburg and James Melton, 'Does the constitutional amendment rule matter at all? Amendment cultures and the challenges of measuring amendment difficulty', (2015) 13 *International Constitutional Law Review* 697.

4 Rosalind Dixon, 'Constitutional Amendment Rules: A Comparative Perspective', in Tom Ginsburg and Rosalind Dixon, *Comparative Constitutional Law* (Edward Elgar 2011) 107–108; Vicky C. Jackson, 'The (myth of un)amendability of the US Constitution and the democratic component of constitutionalism', (2015) 13 *International Journal of Constitutional Law* 575–605. See also Albert, (n 2) 97.

5 Xenophon Contiades and Alkmene Fatiadou, 'Models of Constitutional Change', in Xenophon Contiades (ed), *Engineering Constitutional Change* (Routledge 2013) 426.

6 Ginsburg and Melton (n 3)709–711. See Albert (n 2) 111–119 for a refinement of the concept of amendment culture.

7 Victor Ferreres Comella, *The Constitution of Spain. A contextual analysis* (Hart 2013) 59.

8 Ginsburg and Melton (n 3) 711.

9 Arthur Benz, 'Dimensions and Dynamics of Federal Regimes', in Arthur Benz and Jörg Broschek (eds), *Federal Dynamics. Continuity, Change, & the Varieties of Federalism* (Oxford University Press 2013) 84.

of players holding a veto, which ensures resistance against unilateral pushes for change. A cohesive procedure is, therefore, an indicator of robust institutional change. This might explain why political constraints – i.e., numerous veto players with opposing interests – correlate with an increased amendment rate.[10] Admittedly, an amendment rate is not a good proxy for successful institutional change. Amendments may concern issues that have nothing to do with the federal balance. Moreover, if institutions and social structure converge, there is no need for constitutional revision. A slow but regular amendment rate seems to be more indicative of successful institutional change.

Even if the procedure is cohesive and all parties agree, additional obstacles may prevent formal change from occurring. For example, in Belgium, the constitution first requires that the government and a majority in the House of Representatives and the Senate compose a list of provisions that may be changed. Elections are held next. In the second phase, the listed provisions can be changed with a two-thirds majority in both houses.[11] This means that parties can obstruct constitutional reform by going to elections without a list, or with a minimalist list. Therefore if an agreement for federal reform is secured after the elections, this agreement is excluded from formal change if the parties previously (before the elections) locked the constitution. This is what happened in 1999. Elections opened the possibility for a fifth state reform, but the parties were confronted with a locked constitution. The fifth state reform took place anyway through special majority laws, without any constitutional amendments.

The evidence about these procedures leads to five conclusions.

1 The involvement of SNEs in the constitutional amendment procedure is not merely a feature of federal systems aimed at preserving subnational autonomy. It is actually a feature that enhances robust institutional change. In other words, it is change itself that keeps the system stable, because it reflects a shared view on what the proper power balance is in a particular system. This does not transform cohesion into a normative principle for MTSs. Even in decentralized systems that are not aiming for cohesion, the amendment procedure may be cohesive. For example, in the Netherlands, which presents itself as a decentralized system, constitutional amendments require a two-thirds majority in the upper chamber. The upper chamber is made up of representatives from decentralized provinces.[12] Moreover, the preference for a cohesive amendment procedure presupposes that the different tiers have opposing interests. The more this is the case, the more the involvement that will be required;
2 Hurdles that obstruct institutional change, despite a broad agreement between the different tiers, should be well-reasoned. If rigidity is their only

10 *Ibid* 711.
11 Art. 195 Belgian Constitution.
12 Art. 137(4) Dutch Constitution.

rationale, they risk missing a window for successful and timely change. Ultimately, the rate at which amendments are made will probably remain unaffected. A concern for democratic legitimacy often explains additional hurdles. However, there are multiple ways to secure legitimacy – for example, through elections,[13] consultations,[14] or popular vote[15] – some of which may be less obstructive than others. Additionally, different tracks can be designed for provisions that concern the relationships between the different tiers and with other provisions. One option is to insert multiple tracks for constitutional amendment. For example, in the Netherlands, a more lenient procedure is inserted to enable the conclusion of international treaties that are contrary to the constitution.[16] Another option is to delegate the first type of provisions to other instruments. In Belgium, for instance, most provisions concerning the organization of (most of) the Communities and Regions are regulated by special majority laws. These have more rigid joint-decision requirements but no additional hurdles. This type of deconstitutionalization is discussed further below;

3 A cohesive amendment procedure advances incremental or gradual change. This suggests continuity, which presupposes that the social structure and political constellation are relatively stable. For example, in Switzerland, it has been argued that the frequent constitutional amendments never affect the stability of the system and its basic principles.[17] Yet, incremental change is not a synonym for continuous change. Albert defines continuous constitutional change as a change that occurs within the existing framework of a legal order, whereas discontinuous change is a change in trajectory and identity that results in a new legal order.[18] An alteration in the balance of cohesion and autonomy, which transforms a system into a new form of state, would imply discontinuous change. Where the basic structure is under an eternity clause, discontinuous change would amount to an unconstitutional amendment. However, if the passage from one form of state to another is gradual, it is difficult to identify which precise amendment constitutes the tipping point. For example, in Germany, the eternity clause prohibits the transformation of the federation into a unitary state. It also demands a multi-tiered structure with Länder as constituent units and guarantees the participation of the Länder in the legislative process.[19] However, all this

13 E.g., Art. 195 Belgian Constitution.
14 E.g., Art. 74(5)(a) and (6) South African Constitution.
15 E.g., Art. 128 Australian Constitution.
16 Art. 91(3) Dutch Constitution.
17 Thomas Fleiner, 'Constitutional Revision: The Case of Switzerland', in Contiades (n 5) 340.
18 Albert (n 2) 150.
19 Jens Woelk, 'Germany', in Dawn Oliver and Carlo Fusaro (eds) *How Constitutions Change: A Comparative Study* (Hart 2011) 149.

still leaves room for sliding between the different forms of state that were distinguished in Chapter 2;

4 Crises or other critical junctures may turn everything upside down and trigger calls for immediate transformative change. Eternity clauses prohibit reform through constitutional amendments. In other systems, amendment procedures may complicate global reform. For example, in Belgium, there can only be change to those provisions that were opened for revision by the preceding parliament. This enables detailed adjustments to be made, but it complicates more comprehensive state reforms that are agreed upon after elections. In the past, this necessitated various tricks to give legal form to political agreements.[20] In cases of both eternity clause and restrictive procedures, immediate transformative change can still take place by using an alternative track specifically for partial or total revisions. In Austria, for example, this track implies the need for a referendum.[21] So far, only Austria's accession to the EU (i.e., embedding the country into a new multi-tiered structure) was considered to be a fundamental revision of the constitution that required a referendum.[22] In the United States, it has been suggested that the technique of constitutional conventions could be employed specifically for fundamental revisions.[23] In the absence of an alternative track, another option is to adopt an entirely new constitution. This has the advantage of clarity, but it may also scare the public off;

5 In an unstable context, the power balance between opposing parties may be so fluid that joint decision-making processes are either unbalanced or end up in a deadlock. This has three consequences.

First, democratic legitimacy concerns gain more weight, especially if the new balance of forces has not yet settled. The public then acts as a safeguard against overly drastic changes.[24]

Second, to avoid the entrenchment of fundamental choices about sensitive issues and to bring the debate back to ordinary politics, delaying deconstitutionalization may be preferred.[25] An example is the Iraqi constitution, where the constitution left several issues unresolved. While the Iraqi constitution claims to have a federal structure, it only recognizes the Kurdistan Region and

20 See for instance the transitory provision that was added to the amendment procedure in Art. 195 to enable the sixth state reform in 2012–2013.
21 Art. 44(3) Austrian Constitution: optional in the case of a partial revision, obligatory in the case of a total revision.
22 Manfred Stelzer, 'Constitutional Change in Austria', in Contiades (n 5) 9.
23 John R. Vile, 'Constitutional Revision in the United States of America', in Contiades (n 5) 398.
24 Jenna Bednar, 'Constitutional Change in Federations: The Role of Complementary Institutions', in Benz and Broschek, (n 9) 279.
25 Hanna Lerner, 'Constitution-writing in deeply divided societies: the incrementalist approach', (2010) 16 *Nations and Nationalism* 68–88.

merely allows the hypothetical establishment of future regions.[26] Likewise, in 1970 the Belgian Constitution provided a basis for the establishment of Regions. It took a special majority law ten years later to bring the Regions alive and determine their status and competences.[27] However, there are some risks attached to this. For example, there might be a polarizing effect on other branches of government (parliaments and courts) that are left to decide contentious issues in the absence of any constitutional guidance.[28]

Third, exit options may provide a way out of a deadlock. One example is a secession clause, another is constitutional asymmetry. A different arrangement for one specific group can take many forms. One option has a basis in the constitution itself: the constitution provides asymmetrical arrangements for particular entities,[29] opt-in or opt-out clauses,[30] or allows for constitutional amendments that apply to one or more (but not all) SNEs.[31] Another option is 'displacement' through bilateral or multilateral agreements. Béland and Lecours illustrate the difference between the two types of agreement. They show how social security remained highly centralized in Belgium due to (amongst others) rigid procedures for change in the opposing Flemish and French-speaking parties. Meanwhile, in Canada, displacement took place through asymmetrical decentralization in order to accommodate Québec nationalism.[32] In the first case, asymmetry is supported by the different groups, in the latter case, it is the result of negotiations between the central government and one particular group. This is discussed further in the next section.

8.2 De-constitutionalization

De-constitutionalization means that important aspects of the organization of MTSs are delegated to instruments other than the constitution. In this case, there are no specific guarantees to entrench institutional arrangements. In some cases, de-constitutionalization gives the federal authorities a stronger grip and reduces the involvement of SNEs. Often, however, alternatives differ from the constitutional amendment process in two ways: they are more flexible, and they show concern for more tailored forms of subnational involvement. This can

26 See Bawar Bammarny, 'Federalism and Decentralisation in Iraq. A Country Study of Constitutional Asymmetry in Iraq', in Patricia Popelier and Maja Sahadžić (eds), *Constitutional Asymmetry in Multinational Federalism* (Palgrave MacMillan 2019) 256, 258–259.

27 Patricia Popelier and Koen Lemmens, *The Constitution of Belgium. A Contextual Analysis* (Hart 2015) 25.

28 Lerner (n 25) 84.

29 E.g., Part XXI Indian Constitution.

30 For an opt-in clause, see e.g., art. 137 Belgian Constitution.

31 E.g., art. 43 Canadian Constitution Act 1982.

32 Daniel Béland and André Lecours, 'Federalism, Nationalist Politics, and Social Policy: How Ideas and Institutions Interact to Produce or Prevent Change', in Benz and Broschek (n 9) 221–2224.

result in (potential or actual) constitutional asymmetry. If important aspects of the multi-tiered structure are delegated, these instruments obtain a quasi-constitutional status of their own. This is why Indexes 2.1 and 2.2 in Chapter 4 makes no *a priori* distinction between formal constitutions and quasi-constitutional acts.

Institutional arrangements can be deferred to ordinary laws, special majority laws, or to intergovernmental agreements. In asymmetric regimes, the same matter is sometimes delegated to different instruments at the same time, depending on the SNE. For example, in Italy, financial autonomy is regulated in more detail in national legislation for the ordinary regions and is regulated through bilateral agreements for the special regions.[33] In Belgium, the organization and powers of the GSC are detailed in an ordinary parliamentary act. By contrast, the same rules for other Communities and Regions are set out in special majority laws.

8.2.1 *Ordinary laws*

Ordinary laws are likely to buttress centralization, especially if there is a weak institutional link with SNEs in the upper house. In the absence of a written constitution, the United Kingdom is the most prominent example of an MTS organized by ordinary Acts of Parliament. There, ordinary laws have created three different models of devolution in varying degrees of subnational autonomy. These reflect the different historical tracks and national sentiments in Scotland, Wales, and Northern Ireland.[34] The central grip on the state structure is substantial, as the UK Parliament retains the power to legislate in devolved matters. The Acts themselves are subject to change by an Act of Parliament, with no institutional representation of the devolved entities required.[35] However, soft law mechanisms put this centralized control into perspective. According to the Sewel Convention, the UK Parliament will not legislate without the consent of the Scottish Parliament.[36]

In a MTS with a written constitution, parts of the structural organization can also be deferred to Acts of Parliament. In some systems, such as Canada's, the constitutional framework is dispersed over several written and unwritten sources.[37] In asymmetric MTSs, the delegation of control to ordinary laws most often concerns the organization and powers of second-order SNEs. For example, in

33 Francesco Palermo and Alice Valdesalici, 'Irreversibly Different. A Country Study of Constitutional Asymmetry in Italy', Popelier and Sahadžić (n 26) 300–301.
34 Stephen Tierney, 'Giving with one hand: Scottish devolution within a unitary state', (2007) 5 Int. J. Const. Law 741–742.
35 Even more, the adoption of the Scotland Act 1998 corrected the previous overrepresentation of the Scottish people, *ibid* 748.
36 Although Scottish practice has turned this into a mechanism with centralizing effects, see below.
37 Allan Hutchinson, 'Constitutional Change and Constitutional Amendment', in Contiades (n 5) 66; Tsvi Kahana, 'Canada', in Oliver and Fusaro (n 19) 9, 11.

Belgium, the institutions and powers of the GSC are regulated in an ordinary law that can be adopted by a simple majority in the House and the Senate. In those legislative bodies, this entity might be represented by only one senator. This illustrates the subordinate position of the GSC, which has no decisive voice in the regulation of its status and competences. This is in sharp contrast to the veto powers of the Flemish and French-speaking parts of Belgium. Formal involvement of SNEs is mostly limited, but informal mechanisms may in fact protect subnational autonomy. For instance in Spain, the financing of the (regular) autonomous communities is laid down in an Organic Law. Amending that law requires an overall majority of the members of Congress, where these communities are poorly represented.[38] Such amendments are in fact agreed upon by an intergovernmental body with ministers of the central state and the autonomous communities.[39] In some cases, the law makes the matter further subject to government rules, marginalizing the involvement of both the central Parliament and the SNEs. This is the case in Italy, where financial regulations regarding ordinary regions are mainly incorporated in executive decrees. Amending these decrees requires negotiations with the SNEs, but that does not secure effective participation.[40]

8.2.2 Special majority laws

Special majority laws offer a different combination of rigidity and subnational involvement. As mentioned in section 8.1., this makes it possible to concentrate on federalism safeguards that are focused on subnational involvement and cut all other impediments in the constitutional amendment procedure. Such instruments are, therefore, more protective of subnational autonomy claims than of central integrity concerns.

For example, in Belgium, the fact that most powers and institutional arrangements of the Communities and Regions are laid down in special majority laws (and ordinary laws for the GSC), enabled a fifth centrifugal state reform outside of the constitutional framework. The amendment procedure for these majority laws is more tailored to the specific needs of Belgian federalism. For example, there was no need for the combination of a detailed list and interim elections, which usually obstructs major state reforms to protect central integrity. Instead, a majority requirement in each language group of both Houses is added to the two-thirds majority requirement.[41] This incorporates veto powers for the two major groups around which Belgian federalism revolves.

38 Art. 81(2) Spanish Constitution.

39 Sara Parolari, 'From a Formal to a Substantial Approach: Sources of Law and Fiscal Federalism', in Valdesalici and Palermo (n 33) 29.

40 *Ibid* 33.

41 Art. 4 Belgian Constitution.

8.2.3 Intergovernmental agreements

In some cases, federalism measures are based on multilateral or bilateral negotiations. Such intergovernmental agreements may serve as an alternative to constitutional reform, which is why Poirier calls them 'para-constitutional engineering'.[42] For example, in Spain, the underrepresentation of the SNEs in constitutional reform at the central level is compensated for by their wide discretion to change their scope of autonomy through their Statutes of Autonomy. These are enacted in agreement with the central government.[43] By identifying specific matters in the Statutes of Autonomy, there is a delineation of central powers that are enumerated in the constitutions – e.g., by distinguishing 'protected nature reserves' from the central power for environmental policy.[44] This so-called 'dispositive principle' completes the block of constitutionality[45] and has brought flexibility in the system despite the extreme robustness of the central constitution.[46]

De-constitutionalization through intergovernmental agreement usually gives executives a more prominent role, to the detriment of Parliament. For example, in Canada and Australia, financial relations are mainly laid down in agreements, rather than legal provisions. This gives executives a dominant role in the organization of fiscal federalism.[47]

Multilateral agreements give all parties equal negotiation powers. This makes them an attractive instrument in a MTS based on equality of the central and SNEs. Belgium is such a system, where multilateral agreements are sometimes preferred over other instruments that are imposed by the Constitution. For example, the Belgian Constitution defers the rules for the conclusion of mixed treaties to a special majority law.[48] These rules are on matters that fall partly

42 Johanne Poirier, 'The Functions of Intergovernmental Agreements: Post-Devolution Concordats in a Comparative Perspective', (2001) *Public Law* 134–157.

43 Cesar Colino, 'Constitutional Change without Constitutional Reform: Spanish Federalism and the Revision of Catalonia's Statute of Autonomy', (2009) 39 *Publius; The Journal of Federalism* 263; Ascensión Elvira, 'Spain', in Oliver and Fusaro (n 19) 295–296; Carles Viver, 'Spain's Constitution and Statutes of Autonomy: Explaining the Evolution of Political Decentralization', in Michael Burgess and G. Alan Tarr (eds), *Constitutional Dynamics in Federal Systems: Sub-national Perspectives* (Montreal & Kingston, McGill-Queen's University Press 2012) 228.

44 Viver (n 43) 224–225.

45 Elisenda Casanas Adam, 'The Constitutional Court of Spain: From System Balancer to Polarizing Centralist', in Nick Aroney and John Kincaid (eds), *Courts in Federal Countries: Federalists or Regionalists?* (University of Toronto Press 2017) 372; Viver (n 43) 222–223. The latter author prefers the term 'propositional' over 'dispositional' principle, since they can propose, but not decide without the central authorities' consent, *ibid* at p. 227.

46 Colino (n 43) 263.

47 Parolari (n 39) 35.

48 Art. 167, § 4 Belgian Constitution.

under central powers and partly under subnational powers. In fact, these matters are regulated by an intergovernmental agreement.[49]

Negotiated bilateral statutes and agreements are typical for systems with constitutional asymmetry. In these cases, the position of the SNE depends upon its particular negotiating power. Negotiated agreements come in different forms. In some systems, such as Spain and Italy, the agreements are laid down in statutes approved by the central legislature. In Russia, agreements with the President were ultimately put under Parliamentary approval.[50] In still other systems, such as the United Kingdom, the agreements are not laid down in legal documents: they remain political instruments.

Even if the central government is the dominant actor, these agreements give SNEs some say in institutional developments. For example, in the United Kingdom, the ordinary acts on devolution are complemented by informal bilateral (and quadri) concordats. These manage cooperation and dispute resolution between the central and devolved levels of government, they secure the consultation of the devolved entities in EU affairs, and hold the Westminster Parliament back from legislating in devolved matters without the consent of the subnational Parliament.[51] While the latter convention secures subnational involvement, this has in Scotland resulted in the unexpected practice of authorizing 'Sewel resolutions'.[52] However, this is a deliberate practice of the Scottish Parliament, and therefore, does not affect its ability to control central interference.

In most cases, a system of bilateral negotiations tends to stimulate compartmentalization. SNEs negotiate in their own interest instead of building collective blocks,[53] and the central government is put in a position that allows it to make concessions to individual SNEs that it cannot afford to make at a wider level.[54] This benefits stronger SNEs and encourages them to take a more (sub)nationalist stance and push for more asymmetry. Where the central government loses control, federalism through bilateral negotiations may accelerate centrifugal dynamics.[55] For example, in Russia, there is the possibility to conclude agreements between the central and subnational authorities to give more detail to the

49 Intergovernmental Agreement of 8 March 1993.

50 Elena A. Kremyanskaya, 'Constitutional Asymmetry in Russia: Issues and Developments', in Popelier and Sahadžić (n 26) 408.

51 Andrew Scott, 'The Role of Concordats in the New Governance of Britain: Taking Subsidiarity Seriously', (2001) 21 *Edinburg L. Rev.* 24.

52 Tierney (n 34) 750; Barry Winetrobe, 'Counter-Devolution? The Sewel Convention on Devolved Legislation at West-minster', (2001) 6 *Scot. L. & Prac. Q.* 286.

53 Ramon Maiz, Francisco Caamaño and Miguel Azpitarte, 'The Hidden Counterpoint of Spanish Federalism: Recentralization and Resymmetrization in Spain (1978–2008)', (2010) 20 *Regional & Federal Studies* 77.

54 Colino (n 43) 263.

55 For Russia, see Kremyanskaya (n 50) 400. This concern was also voiced in the Spanish debate, see Colino (n 43) 265.

allocation of powers. In the 1990s this resulted in far-reaching asymmetry and sovereignty claims, which has been called the era of 'wild federalism'.[56]

However, the central authorities, as the central actors in all negotiations, have the keys to control the level of asymmetry. As a result, negotiated arrangements can instigate a-symmetrization as well as symmetrization processes.[57] In the end, asymmetrical arrangements will only last for as long as the under-privileged entities accept them.[58]

8.3 Allocation techniques

In Chapter 5, the (de)centralizing and (dis)integrationist effects of power allocation techniques were discussed. This means that the allocation technique is another way of creating a hub for changes in the relationship between central and subnational authorities. The preponderance of exclusive or shared powers gives a mandate for central authorities to intervene in subnational policy spheres. Interpretative tools impact the flexibility of the system.

As mentioned in Chapter 5, exclusive powers are a device typical to dual federalism. They simultaneously create a static system, inviting other mechanisms such as judicial interpretation to enable adjustments. For instance, when exclusivity leads to a fragmentation of powers that then hinders coherent policy-making to address societal problems. For example, in Canada, the Supreme Court has adopted the so-called 'double-aspect' doctrine. This allows both levels to legislate on the same subject matter, each from their own angle.[59] This way, the Court has moved away from an essentially dualist approach to cooperative federalism, leading to more overlaps. In the case of inconsistency, these overlaps are adjudicated in favor of federal paramountcy.[60] This doctrine, which gives legislative space to both levels, has also been recognized in Belgian Constitutional Court case law.[61] Other techniques used by the Belgian Court to allow for coherent policy-making are implied powers and the loyalty principle. The latter principle promotes intergovernmental coordination and cooperation.

As Steytler observed, shared powers have the advantage of giving the power allocation system some degree of flexibility. This enables the central government "to postpone the exercise of potential authority in a particular field until the

56 Kremyanskaya (n 50) 400, 403–405.

57 Colino (n 43) 264. For Italy, see Palermo and Valdesalici, (n 33) 288–289.

58 Augustias Hombrado, 'Learning to Catch the Wave? Regional Demands for Constitutional Change in Contexts of Asymmetrical Arrangements', (2011) 21 *Regional & Federal Studies*, 496.

59 Eugénie Brouillet, 'The Supreme Court of Canada: The Concept of Cooperative Federalism and its Effect on the Balance of Power', in Aroney and Kincaid (n 45) 142; Hutchinson (n 37) 62.

60 Brouillet (n 59) 141–142.

61 Jürgen Vanpraet, *De Latente tSaatshervorming* (Bruges, die Keure 2011).

latter becomes a matter of federal importance".[62] In the case of framework powers, much depends upon what can be considered a 'general framework', mostly articulated in terms of 'basic norms'. The more broadly this is used and interpreted by the central authorities – and confirmed by courts – the more power relations are shifted toward centralization. In the case of concurrent powers, subnational autonomy is inversely proportional to the extent to which central authorities use their powers.

Chapter 5 already mentioned how counterbalances can be built into the system to protect subnational autonomy. One technique is the involvement of SNEs. Another consists of qualifications to the priority rule, for example, by giving SNEs the right to deviate.[63] Other techniques, which are more reliant upon judicial enforcement, are a well-defined subsidiarity or necessity clause and a mutual loyalty principle.

Very few constitutions explicitly articulate a subsidiarity principle for domestic intergovernmental relations.[64] In Italy, the Constitution links this with administrative competences, but the Constitutional Court has extended this to legislative powers.[65] However, judicial safeguards for subsidiarity have so far proved ineffective. Often, this is perceived to be a consequence of the political nature of the subsidiarity principle.[66] In reality, judicial enforcement can be made effective under two conditions: a more detailed definition of the subsidiarity principle with concrete criteria, and the production of impact assessments or other evidence to explain the reasons for interference.[67]

The loyalty principle, also discussed in Chapter 5, is mostly known as a principle for ensuring the integrity of the system. This is achieved by imposing a duty upon SNEs to act in consideration of the central state's interests, but with a reciprocal duty placed on central authorities (acting within their sphere of competences) to take into account subnational interests.[68] In concrete cases, this may be translated into a duty to involve SNEs in the lawmaking procedure, even

62 Nico Steytler, 'The Currency of Concurrent Powers in Federal Systems', in Nico Steytler (ed), *Concurrent Powers in Federal Systems. Meaning, Making, Managing* (Brill Nijhoff 2017) 3.

63 For example in Germany, in a limited range of six policy domains: Art. 72(3) German Constitution.

64 Art. 270 Bolivian Constitution; Art. 288 and 356 Colombian Constitution; Art. 238 Constitution of the Dominican Republic; Art. 238, 269, and 270 Constitution of Ecuador; Art. 118 and 120 Italian Constitution; Art. 169 Constitution of South Sudan; Schedule F to the Constitution of Sudan; Art. 5A Swiss Constitution; Art. 134 Tunisian Constitution.

65 Carlo Fusaro, 'Italy', in Oliver and Fusaro (n 19) 224–225.

66 For a discussion of the objections against judicial review of the subsidiarity review: Werner Vandenbruwaene, 'Multi-Tiered Political Questions: The ECJ's Mandate in Enforcing Subsidiarity', (2012) 6 *Legisprudence* 321–346.

67 *Ibid* 65–68.

68 Lidija R. Basta Fleiner and Jean-François Gaudreault-DesBiens, 'Federalism and autonomy', in Mark Tushnet, Thomas Fleiner and Cheryl Saunders (eds), *Routledge Handbook of Constitutional Law* (Routledge 2015)151; Anna Gamper, 'On Loyalty and the (Federal) Constitution', (2010) 4 *Vienna Online J. on Int'l Const. L.* 160–161.

where the constitution or (organic) legislation does not prescribe this. This is not only a way to curb misuse of shared powers, but also controls the use of exclusive powers. For example, even before the Belgian Constitutional Court was given the power to review acts against the loyalty principle laid down in the Constitution, it developed a theory of proportionality as part of the system of allocation of powers. This places a mutual loyalty principle upon all levels of government. As a result, if the federal legislator is about to pass legislation that cuts across subnational policies, the SNEs must be involved, and vice versa. In some cases, the Court even requires the conclusion of an intergovernmental cooperation agreement.[69]

All this shows that the effect of allocation techniques as hubs for change depends on both political practice and the courts. Courts use interpretative tools to make the power allocation system more flexible. They construct principles such as the principle of subsidiarity, loyalty, and proportionality. And they develop doctrines that reinforce or moderate the (de-)centralist effects of the constitutional allocation of powers. One example is the 'double-aspect doctrine', which has already been discussed. Another is the implied powers doctrine that enables authorities to regulate a matter that strictly speaking falls beyond their sphere of competences, but must necessarily be dealt with in order to regulate a matter within their powers. In the United States, the term 'capable federalism' is used to describe the doctrine that considers "that the federal government is fully empowered to address all national problems, in particular those that cannot be adequately addressed at the state or local level".[70] Courts also choose a narrow or broad interpretation of assigned powers. Such tools may be used in favor of SNEs, or in favor of both SNEs and the central authority. In practice, however, they often produce a centralizing effect.[71] This brings us to the issue discussed in the next section: the variables that push courts toward a centralist or non-centralist stance.

8.4 Adjudicating federalism conflicts

Constitutional interpretation allows authorities to continuously define and redefine vertical power relations.[72] As interpreters of the constitution, judicial and nonjudicial authorities that adjudicate federalism conflicts are simultaneously the safeguards of power relations and hubs for change.

69 E.g., Const. Court Nos 132/2004, 14 July 2004 and 128/2005, 13 July 2005.

70 David S. Schwartz, 'A Question Perpetually Arising: Implied Powers, Capable Federalism, and the Limits of Enumerationism', (2017) 59 *Arizona L. Rev.* 576.

71 Francesco Palermo and Karl Kössler, *Comparative federalism: Constitutional Arrangements and Case Law* (Hart 2017) 156.

72 Francesco Palermo, 'Italy: A Federal Country without Federalism?', in Burgess and Tarr (n 43) 248 notes that 'constitutional adjudication has shaped the contours of Italian regionalism much more than constitutional amendments have'.

8.4.1 Judicial adjudicators

It is widely considered that courts in federal systems have a centralizing effect because they shift powers to the benefit of the central level. Some scholars regard this as an empirical truism,[73] while others upgrade it to a normative device.[74]

In reality, not all courts have a centralizing impact, and not all courts with a centralizing impact have this effect in any given period.[75] For example, Aroney distinguishes three phases in the jurisprudence of the Australian High Court. In the first phase an approach was taken that was protective of the SNEs, followed by a highly centralist position, and, gradually, some qualifications in support of subnational autonomy.[76] In Canada, the Judicial Committee of the Privy Council revealed a more dualist and decentralist approach compared to the more balanced and cooperative approach adopted by the Supreme Court, which tends to favor the federal government.[77] In the United States of America as well, several periods have been identified in which the Supreme Court took varying positions on the scope of Congressional powers. Overall a centralist trend is clearly visible, particularly because the Court has been almost invariably restrictive as to State powers.[78]

Courts in centrifugal multinational systems tend to take a more balanced position.[79] In Belgium, an examination of all judgments on federalism disputes of the Belgian Constitutional Court shows that almost half of the judgments are decided in favor of the federal authorities, and half are decided in favor of the subnational Communities and Regions.[80] By contrast, the Spanish Constitutional have ruled mostly in favor of the central government or in favor of both parties, while fewer rulings have been made in favor of the Autonomous Communities alone.[81] This points to a more centralist approach.

73 Martin Shapiro, *Courts: A Comparative And Political Analysis* (Chicago, University of Chicago Press 1981) 55.

74 André Bzdera, 'Comparative Analysis of Federal High Courts: A Political Theory of Judicial Review', (1993) 26 *Canadian J. of Pol. Sc.* 19.

75 For an overview of courts worldwide, see Aroney and Kincaid (n 45) 10.

76 Nick Aroney, 'The High Court of Australia: Textual Unitarism vs Structural Federalism', in Aroney and Kincaid (n 45) 52–65.

77 Brouillet (n 59) 135, 152–159.

78 Ilya Somin, 'The Supreme Court of the United States: Promoting Centralization More than State Autonomy', in Aroney and Kincaid (n 45) 448–477.

79 Patricia Popelier, 'Federalism Disputes and the Behavior of Courts: Explaining Variation in Federal Courts' Support for Centralization', (2016) 47 *Publius: The Journal of Federalism* 41–44.

80 Patricia Popelier and Samantha Bielen, 'How Courts Decide Federalism Disputes: Legal Merit, Attitudinal Effects, and Strategic Considerations in the Jurisprudence of the Belgian Constitutional Court', (2018) *Publius: The Journal of Federalism* 595–596.

81 Julio López-Laborda, Fernando Rodrigo and Eduardo Sanz-Arcega, 'Is the Spanish Constitutional Court an instrument of the central government against the Autonomous Communities?', (2018) 29 *Constitutional Political Economy* 321–322.

Most studies that examine the factors which explain the position of courts in federalism studies concentrate on one specific court. In most cases, this is the US Supreme Court,[82] more rarely apex courts in European or Latin-American jurisdictions.[83] Most often, this research is performed by political or economic scientists with a specific interest in the impact of judges' political preferences. Legal factors are more difficult to measure and have, therefore, been widely ignored. However, a more comprehensive approach is needed to establish how constitutional engineering may impact upon the position courts take.

In this section, three sets of factors are discussed: legal-structural factors; ideology or attitudinal preferences; and strategic considerations. To legal scholars, it may seem a banal fact that court outcomes are based on legal analysis. However, judicial interpretation may lead to different outcomes, and political, strategic, or structural considerations may guide the choice for one interpretation over the other. A political take links the outcome with the judges' preferences for a centralist or a decentralist state. According to a strategic perspective, the court will choose the interpretation that leads to the most preferred outcome by the parties in power – in particular, those that control the Court's powers, organization, and financial means[84] – or the public at large. Structural considerations take into account the basic structure of the system, which links up with the constitutional self-definition discussed in Chapter 4. However, it may also refer to power-sharing arrangements in multinational systems. At the same time, it would be an overstatement to claim that courts use legal analysis merely to cover up political decision-making.[85] The court is still bound by legal constraints, and

82 See, amongst many others, Brady Baybeck and William Lowry, 'Federalism Outcomes and Ideological Preferences: The U.S. Supreme Court and Preemption Cases', (2000) 30 *Publius: The Journal of Federalism* 73–97; Paul M. Collins Jr., 'Towards an Integrated Model of the U.S. Supreme Court's Federalism Decision Making', (2007) 37 *Publius: The Journal of Federalism* 505–531; Frank B. Cross and Emerson H. Tiller, 'The three faces of federalism: An empirical assessment of Supreme Court federalism jurisprudence' (2000) 73 *Southern California Law Review* 741–771; John Dinan, 'The Rehnquist Court's Federalism Decisions in Perspective', (1999) 15 *Journal of Law and Politics* 127–194; Kevin Scott, 'Judicial Behavior and the Rehnquist Court's Federalism Revolution', (2008) 36 *American Politics Research* 85–107.

83 E.g., Carolina Arlota and Nuno Garoupa, 'Addressing Federal Conflicts: An Empirical Analysis of the Brazilian Supreme Court, 1988–2010', (2014) 10 *Review of Law and Economics* 137–168; López-Laborda, Rodrigo and Sanz-Arcega (n 81) 317–337; Popelier and Bielen (n 80) 587–616.

84 This is the dependency-hypothesis: Roland Vaubel, 'Constitutional courts as promoters of political centralization: lessons for the Court of Justice', (2009) 28 *Eu. J. of Law and Economics* 205.

85 As was held by Jeffrey A. Segal and Harold J. Spaeth, *The Supreme Court and the Attitudinal Model Revisited* (Cambridge University Press 2002), 53.

some consistency in the choice of interpretation techniques is essential for the legitimacy of the court.[86]

Hence, while empirical scholars tend to rule out legal factors when variation can be explained by political or strategical variables,[87] in practice it is difficult to disentangle the different factors. For example, if courts respond to decentralist reforms in the constitution, they may at the same time strategically try to please the ruling parties that have agreed upon decentralization. Constitutional narratives developed by constitutional courts are based upon legal texts which embody political agreements, and for this reason, they disclose an inextricable mixture of law and politics. For example, in India, the Supreme Court initially showed restraint in disputes about the use and misuse of the emergency clause by the central government. However, this evolved after an important change in the political party landscape, which also resulted in a more restrictive phrasing of the emergency clause.[88] Here, politics may determine the room for judicial review, but this was shaped in a legal amendment that gave the Court an opportunity to adjust its case law. The triple classification, therefore, aims to give structure. This does not detract from the observation that these factors blend, in practice. This chapter concentrates on those elements that can be constrained by the constitutional framework and subjected to constitutional engineering.

Also, some courts are considered to play a more active role than others. The question of how this relates to the constitutional amendment procedure remains unresolved at present.

Some argue that a rigid amendment system invites courts to play a more active role if this is needed to release tension or to adjust the constitutional framework to political developments.[89] For example, it has been noted that in Canada 'the enormous difficulty of amending the Constitution has made constitutional jurisprudence the preferred way to modify the regime'.[90] In Spain as well, broad constitutional interpretation has been found to sometimes compensate for a political reluctance to start constitutional amendment procedures.[91]

However, this reasoning can be turned around. This is based on what Kumm calls 'vicarious representativeness', referring to the extent to which judicial

86 See also Dieter Grimm, 'What Exactly is Political about Constitutional Adjudication?', in Christine Landfried (ed), *Judicial Power. How Constitutional Courts Affect Political Transformations* (Cambridge University Press 2019) 314.

87 Nuno Garoupa, Fernando Gomez-Pomar and Veronica Grembi. 'Judging under Political Pressure: An Empirical Analysis of Constitutional Review Voting in the Spanish Constitutional Court' (2011) 29 *Journal of Law, Economics and Organization* 513–534.

88 Rekha Saxena and Mahendra P. Singh, 'The role of the federal judiciary in union-state relations in India', in Jan Erk and Wilfried Swenden (eds), *New Directions in Federalism Studies* (Routledge 2010) 54.

89 See below for country-specific examples.

90 Brouillet (n 59) 150. See in this sense also Kahana (n 37) 39.

91 Ferreres Comella (n 7) 58. Likewise: Abraham Barrero Ortega and Irene Sobrino Guijarro, 'Constitutional Change in Spain', in Contiades (n 5) 300; Elvira (n 43) 284.

decisions are endorsed by the legislature.[92] A court may be more inclined to give new meaning to constitutional provisions if it knows that its interpretation can be easily corrected through constitutional amendment. Due to the rigid amendment procedure, it may feel less authorized to do so if correction is left to judicial action only.[93] In Germany, Benz has pointed out how the Constitutional Court tends to follow prevailing discussions in the public sphere, and how the constitutional court and politics mutually influence each other.[94] He concludes that 'constitutional law and politics are closely coupled in Germany', with a Constitutional Court involved in intergovernmental politics and constitutional amendments in response. He claims this leads to 'a rather dense system of rules'.[95]

To resolve the question, we need a clear and workable definition of what activism means.[96] Commentators are easily tempted to label their court as activist. However, what we perceive as activist may simply be strategic behavior by a court that follows the lead of governing political actors. For example, the US Supreme Court has been identified as an activist court against the background of a very rigid constitutional amendment system. Yet, when the Court adapts the constitution to changing circumstances, "it does so only with the permission or acceptance of the political branches".[97] Such docility may, in turn, be questionable if it permits governing majorities that are unable to effect constitutional change by securing the intergovernmental agreement that is necessary for constitutional amendments. For example, in Australia, a centralist shift in power relations has taken place due to the High Court's tendency to affirm the federal government's attempts "to press the scope of their powers up to (and arguably beyond) their constitutional limits".[98] This is in contrast to the failure of several centralist proposals for constitutional amendments in the absence of bipartisan political support. By contrast in India, there has been a more diverse political

92 Mattias Kumm, 'On the Representativeness of Constitutional Courts', in Landfried (n 86) 290.

93 William E. Forbath, 'The Politics of Constitutional Amendment: Obduracy and Amendability – A Comment on Ferejohn and Sager', (2003) 81 *Texas Law Review* 1980–1981. For a similar argument, referring to the possibility of responding to 'error costs' of 'parallel constitutional rules': Rosalind Dixon, 'Updating Constitutional Rules', (2009) *Supreme Court Rev.* 341–342. Ferreres Comella (n 7) 59 also acknowledges that the improbability of overriding the Court through constitutional amendment, brings the Spanish Constitutional Court in a delicate position.

94 Arthur Benz, 'The Federal Constitutional Court of Germany: Guardian of Unitarism and Federalism', in Aroney and Kincaid (n 45) 215, 220, 221.

95 *Ibid* 219.

96 Seventeen parameters are provided by Margit Cohn and Mordechai Kremnitzer, 'Judicial Activism: A Multidimensional Model', (2005) 18 *Can. J. L. & Juris* 333, 336, but they are difficult to operationalize, especially in comparative research. On the problem to measure activism, see Nuno Garoupa, 'Comparing Judicial Activism – Can We Say that the US Supreme Court is more Activist than the German Constitutional Court?' (2016) 72 *Revista Portuguesa de Filosofia* 1089–1106.

97 Stephen M. Griffin, 'Constitutional Theory Transformed', (1999) 108 *Yale L. J.* 2138.

98 Aroney (n 76) 33.

specter resulting from the transformation of a one-party dominant system into a multi-party system. This gave the judiciary room for more activist judicial review to curb the power of the executive and parliament. A side effect is the commandeering of Indian federalism by centralist dynamics.[99]

More empirical analysis is required to identify activist courts. Until then, the most plausible hypothesis is that courts are more activist in less rigid systems. The reason for this is that a comparative study showed that systems with judicial review have a higher constitutional amendment rate.[100]

In some jurisdictions, courts have the power to scrutinize draft legislation. In Belgium, it is standard procedure for the Council of State to give a nonbinding opinion on the legality of draft statutes and regulations initiated by the central or subnational government. Elsewhere, authorities may request that the Court assesses whether a draft falls within the ambit of the other entity's competences.[101] In the next section, there is a focus on judicial adjudication of federalism disputes *ex post*. The conclusions can also be applied to *ex ante* scrutiny. Where *ex ante* and *ex post* scrutiny is handled by different courts, a judicial dialogue between both courts may influence the course of the case law.

In the next section, there is a focus on the role of courts in delineating the powers of national and regional authorities. So far, less attention has been paid to the courts' position on intergovernmental conflicts between central (national and/or regional) and local authorities. It is, therefore, unclear whether courts that take a centralist stance in national-regional relations are equally centralist when it comes to national/regional-local relations. For example, in South Africa, the Constitutional Court is considered to be protective of both provincial and local autonomy.[102] This kind of convergence does not necessarily exist in other systems.

8.4.1.1 Legal-structural factors

CONSTITUTIONALLY CONSISTENT INTERPRETATION

Legal merit plays a role when courts consistently choose a particular interpretation method out of a set of available methods. One generally accepted method is consistent interpretation. Faced with the counter-majoritarian difficulty, courts prefer to apply Acts of Parliament rather than criticize them. Courts will therefore uphold the Act if it is possible to interpret it in conformity with the Constitution. This should not be confused with a purely strategic approach, in an effort to please the governing coalition. First, two governments may oppose

99 Saxena and Singh (n 88) 51.
100 Ginsburg and Melton (n 3) 711.
101 For an overview, see Palermo and Kössler (n 71) 261–263.
102 Comp. Victoria Bronstein, 'The Courts and the Provinces in South Africa', in Fessha and Kössler (eds), *Federalism and the Courts in Africa* (Routledge 2020) 98 and Oliver Fuo, 'The Courts and Local Governments in South Africa', in *ibid*, 104, 121.

one another in federalism disputes. Second, constitution-consistent interpretation does not necessarily lead to the government's preferred outcome. This is because the Court may shift the Act's meaning from what the legislature originally intended.[103]

A striking example of courts' preferences for consistent interpretation can be found in the case law of the Spanish Constitutional Court, where it partially upheld the Catalan Declaration of sovereignty. The Constitutional Court held that 'the right to decide' proclaimed in this Declaration can be read in conformity with the constitutional framework. In other words, it can be read as a political program, under the condition of constitutional amendment. However, it was clear that the Declaration's proclaimers had no intention to remain within the limits of the Spanish Constitution. Ferreras Comella qualified this as "a heroic effort at preserving the existing constitutional order, in spite of the political crisis that the Catalan developments have caused".[104] In South Africa, the Constitution seems to impose consistent interpretation. This is particularly the case in federalism disputes, where courts must issue interpretations that result in a finding of no conflict between national and provincial legislation, in preference to any alternative interpretation that results in a conflict.[105]

If this legal method is prevalent, a false impression about the court's stance in federalism disputes may result. Where predominantly federal acts are challenged, the court will mostly uphold them, and thus decide in favor of central authorities. This paints a false picture of a centralist court. In the reverse situation, where predominantly subnational acts are challenged, an impression of a decentralist court emerges.

These impressions are a significant factor that explains the Belgian Constitutional Court's stance in federalism disputes.[106] If the same observation can be made for other courts,[107] this would mean that we might expect a decentralist tendency in systems where only subnational Acts of Parliament can be challenged before the court, to the exclusion of federal Acts of Parliament. Examples of this would include Switzerland and the United Kingdom. However, systems that prohibit judicial review of central statutes clearly distinguish between central and subnational Acts. This applies a sheen of inviolability and sovereignty to central acts only. This might curb a court's inclination to uphold a challenged subnational Act. Empirical research is required to find out which

103 Victor Ferreras Comella, 'The Consequences of Centralizing Constitutional Review in a Constitutional Court: Some Thoughts on Judicial Activism', (2003–2004) 82 *Texas L. Rev.* 1725.

104 Victor Ferreras Comella, 'The Spanish Constitutional Court Confronts Catalonia's "Right to Decide" (Comment on the Judgment 42/2014)', (2014) 10 *Eu. Const. L. Rev.* 585.

105 Art. 150 South African Constitution.

106 Popelier and Bielen (n 80) 607–608.

107 This, however, seems not to be the case in Spain: López-Laborda, Rodrigo and Sanz-Arcega (n 81) 330.

mechanism normally prevails. Meanwhile, the fact that SNEs (unlike the central government) have no legal means for redress in the case of unconstitutional intrusion into their autonomy, was found to harm the court's image as a neutral and unbiased arbitrator of federalism disputes in Switzerland.[108]

Either way, consistent interpretation is not the only explanatory factor. Other factors, such as strategic considerations, also play a role.

BASIC STRUCTURE

The system's basic structure may turn out to be a relevant driver that explains the court's position. Structuralists hold that it is ultimately social structure that explains the long-term patterns of federalism case law. Hence, it has been claimed that the US Supreme Court's centralist position mirrors the preexisting American *demos*.[109] Again, it is difficult to disentangle the impact of social structure, political discourse, and the constitutional system, as these factors are all closely interwoven. As a judicial body, however, the court must find some angles in the constitution for legal interpretation and challenge.

The court may refer to explicit structure clauses, possibly in combination with doctrinal theories. This allows the development of constitutional narratives that push its decision toward a more centralist or decentralist interpretation. A comparative analysis points to the combination of a multinational and centrifugal system as a variable that makes a balanced position more probable unless the country is under threat of violence and secessionism.[110]

An empirical analysis of the Belgian Constitutional Court's case law in federalism disputes confirms this. Belgium is a centrifugal, multinational system with a Constitutional Court that takes a balanced position in federalism disputes. With every state reform that has pushed the system toward more decentralization, the Court has taken a less centralist stance.[111] In Germany, the Constitutional Court is said to be respectful of the basic structure of federalism, because it has developed a theory of unitary federalism. This theory has enabled an integrated welfare state that is constrained by a vertical division of powers on the basis of partnership.[112] In German case law, the court safeguards the position of the Länder in the upper house rather than the autonomy of the

108 Eva Maria Belser, 'Concurrent Powers as Doors to Legislative Innovation, Conditional Powers as Gates to the Blind Alley: Some Swiss Illustrations', in Steytler (n 62) 51.

109 Jan Erk, 'Still in Search of the Federal Spirit: The US Supreme Court and Federalism', in Alain-G. Gagnon, Soeren Keil and Sean Mueller (eds), *Understanding Federalism and Federation* (Routledge 2015) 94–99.

110 Popelier (n 79) 41–43.

111 Popelier and Bielen (n 80) 605–607. This was only the case in disputes with political conflicts, involving two opposing governments. It did not occur in the absence of political conflict, when third parties challenged the act before the Constitutional Court. This points to a strategic position rather than legal merit. However, as mentioned above, law and politics are interwoven in this case.

112 Benz (n 94) 209–210.

Länder *per se*. This upholds the idea of cooperative federalism, which has pervaded the constitutional practice since the 1960s, but was challenged by SNEs after reunification[113].

By contrast, if the constitution's basic structure points more toward a centralist form, courts will be more inclined to take a centralist position. For example, the Spanish structure clause, with its emphasis on unity, was referred to by the Spanish Constitutional Court to illustrate characteristics of the Spanish 'composite' state.[114] In South Africa, the Constitutional Court explicitly referred to the constitutional self-definition of the country as 'one sovereign, democratic state' in order to support 'cooperative government' with a unitary emphasis.[115] This may also explain the Italian Constitutional Court's tendency to introduce mechanisms to protect national unity in the relationship between the central and subnational authorities.[116]

Aside from this, courts may also react to structural components of the political system in which they operate. For example, courts may take into account the position of SNEs in central decision-making. According to the theory of political safeguards that was developed in the United States to curb judicial limitation of federal government power, courts should take a more deferential stance toward federal acts as opposed to subnational acts. This is because institutional and political safeguards, involving SNEs in central decision-making, already protect SNEs against federal authorities overstepping their powers.[117] This might explain the centralist stance of courts in systems with strong political safeguards, either through the participation of SNEs in the upper house[118] or through political parties.[119] An example of the latter is when subnational (branches of) parties are structurally linked with and influence centrally-organized parties.[120] In contrast, comparative analysis suggests that courts are inclined to compensate for the weak representation of SNEs in the upper house by taking a less centralist stance. However, the political party system seems even more influential in the

113 Benz (n 94) 211–213.

114 Casanas Adam (n 45) 389–390.

115 Const. Court, 6 September 1996, re Certification of the Constitution of the Republic of South Africa 1996, 1996 (10) BCLR 1253 (CC) para 287–290. See Nico Steytler, 'The Constitutional Court of South Africa: Reinforcing an Hourglass System of Multi-Level Government', in Aroney and Kincaid (n 45) 349.

116 For this tendency: Tania Groppi, 'Constitutional Revision in Italy', in Contiades (n 5) 219.

117 Jesse H. Choper, 'The Scope of National Power Vis-à-vis the States: The Dispensability of Judicial Review', (1977) 86 *Yale L. Rev.* 1552–1621; Larry D. Kramer, 'Putting the Politics Back Into The Political Safeguards of Federalism', (2000) *Col. L. Rev.* 215–293; Herbert Welscher, 'The Political Safeguards of Federalism', (1954) 54 *Columbia L. Rev* 543–560.

118 See Welchser (n 117) 546–548

119 Kramer (n 117) 278–279, 284.

120 Lori Thorlakson, 'Patterns of Party Integration, Influence and Autonomy in Seven Federations', (2009) 15 *Party Politics* 160.

opposite direction: courts seem more likely to take a non-centralist stance if the political party system ensures the protection of subnational interests by the central governing parties.[121]

8.4.1.2 Attitudinal preferences

While vast amounts of literature have pointed to the undeniable role of a judge's political preferences in case outcomes, the actual impact varies. In the United States, political preferences seem to have an important impact on the Supreme Court's position, whereas in constitutional courts the impact of this variable, while still significant, is more moderate.[122] This may be due to the fact that attitudinal effects are harder to identify in systems that do not reveal the voting position of the individual judges. Either way, institutional design does seem to matter: where the court is balanced, and populated by judges that have different (assumed) policy preferences, attitudinal effects cancel each other out. This, of course, is more difficult to achieve in majority two-party systems. Arguably, in those systems, political parity in the bench would be more likely to reduce attitudinal effects.

Unlike in the United States, few studies have measured the impact of judges' political preferences on the European courts' (de)centralist stance in federalism disputes.[123] In Belgium, the Constitutional Court is composed of twelve judges, based on language parity. Two presidents chair the Court, with annually alternating roles as the sitting chair that has a decisive say in the case of a split vote. Judges are theoretically appointed, alternately, by a two-thirds majority in the House or the Senate. However, they are in fact selected by political parties according to a proportional system. Empirical study shows that the linguistic role and political preferences of the president and reporters do not seem to impact upon the court's centralist stance, but the majority on the bench does. For example, a predominantly Christian-democratic bench leads to more centralist outcomes,

121 Popelier (n 79) 36 and 38.

122 See the empirical studies on the effects of judicial preferences on case outcomes in European Constitutional Courts: Lucia Dalla Pellegrina and Nuno Garoupa, 'Choosing between the government and the regions: An empirical analysis of the Italian constitutional court decisions', (2013) 52 *European Journal of Political Research* 558–580; Lucia Dalla Pellegrina, Jef De Mot, Michael Faure and Nuno Garoupa, (2016) 13 'Litigating Federalism: An Empirical Analysis of Decisions of the Belgian Constitutional Court', *European Constitutional Law Rev* 305–346; Garoupa, Gomez-Pomar and Grembi (n 87) 513–534; Pedro C. Magalhães, *The limits of judicialization: legislative politics and constitutional review in the Iberian Democracies* (Colombus, Ohio State University, Ph.D. thesis, 2003) 271–320.

123 Even if the study is limited to judgments on federalism disputes, this does not mean that the court's centralist stance is examined. For example, in Dalla Pellegrina, De Mot, Faure and Garoupa (n 122) only federalism disputes were examined, but the authors were interested in attitudinal effects on the case outcome, irrespective of what this meant in terms of centralism or decentralism.

whereas a predominantly socialist bench results in more decentralist outcomes. As the bench make-up varies in each case, these influences balance each other out in the long run.[124]

Institutional design may also matter with regard to the judge selection process. In federalism disputes, we might expect that judges that are selected by parties with a centralist program will prefer centralist outcomes, whereas judges that are selected by parties with a decentralist program, share a preference for decentralist outcomes. Comparative analysis suggests that a low representation of SNEs in the selection of judges or the composition of courts may indeed further a more centralist stance, even though there is no conclusive evidence for this hypothesis.[125]

For example, in Italy, where the regions are not involved in the selection of judges of the Constitutional Court nor reflected in its composition, the centralizing effects of the Constitutional Court's case law have been noted.[126] In the United States, the President's dominant role in selecting federal judges makes it difficult for federal courts to play an active role in reviewing and invalidating federal legislation.[127] This, however, implies congruence between the President in power and the political preferences of the court bench majority. In Brazil, empirical research has indicated that there is indeed some alignment between Presidential appointment and judicial behavior in federalism disputes, although the effect is not as strong as expected.[128]

This means that subnational involvement in the selection of judges becomes an important stimulus for a non-centralist stance. The strongest subnational involvement in the selection of judges of the Constitutional Court can be found in Bosnia and Herzegovina. There, most judges are elected by the legislative assemblies of the two SNEs: four by the Federation of Bosnia and Herzegovina, and two by the Republic of Srpska. The only exceptions are the three judges elected by the President of the European Court of Human Rights after consultation with the B&H Presidency. In practice, this leads to the representation of the main ethnic groups (Bosniaks, Croats, and Serbs).[129] The Constitutional Court is nevertheless sometimes quite centralist, but this does not refute the hypothesis that subnational involvement moderates a court's centralist position. This is because in the Bosnian case, the general political disposition of Bosniaks is more centralizing, and because three additional international judges are appointed by the President of the European Court of Human Rights, which prefers a more integrationist stance.[130]

124 Popelier and Bielen (n 80) 609, 612.
125 Popelier (n 79) 40.
126 Palermo and Valdesalici (n 33) 298–299.
127 Somin (n 78) 478.
128 Arlota and Garoupa (n 83) 158
129 See Maja Sahadžić, 'Mild Asymmetry and Ethnoterritorial Overlap In Charge of the Consequences of Multinationalism', in Popelier and Sahadžić (n 26) 64–65.
130 Dawn Walsh, 'Constitutional courts as arbiters of post-conflict territorial self-government: Bosnia and Macedonia', (2019) 29 *Regional & Federal Studies* 81.

An alternative is a representation requirement: judges that represent SNEs with specific features can be expected to have more affinity with that SNE's interests. Even in systems where SNEs have no say in the selection procedure, informal mechanisms may impose some representation of SNEs or subnational groups.[131] In Belgium, political parties have a prominent role in the selection of the judges of the Constitutional Court. As political parties in Belgium are region-based, this implies strong subnational involvement. Moreover, the language groups that are central to the Belgian dyadic federation are actually represented in the court. This is because the court is composed on the basis of language parity. This correlates with a balanced position in federalism disputes. In Germany, half of the judges are elected by a two-thirds majority in the Bundestag and half by the same majority in the Bundesrat. This is found not to impact on the judges' performance, but the result nevertheless is a balanced position in federalism disputes[132].

Even if this effect cannot be generalized in the absence of precise data, we can expect that involvement of SNEs in the selection of judges or subnational representation in the composition of the court generates trust and helps the court to find popular support for its judgments. For example, in Nigeria, the fact that the Supreme Court is professionally recruited but regionally inclusive "has significantly insulated the institution from debilitating sectional bias, fragmentation, or conflict".[133] The opposite is also true: if SNEs are not involved in the selection of judges, this may create distrust about to the Court's impartialness. For example, in the United Kingdom, concerns have been voiced in Scottish circles about the representativeness of the Supreme Court and its centralizing effects.[134] Meanwhile, in Spain, the Organic Act 6/2007 reorganized the selection procedure for the Constitutional Court. This new law required the upper house to elect four judges from amongst the candidates proposed by the Autonomous Community parliaments, with the purpose of creating 'autonomous awareness' within the Court.[135] However, the candidates still need to secure support from a three-fifths majority in the Senate.[136] In reality, party interest takes the upper hand and judges are viewed as being politicized. The conservative judges perceived as centralist, and the progressive judges as more open to subnational claims.[137]

131 E.g., in India: Rajendra K. Pandey, 'Accomodating Diversity, Consolidating Nationhood', in Popelier and Sahadžić (n 26) 219; or in the United Kingdom: Brice Dickson, 'Work in Progress. A Country Study of Constitutional Asymmetry in the United Kingdom', in *ibid* 476.

132 See Benz (n 94) 203.

133 Rotimi T. Suberu, 'The Supreme Court of Nigeria: An Embattled Judiciary More Centralist than Federalist', in Aroney and Kincaid (n 45) 301.

134 Tierney (n 34) 751.

135 Elvira (n 43) 287.

136 See Palermo and Kössler (n 71) 197–198.

137 Casanas Adam (n 45) 383.

8.4.1.3 Strategic considerations

Strategic considerations may impact on case outcomes due to the court's concern about the implementation of its judgments and, more generally, its perceived legitimacy. In the literature, this is identified as an important reason for the centralist position of many courts in federal systems, but it also applies to other MTSs. Interestingly, in Kenya, the apex courts have not clearly picked up on the constitutional transformation from a unitary system into a system of 'devolution'.[138] Strategic reasons seem to play a role, considering the discrepancy between the constitution (with its emphasis on devolution) and political reality (with its culture of centralization).[139]

According to the dependency hypothesis, courts take a centralist position because their statute, powers, or budget depends upon the federal legislator.[140] This assumption does not hold where the federal legislator is governed by region-based parties, which could explain the non-centralist position of the Belgian Constitutional Court. However, Spain, Macedonia, and Bosnia-Herzegovina also disprove this assumption.[141]

Other possible strategic variables to explain the court's position are linked with the assumption that courts in federal systems are interested in securing the stability of the system. The general idea is that stability concerns lead to a more centralist position. This aligns with a trend in federalism theory that equalizes stability with centralization.[142] Associated with this is the hypothesis that courts take a more centralist stance in salient cases. Hence, when the political stakes are high, courts tend to be cautious and not push toward decentralizing dynamics.

Several observations confirm this hypothesis. In South Africa, the Constitutional Court's centralist position was explained as being concerned about nation-building after decades of ethnic and racial divide-and-rule, as well as the need for order.[143] In Belgium, empirical analysis shows that the Constitutional Court takes a more centralist stance in salient cases.[144] In particular, the suggestion that courts take a more centralist position to counter destabilizing centrifugal dynamics is confirmed by a study on the Bosnian Constitutional Court. After threats of secession by the Republika Srpska, the court has taken a centralist position – especially in cases where the SNEs were attempting to create

138 Conrad M. Bosire, 'The Courts and Devolution. The Kenyan Experience', in Fessha and Kössler (n 102) 142.
139 Comp. *ibid* 132.
140 Shapiro (n 73) 55.
141 López-Laborda, Rodrigo and Sanz-Arcega (n 81) 330; Walsh (n 130) 82.
142 See Maja Sahadžić, *Asymmetry, Multinationalism and Constitutional Law* (Routledge 2020) 158–159.
143 Steytler (n 115) 348.
144 Popelier and Bielen (n 80) 609, 612, 613.

ethnically exclusive regions.[145] This might also explain the courts' centralist trends in conflict-prone countries such as India and Nigeria.[146]

Further, courts are expected to acknowledge activist constitutional interpretations that are pushed by political actors if these are based on intergovernmental consensus. In Spain, the Constitutional Court was heavily criticized for rejecting important reforms in Statutes of Autonomy even though they were based on intergovernmental negotiations and ratified by referendum. This action has negatively affected the court's perceived legitimacy and, more importantly, the country's stability.[147]

8.4.1.4 Conclusion

Even if the constitution is entrenched, courts may bring about shifts in power relations between central and subnational authorities. Much depends on extra-legal factors, such as the judge's ideological preferences and the overall stability of the country. However, the court's impact can to some extent be controlled through institutional engineering. Factors that may impact upon the centralist or non-centralist stance of the court include the level of (de)centralism as established in the constitution, the organization of the court and the selection process of the judges, the status of subnational acts compared to central Acts of Parliament, the involvement of SNEs in central decision-making, and the allocation of responsibility for the organization and budget of the court. More empirical research is needed, however, to establish how these various factors relate to one another.

8.4.2 Nonjudicial adjudication of federalism conflicts

The role of courts as hubs for change in MTS varies considerably.[148] In some systems, courts do not play an important role due to a limited number of federalism disputes. This may be due to well-functioning political mechanisms of conflict resolution, single-party domination across both levels, legal culture, or – particularly in the United Kingdom – the political nature of the constitution and the flexible organization of devolution.[149] In Germany, for example, federalism disputes were settled by political negotiation and only rarely reached the Constitutional Court. This was until joint decision-making became more arduous after the 1989 reunification, when social and economic differences

145 Walsh (n 130) 83.
146 Popelier (n 79) 43–44.
147 Casanas Adam (n 45) 395–396, 399.
148 Palermo and Kössler (n 71) 267.
149 See for the United Kingdom, Germany, and South Africa: Alan Trench, 'The Courts and Devolution in the UK', (2012) 14 *BJPIR* 306–307; Benz (n 94) 208; Bronstein (n 102) 87; Steytler (n 115) 344.

raised redistributive conflicts.[150] In some systems, admissibility of a request is conditional on prior efforts to settle the federalism dispute through nonjudicial, intergovernmental mechanisms.[151]

On this premise, the political safeguards theory was developed in US doctrine as a normative device, as an argument against the judicial limitation of federal government power.[152] Courts should assume that the federal legislature remained within the boundaries of its competences because political control is exercised by the states that participate in federal lawmaking through the Senate. However, political safeguards are not necessarily, or exclusively, located in an upper house. Kramer pointed out that in the United States, states do also influence federal decision-making through informal mechanisms (e.g., via political parties) rather than through formal representation in the Senate.[153]

If nonjudicial mechanisms have the upper hand over judicial adjudication of federalism conflicts, the question arises as to how this impacts on intergovernmental power relations. If political mechanisms are effective in keeping federalism disputes from becoming judicialized, we can expect that they produce outcomes based on intergovernmental consensus. This is different if there is no judicial review available as a last resort to secure balanced decisions.

Ethiopia is the most prominent example of a jurisdiction where federalism conflicts between the federal government and the state are exclusively adjudicated by a nonjudicial body. The reason is that the interpretation of the constitution was regarded as a political function that should not be entrusted to an unelected and unaccountable judiciary.[154] In addition, the judiciary was perceived as a body of the former regime and unsympathetic to the new regime of ethnofederalism. The judiciary was therefore suspected of shifting power relations contrary to the constituents' intentions.[155] The House of Federation is the nonlegislative upper house in the Ethiopian Parliament. It is composed of representatives of ethnic communities, but operates *de facto* as a SNE house of representatives.[156] It is assisted by the Council of Constitutional Inquiry in its tasks of constitutional interpretation.[157] This Council is composed of the President and

150 Benz (n 94) 193, 209, 212.

151 E.g., Art. 41(1)(h)vi South African Constitution, urging governments to avoid legal proceedings against one another. See Steytler (n 115) 344. This was already mentioned in chapter 5.

152 Choper (n 117); Wechsler (n 117).

153 Kramer (n 117) 278–279, 294.

154 Yonatan T. Fessha and Zemelak Ayele, 'Giving "Shape and Texture" to a Federal System? Ethiopia's Courts and its Unusual Umpire', in Fessha and Kössler (n 102) 58.

155 Gedion T. Hessebon and Abduletif K. Idris, 'The Supreme Court of Ethiopia: Federalism's Bystander', in Aroney and Kincaid (n 45) 184. See also Assefa Fiseha, 'Constitutional Adjudication in Ethiopia: Exploring the experience of the House of Federation (HOF)', (2007) 1 *Mizan. L. Rev.* 10–11.

156 Yonatan T. Fessha and Biniyam N. Bezahib, 'Federation among Unequals', in Popelier and Sahadžić (n 26) 149.

157 Art. 62(2), 82 and 83 Ethiopian Constitution.

the Vice-President of the Federal Supreme Court, six legal experts appointed by the President of the Republic (on the recommendation of the lower house), and three members of the House of Federation.[158] Few petitions have been submitted so far, and most of them were rejected; cases are handled with little transparency and the outcomes are not published consistently.[159] Federalism-related cases, in particular, are rare and are not dealt with on the basis of general criteria or guidelines.[160] The House of Federation and the Council of Constitutional Inquiry have thus not played a prominent role in the adjudication of federalism conflicts. This is explained by the dominance – so far[161] – of the central political party, such that disputes are settled within party structures and behind closed doors.[162] For the same reason, individuals are not easily tempted to bring a case before the House of Federation, which, as a political body, is not perceived as a neutral arbiter.[163] Where the House dealt with federalism conflicts in its role as an advisor on draft legislation, its opinions clearly favored the federal government.[164]

In post-conflict treaties, the establishment of political arbitration committees is recommended for settling federalism issues that are considered (especially at this stage) to be political rather than legal questions.[165] The purpose is to avoid situations where courts invalidate a law in controversial cases, but no political agreement can be reached to remedy the situation.[166] These arbitration committees, however, are national bodies that cannot defuse situations that flow from a judgment by an international court. An example is the *Sejdic-Finci* judgment, where the Grand Chamber of the European Court of Human Rights held Bosnia's ethnic federal system to be incompatible with the European Convention of Human Rights.[167] This brings us to the next section on global governance.

8.5 Global governance

Global governance can be a hub for shifts in the relationship between central and subnational powers in several ways: by legislating through international treaties, transferring powers to international bodies, and creating new hubs for

158 Art. 82(2) Ethiopian Constitution.
159 Hessebon and Idris (n 155) 182–183.
160 Hessebon and Idris (n 155) 185–188. Fiseha (n 155) 14 also observes that the CCI's opinions are brief and not well-articulated.
161 Fessha and Ayele (n 154) 65 refer to recent developments that have opened the political space.
162 Hessebon and Idris (n 155) 188–189. See also Fessha and Ayele (n 154) 64–65.
163 Hessebon and Idris (n 155) 190–191. Also doubtful, but less conclusive, on the impartiality of the HoF: Fiseha (n 155) 31.
164 Fessha and Ayele (n 154) 62.
165 Walsh (n 130) 86.
166 *Ibid* 86.
167 ECtHR [GC] 22 December 2009, Case Nos. 27996/06 and 34836/06, *Sejdic and Finci v Bosnia-Herzegovina*.

shifts in power relations in the form of an international court. The EU is the most powerful example of the latter two mechanisms.

8.5.1 International treaties

International treaties may impact on the form of state. Fundamental rights treaties may call into question the validity of privileged groups in ethnically-based MTS. Other treaties may articulate constraints on the exercise of powers allocated to the SNEs. Further, international obligations may induce central intervention in subnational policy domains.[168] This is particularly the case where the central authority has the power to conclude international treaties in the sphere of subnational competences, and the implementation of a treaty is considered part of the treaty-making power.[169] For example, scholars have pointed out how this has been used to significantly alter the Spanish territorial structure without any formal constitutional change.[170]

If SNEs make use of their (mostly limited)[171] power to conclude their own international treaties within their sphere of competences, this does not redefine the relations between the central and subnational authorities. International treaties are only a hub for shifts in power relations between central and SNEs if the treaty concerns subnational matters, and if the treaty is concluded by the central government. As was discussed in Chapter 4, more centralist systems conclude the treaties without the involvement of SNEs, or only under an obligation to consult. The predominant view in those systems is that subnational interference is harmful to the national interest.[172] More integrationist systems combine the involvement of SNEs, most often through the Upper House. Decentralist systems require the individual SNE's approval. In the latter systems, subnational interests prevail over the national interest, as any SNE may veto a treaty that is considered beneficial to the entire nation.[173]

If the interference in power relations amounts to an alteration of the constitution, the question arises as to whether a constitutional amendment is required before ratification or not. Institutional engineering may accommodate or

168 See Mahendra Pal Singh, 'India', in Oliver and Fusaro (n 19) 189 on how WTO obligations resulted in central legislation on agriculture, which is an exclusive competence of the States.

169 As is the case in the United States of America, see Palermo and Kössler (n 71) 427–428, 447.

170 Barrero Ortega and Sobrino Guijarro (n 91) 314 and Elvira (n 43) 296–298.

171 For an overview, see Nikos Skoutaris, 'Comparing the Subnational Constitutional Space of the European Sub-State Entities in the Area of Foreign Affairs', (2012) 4 *Perspectives of Federalism* 243–346.

172 For an overview of this view in US doctrine and case law, see Daniel Halberstam, 'The Foreign Affairs of Federal Systems: A National Perspective on the Benefits of State Participation', (2001) 46 *Villanova L. Rev.* 1022–1027.

173 Critical for this reason: *ibid* 1056.

obstruct political preferences to change the constitution through international treaties. For example, until 2008 the Austrian Constitution could be changed by means of a treaty approved by a two-thirds majority in Parliament.[174] In the Netherlands, a special procedure was inserted in the Constitution to allow treaties that contradict the constitution to be implemented without formal constitutional change.[175] In Belgium, discussions arose when an EU Directive required giving non-Belgian EU residents a vote in local elections, contrary to Art. 8 of the Constitution. The prescribed procedure – including general elections – was considered too slow and arduous for immediate compliance. In the end, the solution was a ban on the constitutionality review of Acts of Parliament that give approval to EU Treaties or the European Convention of Human Rights.[176] This particular selection of treaties has a supranational nature, which is discussed in the next section.

8.5.2 Conferral of powers

The central government may transfer powers, ordinarily allocated to the SNEs, to international bodies with legislative powers. In this way, SNEs have to share their powers with international bodies and may be obliged to implement international rules.

The most pronounced example is the transfer of powers to the EU. EU governance has been identified as an important constraint on SNEs, as many EU competences concern matters devolved to the SNEs.[177] Here, the involvement of SNEs – discussed in Chapter 4 – is a two-step system. It concerns firstly their involvement in the conclusion of the power transferal treaty, and secondly their involvement in EU lawmaking. The EU does not impose any procedure to give SNEs a role in decision-making. The only possible exception is under the Early Warning Mechanism that provides a subsidiarity check to national parliaments, where the parliaments' votes are mandatorily spread over both houses in bicameral systems.[178] Instead, by respecting for the member states' varying structures,[179] the EU facilitates both weak and strong subnational involvement. Again, a distinction can be made between more centralist, integrationist, and confederal approaches.[180]

174 Stelzer (n 22) 9 and 22.
175 Art. 91(3) Dutch Constitution.
176 Art. 26, §1*bis* Special Law on the Constitutional Court.
177 Ornella Porchia, 'Sub-national Units, Member States, and the European Union', in Burgess and Tarr (n 43) 283; Tierney (n 34) 741. See also with regard to Spain: Maiz, Caamaño and Azpitarte (n 53) 78.
178 Art. 7 Protocol No 2 on the Application of the Principles of Subsidiarity and Proportionality.
179 As imposed by Art. 4(2) TEU.
180 For more detail, see Patricia Popelier, 'Subnational multilevel constitutionalism', (2014) 6 *Perspectives on Federalism* 9–18.

The United Kingdom was a model of a centralist approach. The UK European Act 2011 required the delegation of powers to the EU to be approved by an Act of Parliament and, in principle, a popular referendum.[181] Similarly, the withdrawal from the EU, which was considered to be a 'hugely significant constitutional shift',[182] resulted from a popular referendum that was controlled by the central authorities. The Supreme Court, while giving the UK Parliament control over the triggering of the exit procedure, denied that there was a duty for the UK Parliament to ask the SNEs approval.[183] The procedure was criticized for ignoring 'remain' preferences in Scotland (and Northern Ireland).[184] It was certain to have implications for the system of devolution and the relations between the central and Scottish authorities.[185] In particular, the SNEs would gain autonomous space in those subnational policy fields in which the EU was normally active. This is because Sewel resolutions, which the Scottish Parliament uses to authorize the UK Parliament to legislate in devolved matters, are used to give effect to EU legislation.[186] However, the identification of areas where UK-wide frameworks are considered necessary resulted in discussions on how to preserve intergovernmental balances.[187] Meanwhile, the SNEs were only included in an informal way, for example, through the Joint Ministerial Committee. This committee functions as a venue for the consultation of devolved entities on UK positions on EU matters that in turn affect subnational matters.[188] The Concordat on the coordination of EU policy issues provided for a consultation mechanism through the Joint Ministerial Committee and allowed for a mixed delegation at the European Council, but the UK lead Minister retained overall responsibility. Subnational involvement was qualified in the literature as 'dependent' and 'conditional'.[189] Under the Early Warning Mechanism, subnational parliaments were

181 Section 2, European Union Act 2011.
182 Dickson (n 131) 461.
183 *R (Miller) v Secretary of State for Exiting the EU* [2017] UKSC 5, [2018] AC 61. See also Dickson (n 131) 477–478.
184 Aileen McHarg and James Mitchell, 'Brexit and Scotland', (2017) 19 *Br. J. Pol. Int. Rel.* 512–526.
185 See Robert Hazell and Alan Renwick, *Brexit: Its Consequences for Devolution and the Union*, UCL Constitution Unit Briefing Paper (UCL 2016); Tony Travers, *Implications of a Brexit for UK National Governance and Local Government*, Report of the hearing held on 13th April, 2016 (LSE Commission on the Future of Britain in Europe, 2016).
186 Stephen Tierney, 'Quiet Devolution: Sub-State Autonomy and the Gradual Reconstitution of the United Kingdom', in Burgess and Tarr (n 43) 212.
187 Dickson (n 131) 474–475.
188 Concordat on coordination of European Union policy issues, March 2010.
189 Simon Bulmer, Martin Burch, Patricia Hogwood and Andrew Scott, 'UK Devolution and the European Union: A Tale of Cooperative Asymmetry?', (2006) 36 *Publius: The Journal of Federalism*, 86.

welcome to submit comments on their own initiative, but the UK Parliament had the final say.[190]

A more integrationist approach is taken in Germany, where participation of the SNEs in EU decision making has compensated for the loss of competences.[191] An EU Treaty that involves a delegation of powers requires a two-thirds majority in both the *Bundestag* and the *Bundesrat*.[192] The *Bundesrat* has to be kept informed throughout the treaty negotiation procedure to enable it to take a position.[193] The Constitution provides for a differentiated approach on the involvement of the SNEs in the Council of Ministers. In some cases, representatives of the *Länder* are assigned by the *Bundesrat* as the German delegate. In other cases, subnational representatives participate in the delegation 'if possible'. Under some circumstances, the federal government represents Germany, but it has to consider the statement of the *Bundesrat*. As soon as a proposed measure would, as a domestic law, have been within the competence of the *Länder* or have had required the participation of the *Bundesrat*, a regional representative assigned by the *Bundesrat* is involved in the discussions to define which position Germany will take in the Council of Ministers.[194] SNEs are involved in the Early Warning Mechanism through the *Bundesrat*. However, this is made up of representatives of the subnational Executives, not the Parliaments.[195]

Likewise in Austria, the Constitution was amended to counterbalance power shifts flowing from the accession to the EU.[196] According to the Constitution, a representative of the *Länder* can be delegated to the Council of Ministers to discuss matters within the competence of the SNEs. The *Länder* can issue a unified statement of position in matters within their competence that binds the federal government in negotiations and voting in the EU, unless foreign policy and integration policy reasons can be invoked.[197]

By contrast, Belgium takes a more confederalist position. SNEs have an individual veto right for the approval of EU treaties, as with any other mixed treaty concluded by the federal government. In exclusively subnational matters, a subnational minister (as a rule) is the Belgian delegate and appointed under a rotation system. In 'mixed' matters Belgium is represented by a mixed delegation led by the federal or the subnational minister, depending on the matter. In all cases,

190 Karolina Borońska-Hryniewiecka, 'Regions and subsidiarity after the Treaty of Lisbon: overcoming the "regional blindness"?', in Marta Cartabia, Nicola Lupo and Andrea Simoncini (eds), *Democracy and Subsidiarity in the EU* (Bologna, Il Mulino, Bologna 2013) 360.

191 Woelk (n 19) 162.

192 Art. 23(1) combined with Art. 79(2) German Constitution.

193 Paras. 2 and 3 of the *Gesetz über die Zusammenarbeit von Bund und Länder in Angelegenheiten der Europeäischen Union (GZBLAEU).*

194 Art. 23(6) German Constitution and Art. 4(1), 6(1) and 23(5) GZBLAEU

195 Magdalena Suszycka-Jasch and Hans-Christian Jasch, 'The Participation of the German Länder in Formulating German EU-Policy', (2009) 9 *German Law Journal* 125.

196 Stelzer (n 22) 11.

197 Art. 23(d) Austrian Constitution.

subnational and central ministers meet beforehand to agree upon the Belgian stance, with a veto right for every actor.[198] If no consensus is found, Belgium will abstain in the Council of Ministers. Under the Early Warning Mechanism, the Belgian Declaration No 51 applies. This states that in the Belgian legal order, the term 'national parliaments' in the EU treaties includes the subnational parliaments. According to a cooperation agreement,[199] each subnational Parliament can submit a reasoned statement and votes are cast in such a way that the positions of each federal or subnational legislative assembly are positioned next to each other, without fostering institutional dialogue.[200]

8.5.3 International courts

An extra hub can be created in the form of an international court. This may shift power relations between the national member state and the international (or supranational) system of which it forms part. It may also impact upon the form of state and the power relations between the central and subnational authorities within the member state.

One example is the European Court of Human Rights. As mentioned above, ethnic federalism may contradict individual rights-based treaties, if privileges are granted to specific groups but discriminate against others. The *Sejdic-Finci* judgment mentioned above, as well as the subsequent *Zornic* judgment,[201] have remained unactionable. This is because compliance would involve a fundamental redesigning of the multi-tiered structure of Bosnia and Herzegovina.[202] Graziadei remarks that on the basis of these judgments, power-sharing arrangements in Northern Ireland, South Tyrol, and Belgium can be called into question.[203] Isacharoff warns against prioritizing individual rights as a principle if this destabilizes the entire country.[204] While national courts have the inclination to secure national stability, more distant courts may take a more principled stance. Graziadei, therefore, developed the 'integrative democracy tolerance test' with five guidelines for courts to deal with 'first-order' cases that challenge the

198 Cooperation agreement of 8 March 1994. In practice, according to a gentleman's agreement, the veto right is only used by actors with competences in the concrete matter. See Peter Bursens, 'Het Europese beleid in de Belgische federatie', (2005) 47 LV *Res Publica* 67.

199 Subsidiarity – Inter-Parliamentary Cooperation Agreement of 29 March 2017.

200 Patricia Popelier and Werner Vandenbruwaene, 'The Subsidiarity Mechanism as a Tool for Inter-Level Dialogue in Belgium', (2011) 7 *Eu. Const. L. Rev.* 223.

201 ECtHR 15 July 2014, Case No. 3681/06, Zornic v BiH.

202 For a discussion of implications and reform proposals, see Hildur Boldt, 'Ending Consociational Power-Sharing. The Sejdic and Finci Case and the Prospects for Constitutional Reform in Bosnia and Herzegovina', (2012) 6 *Vienna Online J. on Internat. Const. L.* 489–547.

203 Stefan Graziadei, 'Democracy v Human Rights? The Strasbourg Court and the Challenge of Power Sharing', (2016) 12 *Eu. Const. L. Rev.* 70–71.

204 Samuel Issacharoff, 'Democracy and collective decision making', (2008) 6 *I-CON* 261.

structure of a state: (1) the democratic and constitutional legitimacy criterion holds that the higher the majorities that supported the law, the more recent the agreement is, and the higher the legal norm on which it is built on, the more courts should use restraint; (2) the legal consistency criterion requires courts to overturn precedent only when backed by strong reasoning; (3) judicial intervention should unwind the state structure only gradually; 4) judges have to show "a keen sense of political judgment", anticipating the risk of non-implementation; and (5) courts should consider whether their judgments will contribute to the integration of the society.[205] This test reveals different aspects that determine the functioning of (international) courts as a hub for change: it can be influenced by institutional engineering (criterion 1), depends on strategic considerations already discussed in section 8.4 (criteria 4 and 5), and is more effective if it induces incremental change (criterion 3).

The strongest example of an international court that impacts on the form of state is the Court of Justice of the European Union (ECJ). This court has been criticized for not taking proper account of the structure of multi-tiered member states, which may alter power relations within these states.

For example, in its initial case law, it considered that tax benefits granted within one region only amounted to state aid, thereby emptying subnational authorities of their tax powers. Later, it adjusted this case law under some conditions that do not take due account of asymmetric MTSs.[206]

In another case, it undermined the Belgian system for the allocation of powers by imposing the employment criterion to determine the locus of competence for a system of social care insurance instead of the usual residence criterion. This related to persons who had made use of their right of free movement. The Advocate General had even considered the use of the employment criterion in purely internal relations, but the ECJ toned this down to a mere suggestion.[207]

In this case, an extra dimension is added to the debate on the factors that influence the position of the court that was previously discussed in section 8.3. For example, the question arises as to whether the European level, the national authorities, and the SNEs all have some control over the selection of judges and the organization of the court, or only one or two of these levels have some control. Another question is whether all entities have equal access to the Court.

205 Graziadei (n 203) 75–83.

206 For a discussion, see Saturnina Moreno Gonzalez, 'Regional Fiscal Autonomy from a State Aid Perspective: The ECJ's Judgment in *Portugal v Commission*', (2007) 47 *European Taxation* 328–338 and Bruno Peeters, 'European legal limitations to the repartition of fiscal competences in a federal state structure', in Bea Cantillon, Patricia Popelier and Ninke Mussche (eds) *Social Federalism: The Creation of a Layered Welfare State* (Antwerp, Intersentia 2011) 232–235.

207 Case C-212/6, Government of the French Community and Walloon Government v Flemish Government, 1 April 2008, with the conclusion of Advocate General Sharpston.

Where no formal procedure is drawn up, such as in Italy and Spain, the nomination is largely in the hands of the central government alone.[208] In the United Kingdom, the Constitutional Reform Act 2005 does not explicitly apply to the EU Courts, but informally judicial advisory boards were established for such nominations. In 2012, this commission was headed by the Chair of the Judicial Appointments Board of Scotland,[209] but the involvement of SNEs was not secured.

Austria is the only member state that has inserted into its constitution a requirement of parliamentary consent for the nomination of the Austrian judge in the EU Courts. The constitution states that the Austrian participation in the nomination of members of the EU courts (and other institutions) is incumbent upon the federal government. The consent of the Main Committee (a body within the National Council) *or* the Federal Council (upper house) is required, and the Federal Council has to be kept informed.[210]

In other member states, balanced mechanisms are inserted in other legal acts. For example, in Germany, the Federal Government selects the candidate nominated by the Judicial Selection Committee, which consists of federal and subnational executive representatives.[211]

Even when SNEs are responsible for compliance with international law – e.g., the implementation of EU Directives or the execution of EU Regulations – in exterior relations it is the national state that is held responsible for non-compliance. For this reason, mechanisms are sometimes created that allow the central authorities to take measures instead of shortchanging SNEs. Such a mechanism may come down to a system of distributing the fines imposed upon the national state. In a centralist system, the central authorities control the proceedings before the international court and the measures to be taken. In a more integrationist approach, SNEs are involved in the judicial proceedings and the national state will not substitute for the SNEs to ensure compliance. However, the national state will negotiate with the SNEs on a fair distribution of possible fines. In some systems, such as Germany, redistribution is based upon well-defined criteria; in other systems, such as Belgium and the United Kingdom, it depends upon bi or multilateral negotiations.[212]

208 See Tómas Dumbrovský, Bilyana Petkova and Marijn Van der Sluis, 'Judicial Appointments: The Article 255 TFEU Advisory Panel and Selection Procedures in the Member States', (2014) 51 *Common Market Law Rev.* 467–469.

209 *Ibid* 471.

210 Art. 23c(2) Austrian Constitution.

211 *Richterwahlgesetz*, as amended by law of 22 September 2009, *Offical Gazette* I, No 60 (*Gesetz über die Ausweitung und Stärkung der Rechte des Bundestages und des Bundesrates in Angelegenheiten der Europäischen Union*).

212 For an overview of different mechanisms, see Werner Vandenbruwaene, Patricia Popelier and Liesbeth Janssens, 'Article 260 TFEU Sanctions in Multi-Tiered Member States', (2015) 7 *Perspectives on Federalism* 146–150.

8.6 Conclusion

This chapter showed how constitutions facilitate or curb the dynamics of MTS and how constitutional engineering can impact on this. It is the constitution that first defines and organizes the basic structure of the system. It is also the constitution that defines and organizes the power relations between central and subnational authorities, in a centralist, balanced, or confederalist manner. At the same time, the constitution creates hubs for shifts in these power relations. This is via constitutional amendment, de-constitutionalization, mandating courts to adjudicate federalism disputes, the technique for the allocation of powers, and participation in systems of global governance. These hubs can adjust power relations beyond the original intention of the constituent, but within political control. Even when courts make decisions, strategic considerations ensure that judicial outcomes, in the long run, align with political majority preferences. These considerations often tend to be the preferences of central governing parties. However, if these mechanisms are to find a new equilibrium, they must ultimately include federalism safeguards to ensure that changes are considered legitimate by the actors at the different levels of authority. This is particularly difficult in asymmetric processes of change, unless diversity between SNEs is supported by all actors.[213]

If constitutional change, then, is 'an organic process in which societies shape and reshape their institutional arrangements',[214] this process does not entirely escape the constitutional machinery. The constituent bodies can, to some extent, direct centralist or non-centralist shifts through constitutional engineering, even beyond the mechanisms for constitutional amendment. In this chapter, several instruments of control in one or the other direction were identified, such as:

1. the self-definition that steers constitutional narratives by courts;
2. the level of (de)centralism established by the constitution;
3. the detail or indeterminacies[215] in the organization of statute, powers, and fiscal federalism;
4. the choice of instruments that are created as hubs for power shifts and the federalism safeguards built into these instruments, such as subnational involvement and effective subsidiarity mechanisms;
5. the organization of the court and the selection process of the judges;
6. the status of subnational acts compared to central Acts of Parliament;
7. the involvement of SNEs in central lawmaking,
8. the involvement of SNEs in the conclusion of international treaties;
9. the involvement of SNEs in EU decision-making; and

213 Nathalie Behnke and Arthur Benz, 'The Politics of Constitutional Change between Reform and Evolution', (2009) 39 *Publius: The Journal of Federalism* 233–234.

214 Hutchinson (n 37) 61.

215 See Fusaro and Oliver (n 19) 432.

10 the access to and involvement of SNEs in proceedings before international or supranational courts.

In summary, as said by Behnke and Benz: "even if a constitution cannot guarantee stability of federalism, constitutional policy has to be regarded as an important mechanism determining the balance of stability and flexibility of federal systems".[216]

The various mechanisms for change complement each other.[217] They can either reinforce each other or balance one another out.

For example, rigid constitutional amendment systems encourage constitutional change by other means. They may influence judicial activism – although up to now there is no consensus as to whether the relation is inversely proportional or not – or they may bring about changes through negotiated agreements or other mechanisms. In contrast, where subnational involvement in constitutional amendment procedures is lacking, negotiated agreements may compensate for this by creating an instrument for constitutional change based on intergovernmental consensus.[218]

At one extreme, a fundamentally centralist MTS entrenches the unitary character of the system in the constitution (preferably in an eternity clause), controls the organization of the system in the constitution or through Acts of Parliament with little involvement of SNEs, emphasizes the sovereignty of central Acts of Parliament as opposed to subnational acts, allocates powers to SNEs on a shared basis, denies courts the power to adjudicate federalism disputes or controls the selection, organization, and budget of the court, and monopolizes external relations. This model risks radical or even violent opposition if subnational autonomy claims find no legal channel to push for an adjustment of power relations.

At the other extreme, in a radically decentralist constellation, the autonomy of the SNEs is secured in the constitution which can only be amended with the approval of subnational legislatures, the organization of power relations is deferred to negotiated bilateral agreements, powers are allocated on the basis of exclusivity and equality, SNEs are given control over the selection of judges and the organization and budget of courts, their individual approval for the conclusion of treaties is required, and they are involved in supranational decision-making and proceedings before international or supranational courts. In this model, the central authority risks losing control over decentralist dynamics.

An integrative position implies the inclusion of both integrity and subnational autonomy safeguards, with a preference for the collective involvement of SNEs in central, EU, and international decision making through a strong and representative upper house. This seems the most promising model to secure dynamic stability over time. Switzerland, for example, has enabled a centralization shift

216 Behnke and Benz (n213) 214, 232–233.
217 See also *ibid* 219.
218 For Italy, see Palermo and Valdesalici (n 33) 296.

through constitutional amendment, supported by the SNEs.[219] It may, however, not be the best model for multinational MTS, which are often characterized by constitutional asymmetry.[220]

In the end, as discussed in Chapter 7, institutional safeguards are not the only variables that determine the direction of power shifts within an MTS. In particular, the political party system, with a centralized one-party system at one extreme, and region-based political parties at the other, is an important driver for change. This can only partially be influenced through the adjustment of the electoral system. The economic context is another element: if SNEs have insufficient resources, they will be less inclined to exercise optional powers and more inclined to use programs funded and conditioned by the central government. Other external factors can be added, such as the multinational or homogeneous disposition of society. All this does not entirely rule out the impact of institutional factors. Instead, we can suspect a mutual relationship: that external factors will determine the choice for the institutional architecture and the use of hubs for change, and that institutional factors, in turn, constrain or strengthen the impact of external factors.

219 See Giovanni Biaggini, 'Switzerland', in Oliver and Fusaro (n 19) 319.
220 For the link between asymmetry and multinationalism, see Sahadžić (n 26) 83, 88, 95–96.

Conclusion: findings and way forward

Findings

The purpose of this book was to develop a theory of federalism that encompasses all forms of MTSs. The contours of this theory were developed in Part I.

Chapter 1 explained why traditional theory fails to meet this requirement and collected building blocks for a new theory of dynamic federalism. This new theory was outlined in Chapter 2. Federalism as a value concept seeks a response to tensions between the central authorities and territorial sub-entities in the search for a proper balance between autonomy and cohesion. So far, the dichotomy of self-rule and shared rule was considered to be the core principle of federalism, and cohesion was a basic requirement for stability. A theory of dynamic federalism shifts the focus to the dichotomy of autonomy and cohesion. Shared rule is an indicator of autonomy if it refers to a particular SNE, and it is an indicator of cohesion if all relevant tiers are included. On this basis, nine forms of state (including federations) were distinguished, in line with varying balances of autonomy and cohesion. The theory is called 'dynamic' for two reasons. First, forms of states are no longer defined on the basis of defining institutional features. Instead, institutional features are indicators of autonomy and cohesion. This means that stability – defined in this book as continuity in the form of state – can be dynamic in itself: if several institutional changes cancel each other out, the form of state remains stable. Second, the proper balance between autonomy and cohesion is considered an essentially contested notion, which means that this balance varies over time. Where scholars used to examine change as a matter of de/centralization, a theory of dynamic federalism points to two different but related dynamics: de/centralization and dis/integration.

It follows from this that a theory of dynamic federalism requires the construction of indicators to measure cohesion and autonomy. It also follows that in its core, a theory of dynamic federalism is a theory of change. The first finding was dealt with in Part II and the second in Part III.

The indexes proposed in Part II were constructed under three categories: status (Chapter 4), powers (Chapter 5), and fiscal arrangements (Chapter 6). They were built on the basis of comparative federalism literature and refined by applying them to the Belgian case. The results of this case study show the potential of these indicators and are discussed in Chapter 3. They show how the institutional designers imagined the proper balance between autonomy and cohesion. They also show where exactly institutional engineering may trigger a shift toward more or less centralization, and more or less integration. The results of the Belgian case study – with high autonomy and medium cohesion – align with existing perceptions about the Belgian architecture. This gives some indication that the indexes are robust, but it is not sufficient to merely validate the indexes. To turn a new index into a credible instrument, it should be tested on numerous cases and over a longer period.[1] This means that more case studies are needed to validate and refine the model.

Part III only offers a brief outline of a theory of (federal) change. The reason for this is that such a theory is essentially a multi-disciplinary endeavor. The topic has recently received much attention, particularly in nonlegal literature. Legal scholarship has until now lagged behind by clinging to the more traditional and static theory of federalism. Chapter 7 and 8, therefore, emphasize why an institutionalist approach is important, despite the importance of noninstitutional drivers.

Chapter 7 showed how the indexes, constructed in Part II, help to measure institutional change, constitutional asymmetry, and the difference between 'law in the books' and how MTSs actually function. However, more research is needed to construct an adequate model to measure the 'actual' balance of autonomy and cohesion. Again, this requires an interdisciplinary study. The overview of sources, catalysts, strategies, and actors revealed that federal dynamics are not, or not necessarily, "natural pendulum-like swings". On the contrary, incremental change may create dynamics that fundamentally change the form of state over time. The research into the sources of multi-tiered construction remains important because they will determine the optimal balance of cohesion and subnational autonomy in that system over a specific period of time. The strategies chosen to adjust the system to reflect the optimal balance will depend on the constellation of actors, the hubs for changes built in the system, and the robustness of the system's institutions, as well as external coincidences. On the basis of this overview of theories of change, a hypothesis was formulated that the stability of MTSs is dependent on two criteria. The first is a criterion of congruence: systems need institutional mechanisms, through which institutional power relations can be kept congruent in a harmonious manner with social power relations. If these mechanisms are lacking, change will be enforced in a more radical and informal way. The second is a criterion of incongruence. Taking into account the self-reinforcing effects of institutional change, congruence must remain imperfect so as to stabilize social dynamics. It is still necessary to test the hypothesis that cohesive instruments may help that effect.

The institutional hubs for change referred to in Chapter 7 are analyzed in Chapter 8. These are constitutional amendments, instruments for de-constitutionalization, techniques for the allocation of competences, judicial and

1 András Jakab and Viktor Lórincz, *International Indices as Models for the Rule of Law Scoreboard of the European Union: Methodological Issues,* MPIL Research Papers Series No 2017–21 (Max Planck Institute 2017) 11.

nonjudicial adjudicators of federalism conflicts, and institutionalization of global governance. As these are also federal safeguards, they were already included in the indexes constructed in Part II. In Chapter 8, there is a discussion of the institutional and noninstitutional factors that determine how these instruments will actually function. The chapter shows how these instruments may facilitate or curb federal dynamics, mostly but not exclusively, using political control. Strategy will influence which instrument turns out to be the most important hub for change, and this is discussed in Chapter 7. At the same time, the choice of instrument may determine the legitimacy of change and its robustness. The hypothesis formulated in Chapter 7 also applies here: change based on cohesion – i.e., in the joint agreement between the relevant parties – is more robust, irrespective of the instrument. For example, change through judicial interpretation is legitimate and robust if it is based not only on legal reasoning, but also reflects intergovernmental agreement.

The way forward

The preceding summary of findings already shows where follow-up research is needed. The theory of dynamic federalism proposed in this book is by no means complete and final. It gratefully uses existing insights made by other scholars. The book invites the federalism research community to help improve and complete the theory and to bring it into practice.

The research agenda for the further development of a theory of dynamic federalism is loaded. At this point, I would like to highlight three items in particular: (1) the refinement of indicators; (2) the specification of multi-level relations; and (3) the meaning of dynamic federalism for multinational MTSs.

1 'The refinement of indicators'. As mentioned previously, more country studies are needed to validate the model and to refine the indicators to suit all systems, regardless of their institutional variety. Such an exercise may simultaneously highlight which are the most relevant indicators. This would enable us to thin out the model or to give more weight to some indicators rather than others. Ideally, these kinds of country studies are performed by country experts. Therefore, the next step is an edited volume with country studies. Such a volume will allow the comparative study of multi-tiered institutions. It will also serve as the basis for measuring institutional as well as factual change.
2 'The specification of multi-level relations'. This book mostly analyzed federalism in terms of central and subnational relations. Only in specific cases was there explicit reference to relationships between multiple tiers of authority. However, the relations between local, regional, national, and supranational levels of authority are bound to create more complex dynamics that need to be untangled.

The impact of the EU on the relationships between national and subnational authorities has already been examined. The mechanisms of upward and downward transfers of powers have mostly been tackled by political scientists through the concept of multilevel governance, given the propensity to avoid the notion of federalism in relation to the EU.[2] Legal scholars, however, have shied away from the concept of multilevel governance, because of its conceptual vagueness and normative weakness.[3] In a theory of dynamic federalism, the units of analysis are MTSs. This means that there is no need to use the term 'federation' to describe the EU. The indexes can be used to qualify the EU, which has the advantage of analytical preciseness. It also allows us to observe the European construction in terms of balance and institutional change. Analyzing multiple dynamics is a more complex enterprise, which requires the combination and comparison of national-EU, subnational-national, and subnational-EU relations. It must also be kept in mind that this captures only one aspect of the system of multilevel governance that forms the essence of the EU. In particular, multilevel governance adds a sideway reallocation of authority. This includes private actors in the network of multilevel decision-making, as well as a blurring of the national and international legal spheres.[4]

The impact of the EU on domestic power relations has already been the object of a wide range of studies. The dynamics of local-regional-national relations have remained under the radar so far, as well as the impact of supranational developments. The studies that have been undertaken so far have revealed important insights. For example, central governments sometimes use municipal decentralization to weaken regional levels of government.[5] Assertive local governments that gain their seat as a partner in intergovernmental decision-making processes may curb the regional authorities' position.[6] By contrast, the focus on regional decentralization may lead to a neglect of local entities, as seems to have been the case in Belgium.

3 'Multinational MTSs'. There is already a wide range of literature on multinational federalism. It is noticeable, however, that focus has centered on the empowerment of ethnic groups through institutional arrangements. Less attention has been given to the position of the central government once these groups have gained control.[7] This means that the preferred balance

2 Erik Fossum and Markus Jachtenfuchs, 'Federal challenges and challenges to federalism', (2017) 24 *Journal of Eu. Public Policy* 474–475.

3 Giacinto della Cananea, 'Is European Constitutionalism Really "Multilevel"?', (2010) 70 *Zeitschriftfür ausländisches* öffentliches *Recht und Völkerrecht* 283–284. Comp. Michael Keating, 'Europe as a multilevel federation', (2017) 24 *Journal of European Public Policy* 621.

4 Patricia Popelier, 'A multilevel governance perspective on distintegrative dynamics within EU member states', in Patrizia Latarullo *et al.* (eds), *The regions of Europe among local identities, new communities and territorial disparities* (FrancoAngeli 2019) 37.

5 J. Tyler Dickovick, 'Municipalization as Central Government Strategy: Central-Regional-Local Politics in Peru, Brazil, and South Africa', (2006) 37 *Publius: The Journal of Federalism* 1–25.

6 John Kincaid, 'The Rise and Characteristics of Coercive Federalism in the United States', in Giancarlo Pola (ed.), *Principles and Practices of Fiscal Autonomy* (Ashgate 2015, reissue Routledge 2017) 59.

7 Philip G. Roeder, 'Ethnofederalism and the Mismanagement of Conflicting Nationalisms', in Jan Erk and Lawrence M Anderson, *The Paradox of Federalism* (2010) 18.

between autonomy and cohesion is particularly relevant for multinational systems.

The divide in power-sharing literature between 'integrationists' and 'consociationalists', referred to in Chapter 2, can be reinterpreted in terms of the preferred balance of autonomy and cohesion. Important here is the extent to which cohesion is possible in a deeply divided system. The notion of 'distrust federalism', coined by Requejo, may offer conceptual guidance.[8] In systems characterized by distrust between the different tiers, Requejo says trust can be created. He points to the participation of the SNEs in central decision-making and protection of SNEs against central action, and by giving SNEs outlets to change power relations and hold exit options such as secession clauses.[9] However, the author used Spain as a reference point, and clearly had in mind systems in which minority nations feel oppressed by the central government that represents the majority nation. By contrast, in dyadic systems, distrust affects horizontal relations, and shared decision-making by two more or less equally strong groups easily leads to a deadlock. Belgium is a prominent example. Here, the strategy has been to organize the system as a form of dual federalism to avoid intergovernmental cooperation as much as possible[10] and to organize power-sharing mechanisms rather than integrationist systems of decision-making at the central level. In the absence of trust, suboptimal cohesion might be the best device for multinational systems.

Nevertheless, trust has been identified as an important quality of MTSs to maintain cohesion and stability.[11] It is defined as the reliance of the different tiers "on the integrity of one another and an overall commitment to the maintenance of the partnership".[12] So far, federalism literature has gone no further than this. It has made some assumptions on how to create or maintain trust, but this was never based on empirical studies or on the findings of the growing conceptual empirical literature on political trust. Conversely, trust scholars have neglected the federal dimension of trust in MTSs. A wealth of insights is to be gained from a combination of both strands of literature.

8 Ferran Requejo, *Multinational Federalism and Value Pluralism* (Routledge 2005) 74.

9 *Ibid* 74; Ferran Requejo, 'Federalism and democracy. The case of minority nations: a federal deficit', in Michael Burgess and Alain-G. Gagnon (eds), *Federal Democracies* (Routledge 2010) 290–291.

10 Wilfried Swenden and Maarten T. Jans, 'Will it stay or will it go?' Federalism and the sustainability of Belgium', (2006) 29 *West European Politics* 886; Ilke Adam, 'Defying the traditional theses: Intergovernmental relations on immigrant integration in Belgium', (2019) 29 *Regional & Federal Studies* 591

11 Maja Sahadžić, *Asymmetry, Multinationalism and Constitutional Law* (Routledge 2020) 160–161, 164.

12 Jan Erk and Alain-G. Gagnon, 'Constitutional ambiguity and federal trust: Codification of federalism in Canada, Spain and Belgium', (2000) 10 Regional & Federal Studies 94.

Appendix: The Belgian showcase

In what follows:

- 'converted scores' are the scores of subdivisions (A, B, C, …) that are brought down to the same factor as the first subdivision. This way, all subdivisions have equal weight;
- 'value' is the total score brought down to factor 1;
- the more detailed indexes for each dimension are followed by an overall table;
- the term 'Flemish Community (FLC)' points to the entity that holds the competences of both the FLC and the Flemish Region, since the merger of institutions.

1 STATUS

Table A.1.1 Overview status Belgium – cohesion index

Category	*A*	*B*	*C*	*D*	*E*	*Total*	*Max*	*Value*
Constitutional self-identification	2	na	na	na	na	2	4	0.50
Constitutional reform	1	na	na	na	na	1	6	0.17
Subnational constitutional autonomy	0	na	na	na	na	0	5	0.00
The legislative level	1	na	na	na	na	1	4	0.25
The executive level	2	na	na	na	na	2	6	0.33
International treaties: central	1	na	na	na	na	1	7	0.14
International treaties: subnational	4	na	na	na	na	4	4	1.00
EU Treaties	1	na	na	na	na	1	7	0.14
EU Council of Ministers	4	na	na	na	na	4	5	0,80
The organization of courts	3	na	na	na	na	3	3	1.00
Total								**0.43**

Table A.1.2 Overview status FLC – autonomy index

Category	*A*	*B*	*C*	*D*	*E*	*Converted total*	*Converted max*	*Value*
Constitutional self-identification	3	1	na	na	na	4	8	0.50
Constitutional reform	7	na	na	na	na	7	9	0.78
Subnational constitutional autonomy	1	3,75	na	na	na	4,75	10	0.53
The legislative level	5	6	na	na	na	11	14	0.78
The executive level	2	4	na	na	na	6	12	0.50
International treaties: central	4	na	na	na	na	4	5	0.92
International treaties: subnational	7	na	na	na	na	7	8	0.87
EU Treaties	5	na	na	na	na	5	5	1.00
EU Council of Ministers	8	na	na	na	na	8	8	1.00
The organization of courts	3	na	na	na	na	3	5	0.60
Total								**0.75**

Index

Table A.1.3 Overview status German-Speaking Community (GSC) – autonomy index

Category	*A*	*B*	*C*	*D*	*E*	*Total*	*Max*	*Value*
Constitutional self-identification	3	1	na	na	na	4	8	0.50
Constitutional reform	1	Na	na	na	na	1	9	0.11
Subnational constitutional autonomy	1	3,75	na	na	na	4,75	10	0.47
The legislative level	4	7	na	na	na	11	14	0.78
The executive level	1	6	na	na	na	7	12	0.58
International treaties: central	4	Na	na	na	na	4	5	0.80
International treaties: subnational	7	Na	na	na	na	7	8	0.87
EU Treaties	5	Na	na	na	na	5	5	1.00
EU Council of Ministers	8	Na	na	na	na	8	8	1.00
The organization of courts	0	Na	na	na	na	0	5	0.00
Total								**0.61**

1.1 Cohesion index

Table A.1.4 Detailed status Belgium – cohesion index

Constitutional self-identification	The constitutional act defines the system as a form of co-government	2
Constitutional reform	As a rule, the constitution is amended by institutional representatives of the SNEs and/or representatives of their electorates only	1
Subnational constitutions	There is no homogeneity clause	0
The legislative level	As a rule, laws are discussed and adopted by institutional representatives of the SNEs or their electorates only	1
The executive level	The executive council is accountable to bodies representative of the SNEs' electorates	1
	The executive council is composed in such a way that only particular groups with traits characteristic of SNEs are represented	1
International treaties concluded by the central government	As a rule, international treaties concluded by the central authority are approved by institutional representatives of the SNEs or representatives of their electorates only	1
International treaties concluded by the subnational government	The SNE can conclude international agreements but the central authorities can interfere to avoid that treaties are concluded that jeopardize the coherency of international policy or violate international obligations, conditional to intergovernmental dialogue	4
The European Union EU Treaties	As a rule, EU-treaties are approved by institutional representatives of the SNEs or representatives of their electorates only	1
The European Union Council of Ministers	The Member State's position is based on intergovernmental agreement, with a veto right for individual entities resulting in an abstention	2
	The Member State is represented in the Council by a mixed delegation	1
	There is room for reconsideration of the Member State's position after inter-governmental consultation	1
The organization of courts	A centrally organized court is the supreme court for all cases directly or indirectly related to central legislation and central constitutional law	2
	The centrally organized court is composed of judges that are, in terms of identity markers, representative for the (major) SNEs	1

1.2 Autonomy index

1.2.1 The Flemish Community

Table A.1.5 Detailed status FLC – autonomy index

Category	*Indicator*	*Application*	*Score*	*Converted total score*
Constitutional self-identification	A. Recognition	The particular SNE is recognized as autonomous constituent part of the system	3	3
	B. Secession	There is no (written or unwritten) secession clause	1	1
Constitutional reform	The individual SNE can veto constitutional reform		6	7
	The SNE can propose constitutional reform		1	
Subnational constitutions	A. Content	The SNE can make non-substantial arrangements in some of the 4 categories	1	1
	B. Procedure	The SNE can adopt its own constitution without central interference according to a procedure designed at the central level	3	3,75
The legislative level	A. Representation in the central lawmaking body	The electorate of the SNE can veto the law	4	5
		The SNE is consulted in matters that affect its interests or competences	1	
	B. Subnational representation	The SNE has a directly elected assembly	3	7
		The subnational assembly, as a rule, makes laws without central oversight	2	
		The SNE's lawmaking assembly cannot be dissolved by a central body	1	
The executive level	A. Representation in the central executive body	The SNE's electorate is indirectly represented in the central executive body through geographical or identitarian criteria that overlap with the SNE	1	2
		The SNE is consulted for matters that affect its interests or competences	1	
	B. Subnational representation	The SNE has an executive appointed by a subnational assembly or directly elected	2	6
		The subnational executive, as a rule, makes decisions without central oversight	2	

(*Continued*)

Table A.1.5 Detailed status FLC – autonomy index (*Continued*)

Category	*Indicator*	*Application*	*Score*	*Converted total score*
International treaties concluded by the central government		As a rule, the SNE can veto international treaties concluded by the central authority that affect subnational interests or competences	4	4
Subnational international treaties		The SNE has the power to conclude international agreements in all matters within their competences	5	7
		The SNE has the (additional) power to participate in trans-border institutions	1	
		The central authority's prior consent is not required to conclude these agreements	1	
EU Treaties		As a rule, the SNE can veto the conclusion of EU-treaties	4	5
		SNEs have to be kept informed of negotiation procedures for EU treaties	1	
EU Council of Ministers Council of Ministers		The SNE alone can strongly impact the Member State's position in the Council	4	8
		The SNE represents the Member State for (most) matters within its exclusive competences, as a rule or on a rotation basis	3	
		The Member State cannot change its position in the Council without consulting the SNE	1	
The organization of courts		Courts are organized at the central level, but in such a way that they are embedded within the subnational legal space	2	
		The SNE is represented in central courts that acts as last resort, through regional criteria or relevant identity markers, at least in panels that hear subnational cases	1	

1.2.2 The German-Speaking Community

Table A.1.6 Detailed status GSC – autonomy index

2. Category	*Indicator*	*Application*	*Score*	*Converted total score*
Constitutional self-identification	A. Recognition	The particular SNE is recognized as autonomous constituent part of the system	3	3
	B. Secession	There is no (written or unwritten) secession clause	1	1
Constitutional reform	The SNE can propose constitutional reform		1	1
Subnational constitutions	A. Content	The SNE can make non-substantial arrangements in some of the 4 categories	1	1
	B. Procedure	The SNE can adopt its own constitution without central interference according to a procedure designed at the central level	3	3,75
The legislative level	A. Representation in the central lawmaking body	The SNE alone can initiate or create hurdles	3	4
		The SNE is consulted in matters that affect its interests or competences	1	
	B. Subnational representation	The SNE has a directly elected assembly	3	7
		The subnational assembly, as a rule, makes laws without central oversight	2	
		The SNE's lawmaking assembly cannot be dissolved by a central body	1	
The executive level	A. Representation in the central executive body	The SNE is not represented in the central executive body and is not involved in its appointment	0	1
		The SNE is consulted for matters that affect its interests or competences	1	
	B. Subnational representation	The SNE has an executive appointed by a subnational assembly or directly elected	2	6
		The subnational executive, as a rule, makes decisions without central oversight	2	

(*Continued*)

Table A.1.6 Detailed status GSC – autonomy index (*Continued*)

2. Category *Indicator*	*Application*	*Score*	*Converted total score*
International treaties concluded by the central government	As a rule, the SNE can veto international treaties concluded by the central authority that affect subnational interests or competences	4	4
Subnational international treaties	The SNE has the power to conclude international agreements in all matters within their competences	5	7
	The SNE has the (additional) power to participate in trans-border institutions	1	
	The central authority's prior consent is not required to conclude these agreements	1	
EU Treaties	As a rule, the SNE can veto the conclusion of EU-treaties	4	5
	SNEs have to be kept informed of negotiation procedures for EU treaties	1	
EU Council of Ministers Council of Ministers	The SNE alone can strongly impact the Member State's position in the Council	4	8
	The SNE represents the Member State for (most) matters within its exclusive competences, as a rule or on a rotation basis	3	
	The Member State cannot change its position in the Council without consulting the SNE	1	
The organization of courts	Courts are entirely organized at the central level	0	0

2 POWERS

Table A.1.7 Overview powers Belgium – cohesion index

Topic	*A*	*B*	*C*	*D*	*E*	*Total*	*Max*	*Value*
Scope of powers	3	na	na	Na	na	3	3	1.00
Allocation techniques	0	na	na	Na	na	0	6	0.00
Allocation principles	4	na	na	Na	na	4	6	0.67
Political dispute resolution	3	na	na	Na	na	3	5	0.60
Judicial dispute resolution	2	na	na	Na	na	2	5	0.40
Total								**0.53**

Table A.1.8 Overview powers FLC – autonomy index

Topic	*A*	*B*	*C*	*D*	*E*	*Total*	*Max*	*Value*
Scope of powers	5	na	na	Na	na	5	6	0.83
Allocation techniques	6	na	na	Na	na	6	6	1.00
Allocation principles	10	na	na	Na	na	10	10	1.00
Political dispute resolution	5	na	na	Na	na	5	5	1.00
Judicial dispute resolution	6	na	na	Na	na	6	6	1.00
Total								**0.97**

Table A.1.9 Overview powers GSC – autonomy index

Topic	*A*	*B*	*C*	*D*	*E*	*Total*	*Max*	*Value*
Scope of powers	3	na	na	Na	na	3	6	0.50
Allocation techniques	6	na	na	Na	na	5	5	1.00
Allocation principles	10	na	na	Na	na	10	10	1.00
Political dispute resolution	4	na	na	Na	na	4	5	0.80
Judicial dispute resolution	3	na	na	Na	na	3	6	0.50
Total								**0.76**

2.1 Cohesion index

Table A.1.10 Detailed powers Belgium – cohesion index

Scope of powers	The central level has substantial powers in all categories of security, economic and monetary union, and solidarity	3
Allocation techniques	Powers are predominantly allocated on the basis of exclusivity	0
Allocation principles	There is a federal loyalty principle in place that comprises two of three components	2
	The federal loyalty principle binds both central and subnational authorities equally	2
Political dispute resolution	The political dispute resolution mechanism implies balanced intergovernmental dialogue	3
Judicial dispute resolution	The court is composed of judges appointed by the subnational authorities only	1
	The court, as a rule, decides in a mixed chamber	1

2.2 Autonomy index

2.2.1 The Flemish Community

Table A.1.11 Detailed powers FLC – autonomy index

Scope of powers	The SNE has substantial powers in four of the categories: economic purposes, political control, multinational conflict management, and territorial management	5
Allocation techniques	The SNE has mostly exclusive powers	5
	There is no central oversight	1
Allocation principles	The central government has no overriding powers targeting a particular SNE, to keep a particular SNE in line	10
Political dispute resolution	The particular SNE has a dominant position in the political dispute resolution mechanism	4
	The SNE can initiate the political dispute resolution mechanisms if the central authorities have harmed its interests or exceeded its competences, or are about to do so	1
Judicial dispute resolution	The SNE is involved in the appointment of judges, with an individual veto right	4
	In cases that affect the SNE, the court decides in a chamber with a judge that is, in terms of geography or identity markers, representative for the SNE	1
	The SNE has a substantial say in the rules that determine the functioning of the court	1

2.2.2 *The German-Speaking Community*

Table A.1.12 Detailed powers GSC – autonomy index

Scope of powers	The SNE has substantial powers in two of the categories: multinational conflict management and territorial management	3
Allocation techniques	The SNE has mostly exclusive powers	5
Allocation principles	The central government has no overriding powers targeting a particular SNE, to keep a particular SNE in line	10
Political dispute resolution	The political dispute resolution mechanism implies unbalanced intergovernmental dialogue, with a prominent representation for SNEs	3
	The SNE can initiate the political dispute resolution mechanisms if the central authorities have harmed its interests or exceeded its competences, or are about to do so	1
Judicial dispute resolution	The SNE is involved in the appointment of judges, through collective vote	3

3 FISCAL ARRANGEMENTS

Table A.1.13 Overview status Belgium – cohesion index

Category	*A*	*B*	*C*	*D*	*E*	*Converted total*	*Converted max*	*Value*
Equalization and other cohesive arrangements	3	3,43	na	na	na	6,43	8	0.80

Table A.1.14 Overview status FLC – autonomy index

Category	*A*	*B*	*C*	*D*	*E*	*Converted total*	*Converted max*	*Value*
Revenues and spending powers	6	5,33	8	6,67	7	33	40	0.82

Table A.1.15 Overview status GSC – autonomy index

Topic	*A*	*B*	*C*	*D*	*E*	*Converted Total*	*Converted Max*	*Value*
Revenues and spending powers	4	5,33	2,67	6,67	4	22,67	40	0.57

3.1 Cohesion index

Table A.1.16 Detailed fiscal arrangements Belgium – cohesion index

Category	*Application*	*Score*	*Converted total score*
A. Equalization mechanism	An equalization mechanism is in place, based on criteria that take into account subnational fiscal revenue capacity and needs	1	3
	Central equalization criteria are determined jointly by the central government and SNEs or their electorates	2	
B. Other cohesive arrangements	The central government has the power to raise taxes on mobile factors and tradeable goods as well as progressive redistributive taxes	2	3,43
	Fiscal discipline rules are in place to protect the stability of the common currency	1	
	Rules and procedures are in place to constrain horizontal double taxation	1	
	Other rules are in place to avoid unfair inter-regional tax competition	1	
	SNEs are prohibited to raise protectionist subnational taxes	1	

3.2 Autonomy index

3.2.1 The Flemish Community

Table A.1.17 Detailed fiscal arrangements FLC – autonomy index

Category	*Application*	*Score*	*Converted total score*
A. Subnational taxes	The SNE has the power to set the base and/or rate of at least one major tax (personal income, corporate, value added, or sale tax) with constraints set by the central authority	3	6
	The SNE has the power to introduce new taxes	1	
	The SNE has the power to set tax reliefs	1	
	The levying of specific taxes is reserved to the SNE	1	
B. Borrowing powers	The SNE has borrowing powers, subject to prior authorization	2	5,33
	Some of the substantive and procedural restrictions can only be imposed on a temporary basis	1	
	Most substantive or procedural restrictions can only be imposed after involvement of the SNE	1	
C. Shared tax revenue	The SNE alone can veto the law	6	8
D. Conditional grants	The central government can only issue general-purpose contributions	4	6,67
	Conditions can only be imposed after involvement of the SNE	1	
E. Fiscal discipline rules	The central government has no supervisory powers that limit the SNE's spending powers	4	7
	The SNE has a veto right for fiscal discipline rules imposed by the central government	3	

3.2.2 *The German-Speaking Community*

Table A.1.18 Detailed fiscal arrangements GSC – autonomy index

Category	*Application*	*Score*	*Converted total score*
A. Subnational taxes	The SNE has the power to set the base and/or rate of minor taxes only without limitations set by the central authority	2	4
	The SNE has the power to introduce new taxes	1	
	The SNE has the power to set tax reliefs	1	
B. Borrowing powers	The SNE has borrowing powers, subject to prior authorization	2	5,33
	Some of the substantive and procedural restrictions can only be imposed on a temporary basis	1	
	Most substantive or procedural restrictions can only be imposed after involvement of the SNE	1	
C. Shared tax revenue	The revenue split is determined by the central government only, but less frequently than once a year	2	2,67
D. Conditional grants	The central government can only issue general-purpose contributions	4	6,67
	Conditions can only be imposed after involvement of the SNE	1	
E. Fiscal discipline rules	The central government has no supervisory powers that limit the SNE's spending powers	4	4

4 OVERALL

Table A.1.19 Belgium – overall results

	Cohesion	*Autonomy FLC*	*Autonomy GSC*
Status	0.39	0.75	0.61
Powers	0.53	0.97	0.76
Fiscal Arrangements	0.80	0.82	0.57
Overall	**0.57 (M)**	**0.85 (H)**	**0.65 (M)**

Bibliography

Agranoff, R., 'Power Shifts, Diversity and Asymmetry', in R. Agranoff (eds), *Accomodating Diversity: Asymmetry in Federal States* (Nomos 1999)

Alber, E., 'Intergovernmental Financial Relations: Institutions, Rules and Praxis', in A. Valdesalici and F. Palermo (eds), *Comparing Fiscal Federalism* (Brill 2018)

Albert, R., 'The structure of constitutional amendment rules', (2014) *Wake Forrest L Rev.* 913–976

Albert, R., *Constitutional Amendments. Making, Breaking, and Changing Constitutions* (Oxford University Press 2019)

Ambrosanio, M.F., P. Balduzzi and C. Peiti, 'Accountability and Revenue Assignment across Levels of Government: Rules, Practices and Challenges', in A. Valdesalici and F. Palermo (eds), *Comparing Fiscal Federalism* (Brill 2018)

Antonio Rodrigues, G.M., M.A. Garcia Lopes Lorencini and A. Zimmerman, 'The Supreme Federal Court of Brazil: Protecting Democracy and Centralized Power', in N. Aroney and J. Kincaid (eds), *Courts in Federal Countries. Federalists or Regionalists?* (University of Toronto Press 2017)

Arlota, C. and N. Garoupa, 'Addressing federal conflicts: an empirical analysis of the Brazilian supreme court, 1988-2010' (2014) 10 *Review of Law and Economics* 137–168

Aroney, N., 'Formation, representation and amendment in federal constitutions', (2006) 54 *Am. J. Comp. L.* 277–336

Aroney, N., 'The High Court of Australia: Textual Unitarism vs Structural Federalism', in N. Aroney and J. Kincaid (eds), *Courts in Federal Countries: Federalists or Regionalists?* (University of Toronto Press 2017)

Aroney, N. and J. Kincaid (eds), *Courts in Federal Countries: Federalists or Regionalists?* (University of Toronto Press 2017)

Aubert, J.-F., 'Essai sur le fédéralisme' (1963) *Revue de droit public* 401–452

Baier, G., 'Canada: Federal and Sub-national Constitutional Practices', in M. Burgess and G. Alan Tarr, *Constitutional Dynamics in Federal Systems. Subnational Perspectives* (Montreal & Kingston, McGill-Queen's University Press 2012)

Baldi, B., *Federalism by degree* (Working Paper Institute of Governmental Studies, University of California, 1999)

Bammarny, B., 'Federalism and Decentralisation in Iraq. A Country Study of Constitutional Asymmetry in Iraq', in P. Popelier and M. Sahadžić (eds), *Constitutional Asymmetry in Multinational Federalism* (Palgrave MacMillan 2019)

Barnett, R.E., 'Three Federalisms', (2008) 39 *Loy. U. Chi. L. J.* 285–294

Barrero Ortega, A. and I. Sabrino Guijarro, 'Constitutional Change in Spain', in X. Contiades (ed), *Engineering Constitutional Change* (Routledge 2013)

Basta Fleiner, L.R. and J.-F. Gaudreault-DesBiens, 'Federalism and Autonomy', in M. Tushnet, T. Fleiner and C. Saunders (eds), *Routledge Handbook of Constitutional Law* (London, Routledge 2015)

Baybeck, B. and W. Lowry, 'Federalism Outcomes and Ideological Preferences: The U.S. Supreme Court and Preemption Cases' (2000) 30 *Publius: The Journal of Federalism* 73–97

Bednar, J., 'Constitutional Change in Federations: the Role of Complementary Institutions', in A. Benz and J. Broschek (eds), *Federal Dynamics. Continuity, Change & the Varieties of Federalism* (Oxford University Press 2013)

Bednar, J., 'Federalism Theory: the Boundary Problem, Robustness and Dynamics', in J. Kincaid (ed), *A Research Agenda for Federalism Studies* (Edward Elgar 2019)

Behnke, N. and A. Benz, 'The Politics of Constitutional Change between Reform and Evolution' (2009) 39 *Publius: the Journal of Federalism* 213–240

Béland, D. and A. Lecours, 'Federalism, Nationalist Politics, and Social Policy: How Ideas and Institutions Shape Federal Dynamics', in A. Benz and J. Broschek (eds), *Federal Dynamics. Continuity, Change & the Varieties of Federalism* (Oxford University Press 2013)

Belser, E.M., 'Concurrent Powers as Doors to Legislative Innovation, Conditional Powers as Gates to the Blind Alley: Some Swiss Illustrations', in N. Steytler (ed), *Concurrent Powers in Federal Systems. Meaning, Making, Managing* (Brill Nijhoff 2017)

Benz, A., 'Dimensions and Dynamics of Federal Regimes', in A. Benz and J. Broschek (eds), *Federal Dynamics. Continuity, Change & the Varieties of Federalism* (Oxford University Press 2013)

Benz, A., 'The Federal Constitutional Court of Germany: Guardian of Unitarism and Federalism', in N. Aroney and J. Kincaid (eds), *Courts in Federal Countries: Federalists or Regionalists?* (University of Toronto Press 2017)

Benz, A. and J. Broschek (eds), *Federal Dynamics. Continuity, Change & the Varieties of Federalism* (Oxford University Press 2013)

Benz, A. and J. Broschek, 'Federal Dynamics: Introduction', in A. Benz and J. Broschek (eds), *Federal Dynamics. Continuity, Change & the Varieties of Federalism* (Oxford University Press 2013)

Benz and J. Broschek, 'Conclusion: Theorizing federal dynamics', in A. Benz and J. Broschek (eds), *Federal Dynamics. Continuity, Change & the Varieties of Federalism* (Oxford University Press 2013)

Beyers, J. and P. Bursens, 'The European rescue of the federal state: how Europeanization shapes the Belgian state' (2006) 29 *West European Politics* 1057–1078

Bhattacharyya, *Federalism in Asia* (Routledge 2010)

Bhattacharyya, H., 'Federalism in Asia: Beyond the Diversity Problematic', in J. Kincaid (ed), *A Research Agenda for Federalism Studies* (Edward Elgar 2019)

Biaggini, G., 'Switzerland', in D. Oliver and C. Fusaro (eds), *How Constitutions Change. A Comparative Study* (Oxford, Hart 2011)

Birch, A.H., 'Approaches to the Study of Federalism', (1966) XIV *Political studies* 15–33, reprinted in J. Kincaid (ed), *Federalism* (Sage 2011, Vol. 1)

Boldt, H., 'Ending Consociational Power-Sharing. The Sejdic and Finci Case and the Prospects for Constitutional Reform in Bosnia and Herzegovina', (2012) 6 *Vienna Online J. on Internat. Const. L.* 489–547

Borońska-Hryniewiecka, K., 'Regions and subsidiarity after the Treaty of Lisbon: overcoming the "regional blindness"?', in M. Cartabia, N. Lupo and A. Simoncini (eds), *Democracy and Subsidiarity in the EU* (Bologna, Il Mulino, Bologna 2013)

Bosire, C.M. 'The courts and devolution. The Kenyan experience', in Y.T. Fessha and K. Kössler (eds), *Federalism and the courts in Africa* (Routledge 2020)

Bossacoma Busquets, P., *Morality and Legality of Secession* (Palgrave MacMillan 2020)

Bossacoma Busquets, P. and Marc Sanjaume-Calvet, 'Asymmetry as a Device for Equal Recognition and Reasonable Accommodation of Majority and Minority Nations. A Country Study on Constitutional Asymmetry in Spain', in P. Popelier and M. Sahadžić (eds), *Constitutional Asymmetry in Multinational Federalism* (Palgrave MacMillan 2019)

Braun, D. and P. Trein, 'Federal Dynamics in Times of Economic and Financial Crisis', (2014) 53 *Eu.J.Pol.Research* 803–821

Braun, D. and P. Trein, 'Economic Crisis and Federal Dynamics', in A. Benz and J. Broschek (eds), *Federal Dynamics. Continuity, Change & the Varieties of Federalism* (Oxford University Press 2013)

Breen, M.G., 'Asymmetry or Equality? Ethnic Nationalities in a Bamar-Dominated State', in P. Popelier and M. Sahadžić (eds), *Constitutional Asymmetry in Multinational Federalism* (Palgrave MacMillan 2019)

Bronstein, V., 'The courts and the provinces in South Africa', in Y.T. Fessha and K. Kössler (eds), *Federalism and the courts in Africa. Design and impact in comparative perspective* (Routledge 2020)

Brouillet, E., 'The Supreme Court of Canada: the Concept of Cooperative Federalism and its Effect on the Balance of Power', in N. Aroney and J. Kincaid (eds), *Courts in Federal Countries: Federalists or Regionalists?* (University of Toronto Press 2017)

Broschek, 'Conceptualizing and theorizing constitutional change in federal systems. Insights from historical institutionalism', (2011) 21 *Regional and Federal Studies* 539–559

Broschek, J., 'Between Path dependence and gradual change: Historical institutionalism and the study of federal dynamics', in A. Benz and J. Broschek (eds), *Federal Dynamics. Continuity, Change & the Varieties of Federalism* (Oxford University Press 2013)

Brosio, G. and J.P. Jiménez, 'Federalism and Oil: the Challenges of Intergovernmental Revenue-sharing in Argentina and Brazil', in G. Pola (ed), *Principles and Practices of Fiscal Autonomy* (Ashgate 2015, reissue Routledge 2017)

Bulmer, S., M. Burch, P. Hogwood and A. Scott, 'UK Devolution and the European Union: a tale of cooperative asymmetry?' (2006) 36 *Publius: The Journal of Federalism* 75–93

Burgess, M., *Comparative Federalism: Theory and Practice* (London, Routledge, 2006)

Burgess, M., *In Search of the Federal Spirit* (Oxford University Press 2012)

Burgess, M., 'The Penumbra of Federalism', in J. Loughlin, J. Kincaid and W. Swenden (eds), Routledge Handbook of Regionalism and Federalism (Routledge 2013)

Burgess, M. and J. Pinder (eds), *Multinational Federations* (London-New York, Routledge, 2007)

Burgess, M. and G.A. Tarr (eds), *Constitutional Dynamics in Federal Systems. Sub-national Perspectives* (McGill-Queen's University Press 2012)

Burgess, M. and G. Alan Tarr, 'Introduction: Sub-national Constitutionalism and Constitutional Development', in M. Burgess and G. Alan Tarr (eds), *Constitutional Dynamics in Federal Systems. Subnational Perspectives* (Montreal & Kingston, McGill-Queen's University Press 2012)

Bursens, P., 'Het Europese beleid in de Belgische federatie', (2005) LV *Res Publica* 58–79

Butt, S., 'Provincial Asymmetry in Indonesia: What Is so 'Special' About It? A Country Study of Constitutional Asymmetry in Indonesia', in P. Popelier and M. Sahadžić (eds), *Constitutional Asymmetry in Multinational Federalism* (Palgrave MacMillan 2019)

Bzdera, A., 'Comparative Analysis of Federal High Courts: A Political Theory of Judicial Review' (1993) 26 *Canadian J of Pol. Sc.* 3–29
Cameron, D., 'The Paradox of Federalism: Some Practical Reflections', in J. Erk and L. M. Anderson (eds), *The Paradox of Federalism* (Routledge 2010).
Cameron, M.A. and T.G. Falleti, 'Federalism and the Subnational Separation of Powers', (2005) *Publius: the Journal of Federalism* 245–271
Della Cananea, G., 'Is European Constitutionalism Really "Multilevel"?' (2010) 70 *Zeitschrift für ausländisches öffentliches Recht und Völkerrecht*, 283–317
Cantillon, B., P. Popelier and N. Mussche (eds), *Social Federalism: The Creation of a Layered Welfare State* (Intersentia 2011).
Casanas Adam, E., 'The Constitutional Court of Spain: From System Balancer to Polarizing Centralist', in N. Aroney and J. Kincaid (eds), *Courts in Federal Countries. Federalists or Regionalists?* (University of Toronto Press 2017) 367–403
Castells, A., 'Catalonia and Spain at the crossroads: financial and economic aspects' (2014) 30 *Oxford Review of Economic Policy* 277–296
Castells, A., 'The Relation Catalonia/Spain: Some Financial and Economic Aspects', in G. Pola (ed), *Principles and Practices of Fiscal Autonomy* (Asgate 2015, reissued Routledge 2017)
Chemerinsky, E., 'Cases under the guarantee clause should be justiciable' (1994) 65 *U.Colo.L.Rev.* 849–880
Chemerinsky, E., 'The Values of Federalism', (1995) 47 *Florida L.Rev.* 499–540
Choper, J.H., 'The Scope of National Power Vis-à-vis the States: Dispensability of Judicial Review', (1977) 86 *Yale L Journal* 1552–1621
Choudry, S. and N. Hume, 'Federalism, devolution and secession: from classical to post-conflict federalism', in T. Ginsburg and R. Dixon (eds), *Comparative Constitutional Law* (Cheltenham, Edward Elgar 2011)
Cochrane, F., N. Loizides and T. Bodson, *Mediating Power Sharing* (Routledge 2018)
Cohn, M. and M. Kremnitzer, 'Judicial Activism: A Multidimensional Model', (2005) 18 *Can. J.L. & Juris* 333–356
Colino, C., 'Constitutional Change without Constitutional Reform: Spanish Federalism and the Revision of Catalonia's Statute of Autonomy', (2009) 39 *Publius; the Journal of Federalism* 262–288
Colino, C., 'Introduction: the study of change in federations', in J. Erk and W. Swenden (eds), *New directions in federalism studies* (2010)
Colino, C., 'Varieties of federalism and propensities for change', in A. Benz and J. Broschek (eds), *Federal Dynamics. Continuity, Change & the Varieties of Federalism* (Oxford University Press 2013)
Collins P.M. Jr., 'Towards an integrated model of the U.S. Supreme Court's federalism decision making' (2007) 37 *Publius: The Journal of Federalism* 505–531
Collins R.B., 'Economic Union as a Constitutional Value' (1988) 63 *NYU L. Rev* 43–130
Contiades, X. (ed), *Engineering Constitutional Change* (Routledge 2013)
Contiades, X., 'Constitutional Change Engineering', in X. Contiades (ed), *Engineering Constitutional Change* (Routledge 2013)
Contiades, X. and A. Fatiadou, 'Models of Constitutional Change', in X. Contiades (ed), *Engineering Constitutional Change* (London, Routledge 2013)
Couwenberg, S.W., 'Staatsvorming, soevereiniteit en subsidiariteit', in J. Velaers (ed), *Publiek Recht, Ruim Bekeken* (Maklu 1994)

Cross, F.B. and Emerson H Tiller, 'The three faces of federalism: an empirical assessment of Supreme Court federalism jurisprudence' (2000) 73 *Southern California Law Review* 741–771

Dafflon, B., 'Swiss Fiscal Federalism: New Roads after the Reforms of the Constitution', in G. Pola (ed), *Principles and Practices of Fiscal Autonomy* (Asgate 2015, reissued Routledge 2017)

Dahl, R., *Democracy, Liberty, and Equality* (Norwegian University Press, 1986)

Dalla Pellegrina, L. and N. Garoupa, 'Choosing between the government and the regions: an empirical analysis of the Italian Constitutional Court decisions, (2013) 52 *European Journal of Political Research*, 558–580

Dalla Pellegrina, L., J. De Mot, M. Faure and N. Garoupa, 'Litigating Federalism: An Empirical Analysis of Decisions of the Belgian Constitutional Court', (2016) 13 *European Constitutional Law Rev*, 305–346

Dardanelli, P. *et al.*, 'Dynamic Decentralization in Federations: Comparative Conclusions' (2018) 49 *Publius: the Journal of Federalism* 194–219

Dardanelli, P., 'Decentralization', in J. Kincaid (ed), *A Research Agenda for Federalism Studies* (Edward Elgar 2019)

De Baere G. and T. Roes, 'EU loyalty as good faith', (2015) 64 *ICLQ* 829–874

Delaney, E.F. 'Judicial Federalism in Comparative Perspective', in Y.T. Fessha and K. Kössler (eds), *Federalism and the courts in Africa. Design and impact in comparative perspective* (Routledge 2020)

Deschouwer, 'The Rise and Fall of the Belgian Regionalist Parties', (2009) 19 *Regional and Federal Studies* 559–577

De Sousa, L., 'Understanding European Cross-border Cooperation: A Framework for Analysis' (2013) 35 *Journal of European Integration* 669–687

De Visser, J., 'Concurrent Powers in South Africa' in N. Steytler (ed), *Concurrent Powers in Federal Systems. Meaning, Making, Managing* (Brill Nijhoff 2017)

De Witte, B., 'The European Treaty Amendment for the Creation of a Financial Stability Mechanism', (2011) 6 *European Policy Analysis* 1–8

Diamond, M., 'The Ends of Federalism', (1973) 3 *Publius: the Journal of Federalism*, 129–152.

Dicey, A.V. *Introduction to the study of the law of the constitution* (MacMillan, 1915, 8th ed.)

Dickovick, J.T., 'Municipalization as Central Government Strategy: Central–Regional-Local Politics in Peru, Brazil, and South Africa', (2006) 37 *Publius; the Journal of Federalism* 1–25

Dickovick, J.T., 'Federalism in Africa: Origins, Operation and (In)Significance', (2014) 24 *Regional & Federal Studies*, 553–570

Dickson, R., 'Work in Progress. A Country Study of Constitutional Asymmetry in the United Kingdom', in P. Popelier and M. Sahadžić (eds), *Constitutinal Asymmetry in Multinatinoal Federalism* (Palgrave Macmillan 2019)

Dietze, G., 'Hamilton's Federalist – Treatise for Free Government' (1957) 42 *Cornell Law Quarterly*, 307–328

Dinan, J., 'The rehnquist court's federalism decisions in perspective' (1999) 15 *Journal of Law and Politics* 127–194

Dinan, J., 'State Constitutions and American Political Development', in M. Burgess and G. Alan Tarr (eds), *Constitutional Dynamics in Federal Systems. Subnational Perspectives* (Montreal & Kingston, McGill-Queen's University Press 2012)

Dixon, R., 'Updating constitutional rules', (2009) *Supreme Court Rev.* 319–346

Dixon, R., 'Constitutional Amendment Rules: A Comparative Perspective', in Tom Gonsburg and Rosalind Dixon (eds), *Comparative Constitutional Law* (Edward Elgar 2011)
Doria, G., 'The Paradox of Federal Bicameralism' (2006) 5 *European Diversity and Autonomy Papers* 1–43
Dougherty, S., M. Harding and A. Reschovsky, *Twenty years of tax autonomy across levels of government: measurement and applications*, OECD Working Papers on Fiscal Federalism N° 29 (OECD Fiscal Network, 2019)
Duchacek, I., *Comparative Federalism: The Territorial Dimension of Politics* (New York, Holt, Rinehart and Winston 1970, reissued by University Press of America, 1987)
Duchacek, I., 'Consociational Cradle of Federalism', (1985) 15 *Publius: the Journal of Federalism* 35–48
Dumbrovský, T., B. Petkova and M. Van der Sluis, 'Judicial Appointments: The Article 255 TFEU Advisory Panel and Selection Procedures in the Member States', (2014) 51 *Common Market L. Rev.* 455–482
Dziedzic, A. and C. Saunders, 'The Meanings of Concurrency', in N. Steytler (ed), *Concurrent Powers in Federal Systems. Meaning, Making, Managing* (Brill Nijhoff 2017)
Elazar, D.J. 'Federalism vs Decentralization: the Drift from Authenticity', (1976) 6 *Publius: the Journal of Federalism* 9–19
Elazar, D.J., 'The Political Theory of Covenant: Biblical Origins and Modern Developments', (1980) 10 *Publius: the Joirnal of Federalism* 3–30
Elazar, D.J., 'Federalism and Consociational Regimes'. (1985) 15 *Publius: the Journal of Federaliusm* 17–34
Elazar, D.J. *Exploring Federalism* (University of Alabama Press, 1987 – ed. 1991)
Elazar, D.J., *Constitutionalizing Globalization: The Postmodern Revival of Confederal Arrangements* (Rowman & Littlefield Publishers 1998)
Elazar, D.J., 'The New Europe: a Federal State or a Confederation of States?', (1998) 4 *Swiss Pol. Sc. Rev.* 119–138
Elvira, A., 'Spain', in D. Oliver and C. Fusaro (eds), *How Constitutions Change. A Comparative Study* (Oxford, Hart 2011)
Erk, J., *Explaining Federalism. State, society and congruence in Austria, Belgium, Canada, Germany and Switzerland* (Routledge 2008)
Erk, J., 'Federalism and Decentralization in Sub-Saharan Africa: Five Patterns of Evolution', (2014) 24 Regional & Federal Studies, 535–552
Erk, J., 'Still in Search of the Federal Spirit: The US Supreme Court and Federalism', in A.-G. Gagnon, S. Keil and S. Mueller (eds), *Understanding Federalism and Federation* (Routledge 2015)
Erk, J. and L.M. Anderson (eds), *The Paradox of Federalism. Does Self-Rule Accommodate or Exacerbate Ethnic Divisions?* (Routledge 2010)
Erk, J. and L. Anderson, 'The Paradox of Federalism: Does Self-Rule Accommodate or Exacerbate Ethnic Divisions?', in J. Erk and L.M. Anderson (eds), *Thee Paradox of Federalism* (Routledge 2010)
Erk, J. and A-G. Gagnon, 'Constitutional ambiguity and federal trust: codification of federalism in Canada, Spain and Belgium', (2000) 10 *Regional & Federal Studies* 92–111
Erk, J. and E. Koning, 'New Structuralism and Institutional Change: Federalism between Centralization and Decentralization', (2010) 43 *Comp. Pol. Studies* 353–378
Erk, J. and W. Swenden (eds), *New Directions in Federalism Studies* (Routledge 2010)
Erk, J. and W. Swenden, 'The new wave of federalism studies', in J. Erk and W. Swenden (eds), *New Directions in Federalism Studies* (Routledge 2010)

Esman, M.J., 'Federalism and Modernization: Canada and the United States', (1984) 14 *Publius* 21–38

Fabbrini, F., 'The Fiscal Compact, the Golden Rule, and the Paradox of European Federalism' (2013) 36 *Boston College Int'l & Comp L Rev* 1–38

Färber, G., 'Taxing Powers of Subnational Entities: Between Domestic and Supranational Constraints', in A. Valdesalici and F. Palermo (eds), *Comparing Fiscal Federalism* (Brill 2018)

Fasone, C., 'What Role for Regional Assemblies in Regional States? Italy, Spain and the United Kingdom in Comparative Perspective', (2012) 4 *Perspectives on Federalism* 171–216

Ferejohn J. and P. Pasquino, 'The Law of Exception: A typology of Emergency Powers', (2004) 2 I.CON 210–239

Ferreras Comella, V., 'The consequences of centralizing constitutional review in a constitutional court: some thoughts on judicial activism', (2003–2004) 82 *Texas L. Rev.* 1705–1736

Ferreres Comella, V., *The Constitution of Spain* (Oxford, Hart 2013)

Ferreras Comella, V., 'The Spanish constitutional court confronts catalonia's right to decide (Comment on the Judgment 42/2014)' (2014) 571–590

Fessha, Y.T., 'Constitutional Déjà vu: Reading Subnational Constitutions in Ethiopia', in P. Popelier, G. Delledonne and N. Aroney (eds), *The Routledge Handbook of Subnational Constitutions and Constitutionalism* (Routledge 2021).

Fessha, Y.T. and Z. Ayele, 'Giving 'shape and texture' to a federal system? Ethiopia's courts and its unusual umpire', in Y.T. Fessha and K. Kössler (eds), *Federalism and the courts in Africa. Design and impact in comparative perspective* (Routledge 2020)

Fessha, Y.T. and Biniyam N Bezahib, 'Federation among Unequals', in P. Popelier and M. Sahadžić (eds), *Constitutinal Asymmetry in Multinatinoal Federalism* (Palgrave Macmillan 2019)

Fessha, Y.T. and K. Kössler (eds), *Federalism and the Courts in Africa. Design and Impact in Comparative Perspective* (Routledge 2020)

Filippov, M., P.C. Ordeshook and O. Shvetsova, *Designing Federalism* (Cambridge University Press 2004)

Fiseha, A. and Z. Ayele, 'Concurrent Powers in the Ethiopian Federal System', in N. Steytler (ed), *Concurrent Powers in Federal Systems. Meaning, Making, Managing* (Brill Nijhoff 2017)

Fleiner, T., 'Constitutional Revision. The Case of Switzerland', in X. Contiades (ed), *Engineering Constitutional Change* (London, Routledge 2013)

Forbath, 'The politics of constitutional amendment: obduracy and amendability – a comment on Ferejohn and Sager' (2003) *Texas Law Review* 1965–1984

Fossum, E. and M. Jachtenfuchs, 'Federal challenges and challenges to federalism' (2017) 24 *J of Eu Public Policy* 467–485

Fuo, O, 'The courts and local governments in South Africa', in Y.T. Fessha and K. Kössler (eds), *Federalism and the courts in Africa. Design and impact in comparative perspective* (Routledge 2020)

Frey B.S. and I. Bohnet, 'Democracy by competition: referenda and federalism in Switzerland', (1993) 23 *Publius: the Journal of Federalism* 71–80.

Friedrich C.J. 'New tendencies in federal theory and practice', (1965) 14 Jahrbuch des Öffentliches Rechts 1–14

Friedrich C.J. *Constitutional Government and Democracy: Theory and Practice in Europe and America* (Blaisdell Publishing Company 1968)

Friedrich C.J. *Trends of Federalism in Theory and Practice* (Frederick A. Praeger 1968)

Gabriel Carranza, G., 'Subnational constitutionalism in Spain', in P. Popelier, G. Delledonne and N. Aroney (eds), *The Routledge Handbook of Subnational Constitutions and Constitutionalism* (Routledge 2021).
Gagnon, A.-G., *The Case for Multinational Federalism* (Routledge 2010)
Gagnon A.-G. and A. Tremblay; 'Federalism and diversity: a new research agenda', in J. Kincaid (ed), *A Research Agenda for Federalism Studies* (Edward Elgar 2019)
Gamper, A., 'Homogeneity and democracy in Austrian federalism: the constitutional court's ruling on direct democracy in Vorarlberg' (2003) 33 *Publius: the Journal of Federalism* 45–57
Gamper A., 'A 'global theory of federalism'? The nature and challenges of a Federal State' (2005) 6 *German Law Journal* 1297–1318
Gamper, A., 'On Loyalty and the (Federal) Constitution', (2010) 4 *Vienna Online J. on Int'l Const. L.* 157–170
García Morales, M.J., 'Federal execution, article 155 of the Spanish Constitution and the crisis in Catalonia' (2018) 73 Zeitschrift für Öffentliches Recht 791–830
Gardner, J., 'In Search of Sub-National Constitutionalism', (2008) 4 *Eu.Const.L.Rev.* 325–343
Gardner, J., 'The Theory and Practice of Contestatory Federalism', (2018) 60 *William & Mary L. Rev.*, 507–588
Gardner, J., 'Subnational constitutionalism in the United States', in P. Popelier, G. Delledonne and N. Aroney (eds), *The Routledge Handbook of Subnational Constitutions and Constitutionalism* (Routledge 2021)
Garoupa, N., 'Comparing Judicial Activism – Can We Say that the US Supreme Court is more Activist than the German Constitutional Court?' (2016) 72 *Revista Portuguesa de Filosofia* 1089–1106
Garoupa, N., F. Gomez-Pomar and V. Grembi. 'Judging under Political Pressure: An Empirical Analysis of Constitutional Review Voting in the Spanish Constitutional Court' (2011) 29 *Journal of Law, Economics and Organization* 513–534
Gaudreault-DesBiens, J-F. 'Cooperative Federalism in Search of a Normative Justification: Considering the Principle of Federal Loyalty' (2014) 23 Const Forum, 1–19
Gaudreault-Desbiens, J.-F. and F. Gélinas, 'Prolégomènes à une étude renouvelée du fédéralisme', in J.-F. Gaudreault-Desbiens and F. Gélinas (eds), *Le fédéralisme dans tous ses états* (Brussels, Bruylant 2005)
Ginsburg, T. and J. Melton, 'Does the constitutional amendment rule matter at all? Amendment cultures and the challenges of measuring amendment difficulty', (2015) 13 *International Constitutional Law Review* 686–713
Graziadei, S., 'Power Sharing Courts', (2016) 3 Contemporary Southeastern Europe, 66–105
Graziadei, S., 'Democracy v Human Rights? The Strasbourg Court and the Challenge of Power Sharing', (2016) 12 *Eu. Const. L. Rev.*
Grewe, C., 'Methods of identification of national constitutional identity', in A. Saiz Arnaiz and C. Alcoberro Llivina (eds), *National Constitutional Identity and European Integration* (Cambridge, Intersentia 2013)
Griffin, S.M., 'Constitutional Theory Transformed', (1999) 108 *Yale L.J.* 2115–2164
Grimm, D., 'What Exactly is Political about Constitutional Adjudication?', in Christine Landfried (ed), *Judicial Power. How Constitutional Courts Affect Political Transformations* (Cambridge University Press 2019)
Groppi, T., 'Constitutional Revision in Italy', in X. Contiades (ed), *Engineering Constitutional Change* (London, Routledge 2013)

Gunlicks, A., *The Länder and German Federalism* (Manchester University Press 2003)

Gunlicks, A.B., 'Legislative Competences, Budgetary Constraints, and the Reform of Federalism in Germany from the Top Down and the Bottom Up', in M. Burgess and G.A. Tarr (eds), *Constitutional Dynamics in Federal Systems* (McGill-Queen's University Press 2012)

Haag, M., 'Horizontal Tax Coordination: The Canadian Perspective and a Few General Observations', in M. Lang, P. Pistone, J. Schuch and C. Staringer (eds), *Horizontal Tax Coordination* (IBFD 2012)

Häberle, P., 'Legal comparison for constitutional development – the relevance of federalism and regionalism', in Luther Jörg., Passaglia Paolo and Tarchi Rolando (eds), *A world of second chambers* (Giuffrè Editore, 2006)

Habtu, A., 'Multiethnic Federalism in Ethiopia: A Study of the Secession Clause in the Constitution', (2005) *Publius: the Journal of Federalism* 313–335

Halberstam, D., 'The foreign affairs of federal systems: national perspective on the benefits of state participation' Villanova Law Review (2001) 46 (5), 1015–1068

Halberstam, D., 'Comparative Federalism and the Role of the Judiciary', in K.E. Whittington, R.D. Kelemen and G.A. Caldeira (eds), *The Oxford Handbook of Law and Politics* (Oxford, Oxford University Press 2010)

Halberstam, D., 'Federalism: History, Policy, Law' in M. Rosenfeld and A. Sajo (eds), *The Oxford Handbook of Comparative Constitutional Law* (Oxford University Press 2012)

Halberstam, D. and R.M. Hills, 'State Autonomy in Germany and the United States', (2001) *Annals AAPSS* 173–184

Hazell, R. and A. Renwick, *Brexit: Its Consequences for Devolution and the Union*, UCL Constitution Unit Briefing Paper (UCL 2016)

Hellerstein, W., 'Tax Coordination between the US States – The Role of the Courts', in M. Lang, P. Pistone, J. Schuch and C. Staringer (eds), *Horizontal Tax Coordination* (IBFD 2012)

Hessebon, G.T. and A.K. Idris, 'The Supreme Court of Ethiopia: Federalism's Bystander', in N. Aroney and J. Kincaid (eds), *Courts in Federal Countries. Federalists or Regionalists?* (University of Toronto Press 2017)

Heun, W., *The Constitution of Germany. A Contextual Analysis* (Hart 2011)

Hoetjes, B.J.S., 'Federaties en federalisme. Een raamwerk voor theorie en onderzoek', (1978) 20 *Res Publica* 33–57.

Hombrado, A., 'Learning to Catch the Wave? Regional Demands for Constitutional Change in Contexts of Asymmetrical Arrangements', (2011) 21 Regional & Federal Studies, 479–501

Hooghe, L., G. Marks and A.H. Schakel, *The rise of regional authority: a comparative study of 42 countries* (Routledge 2010)

Hooghe, L, G. Marks, A.H. Schakel, S. Niedzwiecki, S. Chapman Osterkatz and S. Shair-Rosenfield, *Measuring Regional Authority: A Postfunctionalist Theory of Governance. Volume 1* (Oxford University Press 2016)

Hueglin, T.O., *A political economy of federalism: in search of a new comparative perspective with critical intent throughout* (1990 Queen's University Institute of Intergovernmental relations)

Hueglin, T.O., 'Comparing federalism: Variations or distinct models?', in A. Benz and J. Broschek (eds), *Federal Dynamics. Continuity, Change & the Varieties of Federalism* (Oxford University Press 2013)

Hueglin, T.O. and A. Fenna, *Comparative Federalism. A Systematic Inquiry* (Ontario, Broadview Press 2006)

Hueglin, T.O., 'Federalism and political theory: a case of mutual neglect', in J. Kincaid (ed), *A Research Agenda for Federalism Studies* (Edward Elgar 2019)

Hutchinson, A., 'Constitutional Change and Constitutional Amendment', in X. Contiades (ed), *Engineering Constitutional Change* (London, Routledge 2013)

Inman, R., 'Federalism's Values and the Value of Federalism', (2007) 53 *CESifo Economic Studies* 522–560, reprinted in Kincaid, *Federalism*, Vol. 1

Issacharoff, S., 'Democracy and Collective Decision Making', (2008) 6 *I-CON* 231–266

Ivanyna, M. and A. Shah, *How Close is Your Government to Its People? Worldwide Indicators on Localization and Decentralization*, World Bank Policy Research Working Paper N° 6138 (World Bank 2012)

Jackson, V.C., 'Comparative Constitutional Federalism: Its Strengths and Limits', in J.-F. Gaudreault-Desbiens and F. Gélinas (eds), *Le fédéralisme dans tous ses états* (Brussels, Bruylant 2005)

Jackson, V.C., 'The (myth of un)amendability of the US Constitution and the democratic component of constitutionalism', (2015) 13 *International Jurnal of Constitutional Law* 575–605

Jakab, A. and V. Lórincz, *International Indices as Models for the Rule of Law Scoreboard of the European Union: Methodological Issues*, MPIL Research Papers Series No 2017–21 (Max Planck Institute 2017)

Janoski, T. and B. Gran, 'Political Citizenship: Foundations of Rights', in E.F. Isin and B.S. Turner (eds), *Handbook of Citizenship Studies* (Sage Publications 2002)

Jewkes, M., 'Theorising federal togetherness in multinational states', (2015) 15 *Ethnicities* 323–340

Kahana, T., 'Canada', in D. Oliver and C. Fusaro (eds), *How Constitutions Change. A Comparative Study* (Oxford, Hart 2011)

Karlhofer, F. and G. Pallaver, 'Strength through weakness: state executive power and federal reform in Austria' (2013) 19 *Swiss Political Science Review* 41–59

Keating, M., 'Why no Federalism in the United Kingdom?', in A.-G. Gagnon, S. Keil and S. Mueller (eds), *Understanding Federalism and Federation* (2016)

Keating, M. 'Europe as a Multilevel Federation', (2017) 24 *J of Eu Public Policy* 615–632

Keil, S., 'Federalism as a Tool of Conflict Resolution', in J. Kincaid (ed), *A Research Agenda for Federalism Studies* (Edward Elgar 2019)

Kelemen, R.D. and Teo, T.K., 'Law, focal points, and fiscal discipline in the United States and the European Union', (2014) 108, *Am. Pol. Sc. Rev* 355–370

Kerremans, B., 'Determining a European policy in a multi-level setting: The case of specialized co-ordination in Belgium', (2000) 10 *Regional and Federal Studies* 36–61

Kese V., N. Küster, T. Oelmaier, C. Peschl, M. Werner and E. Yologlu, *Steigerung der Europafähigkeit der Landkreise - Notwendigkeit strategischer Steuerung* (Ludwigsburg: Institut für Anpassungsherausforderungen durch europäische Politiken und weltweite Migration, 2018)

Kincaid, J., 'Values and Value Tradeoffs in Federalism', (1995) 25 *Publius: the Journal of Federalism* 29–44

Kincaid J., 'Economic Policy-Making: Advantages and Disadvantages of the Federal Model' (2001) *International Social Science Journal* 85–92

Kincaid, J., 'Editor's Introduction: Federalism as a Mode of Governance', in J. Kincaid (ed), *Federalism* (Sage 2011, Vol. 1)

Kincaid, J., 'From Dualistic Autonomous Concurrency to Marbleised Permissive Concurrency in American Federalism' in N. Steytler (ed), *Concurrent Powers in Federal Systems. Meaning, Making, Managing* (Brill Nijhoff 2017)

Kincaid, 'The Rise and Characteristics of Coercive Federalism in the United States', in G. Pola (ed), *Principles and Practices of Fiscal Autonomy* (Ashgate 2015, reissued Routledge 2017)

King, P., *Federalism and Federation* (Croom Helm 1982)

Klamert, M., *The principle of loyalty in EU law* (Oxford University Press 2014)

Kössler, K. and Y.T. Fessha, 'Introduction', in Y.T. Fessha and K. Kössler (eds), *Federalism and the Courts in Africa* (Routledge 2020)

Kössler, K. and M. Trettel, 'Fiscal Federalism in Times of Crisis: an Iron Law of Centralisation?', in A. Valdesalici and F. Palermo (eds), *Comparing Fiscal Federalism* (Brill 2018)

Kotzur, M., 'Federalism and bicameralism – the German 'Bundesrat' (Federal Council) as an atypical model', in J. Luther, P. Passaglia and R. Tarchi (Giuffrè Editore, Milano 2006) A World of Second Chambers. Handbook for Constitutional Studies on Bicameralism

Kotzur, M., 'Constitutional Amendments and Constitutional Changes in Germany', in X. Contiades (ed), *Engineering Constitutional Change* (London, Routledge 2013)

Kramer, L.D. 'Putting the Politics back into Political Safeguards of Federalism', (2000) *Col. L. Rev.* 215–293

Kremyanskaya, E.A., T.O. Kuznetsova, I.A. Rakitskaya, *Russion Constitutional Law* (Cambridge Scholars Publishing 2014)

Kremyanskaya, E.A., 'Constitutional Asymmetry in Russia: Issues and Developments', in P. Popelier and M. Sahadžić (eds), *Constitutional Asymmetry in Multinational Federalism* (Palgrave MacMillan 2019)

Kress, A., 'Accomodating Diversity While Guaranteeing Stability: The Role of Financial Arrangements', in A. Valdesalici and F. Palermo (eds), *Comparing Fiscal Federalism* (Brill 2018)

Kumm, M., 'On the Representativeness of Constitutional Courts', in C. Landfried (ed), *Judicial Power. How Constitutional Courts Affect Political Transformations* (Cambridge University Press 2019)

Kwasi Tieku T., 'African Union From Practical Federalism to Fantasy Union', in J. Loughlin, J. Kincaid and W. Swenden (eds), Routledge Handbook of Regionalism and Federalism (Routledge 2013)

Labanca Corrêa de Araújo, M., 'Subnational constitutionalism in Brazil', in P. Popelier, G. Delledonne and N. Aroney (eds), *The Routledge Handbook of Subnational Constitutions and Constitutionalism* (Routledge 2021)

López-Laborda, J., F. Rodrigo and E. Sanz-Arcega, 'Is the Spanish Constitutional Court an instrument of the central government against the Autonomous Communities?' (2018) 29 *Constitutional Political Economy* 317–337

Lane J. and S. Ersson, 'The riddle of federalism: does federalism impact on democracy?,' (2005) 12 *Democratisation* 163–182

Law, J., 'How Can We Define Federalism?' (2013) 5 *Perspectives on Federalism* 88–120

Lecou, A., 'Federalism and Nationalism', in J. Kincaid (ed), *A Research Agenda for Federalism Studies* (Edward Elgar 2019)

Lépine, F., 'Federalism: Essence, Values and Ideologies', in A.-G. Gagnon, S. Keil and S. Mueller (eds), *Understanding Federalism and Federation* (Routledge 2015)

Lerner, H., 'Constitution-writing in deeply divided societies: the incrementalist approach', (2010) 16 *Nations and Nationalism* 68–88

Leslie, P., 'European Futures: The Unbearable Heaviness of Thinking Federally', in T.J. Courchene *et al.* (eds), *The Federal Idea. Essays in Honour of Ronald L. Watts* (McGill-Queen's University Press 2011)

Lev, A., 'Introduction. Federalism and Public Law Theory', in A. Lev (ed), *The Federal Idea. Public Law Between Governance and Political Life* (Hart 2017)
Leyland, P., 'The Multifaceted Dynamics of UK Devolution' (2011) 9 *International Journal of Constitutional Law* 251–273
Lienhard, A. *et al.*, 'The Federal Supreme Court of Switzerland: Judicial Balancing of Federalism without Judicial Review', in N. Aroney and J. Kincaid (eds), *Courts in Federal Countries. Federalists or Regionalists?* (University of Toronto Press 2017)
Lijphart, A., 'Non-majoritarian Democracy: A Comparison of Federal and Consociational Theories', (1985) 15 *Publius: the Journal of Federalism* 3–15
Livingston, W.S., 'A Note on the Nature of Federalism', (1952) 67 *Political Science Quarterly* 81–95
Livingston, W.S., *Federalism and Constitutional Change* (Oxford University Press 1956)
Loughlin, J., 'Reconfiguring the nation-state. Hybridity vs. uniformity', in J. Loughlin, J. Kincaid and W. Swenden (eds), *Routledge Handbook of Regionalism and Federalism* (Routledge, 2013)
Lysyk K. 'Constitutional reform and the introductory clause of section 91: residual and emergency law-making authority' (1979) 57 Can B Rev 531–575
Mader, O., 'Enforcement of EU values as a political endeavour: constitutional pluralism and value homogeneity in times of persistent challenges to the rule of law', (2019) 11 *Hague J on the Rule of Law* 133–170
Magalhães, *The limits of judicialization: legislative politics and constitutional review in the Iberian Democracies* (Colombus, Ohio State University, Ph.D. thesis, 2003)
Maiz, R., F. Caamaño and M. Azpitarte, 'The Hidden Counterpoint of Spanish Federalism: Recentralization and Resymmetrization in Spain (1978–2008)', (2010) 20 *Regional & Federal Studies* 63–82
McHarg, A. and J. Mitchell, 'Brexit and Scotland', (2017) 19 *Br.J.Pol.Int.Rel.* 512–526
McKenna, M., A. Simpson and G. Williams, 'First Words: the Preamble to the Australian Constitution', (2001) 24 *U.N.S.W.L.J.* 382–400
McNulty, D., 'Fiscal Decentralization for Scotland: Risks and Consequences for the UK', in G. Pola (ed), *Principles and Practices of Fiscal Autonomy* (Asgate 2015, reissued Routledge 2017)
Merritt, J.D., 'The Guarantee Clause and State Autonomy: Federalism for a Third Century', (1988) 88 *Columbia Law Rev.* 1–78
Michelmann, H., 'Introduction', in H. Michelmann (ed), *Foreign relations in federal countries* (McGills-Queen's Univ 2009)
Moore C., W. Jacoby and A.B. Gunlicks, 'Introduction: German Federalism in Transition?', (2008) XVII *German Politics* 396–408
Moreno Gonzalez, S., 'Regional Fiscal Autonomy from a State Aid Perspective: the ECJ's Judgment in *Portugal v Commission*', (2007) 47 *European Taxation* 328–338
Morris, A., 'Commonwealth of Australia', in A. Shah and J. Kincaid (eds), *The Practice of Fiscal Federalism: Comparative Perspectives* (McGill-Queen's University Press 2007)
Mussche N., 'Social Citizenship vs. The Territoriality Principle: Lessons for Flanders' Solidarity Circle', in B. Cantillon, P. Popelier and N. Mussche (eds), *Social Federalism: the Creation of a Layered Welfare State* (Intersentia 2011)
Mueller, S., 'Switzerland: Federalism as an Ideology of Balance', in A. Gagnon, S. Keil and S. Mueller (eds), *Undertsanding Federalism and Federation* (Routledge 2015)
Mueller, S. *Theorising decentralisation* (ECPR Press 2015)
Mueller, S., 'Federalism and the politics of shared rule', in J. Kincaid (ed), *A Research Agenda for Federalism Studies* (Edward Elgar 2019)

Muñoz, J. and R. Tormos, 'Economic expectations and support for secession in Catalonia: between causality and rationalization' (2015) 7 *Eu. Pol. Sc. Rev.* 315–341

Murray, C. and R. Simeon, 'Promises Unmet – Multi-level Government in South Africa', in R. Saxena (ed), *Varieties in Federal Governance: Major Contemporary Models* (Foundation Books 2011)

Neitsch A.T., 'A Tradition of Vigilance: the Role of Lieutenant Governor in Alberta', (2007) *Canadian parliamentary Review* 19–28

Oliver, D. and C. Fusaro (eds), *How Constitutions Change. A Comparative Study* (Oxford, Hart 2011)

Osoghae, E., 'Purpose and functioning of the Senate', in Bertus De Villiers, Frank Delmartino Frank and André Alen (eds), *Institutional Development in Divided Societies* (Human Rights Research Council, 1998)

Pal Singh, M., 'India', in D. Oliver and C. Fusaro (eds), *How Constitutions Change. A Comparative Study* (Oxford, Hart 2011)

Palermo, F., 'Italy: A Federal Country without Federalism?', in M. Burgess and G.A. Tarr (eds), *Constitutional Dynamics in Federal Systems. Sub-national Perspectives* (McGill-Queen's University Press 2012)

Palermo, F., 'Beyond Second Chambers: Alternative Representation of Territorial Interests and their Reasons' (2018) 10 *Perspectives on Federalism* 49–70

Palermo, F., 'Federalism and the European Union: asymmetry, policies and some recurring federal dilemmas', in John Kincaid (ed), *A Research Agenda for Federalism Studies* (Edward Elgar 2019)

Palermo F. and K. Kössler, *Comparative Federalism. Constitutional Arrangements and Case Law* (Oxford, Hart, 2017)

Palermo, F., C. Zwilling and K. Kössler (eds), *Asymmetries in Constitutional Law* (Bozen/Bolzano, Eurac 2009)

Palermo, F. and A. Valdesalici, 'Irreversibly Different. A Country Study of Constitutional Asymmetry in Italy', in P. Popelier and M. Sahadžić (eds), *Constitutional Asymmetry in Multinational Federalism* (Palgrave MacMillan 2019)

Panara, C., 'In the Name of Cooperation: the External Relations of the German Länder and their participation in the EU Decision Making' (2010) 6 *Eu Const L Rev* 59–83

Panara, C., 'Multi-Level Governance as a Constitutional Principle in the Legal System of the European Union' (2016) 16 Croatian and Comparative Public Administration 705–742

Pandey, R.K. 'Accommodating Diversity, Consolidating Nationhood. A Country Study of Constitutional Asymmetry in India', in Patricia Popelier and Maja Sahadžić (eds), *Constitutional Asymmetry in Multinational Federalism* (Palgrave MacMillan 2019)

Parolari, S., 'From a Formal to a Substantial Approach: Sources of Law and Fiscal Federalism', in A. Valdesalici and F. Palermo (eds), *Comparing Fiscal Federalism* (Brill 2018)

Pas, W., 'A Dynamic Federalism Built on Static Principles: The Case of Belgium', in G. Alan Tarr, R. Williams and J. Marko (eds), *Federalism, Subnational Constitutions, and Minority Rights* (Praeger Publishers 2004)

Patino, C.M. and J. Carvalho Ferreira, 'Inclusion and exclusion criteria in research studies; definitions and why they matter', (2018) 44 *J.Bras.Pneumol* N° 2.

Peers, S., 'European Integration and the European Union Act 2011: An Irresistible Force Meets an Immovable Object?' (2012) 58 *Public Law* 119–134

Peeters, B., 'European legal limitations to the repartition of fiscal competences in a federal state structure', in Bea Cantillon, Patricia Popelier and Ninke Mussche (eds), *Social Federalism: the Creation of a Layered Welfare State* (Antwerp, Intersentia 2011)

Peeters, P., 'The Constitutional and Institutional Autonomy of Communities and Regions in Federal Belgium', in M. Burgess and G.A. Tarr (eds), *Constitutional Dynamics in Federal Systems. Sub-national Perspectives* (McGill-Queen's University Press 2012)

Philips, E. 'Drastic Solutions: a Comparative Study of Emergency Powers in the Commonwealth' (1990) 5 *Denning Law Journal* 57–76

Pinder, J., 'Economic and Monetary Union: Pillar of a Federal Polity' (1996) 26 *Publius: the Journal of Federalism* 123–140

Pinder, J., 'Multinational federations. Introduction', in M Burgess and J Pinder (eds), *Multinational Federations* (London-New York, Routledge, 2007)

Poirier, J., 'Intergovernmental Agreements: Post-Devolution Concordats in a Comparative Perspective', (2001) *Public Law* 134–157

Poirier, J., C. Saunders and J. Kincaid (eds), *Intergovernmental Relations in Federal Systems* (Oxford University Press 2015)

Poirier, J. and C. Saunders, 'Conclusion: Comparative Experiences of Intergovernmental Relations in Federal Systems', in J. Poirier, C. Saunders and J. Kincaid (eds), *Intergovernmental Relations in Federal Systems* (Oxford University Press 2015)

Pola, G. (ed), *Principles and Practices of Fiscal Autonomy* (Ashgate 2015, reissued Routledge 2017)

Popelier, P., 'Subnational multilevel constitutionalism', (2014) 6 *Perspectives on Federalism* 1–23

Popelier, 'Europe clauses and constitutional strategies in the face of multilevel governance' (2014) 21 *Maastricht J of Eu and Comp Law* 300–319

Popelier, P., 'Secessionist and Autonomy Movements in Flanders: the Disintegration of Belgium as the Chronicle of a Death Foretold?', in E.M. Belser *et al.* (eds), *States falling apart? Secessionist and Autonomy Movements in Europe* (Stämpfli Verlag 2015)

Popelier, P., 'Federalism Disputes and the Behavior of Courts: Explaining Variation in Federal Courts' Support for Centralization' (2016) 47 Publius: The Journal of Federalism, 27–48

Popelier, 'Asymmetry and Complexity as a Device for Multinational Conflict Management. A Country Study of Constitutional Asymmetry in Belgium', in P. Popelier and M. Sahadžić (eds), *Constitutional Asymmetry in Multinational Federalism* (Palgrave MacMillan 2019)

Popelier, P., 'A Multilevel Governance Perspective on Disintegrative Dynamics within EU Member States', in Patrizia Latarullo *et al.* (eds), *The regions of Europe among local identities, new communities and territorial disparities* (FrancoAngeli 2019)

Popelier, P., 'Exclusive Powers and Self-Governed Entities: A Tool for Defensive Federalism?', in F. Requejo and M. Sanjaume (ed), *Defensive Federalism* (2021)

Popelier, P., N. Aroney and G. Delledonne, 'Subnational Constitutions: an Introduction', in P. Popelier, G. Delledonne and N. Aroney (eds), *The Routledge Handbook of Subnational Constitutions and Constitutionalism* (Routledge 2021).

Popelier, P. and S. Bielen, 'How Courts Decide Federalism Disputes: Legal Merit, Attitudinal Effects, and Strategic Considerations in the Jurisprudence of the Belgian Constitutional Court', (2018) 49 Publius: The Journal of Federalism, 587–616

Popelier, P. and K. Lemmens, *The Constitution of Belgium. A Contextual Analysis* (Hart 2015)

Popelier P. and M. Sahadžić (eds), *Constitutional Asymmetry in Multinational Federalism* (Palgrave MacMillan 2019)

Popelier, P. and M. Sahadžić, 'Linking Constitutional Asymmetry with Multinationalism. An Attempt to Crack the Code in Five Hypotheses', in P. Popelier and M. Sahadžić (eds), *Constitutional Asymmetry in Multinational Federalism* (Palgrave MacMillan 2019)

Popelier, P. and W. Vandenbruwaene, 'The Subsidiarity mechanism as a tool for inter-level dialogue in Belgium', (2011) 7 *Eu. Const. L. Rev.* 204–228

Porchia, O., Sub-national Units, Member States, and the European Union', in M. Burgess and G.A. Tarr (eds), *Constitutional Dynamics in Federal Systems. Sub-national Perspectives* (McGill-Queen's University Press 2012)

Powell, D., 'Constructing a Developmental State in South Africa: the Corporatization of Intergovernmental Relations', in J. Poirier, C. Saunders and J. Kincaid (eds), *Intergovernmental Relations in Federal Systems* (Oxford University Press 2015)

Raffass, *The Soviet Union: federation or empire?* (Routledge 2012).

Reagle, J., 'Following the Joneses: FOMO and conspicuous reality', (2015) 20 *FirstMonday*

Requejo F., *Multinational Federalism and Value Pluralism* (London, Routledge 2005)

Requejo F., 'Federalism and democracy. The case of minority nations: a federalist deficit', in M. Burgess and A. Gagnon (eds), *Federal Democracies* (Routledge 2010) 275–298

Requejo, F., 'Plurinational federalism and political theory', in J. Loughlin, J. Kincaid and W. Swenden (eds), *Routledge Handbook of Regionalism and Federalism* (Routledge, 2013)

Requejo, F., 'National Pluralism, Recognition, Federalism and Secession (or Hegel Was a Clever Guy)', in A.-G. Gagnon, S. Keil and S. Mueller (eds), *Understanding Federalism and Federation* (2016)

Riker, W.R., *Federalism: Origin, Operation, Significance* (Little Brown and Company 1964)

Riker, W.R., 'Federalism' in F.I. Greenstein and N.W. Polsby (eds), *Handbook of Political Science.* Vol.5. Governmental Institutions and Processes (AddisonWesley 1975)

Roche M., 'Social Citizenship: Grounds of Social Change', in E.F. Isin and B.S. Turner (eds), *Handbook of Citizenship Studies* (Sage Publications 2002)

Roeder, P.G. 'Ethnofederalism and the Mismanagement of Conflicting Federalism', in J. Erk and L.M. Anderson (eds), *Thee Paradox of Federalism* (Routledge 2010)

Rothmayr, C., 'Towards the Judicialisation of Swiss politics?' (2001) 24 *West European Politics* 77–94

Rubin, E.L., 'Federalism as a Mode of Governance: Autonomy, Identity, Power, and Rights', in A. Lev (ed), *The Federal Idea. Public Law Between Governance and Political Life* (Hart 2017)

Ruhl, J.B., 'Complexity Theory as Paradigm for the Dynamic Law-and-society System: A Wake-up Call for Legal Reductionism and the Modern Administrative State' (1996) 45 *Duke Law Journal* 849–928

Ruiz-Huerta, J., 'Spanish Decentralization and Fiscal Federalism', in G. Pola (ed), *Principles and Practices of Fiscal Autonomy* (Asgate 2015, reissued Routledge 2017)

Sahadžić, 'Mild Asymmetry and Ethnoterritorial Overlap I Charge of the Consequences of Multinationalism. A Country Study of Constitutional Asymmetry in Bosnia and Herzegovina', in Popelier and Sahadžić (eds), *Constitutional Asymmetry in Multinational Federalism* (Palgrave MacMillan 2019)

Sahadžić, M., *Asymmetry, Multinationalism and Constitutional Law. Making Legitimacy and Stability in Multinational States* (Routledge 2020)

Sala G. 'Federalism without adjectives', (2013) 44 *Publius: the Journal of Federalism* 109–134.

Salleh A, A. Puyok and T. Paridi Bagang, 'Constitutional Asymmetry in Malaysia: A Case Study of Sabah and Sarawak. A Country Study of Constitutional Asymmetry in Indonesia', in P. Popelier and M. Sahadžić (eds), *Constitutional Asymmetry in Multinational Federalism* (Palgrave MacMillan 2019)

Sassen S., 'Towards Post-National and Denationalized Citizenship', in E.F. Isin and B.S. Turner (eds), *Handbook of Citizenship Studies* (Sage Publications 2002)

Saunders, C., "Financial Autonomy vs. Solidarity: A Dialogue between Two Complementary Opposites', in A. Valdesalici and F. Palermo (eds), *Comparing Fiscal Federalism* (Brill 2018)

Saunders, C., 'Federalism and Constitutionalism: challenges presented by dominant conceptions of the unitary state', in J. Kincaid (ed), *A Research Agenda for Federalism Studies* (Edward Elgar 2019)

Saxena, R. and Singh, M.P., 'The role of the federal judiciary in union-state relations in India', in J. Erk and W. Swenden (eds), *New directions in Federalism Studies* (Routledge 2010)

Scheiber H.N., 'Federalism and the Constitution: The Original Understanding', in L.M. Friedman and H.N. Scheiber (eds), *American Law and the Constitutional Order: Historical Perspectives* (Harvard University Press 1988)

Schneider, C.J., 'Political Parties and the German Basic Law of 1949', (1957) 10 *Western Pol. Quarterly* 527–540

Schnellenbach, J., 'Fiscal Sovereignty in a Globalized World: The Pressure of European Economic Governance on Domestic Public Finance', in A. Valdesalici and F. Palermo (eds), *Comparing Fiscal Federalism* (Brill 2018)

Schütze, R., *From Dual to Cooperative Federalism. The Changing Structure of European Law* (Oxford, Oxford University Press 2019)

Schwartz, D.S. 'A Question Perpetually Arising: Implied Powers, Capable Federalism, and the Limits of Enumerationism', (2017) 59 *Arizona L. Rev.* 573–646

Scott, A., 'The Role of Concordats in the New Governance of Britain: Taking Subsidiarity Seriously', (2001) 21 *Edinburg L. Rev.* 21–48

Scott, K., 'Judicial behavior and the Rehnquist Court's federalism revolution', (2008) 36 *American Politics Research* 85–107

Segal, A. and H.J. Spaeth, *The Supreme Court and the Attitudinal Model Revisited* (Cambridge University Press 2002)

Shah, A., 'Introduction. Principles of Fiscal Federalism', in A. Shah and J. Kincaid (eds), *The Practice of Fiscal Federalism: Comparative Perspectives* (McGill-Queen's University Press 2007)

Shapiro, M., *Courts. A Comparative Analysis* (University of Chicago Press 1981)

Sharma, R.P.D. 'In search of the theory of constitutional machinery failure (emergency) models in India and Pakistan: a comparative exploration' (2017) 23 *Comp. L. Rev.* 83–107

Simeon, R., 'Constitutional Design and Change in Federal Systems: Issues and Questions', (2009) 39 *Publius: the Journal of Federalism* 141–161

Simonek, M., 'Tax Coordination Between Cantons in Switzerland – Role of the Courts', in M. Lang, P. Pistone, J. Schuch and C. Staringer (eds), *Horizontal Tax Coordination* (IBFD 2012)

Skoutaris, N., 'Comparing the subnational constitutional space of the European sub-entities in the area of foreign affairs', (2012) 4 *Perspectives on Federalism* 239–268

Skoutaris, N., 'Subnational Constitutionalism in the UK', in P. Popelier, G. Delledonne and N. Aroney (eds), *The Routledge Handbook of Subnational Constitutions and Constitutionalism* (Routledge 2021)

Somin, I., 'The Supreme Court of the United States: Promoting Centralization More than State Autonomy', in in N. Aroney and J. Kincaid, *Courts n Federal Countries. Federalists or Regionalists?* (University of Toronto Press 2017)

Spahn, P.B., 'Measuring Decentralization of Public Sector Activities: Conceptual Issues and the Case of Germany', in Kim *et al.* (eds), *Measuring Fiscal Decentralization: Concepts and Policies* (OECD Publishing 2013)

Stein, M.B., 'Federal Political Systems *World Pol* and Federal Societies' (1968) 20 721–748

Stelzer, M., 'Constitutional Change in Austria', in X. Contiades (ed), *Engineering Constitutional Change* (Routledge 2013)

Stepan, A., 'Federalism and Democracy: Beyond the US Model' (1999) 10 *Journal of Democracy* 19–34

Stepan, A., 'Towards a New Comparative Politics of Federalism, Multinationalism, and Democracy: Beyond Rikerian Federalism', in E.L. Gibson (ed), *Federalism and Democracy in Latin America* (John Hopkins University Press 2004)

Steytler, N., 'Provincial Constitutions in South Africa: an Empty Promise', in P. Popelier, G. Delledonne and N. Aroney (eds), *The Routledge Handbook of Subnational Constitutions and Constitutionalism* (Routledge 2021).

Steytler, N., 'The Constitutional Court of South Africa: Reinforcing an Hourglass System of Multi-Level Government', in N. Aroney and J. Kincaid (eds), *Courts in Federal Countries. Federalists or Regionalists?* (University of Toronto Press 2017)

Steytler, N. (ed), *Concurrent Powers in Federal Systems. Meaning, Making, Managing* (Brill Nijhoff 2017)

Steytler, N., 'The Currency of Concurrent Powers in Federal Systems' in N. Steytler (ed), *Concurrent Powers in Federal Systems. Meaning, Making, Managing* (Brill Nijhoff 2017)

Steytler, N., 'Concurrency of Powers: The Zebra in the Room', in N. Steytler (ed), *Concurrent Powers in Federal Systems. Meaning, Making, Managing* (Brill Nijhoff 2017)

Steytler N., 'Non-centralism in Africa: in search of the federal idea', in J. Kincaid (ed), *A Research Agenda for Federalism Studies* (Edward Elgar 2019)

Steytler, N. and Z.A. Ayele, 'Local Governments in African Federal and Devolved Systems of Government: The Struggle for a Balance between Financial and Fiscal Autonomy and Discipline', in A. Valdesalici and F. Palermo (eds), *Comparing Fiscal Federalism* (Brill 2018)

Steytler, N. and J. Mettler, 'Federalism Arrangements as a Peacemaking Device during South Africa's Transition to Democracy' (2001) *Publius: the Journal of Federalism* 93–106

Sturm, R., 'More courageous than expected? The 2006 reform of German Federalism', in J. Erk and W. Swenden (eds), *New Directions in Federalism Studies* (Routledge 2010)

Suberu, R., 'Federalism in Africa: the Nigerian Experience in Comparative Perspective', (2009) 8 *Ethnopolitics* 67–86

Suberu, R. 'The Supreme Court of Nigeria: An Embattled Judiciary More Centralist than Federalist', in N. Aroney and J. Kincaid (eds), *Courts in Federal Countries. Federalists or Regionalists?* (University of Toronto Press 2017)

Suszycka-Jasch, M. and H.-C. Jasch, 'Participation of the German Länder in Formulating German EU-Policy', (2009) 9 *German Law Journal* 1215–1256

Swenden W., *Federalism and Regionalism in Western Europe. A Comparative and Thematic Analysis* (Palgrave MacMillan 2006)

Swenden W., 'Territorial strategies for managing plurinational states', in J. Loughlin, J. Kincaid and W. Swenden (eds), *Routledge Handbook of Regionalism and Federalism* (Routledge 2013)

Swenden, W. and M.T. Jans, 'Will it stay or will it go?' Federalism and the sustainability of Belgium' (2006) 29 *West European Politics* 877–894

Swenden, W. and B. Maddens, 'Concluding Observations', in W. Swenden and B. Maddens (eds), *Territorial Party Politics in Western Europe* (Palgrave MacMillan 2009)

Tambini, D., 'Post-national citizenship' (2001) 24 *Ethnic and Racial Studies*, 195–217

Tatham, M., 'Going Solo: Direct Regional Representation in the European Union', (2008) 18 *Regional & Federal Studies* 493–515

Thorlakson, L., 'Comparing Federal Institutions: Power and Representation in Six Federations' (2003) 26 *West European Politics* 1–22

Thorlakson, L., 'Patterns of party integration, influence and autonomy in seven federations', (2009) 15 *Party Politics* 157–177

Thorlakson, L., 'Dynamics of change in federal representation', in A. Benz and J. Broschek (eds), *Federal Dynamics. Continuity, Change & the Varieties of Federalism* (Oxford University Press 2013)

Tierney, S., 'Giving with one hand: Scottish devolution within a unitary state', (2007) 5 *Int. J. Const. Law* 730–753

Tierney, S., 'Quiet Devolution: Sub-State Autonomy and the Gradual Reconstitution of the United Kingdom', in M. Burgess and G.A. Tarr (eds), *Constitutional Dynamics in Federal Systems. Sub-national Perspectives* (McGill-Queen's University Press 2012)

Travers, T., *Implications of a Brexit for UK National Governance and Local Government*, Report of the hearing held on 13th April, 2016 (LSE Commission on the Future of Britain in Europe, 2016)

Traversa, E. and B. Vintras, 'Tax Coordination between Regions in Belgium – Role of the Courts', in M. Lang, P. Pistone, J. Schuch and C. Staringer (eds), *Horizontal Tax Coordination* (IBFD 2012)

Trench, A., 'The Courts and Devolution in the UK', (2012) 14 *BJPIR* 303–322

Turgeon, and R. Simeon, 'Ideology, Political Economy and Federalism: the Welfare State and the Evolution of the Australian and Canadian Federation', in A.G. Gagnon, S. Keil and S. Mueller (eds), *Understanding Federalism and Federation* (Routledge 2015)

Tushnet, M., *The Constitution of the United States of America. A Contextual Analysis* (Oxford, Hart 2009)

Ukata, P., 'Federalism and the courts in Nigeria', in Y.T. Fessha and K. Kössler (eds), *Federalism and the Courts in Africa* (Routledge 2020)

Valcke, C., 'Québec civil law and Canadian Federalism', (1996) 21 *Yale J. International Law* 67–123

Valdesalici, A., 'Defining Fiscal Federalism', in Alice Valdesalici and Francesco Palermo (eds), *Comparing Fiscal Federalism* (Leiden, Brill, 2018)

Valdesalici, A., 'The peregrinations of fiscal federalism: past, present and future of a research agenda', in J. Kincaid (ed.), *A Research agenda for federalism studies* (Edward Elgar 2019) 93–105

Valdesalici, A. and F. Palermo (eds), *Comparing Fiscal Federalism* (Brill 2018)

Vandenbruwaene, W., 'Multi-tiered Political Questions: The ECJ's Mandate in Enforcing Subsidiarity' (2012) 6 *Legisprudence* 321–346

Vandenbruwaene, W., 'What Scope for Subnational Autonomy: the Issue of the Legal Enforcement of the Principle of Subsidiarity' (2014) 6 *Perspectives on Federalism* 45–73

Vandenbruwaene, W., P. Popelier and L. Janssens, 'Article 260 TFEU Sanctions in Multi-Tiered Member States', (2015) 7 *Perspectives on Federalism* 133–162

Van Kersbergen, K., 'The politics of solidarity and the changing boundaries of the welfare state', (2006) 5 *European Political Science* 377–394

Vanpraet, J., *De latent staatshervorming* (Bruges, die Keure 2011)

Vaubel, R., 'Constitutional Courts as Promoters of Political Centralization: Lessons for the Court of Justice', (2009) 28 *Eu. J. of Law and Economics* 203–222

Velaers, J., *Federalisme/Confederalisme... en de weg er naar toe* (KVAB Press 2013)

Vermeule, A., 'Does Commerce Clause Review have Perverse Effects?' (2001) 46 *Villanova L. Rev.* 1326–1340

Verney, D.V., 'Federalism, Federative Systems, and Federations: The United States, Canada, and India', (1995) 25 *Publius*

Vernon, R., 'The Principle of Federation: an introduction', reprinted in J. Kincaid (ed), *Federalism* (Sage 2011, Volume 1)

Vile, J.R., 'Constitutional revision in the United States of America', in X. Contiades (ed), *Engineering Constitutional Change* (Routledge 2013)

Viver, C., 'Spain's Constitution and Statutes of Autonomy: Explaining the Evolution of Political Decentralization', in M. Burgess and G. Alan Tarr (eds), *Constitutional Dynamics in Federal Systems. Subnational Perspectives* (Montreal & Kingston, McGill-Queen's University Press 2012)

Viver Pi-Sunyer, C. and M. Corretja Torrens, 'De Facto Concurrency in Spain', in N. Steytler (ed), *Concurrent Powers in Federal Systems. Meaning, Making, Managing* (Brill Nijhoff 2017)

von Krosigk, F., 'A reconsideration of federalism in the scope of the present discussion on European integration', (1970) 9 *Journal of Common Market Studies* 197–223

Walgrave, S., Lefevere, J. *et al.* Note based on the RepResent study, 'Vlamingen en Walen stemden voor verschillende partijen maar verschillen van mening over het beleid dat ze willen', 4–11. Unpublished.

Walker, N., *Final Appellate Jurisdiction in the Scottish Legal System* (Scottish Government 2010)

Walsh, D., 'Constitutional courts as arbiters of post-conflict territorial self-government: Bosnia and Macedonia, (2019) 29 *Regional & Federal Studies*, 67–90.

Watts, R.L., *Comparing Federal Systems* (Queen's University 2008, 3rd ed.)

Watts, R.L., 'The distribution of powers, responsibilities and resources in federations', in A.L. Griffiths (ed), *Handbook of federal countries* (McGill-Queen's University Press 2002) 448–471; included in J. Kincaid, *Federalism* Vol 2, (Sage Publications 2011)199–221.

Watts, R.L., 'The Federal Idea and its Contemporary Relevance', in T.J. Courchene *et al.* (eds), *The Federal Idea. Essays in Hounour of Ronald L. Watts* (McGill-Queen's University Press 2011)

Watts, R.L. 'Typologies of federalism', in J. Loughlin, J. Kincaid and W. Swenden (eds), *Routledge Handbook of Regionalism and Federalism* (Routledge 2013)

Watts, R.L., 'Comparing Federal Political Systems', in A.-G. Gagnon, S. Keil and S. Mueller (eds), *Understanding Federalism and Federation* (Routledge 2015)

Wehner, J., 'Fiscal federalism in South Africa', (2000) 30 *Publius: the Journal of Federalism* 47–72

Welscher, H., 'The political safeguards of federalism', (1954) 54 *Columbia L. Rev* 543–560

Wheare, K.C., *Federal Government* (Oxford University Press 1953)

Whitaker, R., *A Sovereign Idea* (McGill-Queen's University Press 1992)

Wilkins, R.B., 'Federalism: Distance and Devolution', (2004) 50 *Australian J. of Politics and History* 95–101.

Winetrobe, B., 'Counter-Devolution? The Sewel Convention on Devolved Legislation at West-minster', (2001) 6 *Scot. L. & Prac. Q.* 286–292

Woelk, J., 'Germany' in D. Oliver and C. Fusaro (eds), *How Constitutions Change. A Comparative Study* (Oxford, Hart 2011)

Woelk, J., 'Bosnia-Herzegovina: Trying to Build a Federal State on Paradoxes', in M. Burgess and G.A. Tarr (eds), *Constitutional Dynamics in Federal Systems* (McGill-Queen's University Press 2012)

Wolff, S., 'Cases of Asymmetrical Territorial Autonomy', in M. Weller and K. Nobbs (eds), *Asymmetric Autonomy and the Settlement of Ethnic Conflicts* (University of Pennsylvania Press 2010)

Yarbrough, J., 'Rethinking "The Federalist's View of Federalism", (1985) 28 *Publius: the Journal of Federalism* 31–53

Index

For Product Safety Concerns and Information please contact our EU
representative GPSR@taylorandfrancis.com
Taylor & Francis Verlag GmbH, Kaufingerstraße 24, 80331 München, Germany

www.ingramcontent.com/pod-product-compliance
Ingram Content Group UK Ltd.
Pitfield, Milton Keynes, MK11 3LW, UK
UKHW020016200926
475702UK00014B/1914
* 9 7 8 0 3 6 7 6 5 2 9 2 0 *